# The Limits of Moralizing

# The Limits of Moralizing
## Pathos and Subjectivity in Spenser and Milton

David Mikics

Lewisburg
Bucknell University Press
London and Totonto: Associated University Pressesx

© 1994 by Associated University Presses

All rights reserved. Authorization to photocopy items for internal or personal use, or the internal or personal use of specific clients, is granted by the copyright owner, provided that a base fee of $10.00, plus eight cents per page, per copy is paid directly to the Copyright Clearance Center, 222 Rosewood Drive, Danvers, Massachusetts 01923. [0-8387-5285-3/94 $10.00 + 8¢ pp, pc.]

Associated University Presses
440 Forsgate Drive
Cranbury, NJ 08512

Associated University Presses
25 Sicilian Avenue
London WC1A 2QH, England

Associated University Presses
P.O. Box 338, Port Credit
Mississauga, Ontario
Canada L5G 4L8

The paper used in this publication meets the requirements of the American National Standard for Permanence of Paper for Printed Library Materials Z39.48–1984.

Lines from "On the Road Home" by Wallace Stevens are reprinted by permission of Alfred A. Knopf, Inc. Copyright © Holly Stevens.

**Library of Congress Cataloging-in-Publication Data**

Mikics, David, 1961-
 The limits of moralizing : pathos and subjectivity in Spenser and Milton / David Mikics.
  p.   cm.
 Includes bibliographical references and index.
 ISBN 0-8378-5285-3 (alk. paper)
  1. Spenser, Edmund, 1552?-1599--Ethics.  2. English Poetry--Early modern, 1500-1700--History and criticism.  3. Epic poetry, English--History and criticism.  4. Milton, John, 1608-1674--Ethics. 5 . Subjectivity in literature.  6. Pathos in literature.  7. Ethics in literature.  I. Title
PR2367.E8M55    1994
821'.03209--dc20                                    93-39323
                                                     CIP

PRINTED IN THE UNITED STATES OF AMERICA

In memoriam
D. E. M.
Salve, sancte parens, iterum salvete, recepti
nequiquam cineres animaeque umbraeque maternae

# Contents

Acknowledgments — ix

Introduction — 3
1. Pathos and Moralizing in Classical and Renaissance Tradition — 15
2. *The Faerie Queene*, Book 1 — 39
3. *The Faerie Queene*, Book 2 — 64
4. *The Faerie Queene*, Book 3 — 86
5. From Spenser to Milton — 114
6. *Paradise Lost* — 131
7. *Paradise Regained* and *Samson Agonistes* — 159
Conclusion — 189

Notes — 197
Works Cited — 251
Author and Subject Index — 267
Index to Works by Spenser and Milton — 270

# Acknowledgments

One notable tendency of the prolonged and intensive otium that a life of scholarship offers is, to paraphrase John Ashbery, the elevation of fence-sitting to an aesthetic ideal. I must thank those who, preaching commitment, nudged me from the fence while also keeping me off the "grassie grounde." There were more than a few present at the creation. John Hollander's unfailingly generous and spirited wisdom informed his direction of this project in its previous incarnation as a Yale dissertation. Without Perry Meisel's authoritative enthusiasm as a patron and his unrivaled energy as a teacher and friend, I cannot imagine I would have assumed whatever intellectual weight inhabits the following pages. Joshua Scodel and Edward Schiffer, who guided me through graduate school (while, perhaps more important, introducing me to dinner at Malone's and used disco at Rhymes), provided moral authority, hope for the future, and floods of inspirational commentary able to meet skepticism at least halfway. Leslie Brisman, whose teaching instilled in me an ideal of responsibility to texts that I will always cherish, challenged me to do serious justice to poetry in the Miltonic tradition. Also at Yale, Harold Bloom and Martin Price provided irreplaceable teacherly examples, while Ian Duncan, David Kaufmann, and Mary Pat Martin rescued me repeatedly from doubt, danger, overenthusiasm, and other allegorical figures (well, maybe not overenthusiasm). Years later, Melanie Thernstrom and Tom Reiss arranged for me an idyllic sublet in Cambridge where I could await final proofs. Other memorable gifts of reassurance, criticism, and helpful rebuke were provided by my father, Lewis J. Mikics, John Bernard, Donald Cheney, Alexis Quinlan, John Guillory, Elizabeth Gregory, Daniel Javitch, Ernest Gilman, Lawrence Manley, Steve Dillon, Thomas Greene, Lindsay Kaplan, Anne Badger, James Houlihan, Victor Bers, Nancy Wright, and Julia Lupton. Many more students, teachers, and friends helped out. I hope that I have been true to their care and imagination in searching these antique, and modern, springs.

# The Limits of Moralizing

# Introduction

Literary criticism has recently been paying increasing attention to the issue of subjectivity. Yet there have been few investigations of the roles that subjectivity plays within genre. In this book, I address the connection between genre and the subject by examining how two English Reformation poets, Edmund Spenser and John Milton, produce a confrontation between the narrative framework of the epic genre and its depiction of the self. Epic traditionally conveys a providential sense of moral destiny; however, the subjectivity of the epic hero, located above all in moments of tragic and erotic pathos, resists such constraining didacticism. This conflict, which reaches its height in the Reformation, contributes to the formation of a newly modern selfhood. I have chosen to focus on Spenser and Milton, the two central epic poets of English Protestantism, because the debate between pathos and moralism demands to be seen in a Reformation context. *The Faerie Queene*, *Paradise Lost*, *Paradise Regained,* and *Samson Agonistes* exemplify the new literary subjectivity that develops under the pressure of their era's didactic aims.

The Reformation's emphasis on the individual human subject can be traced back to Paul and Augustine, whose self-searching inwardness is revived by Protestant autobiography and confession. This tradition firmly links inwardness to pathos. Augustine's influential reading of Romans 7 insists that the mortal self's emotion, not Stoic or apocalyptic hopes to transcend first-person emotional vulnerability by looking toward a larger, calmer cosmic order, provides the essential setting for religious experience. The intense, introspective Pauline-Augustinian vision of spirituality contrasts with an opposing side of Christianity, one equally crucial to the Reformation: the impulse to subordinate the self to the plot of sacred history. By means of what Leopold Damrosch calls the "sacred plot," Calvinism subjects the individual consciousness of the believer to a divine narrative telos. Calvinist predestination, the subordination of consciousness to divine plan, transcends the reach of subjective human understanding.

These external and internal modes of Christian experience supplement each other, but, as Damrosch writes, they finally prove distinct and even irreconcilable. The active participation in belief that inwardness provides does not bring one closer to the perspective of God, the plot's synoptic director—it even makes the hope that one is involved in a coherent narrative less plausible. But inwardness dramatizes the believer's personal relation to God as the sacred plot cannot. Protestant consciousness originates in the self's inward sense of distance from the divine plan that gives it meaning. This division between the private sense of faith and the grand scheme of sacred history exists long before the Reformation; however, the Reformation makes it permanent and unresolvable.[1]

The Reformation division between the solitary pathos of the Pauline believer and the imposing scale of sacred history also appears in its epic poetry, which poses the self and its passions against the overarching providential structure of epic narrative. This book finds in the major poems of Spenser and Milton, with their explicit negotiations among Reformation theology, poetic genre, and the heroic self, the most profitable arena for studying the interaction between private pathos and suprapersonal moral design. David Norbrook has pointed out that Spenser and Milton share a tradition of Protestant political opinion.[2] While I agree with Norbrook, I locate the *poetic* connection between these Reformation writers in a different realm: their common treatment of inward temptation, despair, and sexual pathos as the formative forces of Protestant subjectivity, which they develop in contrast to a more general or public moralizing narrative.

By setting narrative against the pathos of subjectivity in a way that is consonant with epic, romance, and tragic traditions, as well as Scripture, Spenser and Milton define the English Protestant self as a product of genre. Spenser's major poem is an epic romance; Milton reinvents Christian epic. The confluence and conflicts of epic, romance, and Protestant theology have not been much investigated, because genre study has remained largely on the level of taxonomy. The generic possibilities I mention, all of which centrally involve the presence of pathos or psychologically definitive emotion, go far toward outlining a place for the subjectivity that has recently been neglected, along with the question of genre, by much new historicist reading.

In keeping with the Protestant dialectic between inwardness and moralizing narrative, I read parts of *The Faerie Queene* as stories of narrative's power and other, contrasting sections of the poem as unveilings of a heroic, morally contested psyche. The shifts between these two modes in the 1590 *Faerie Queene* provide the drama in Spenser's allegedly nondramatic art.[3] Milton assumes a division similar to Spenser's between the fragile autonomy of the private subject and the alternately comforting and threatening rigor of institutional, generic, and doctrinal narratives. In Milton, the division intensifies because he, unlike Spenser, claims the stance of a radical Protestant. This study defines radical Protestantism, or Puritanism, as the impulse of Reformation Christianity to detect a disjunction between official ceremony and the private experience of faith. The Puritan assumes some precedence of private faith over public, however much he or she might accommodate personal belief to institutional goals.[4] Historians Peter Lake, Patrick Collinson, and Derek Hirst have recently offered evidence of the ways in which English Puritans balanced their "invisible" or personal spirituality with the "visible" church, despite the often warring demands of private spirit and public order.[5] The fact that the conflicting contexts of institution and individual could be successfully balanced, the main axe that this revisionist view of Puritanism grinds, is less relevant for my purposes than the sheer fact that they are intertwined. Self and institution stake their claims with, and in reaction to, each other. Northrop Frye writes of Paul's Christianity, "What one repents of is sin, a word that means nothing outside a religious and individualized context . . . sin is not illegal or antisocial behavior."[6] Yet the definition of sin and its significance is necessarily provided by the church, a public institution.

In the Reformation as in the early Christianity of Paul, the self responds emotionally to the moralizing regulations that society imposes through terms like *sin*. But, as the foundation of a premoral subjectivity, pathos also resists these terms. To explain why, I draw on Freudian theory, which more than any other intellectual legacy demonstrates the primordial connection between the birth of the self and the pathos of sexual-emotional desire. For Freud, the drive transforms itself into desire, a pathos that is subjective rather than merely automatic or instinctual, when it encounters the loss of satisfaction. This meeting with reality as privation marks the origin of the human, which the subject will later recall and work through in the form of tragedy. The experience of loss creates the self in the only form we know it—as emotional individuality. This individuality, in turn, exists in antagonism to the social forces that argue against it and attempt to construct it as a responsible entity. In Lacan's terms, the Imaginary strives against the Symbolic. The self, if it is to reach a healthy maturity, must try to internalize Symbolic social responsibility.[7] But such internalization can never be complete. Milton, even in his striving for the chaste inwardness of moral autonomy, knows that the superego remains to some degree an alien presence: as William Kerrigan calls it, "a scandal in the eye of the ego."[8] The barbaric justice enacted through Samson, like the brutality of Spenser's Book 5, resonates with the continuing primitiveness of moral law.[9] Milton's poetry, with its emphasis on the tragic situation of a separated or discontinuous self, dramatizes the strife between the superego's authority and a resistant subjectivity. Even when the poet images God's creation or Adam and Eve's marriage as a harmonious continuity, he anxiously predicts a fall away from the law and into separateness.

The conflict that Freud detects between private desire and social obligation, pathos and moral decree, occurs whenever tragic pathos interrupts the narrative design of epic. Epic's tragic instances make visible a confrontation between the passion of heroic personality and the destiny it must follow (often by renouncing pathos for moral duty, as when Aeneas leaves Dido). Destiny here represents society's power to produce judgments that subordinate the self and its desires to collective morality. In Homer and Virgil, characters like Achilles and Dido, by opposing destiny and introducing tragic pathos into epic, propel the heroic self into subversion of epic's didactic agenda. In my first chapter, I describe Plato's worry about the social effects of Achilles' grief-crazed anger, which lives on in Renaissance literary critics' unease over the *Aeneid*'s use of tragic emotion. Spenser and Milton respond to contentious political and theological conditions by sharpening the strife between self and social morality that characterizes this tradition of tragic crises within epic.[10]

Given the dialectical understanding of Spenser and Milton that I have outlined, I will first show how recent criticism of the Renaissance and its genres obscures the relation between subjective pathos and the didactic authority of impersonal narrative. Criticism wants to resolve the ambivalence that supports the text by choosing one term, self or narrative system, as a guide to reading. In doing so, it misses the significance of these terms' confrontational meeting. Turning to the poems of Spenser and Milton, I try to restore a view of what the critics deny, the rich, uncertain strife between subjective pathos and the rules of genre or social morality.

Whereas critics in the Romantic tradition, from Keats to Empson, chose an amoral pathos associated with the self's aesthetic responses as definitive of the essential Spenser and Milton, recent criticism, whether reader response–oriented or new historicist, opts for a systematic power that transcends the self. Stanley Fish's readings of Milton, for example, espouse moral law as it finds embodiment in the force of narrative destiny. A transcendent truth overrides the mortal, weak subjectivity that is our inevitable earthly condition. According to Fish, Milton continually cancels the impact of earthly experience in favor of a truer divine perspective. The poet abstracts his readers from the palpable context of this world in order to make them heed a promise of grace imposed from above. Fish's reading, persuasive as it is, remains partial. He captures only one aspect of Milton, slighting the poet's deep investment in the search for the divine within, rather than beyond, subjective emotion.

There is common ground among Fish, new historicism, and Marxism in their espousal of the efficacy of narrative system, which in Fish's work takes the form of Protestant didacticism. But the contrary Protestant mode, the searching treatment of the soul's emotional reactions, works against the kind of deterministic, impersonal narrative that Fish describes and that new historicism espouses in a more politicized, less theological context. As I will argue in my discussion of Milton, subjectivity may demand a turning of the self toward an unpredictable alterity, a hidden future that providential narrative cannot accommodate.

The demonstration of impersonal authority's effectiveness, whether this authority takes the form of narrative structure or social system, is the reigning form of post-Christian moralism in current literary criticism. Denial of the self's inwardness pursues a didactic clarity similar to that of the Protestant dogmatist. The new historicist celebration of authority moralizes in its need to prove an invariable pattern or structure in events, a necessity that will upbraid and humble human desire. But such claims usually backfire, revealing the inescapable presence of the self that they protest against. Strangely enough, for Jonathan Dollimore the "decentering of man" illustrated by the "radical tragedy" of Reformation England achieves its power only because it attacks a subjectivity that is not yet supposed to exist.[11]

Serious choices remain for contemporary Renaissance Studies, even irreconcilable differences. One such difference is that between Marx on one side and Freud and Nietzsche on the other. Along with Heidegger, these thinkers, mediated by their French heirs, are the reigning spirits of contemporary criticism. But they epitomize two opposed strains of thought that cannot be easily harmonized, despite the efforts of contemporaries like Jameson and Gayatri Spivak. Marx sees the self as a social effect, unlike Freud and Nietzsche, who focus on the self's creative and destructive dramas of interpretation, which for them are animated by a permanent, double-edged conflict between individual desire and society. For the study of ideology, we still need Marx's great achievement. But we must avoid the assumption, common to Marx and Foucault, that ideological systems generate individuals. Despite Foucault's protestations to the contrary, such theories necessarily ignore the way that individuality strives against order.[12] Contemporary criticism's overestimation of ideology, riding roughshod over the particularity of literary- and social-historical moments, is symptomatic of its desire to deny the resonant, uncanny authority of literature, to reduce unique texts to the comfortably predictable results of a system. Such ideological moralism, like the theological variety, obliterates the idiosyncratic, subjective event that occurs between reader and book. It therefore fails to explain, for example, one of the major themes of Milton's late poetry: the urge, realized at the end of both *Paradise Regained* and *Samson Agonistes*, to generate a future different from the past, a surprising and unprecedented narrative outcome. Here I have space only to assert, rather than argue for, the political value of acknowledging the future as difference, as an interruption of historical totality by subjectivity's resistant inclination toward the new.[13] After the breakup of modernism's mythic narratives, a postmodern political culture has turned to a consideration of local contexts of resistance and potential change, centered on individual responses to ideologies and dogmas that have outlived their time. Long before this historical shift, Spenser and Milton share a sense of the gap between rigid or archaic doctrinal patterns and the individual's position that seems oddly contemporary. Though doctrine is far more attractive to these Reformation poets than it is to us, it can seem just as distant from the inner life of subjectivity.

In the rest of this introduction, I will argue against the choice of impersonal authority over the self in current critical practice by looking closely at two influential recent critics. To stake my claim that subjectivity, as well as moral law, speaks through texts, I need to take issue with two recent, and brilliant, champions of the law, Fredric Jameson and Stephen Greenblatt. After seeing why Jameson and Greenblatt, like much of more recent cultural criticism, aim to exclude subjectivity, we will be in a better position to understand the crucial significance of the subject, and the forces that oppose it in Spenser and Milton.

The first sentence of Jameson's *The Political Unconscious*, "Always historicize!" is, says Jameson, spoken by "all dialectical thought," not by the author. This opening remark foreshadows the denial of subjectivity dramatized in the course of *The Political Unconscious*. Jameson claims that he, as object of the historicizing imperative, has no choice but to interpret as he does. But it is not hard to see that Jameson's Hegelian desire to synthesize all interpretative approaches into a totalizing master narrative actually amounts to a desire to be mastered, to credit history with his own remarkable act of critical will. In this way, he obtains the neutral or scientific version of mastery that Marxism still promises as a cure for the unstable idiosyncrasies of postmodern polemic.[14]

Jameson's projection of his critical insights onto history itself has important implications for his definition of narrative as a victory of system or scheme over individual desire. The antisubjective reading of narrative in *The Political Unconscious* at first comes as a surprise. Jameson asserts that he does not want to reject the idea of the self; that he wants, instead, to incorporate it as an aspect of the larger narrative of history. His goal is for Marx to subsume, without denying, Freud. But if we pay close attention to the argument of "Magical Narratives," the chapter of *The Political Unconscious* that deals most explicitly with genre—and that is, therefore, most relevant to my reading of Spenser and Milton—it will be clear that Jameson actually represses the self and its desires. Jameson chooses romance as his central example of genre because he can claim that romance reveals itself as a collective narrative that supersedes the individual.[15] His anti-individualist bias is also clearly visible in his brief treatment of tragic pathos. According to *The Political Unconscious*, tragedy's "fundamental staging of the triumph of an inhuman destiny or fate generates a perspective which radically transcends the purely individual categories of good and evil."[16] In this study I argue, against Jameson, that one can only understand the shock of tragedy if one retains the idea of a subjectivity irreducible to society's Symbolic laws—what Lacan calls the Imaginary. Tragic suffering is not a generalized or collective cosmic force, but the expression of a particular self's separateness from and vulnerability to others.[17] By distorting tragic pathos into a postindividual phenomenon, Jameson effectively excludes subjectivity from his conception of literature.

Jameson's reinvention of genre criticism remains one of the most ambitious and exciting critical projects of recent years. By focusing on its weakest passages, I am not attempting to deny the obvious magisterial inspiration of *The Political Unconscious*. I want, instead, to point out the motive behind its bias against the self, which is widely shared in current historicist interpretation: the trust in narrative system.

One critic who does deal convincingly with the pathos of the self is Stephen Greenblatt, in his *Renaissance Self-Fashioning*. But Greenblatt, who is, as the title of his book suggests, strongly drawn toward the notion of the self, officially claims to share his colleagues' antisubjectivist bias. By continually making theoretical statements to the effect that discursive systems engender and determine individual subjects, Greenblatt wars against his own confessed desire to see a heroic or tragic individualism in the Renaissance. The ambivalence of *Renaissance Self-Fashioning* over the status of the self declines into unequivocal polemic in a later Greenblatt essay, "Psychoanalysis and Renaissance Culture," which tries to exile the self altogether from Renaissance culture. I will discuss Greenblatt's later text, which deals prominently with Spenser, before moving on to a brief analysis of the worried, creative contradictions in *Renaissance Self-Fashioning* that "Psychoanalysis and Renaissance Culture" reductively avoids.

In "Psychoanalysis and Renaissance Culture," Greenblatt argues against psychoanalysis as a tool for understanding the Renaissance.[18] The individual of the Renaissance, according to Greenblatt, is not an ambitious, self-consuming ego, but a far less grandiose creature, the product of social, economic, and political determinations. Greenblatt's comments implicitly oppose the entire tradition in Renaissance studies since Burckhardt of celebrating proud, sometimes even psychopathic, selfhood.

In "Psychoanalysis and Renaissance Culture," Greenblatt offers Book 1 of Spenser's *The Faerie Queene* as his main example of how the Renaissance rejects subjectivity. "Spenser's concern with psychic experience," Greenblatt writes, "is not manifested in the representation of a particular individual's inner life but rather in the representation of the hero's externalized struggle to secure clear title to his allegorical attributes and hence to his name."[19] Spenser's Red Crosse, Greenblatt suggests, is manipulated into reaching the goal of his quest, determined by the conventions of romance and Christian allegory. Red Crosse remains unknown to himself, defined by the Spenserian system without being able to recognize himself in it. We might compare Greenblatt's treatment of Red Crosse as a pawn of allegorical romance form to the historicizing genre criticism practiced by Jameson. Jameson, in his comments on romance in *The Political Unconscious*, notices that "the traditional heroes of Western art-romance . . . show a naïveté and bewilderment that marks them . . . as mortal spectators surprised by supernatural conflict, into which they are unwittingly drawn, reaping the rewards of cosmic victory without ever having been quite aware of what was at stake in the first place."[20]

Greenblatt and Jameson accurately describe one aspect of romance, its portrait of the magically naive hero or heroine adrift in a symbolic world whose author conceals its narrative twists and turns from his characters. The *Orlando Furioso* of Spenser's precursor Ariosto exemplifies such submission of a naive hero to romance plot. Greenblatt is right when he says, in effect, that Book 1 of *The Faerie Queene* is an Ariostan romance in which plot rules character.[21] But, as I will argue at length, later books of *The Fairie Queene* that enshrine character rather than plot are equally true to romance, and epic, tradition. Discussing Book 1 alone eliminates Spenser's shift from Red Crosse, the clumsy innocent victim of narrative, to two fully accomplished, self-directed protagonists, Guyon and Britomart. Spenser's poetics divides him between system and self in a way that Greenblatt in "Psychoanalysis and Renaissance Culture" proves unable to acknowledge.

The simplifying antisubjectivism of "Psychoanalysis and Renaissance Culture" stands in stark contrast to *Renaissance Self-Fashioning*, Greenblatt's pioneering study of Renaissance subjectivity. Like most new historicists, Greenblatt wants social power to precede the self. But the critical practice, as opposed to the theory, of *Renaissance Self-Fashioning* often enables the self to hold its own against new historicist dogma. *Renaissance Self-Fashioning* has had a profound influence on my project because of its productive practice of reading, which poses the internal psychology of the self against the constraints of the powers that surround it. Greenblatt's practice, in fact, contradicts his theoretical desire to resolve this opposition in favor of power. In his virtuosic and profound practical interpretations, Greenblatt reveals himself as a true heir of Burckhardt, the figure who inaugurates the description of the Renaissance as a story of heroic selves created by a simultaneous rebellion against and cathexis onto structures of authority. In his theory, however—which I emphasize here—Greenblatt tries to escape this Burckhardtian legacy.

Noting the root of Greenblatt's trouble in Burckhardt himself will prepare us for a fuller discussion of *Renaissance Self-Fashioning*. Burckhardt recognizes a constitutive relation in the Renaissance between the aggressive ambitions of the self and an absolutist state power, the *system* of despotism, against and through which this self is defined.[22] Absolutism heralds a new objectivity of thought and, with it, a new subjective freedom. As Burckhardt famously writes, "In Italy this veil [of medieval faith] first melted into air; an *objective* treatment and consideration of the state and of all the things of this world became possible. The *subjective* side at the same time asserted itself with corresponding emphasis; man became a spiritual individual, and recognized himself as such."[23] Burckhardt makes new historicists shudder when he hails Renaissance individualism as a reality whose palpable dynamism causes the laws of feudal society to fade into obsolete fictions. But, unlike the "traditional humanist" caricatured by new historicism, he also sees this individualism as dependent for its very existence on a newly impersonal form of state power. According to Burckhardt, the fifteenth-century Italian city-states invent modern mass society: population statistics, passports, and the will to control the lives of their subjects. Yet, somehow, this impersonal, bureaucratic power remains inseparable from the flamboyant individuality of both tyrant and poet.[24]

New historicism wants to escape from the Burckhardtian dialectic between individual and system. For the new historicist, the ambitious

Renaissance individual that Burckhardt described so convincingly is a fiction, but the force of the social system he depicted with equal mastery—namely, Renaissance state power—is not.[25] Jonathan Goldberg writes that Burckhardt "projected modern man," with his anxious, blustering egoism, "back on to the Renaissance."[26] Goldberg and Greenblatt want to exile the Renaissance subject's famous libido, the passions that define his personality for Burckhardt, in favor of the authoritative sway of a system that "situates" individuals, but knows nothing of individual desire or will.

*Renaissance Self-Fashioning* frequently emphasizes the delusory or inauthentic nature of the heroic personality that Burckhardt celebrated and that Renaissance humanists crafted so energetically. In his epilogue to the book, Greenblatt notes that the Renaissance only had access to "selfhood conceived *as a fiction*."[27] For Greenblatt, this fictive self appears a flimsy, defensive creation when compared with the grim authenticity of political power. He corrects Burckhardt by asserting that the Renaissance gives birth, not to a new individualism, but to absolutism, a newly extreme variety of political constraint that, unlike the individual, is anything but a fable. When Greenblatt fictionalizes the Renaissance ego even as he insists on the reality of Renaissance institutional power, he denies the possibility of the reciprocal relation between the two terms that Burckhardt explored. Power becomes the efficient cause of an ephemeral "subject effect," an immovable bottom line. As a result, the self fades into illusion.

The influence of Foucault and Althusser is visible in Greenblatt's derivation of selves from power, the monumental apparatus of the institution. The Foucauldian emphasis on the institutional production of subjectivity appears most clearly in Greenblatt's definition of the Protestant self, which will be directly relevant to my analysis of ascetic subjectivity in Milton. Reformation self-fashioning, writes Greenblatt, necessarily "involves submission to an absolute power or authority situated at least partly outside the self—God, a sacred book, an institution such as church, court, colonial or military administration."[28] The causal character of Greenblatt's definition is striking: submission, or Foucault's "subjectification," produces individuation. Such causality provides the burden of Greenblatt's Tyndale chapter, in which he states that Protestant inwardness stems from the perception of external authority, of a God who threatens the sinner in the same manner as the Antichrist or unholy monarch.[29]

In Greenblatt's account of the self, Wyatt's rebellious Protestant introspection is produced by the logically prior authority of absolutist power that Tyndale evokes in his God.[30] Similarly, Foucault's *History of Sexuality*, which he was planning at the same time that Greenblatt was writing *Renaissance Self-Fashioning,* implausibly sees the modern self as a product of the collective, imposed order of monastic practice.[31] But when Greenblatt moves from Tyndale to Wyatt he is forced, despite his intentions, to admit the utterly private function of pathos, which turns out to be no mere symptom of the courtly power struggle but a fierce power in its own right.[32] Wyatt's versions of the penitential psalms, Greenblatt admits, draw on a long tradition of religious inwardness to bear witness to "an unmistakably *personal* crisis of consciousness," a crisis that endows the self with an authority just as compelling as that of the political system.[33]

The new historicists' resistance to subjectivity can be very useful as a counter to some earlier scholars' invocations of a bland humanist self. But, more often, the extremist character of this resistance leads to interpretative blindness. I will cite one more example: Shakespeare's *Antony and Cleopatra,* a work that shares with *The Faerie Queene* a dialectic between subjective passion and official law. Antony's pathos as a hero lies in the unbalanced character of this contest, as he takes his stand against the irresistible imperial forces embodied in Octavian. Antony remains unassimilated to Octavian's new, efficient rule, his anachronistic heroism never declining into mere nostalgia. Jonathan Dollimore's new historicist interpretation of the lovers' pathos in *Antony and Cleopatra* as a weak shadow of imperialist desires therefore fails. This is precisely Enobarbus's reading, a cynical escapism that snipes from the sidelines because it cannot suffer the brilliant glare of this play's heroic eros.[34]

We can only understand the Renaissance self in the same terms that we understand the Renaissance state's power: as a compelling fiction with real, if variable, historical effects. The reification of power as an inexorable, faceless force in the work of Dollimore, Goldberg, and others is just as predictable an avoidance of history's unevenness, the local peculiarities embodied in individual subjects, as the reification of the individual that they project onto the old-fashioned humanist other.[35]

The Reformation restates the Renaissance's discovery of a stark difference between subjectivity and narrative determinism in critical, newly urgent form. The double character of the Reformation, both humanly private and supernaturally impersonal, intensifies the dynamic of early Renaissance society, with its paradoxical combination, first described by Burckhardt, of aggressive individualism and newly absolute systems of power. The Reformation subject exists alongside power, whether we conceive power as the prerogative of God or as the social authority that cites God's authority for legitimation. This historical conjunction, in turn, suggests the need to reconcile two critical modes, the one attending to subjective psychology and the other to institutional determinations. Here, as I will suggest in the following pages of this discussion, Damrosch's polarity between subjectively empowered and externally determined discourse provides an apt model for the conflict between self and system in Reformation culture and literature.

# 1
# Pathos and Moralizing in Classical and Renaissance Tradition

> O Conscience, into what Abyss of fears
> And horrors hast thou driv'n me; out of which
> I find no way, from deep to deeper plung'd!
> —*PL* 10.815–44

Frantically assuming infinite guilt, Adam in these lines imagines himself at, and as, the end of history. With his speech of suicidal despair in Book 10 of *Paradise Lost*, Adam joins a tradition that begins with Achilles' lament for Patroklos: the elevation of an utterly private pathos above larger historical, moral, and social agendas. This first chapter begins by comparing Homeric and Miltonic pathos, focusing on how Achilles' sublime grief comes under the pressure of one such agenda, Plato's didacticism, and how Michael's moralism similarly surrounds Adam's pathos in the final books of *Paradise Lost*. Plato's critique provides a model for criticism's later objections to the dangerous effects of poetic pathos—objections that have already been internalized by epic poets like Virgil and Milton. To demonstrate this connection between poetic and critical moralizing, I end the chapter with a discussion of pathos in Virgil's *Aeneid,* along with responses to Virgil by three Renaissance critics: Julius Caesar Scaliger, Torquato Tasso, and Philip Sidney.

Milton's Book 10 features an Adam who is oblivious to the future plot of sacred history. He does not know that history will end, not with a "miserable of happy" peripeteia like the one at which he finds himself now (10.720),[1] but with a celebration of his fall as the felix culpa that enables Christ's redemption of mankind. Adam reduces history to the moment, the sensation of despair that now arrives in him: "This [is] the end / Of this new glorious World" (10.720–21). When, in an exquisite phrase that foreshadows the elegiac Tennyson, Adam describes his and Eve's fate as "A long day's dying to augment our pain" (10.964), all human tragedy becomes a perpetual present. The single agonizing now of the fall that is still occurring dies slowly away even as its intensity increases. Adam fails to see the grand design of sacred history that enfolds and distances his all-consuming present pathos. Michael will point out this design to Adam in the final books and by doing so moralize Adam's position, defining him as father of mankind.

Here Milton joins a tradition. Epic incorporates moralizing or philosophizing abstraction in characters like Michael, the dead Anchises in the *Aeneid*, Virgil in the *Divine Comedy*, and the Palmer and Contemplation in *The Faerie Queene*. Poetry inherits such moralizing figures from the often adversarial criticism that philosophy and theology direct toward its exploitation of readerly emotion. In the *Republic*, Plato's Socrates plays the role of moral censor, subordinating Homer's tragic and sublime pathos to philosophy's more general, abstract (and therefore, for Plato, truer) perspective. The remarkable turn from epic convention in Milton's *Paradise Regained* and *Samson Agonistes* is his discrediting of such a censor figure, signifying the poet's rejection of his earlier hope in *Paradise Lost* that doctrine might frame the pathos of Adam and Eve's private experience, enclosing it securely in a moral or historical pattern. As we shall see, though, Milton even in the final books of *Paradise Lost* displays ambivalence in his attitude toward pathos; Michael does not get an unqualified endorsement from his author.

Michael's doctrinal moralism, like Platonic and Stoic invocations of virtue, wants to annul the uniqueness of emotional experience, its particular loves or sorrows, in favor of a theoretical scheme that will distance and (Michael hopes) liberate Adam from such immediate worldly involvements.[2] In this respect Michael resembles the Socrates of the *Republic*—and differs from the Aristotelian critic or the Freudian psychoanalyst, two other interpreters who figure largely in my study. The analyst does not try to estrange the analysand from emotional experience through narrative abstraction. True, the analysand learns to see emotional relations as formulaic or repetitive patterns, but ideally the distance from past emotion that such a perception enables provides the possibility of a new pathos, a sympathy for one's old self—the generous yet objective feeling that Jonathan Lear compares to the pity and fear of the Aristotelian spectator.[3] Plato and the Stoics insist, by contrast, that no such distanced or neutral sophistication of emotion is possible. For them, pathos, whose threat is conveniently underestimated by Freudians and Aristotelians, overflows any moral structure unless morality combats pathos per se as a corrupting force. Plato in the

*Republic* inaugurates the radical philosophical protest against the pathos of subjectivity, as his theory counters subjective impulses with a moralism that transcends the individual.

Plato's Socrates warns most severely against pathos in Book 3 of the *Republic*. Memorably, he recommends that the good *phulax*, or guardian, should practice self-sufficiency and strive to be *autarkês pros to eu zên* (self-reliant in order to live well) by trying not to experience emotion even when confronted with the loss of a brother or son (Rep. 387d-e).[4] Plato demands even more insensitivity from his *arkhôn* (member of the republic's ruling class) than from his guardian. The ruler must eliminate from himself the self-absorbed weakness of his subjects, who are mainly concerned with their own desires and thus incapable of the objective knowledge that enables the ruler's practice of ideal government.[5]

Here it is relevant to consider the social division of the republic's three classes, which correspond to the three parts of the individual soul. Plato writes in Book 9 that the man governing the city in himself (*kubernôn . . . tên en autôi politeian*) must take care not to be "moved from himself" (*mê ti parakinêi autou*) on account of worldly goods (591e). Such material rewards correspond to the feelings exploited by the lowest level of desire in Plato's system, the *epithumia* or lust for possession that dominates the humblest citizens of the *politeia*. Plato associates his rulers with the contrasting power of *logismos*, reason, and his guardians with the *thumos*, the intensely passionate part of the soul between *logismos* and *epithumia*.

The three parts of the soul, and of the city, are not as separate as Plato wants them to be: the *thumos*' emotional force contaminates the rule of reason. Book 3 of the *Republic* makes it clear that the *arkhôn*, or ruler, cannot simply embody the *logismos*' exact truth: he must rely on myth in the same way that he relies on the guardians' *thumos*. Pure, scientific accuracy does not help one to govern. Instead, the ruler must construct and exploit an emotionally powerful fiction. And such a myth necessarily incites the extreme emotional responses of the *thumos*. The ruler's larger lie (*meizon hamartêma*) makes use of the same passionate invention exploited by the poets who write of grief and desire.[6]

Though the philosophical ruler's myth in the *Republic* is supposed to disseminate truth, however disguised, instead of obscuring it as the poet's does, Plato's ironic knowledge of the similarity between his own strategies and poetic ones runs very deep. Socrates' astonishingly beautiful comparison of the republic's education to "a breeze that brings health from salubrious places" (*hôsper aura pherousa apo khrêstôn topôn hugieian*) leading citizens "unawares" (*lanthanêi*) from childhood to love of, resemblance to, and harmony with, the beauty of reason (*eis homoiotêta te kai philian kai sumphonian tôi kalôi logôi*) (401c-d) shows that his project to combat poetry's lies is itself poetic—and deceptive. Plato's lines echo Sophocles' *Ajax* (558–59), in which Ajax says to his young son, "*teôs de kouphois pneumasin boskou, nean/psuchên atallôn, mêtri têide de kharmonên*" ("until [you go to war] feed on delicate breezes, nourishing your young soul, a delight to your mother").[7] Ajax speaks of youthful ignorance as a graceful breeze, an ephemeral and precious period that fragilely resists, until it is violently disrupted by, the heroic and degrading norms of adulthood.[8] Plato reverses the significance of the image, making it describe the mature philosophical knowledge that will lead the republic's citizens out of their present childhood and into the mature remembrance of truth.

Sophocles' words seem to be pointed exactly opposite to the use that Plato makes of them. But there is a strange and telling similarity between the tragic and the philosophical passages. Plato reveals the poetic nature of his philosophy by championing, like Sophocles, the value of ignorance. The citizens' education in the republic, Plato writes, should take effect "unawares" (*lanthanêi*). Plato here refashions *lanthanein*, the deception or deliberate "forgetting" he has associated with the unjust man as well as the poet, into an enlightened, philosophical myth: education in the ideal city.[9] As Plato well knows, his praise of such covert techniques casts him in the same camp as the poet. The philosopher, no less than the poet, recommends the duplicitous persuasion usually stigmatized by his philosophy.[10] And in praising *lanthanein*, Plato also celebrates the power of *thumos*, the sublime and rebellious emotion that poetic dissimulation incites.

Plato's use of poetry in the service of philosophy, his enlisting of *thumos* for the purposes of *logismos*, does not always prove feasible. Specifically, Plato cannot convert Achilles' *thumos* to his philosophy's didactic goals as he can Ajax's.[11] As a result, Plato must amend Homer's portrait of Achilles to play down the fiercely antisocial threat of the emotion that animates this hero. In Book 3 of the *Republic* Plato comments that Homer was inconsistent when he portrayed an Achilles governed both by *aneleutheria*, "cheapness" or "avarice"—the desire for material honors he voices to Agamemnon in Book 1—and *huperêphania*, the heroic "insolence" he shows in reproaching Agamemnon and avenging Patroklos (391c).[12] In a nearby passage, Plato goes even further. Complaining about the fact that Homer's Achilles "will release the corpse of Hector for ransom, but not otherwise" (390e-91a), Plato defines the Achilles of *Iliad* 24 as a creature of *epithumia* rather than *thumos*, avarice and not heroic pride.[13]

Plato's charge that Achilles is out for material gain falsifies Homer's text. When we reach Achilles' great rejection of Agamemnon's pleas in Book 9, the hero's anger definitively surpasses material considerations, the gifts Agamemnon offers him. In the scene with Priam that Plato mentions, from Book 24, Achilles even more clearly displays *thumos* rather than *epithumia*. Here, at the poem's end, Achilles grieves over the loss of the world he knew in Patroklos as Adam laments lost Eden. It is Achilles' recognition that Priam shares with him a grief so extreme that no others can understand it, and not his desire for monetary reward, that allows him to return the corpse of Hector.

Because the material greed of *epithumia*, unlike *thumos*, can be rationalized, submitted to the understanding that *logismos* exercises, Plato misreads Achilles as an epithumic hero. In a "results-culture" like classical Greece (to use A.W. H. Adkins's phrase), a desire for the material signs of status is far more comprehensible than the crazily ambitious tragic emotions, the *huperêphania* or *hubris*, that Greek literature is also obsessed with, and that base themselves on the neglect of publicly justifiable values.[14] The taste for material luxuries that Plato would attribute to Achilles is shallower, more calculating, than the sublime distraction that Achilles actually displays in Book 24. Desire for *timê*, for the rewards that provide visible evidence of social status, is useful, and rationally explicable, in Greek culture. Grief and love are not, in the ancient as in the modern world.

Plato is worried that poetry may be a more serious adversary than he admits, an opponent not easily vanquished by philosophical reason. He therefore does not want to admit that Achilles' grief offers a full-fledged perspective or judgment on the world, that it can rival the judgments of *logismos*. He wants philosophical moralism to defeat the pathos of poetic subjectivity, but this victory is too easy—the philosopher fails to acknowledge the strength of his poetic opponent. By avoiding the *thumos* in his portrait of Achilles, Plato inadvertently testifies to its power. In Homer, *thumos* is not simply a gut reaction that needs *logismos* to render it comprehensible. Instead, emotion thinks.[15]

The hero's subjective pathos enacts a critique of Greek morality as emphatic as the one accomplished by philosophical reason. The grieving Achilles exhibits a *thumos* that is not answerable or even explicable to social law. Already in Book 9, long before the death of Patroklos, Achilles repeatedly refuses Agamemnon's offer of *dôra* (gifts) in amends for his insult. Achilles asks a radical question about Akhaian social values: whether the material rewards promised by war and the social cohesion it ensures are worth killing enemies and allowing friends to die (9.401–16).[16] In Book 24, Achilles even casts doubt on his society's definition of "enemy" when he identifies his father Peleus with Priam and thus, by implication, himself with Hector (24.535–51).

In the later books of the *Iliad* Achilles displays a desperate, intuitive pessimism that threatens the authority of society. Such grief argues against the integrity of society's vision of itself by fixating on the cost of this vision. In the *Republic*, the philosopher's *logismos* champions the authority of social structure against the recalcitrant individuality that Achilles exemplifies. Plato's larger lie is his wish that society would define grief as useless, as a luxury that the ruling mental function, reason, can decide to renounce. But the emotions of an Achilles, or an Oedipus, or a Medea, are not simply self-indulgent in this way— nor are they self-interested. These characters live through extreme trials that question reason by attacking the value of its involvement in systems of social status and material gain. Tragedy, at least in the *Republic*, seems intolerable to Plato because it renders doubtful his hope that individual motivation can be explained as the logical product of narrow-minded desires and rational clarity, *epithumia* interacting with *logismos*. The *thumos* resists allegiance to all socially functional concepts of profitable action, whether egoist or cooperative; it doubts the self-interest of current Greek society as well as the communal interest of the republic.[17] (It is important to note, however briefly, that this is not the whole Platonic story: Plato swerves definitively from the vision of the *Republic* in other dialogues, like the *Symposium*, in which he enshrines both the poetic work of tragedy and the memorability of its heroic examples, conspicuously including Achilles.)

Because Plato wants to trace a society's values back to its educational program, especially insofar as that education includes poetry like the *Iliad*, he de-emphasizes the aspect of the *Iliad* that subverts social norms—its celebration of the individual's heroic *thumos*.[18] Plato refuses the possibility that tragic art from Homer on may not enforce norms, whether good or bad ones, but instead interrogates their worth. In fact, as Plato does not recognize, the disruptiveness of the *thumos* means that poetic pathos refuses to promote *any* system of social values. (Plato's assumption that literature makes social values more efficient or coherent, rather than disorienting them, lingers on in the totalizing ideological approaches of contemporary criticism.)

In the *Republic*, philosophy appropriates poetic deception in order to reduce its threat. The philosopher wants to discipline the pathos of individuality that poetry represents, to make poetry normative rather than subversive by deflecting its emphasis from individual differences to social codes. Without an efficient communal myth to oversee the programmed ignorance of the mass of citizens, the euphemizing and disciplining of emotion cannot occur. Because the surrender to pathos marks the reckless individuation that defines human personality, Plato must find a way to correct pathos, and with it individuation, on a higher social level—one that will radically supersede the privacy that individual identity requires.

Yet the ironic side of Plato knows that his advocacy of an utterly reinvented society comes down to the mood of an individual: the philosopher's outrageous and unrealizable perspective. Irony appears most dramatically in the self-defeating hyperbole of his utopian communism, whose authoritarian style mandates two definitive signs of anarchic ruin, incest and gender confusion (Rep. Books 4–6). When we recognize that Plato hints at the impossibility of his ideal state, his use of poetic dissembling to advocate this state turns as subversive as the tragic poetry he rejects. The philosopher's truth suddenly becomes a partial, self-doubting fiction.

Subjectivity's subversion of the possibility of a stable doctrinal truth occurs in a less playfully ironic, but equally compromising, way in the final books of *Paradise Lost*. When the reader veers away from Michael's pronouncements on sacred history, the official assurance of God's future republic of the saved, and toward the deeper truth of Adam's individual pathos, he or she questions the didactic authority of a divine voice in the name of a humbler, more affecting human one. The lone pathos of Adam proves more truly poetic than Michael's grand theory, as Achilles' *thumos* is more poetic than the universalizing Platonic voice that condemns it. In Homer as in Milton, pathos has our allegiance over didactic morality.

Like Achilles "sailing" in his grief in the *Iliad*'s Book 24 (5–12), and criticized by Plato for his self-abandoned distraction (Rep. 388a), Adam in Book 10 of *Paradise Lost* immerses himself in an ocean of tormented emotion. Adam feels himself "in a troubl'd sea of passion tost" (10.718), exiled from the governance that only the outside authority of God's moralized history can give him. Milton, like Plato, hints at the practical autonomy of human emotion, the way it overtakes moral-theoretical schemes. Both writers react against this priority by trying to secure a didactic supervisor, a moralizing guardian, for their texts. There are texts in which Plato overturns this moralizing project, as does Milton, I will argue, in the conclusions of *Paradise Regained* and *Samson*. In the *Symposium*, for example, Alcibiades unveils the shock of the bewildering and addictive pathos that Socrates incites in his flustered listeners; and Diotima, leaving us stranded in passionate wishfulness at the end of her speech, offers a glimpse of an estranging, unknowable beauty as tantalizing as Alcibiades' portrait of his teacher.[19] The ecstatic, confusing charisma of Socrates cannot be transmuted into a calm Platonic logos.

In *Paradise Lost*'s final books, Milton both acknowledges a conflictual pathos and attempts, through Michael, to supersede it in the name of stable doctrine. Michael tries to cure Adam's loneliness by showing him the history he will father. In the course of this cure, however, Michael, like Socrates, turns back on his own priorities: he introduces subjective passion to present his doctrine, and such passion finally proves more pressing than doctrinal utterance. Michael, before he gives Adam his society, reduces him to utter isolation. When he witnesses the Flood, Adam is left alone, this time like a suddenly childless father rather than the solitary of Book 10 (11.760). Here, Adam's private emotional perception of loss overwhelms all knowledge of the future world that will place him within a collective history; and Adam's emotion is echoed in turn in his son Milton's image of him.[20] As in Book 10, Adam becomes a world of tears. "Thee another Flood," says the poet, "Of tears and sorrow a Flood thee also drown'd, / And sunk thee as thy sons" (11.756–58).

Michael tells Adam that the sons of Seth, who "now swim in joy," will "erelong . . . swim at large" (11.625–26). Michael's severely ironic, punning humor brandishes the literal facts of sacred history that will show up fallen man's emotion. He explodes the selfish pathos that humans mistakenly elevate into reality. Yet at the same time Michael relies on such pathos: he depicts the Flood as a "world of tears," a vast magnification of the human Adam's personal sorrow. God's truth expresses its grandeur, at this moment in Book 11, by pointing to the enormous difference in scale between the collective fact of sacred history and the lone individual, between universal divine intent and a particular person's response to it. But Milton also locates truth in the response, in the affective capacity of this isolated figure, Adam. Still ignorant of scripture's apocalyptic plot, Adam recognizes only his own emotional intensity as a measure of experience. Even when he has learned the plot, he still clings to the first-person singularity of his experiential passions—and so do we. Accordingly, Milton's vision in the final books must finally rely on an individual pathos that overshadows all communal myths. *Paradise Lost* ends by giving us, not a collective apocalypse, but the grieving, solitary Adam and Eve.

In *Paradise Lost*, then, pathos, which embodies the resistant particularity or individuality of the human, survives the moralizing scheme that tries to subsume it, as Achilles outlives Plato's critique. The second half of this chapter explores some of the ways that both poetry and criticism try to overcome the frustrations that the argument between subjectivity and didacticism entails—most often by claiming that the self's passion conveys an immediate moral message.

How does one make didactic meaning out of the pathos of poetic character? This is a central question for the poem whose Renaissance interpretations occupy most of this chapter, Virgil's *Aeneid*. This most imitated example of epic combines its intense attraction to pathos with a regard for morality that encouraged the Renaissance perception of Virgil as a virtual Christian *avant la lettre*. Because it is so widely seen as a great didactic epic, the *Aeneid* provides a particularly crucial example of the intersection of pathos and morality.

The *Aeneid* relies on a harrowing tragic pathos in its depictions of Aeneas, Dido, Turnus and other characters.[21] Virgil, though he wants to combine moralizing and poetic affect through the force of Aeneas's pious character, cannot make these two terms cohere. As we shall see, readers of the *Aeneid* can only moralize their emotional reactions to the poem by drastically underestimating the ways that Virgilian tragic passion upsets the moral judgments Virgil also invites. Virgil, then, finds an incongruity between poetic emotion and its moralizing paraphrase that troubles both himself and his critics.

The critic wants morality to govern pathos. Not that pathos is unimportant to Renaissance critics, who highly esteem the passionate *enargeia*, or startling pictorial imagination, that seizes the reader of poetry. A skillful poet, we are told, exploits the captivating powers of both sadness and delight.[22] Yet critics worry that such imagination lacks the guiding standards of social morality.[23] Renaissance criticism therefore tries, in different ways, to moralize pathos by supplying a didactic explicitness not present in the text itself.

The critic, then, like the poet, finds himself divided between pathos and moralism. Moralizing impulses conflict with criticism's contrary urge toward a recognition of the amoral power of pathos, a heroic sublimity that makes the question of moral virtue secondary. In the case of Dido, for example, pathos' intensity transcends the commonplace moral prejudices of the *doxa*. The inwardness of emotion, which is especially clear in epic's tragic moments, like the Dido episode, implies a sharing of affect between character and reader that transgresses ordinary moral standards by eliciting the reader's intense sympathy.

Renaissance criticism does not reject Virgil's tragic passion in the interest of didacticism, as Plato did Homer's: the Renaissance is too attached to the notion of the heroic force of pathos, even if that force cannot be made fully responsible. Renaissance critics make an effort to avoid posing an external, mechanical moralism against an amoral pathos. Instead, the three critics I examine—J. C. Scaliger, Tasso, and Sidney—try, like Virgil himself, to integrate morality into pathos, asserting that emotion must have an internal didactic meaning. The difficulty of this effort to prove that, as Sidney puts it, the poetic action that "stirreth . . . the mind" also "instructeth" it will be obvious in the discussion that follows. First, though, I will take a brief detour back to the ancients and forward to Freud to suggest some connections between this chapter's focus on tragic pathos in classical epic and the study of Spenser and Milton that follows.

Readers have always wanted to moralize tragic loss, to assert that tragedy's disasters prove a lesson—an effort epitomized by ancient interpretations of the famous phrase from the *Agamemnon, pathei mathos* (learning through suffering). Most classical and modern tragedies, including the *Agamemnon*, resist this moralizing program. Tragic *tukhê* (chance) subverts the optimistic trust in cosmic coherence that didactic morality requires. Because the internal or inherent moralizing of pathos can never be wholly successful, the Renaissance is tempted by the Stoic attitude toward emotion as a monstrous, alien presence.

In my understanding of this failure of didacticism I have relied on Pietro Pucci, who traces the effort to transform pathos into an internal didactic example back to Greek tragedy and its critic Aristotle. Aristotelian pity, Pucci writes, defends against the palpable shock of the tragic encounter. Through pity, the spectator tries to depart from his or her deeply sympathetic involvement in the spectacle of another's pain, which threatens to conflate spectatorial self and suffering protagonist. To fend off such Dionysian vulnerability, the spectator produces the Apollonian emotion of pity as a self-possessed moralizing on the tragic hero's state. Pucci writes: "The pitier attributes his anguish not to the fear that invades his mind but to his own noble or wise temper"—the social values that give meaning to his sense of self-worth.[24]

Pucci outlines the repression or "forgetting" of an earlier form of pathos, fear, and its primal empathy, in favor of a later one, the pity practiced by the calm Aristotelian spectator-judge. A sympathetic anguish precedes pity, a fear for the other as if the other were oneself. But such a passion is too uncontrolled, too captive to what Lacan calls the Imaginary, to serve the ends of morality. It therefore gives way to a new form of pathos, one that can be moralized: mature pity, which implies the self's firm guidance by the demands of social conscience. Such pity is under the control of the socially determined Symbolic self, in contrast to the more basic Imaginary identification with the hero.[25] According to Lacan, the Imaginary *moi* is passionately attached to, and repelled by, an image of the other that it can neither assimilate nor resist. The later Symbolic *je* covers up the ambivalence of Imaginary desire to stake out a role for itself in society.

Samuel Weber's *Return to Freud* contains the most useful version I have encountered of Lacan's distinction between Imaginary and Symbolic. Weber outlines a deep connection, in the Imaginary stage, between image, pathos, and subjective impulse. This connection, as we will see in the careers of Guyon, Britomart, Eve, and even the Son of *Paradise Regained*, constitutes the desiring self:

The process of projective identification with an image, that is: with something other, something external ... this process remains a constitutive force and factor in the ego that develops from it. Thus, although the ego may claim to be self-identical, although it may strive to subordinate and to appropriate heterogeneity as *its* other, it is in fact in constant rivalry with itself and with everything else; aggressive tension is fundamental to it. The autonomy of the ego is constituted only through a misconstruing [*Verkennung*] and denial [*Verleugnung*] of its structural dependence on others.[26]

For Lacan, the Imaginary is essential to the formation of self. In this reading, the self derives from a misconception induced by a primal fascination with the image of the other. In pursuit of the alluring other, the Imaginary misrepresents its difference from otherness as identity, and thereby seeks, often aggressively, to appropriate the image of the other for or as itself. It wants to ground itself autonomously, on the basis of its own will, and erase any dependence on an alien image. Paradoxically, this appropriative desire also wants to purge the other, to repel the other's image by pretending that it is not constitutive for the self. Aggression, then, emerges directly from Imaginary conflict.

As Weber points out, the relations of social prohibition and law that structure the Symbolic make evident the elusiveness of desire's objects in a less self-deceptive or self-frustrating, and therefore less ruinous, way than the Imaginary. In the Symbolic, the subject does not wish to become proper to itself but simply occupies a position in a structure of meaning that could just as well be filled by any other person. Our place is already assigned. We comfort ourselves with the knowledge that the system was there before us, before we knew what it meant. The Symbolic, in other words, unveils the socially prepared, impersonal nature of signification that the Imaginary protests against with its claim to propriety. Symbolic systems rely on sheer positionality and function, not the specific identity of their agents. But the Symbolic needs the Imaginary moment of fixation to assume determinateness, to provide a beginning for any situation at all. So the image of the other remains crucial for self-definition. Similarly, in Pucci's account, the socially approved emotion of pity, which automatically ennobles the spectator who feels it (Symbolic), derives its energy from the more profound experience of fear (Imaginary). The power of fear, unlike that of generalized Symbolic pity, stems from its location in a particular spectator's idiosyncratic response to a particular tragic hero.

The Symbolic alone is not enough. The Imaginary models a particular self for the emulation of others; it figures forth our desire even as it eludes the lucid justifications of the Symbolic order incorporated in the numerous Renaissance handbooks that prescribe the perfectly self-fashioned composure of knight, ruler, or courtier. In this chapter I argue that the Renaissance critic's effort to overcome this disjunction—by envisioning a Symbolic morality embodied in a pathos that would clarify Imaginary passion's public role—proves finally unrealizable.

The discovery of pity as a moralized, Symbolic sublation of pathos that Pucci discerns in Aristotle and Greek tragedy appears in epic as well (for example, in Books 2 and 3 of *The Faerie Queene*). Guyon and Britomart try to compensate for their captivated, empathic bonds to characters like Mordant, Verdant, or Malecasta, who are close images of themselves, by directing a self-distancing pity toward others, like Grylle and Paridell, who represent easily refused social types rather than potential alternate selves. In Britomart's fervent identification with the shadowy image of Arthegall, an unformed figure like herself, or her fascination with Malecasta, a rival aspect of chastity, the poet shows us what needs to be repressed so that she may finally achieve the moral effect of socially responsible pity in the Hellenore-Paridell episode. Spenser, then, embodies vulnerability to the other, which precedes moralizing, in the fact of the hero's, and reader's, empathy.

Morality-as-repression remains in business because of our sense that there are torrential threats it is trying rather desperately to ward off. The incomplete success of morality thus argues for its necessity as a project. My point of view here runs contrary to that of Fish's reader response criticism. According to Fish, the reading process results in the reader's awareness of a correct answer mandated by the text and anticipated by the reader's best, most conscious, self. But Fish overlooks the true force of the pathos that needs to be repressed so that such orthodoxy may appear. Instead of reinforcing the gains from moral consciousness, my reading of Spenser and Milton emphasizes the losses, the cost of such consciousness in its denial of the irrational, empathic basis of the ego. In my discussion of Spenser's Books 2 and 3 I explore further the secondary, Symbolic pathos of moralizing—pity—and its ongoing competition with the prior Imaginary pathos of attraction that the text exerts on the reader, by describing the distance between Fish-style readerly didacticism and Freudian psychoanalysis.

For much of European literary tradition, the Symbolic must somehow circumscribe or guide the Imaginary. The moment of pathos cannot be allowed to stand on its own: it needs to be justified by way of literature's avowed didactic goals. Modern proclamations that celebrate the thrill of an openly amoral aesthetics are, for the most part, alien to the Renaissance, an era that demands from its poets and critics the defense of pathos, and the literary structures in which it is embedded, as a useful didactic force.[26] A similar didactic interest characterizes most classical critics, with the significant exception of the

Alexandrians. Even Longinus, who has lately been seen as adamantly antididactic and aestheticist, has his moralizing agenda.[27]

Criticism's moralizing efforts can never succeed completely. The risks that poetry poses to critical didacticism perhaps appear most clearly when emotional weakness, associated with tragedy, overcomes the virtuous epic hero.[28] One such moment is Aeneas' first appearance in Virgil's *Aeneid*. Sebastian Regulus, in his 1563 commentary on the first book of the *Aeneid*, defends Aeneas' shuddering reaction to the storm that begins the epic against those readers who may worry that Aeneas' passionate distress will tarnish his heroic image. Regulus claims that Aeneas is not really frightened of death at all: he merely fears dying in an undignified, unheroic shipwreck. Aeneas wants to meet his end in a socially approved, edifying manner—on the battlefield.[29] Regulus, echoing a passage from Aristotle's *Nicomachean Ethics*,[30] thus attributes to Aeneas a heroic security and control that he conspicuously lacks in this first scene. In Regulus's reading, Aeneas, like the Son in *Paradise Regained*, or Guyon in Mammon's Cave, does not actually experience fear in any real sense: he feels only the desire to remain a virtuous example by acting in a properly heroic way. Against the evidence of the text, Regulus transforms one of Aeneas's moments of weakness into an example of didactic strength for the benefit of the poem's reader.

The *Aeneid*'s episodes of martial fury and betrayed love raise the possibility of a divergence from moral standards just as much as Aeneas's depressed passivity does in the shipwreck scene. The differences among the various manifestations of tragic pathos in epic—vengeful anger and despair, madness and love—are important. But my major point in this book is more basic: the way in which all forms of poetic affect, whether best described as *delectare* or *movere* (delight or turbulent emotion), strain against the efforts of both critics and poets to convert affect to moral use (*docere*).[31]

Aside from its tragic aspects, there is another element of epic pathos that it is difficult to persuade to moral argument: its decorum, or vision of an impressive range of characters and their passions. In Book 3 of his massive and influential *Poetices* (1561), Julius Caesar Scaliger describes epic poetry as such a spectrum of characters and events. Indulging in the pathos of poetic depiction, the poet-creator gives his readers a panoramic imitation of the scope of nature itself.[32] Scaliger defines Virgil's epic as a mimetic catalog of human character. In the *Aeneid* "personam vero cum habitu multis in locis habes . . . militaris vero in Mezentio, Turno, Aenea: atque aliter in Camilla, et Penthesilea"[33] (you have characters as they really behave in many passages . . . indeed, the character of a soldier in Mezentius, Turnus, Aeneas: and otherwise in Camilla and Penthesilea). Similarly, Scaliger writes, "Quae naturae sunt, ita describenda erunt: ut nihil non verisimile videatur"[34] (whatever things occur in nature must be so described that nothing seems unrealistic [3.20 (p. 106)]).

Virgil's wide-ranging mimesis, as Scaliger defines it,[35] sets the morally dubious Turnus and Mezentius alongside the virtuous Aeneas. But Scaliger claims that Virgil has a means to reconcile the epic's presentation of a variety of heroic, emotionally impressive types with its need to provide clear models of virtue. The poet, writes Scaliger, adds a moral qualification to his presentation of amoral, passionate epic heroism:

> Quemadmodum Poeta Misenum quum Heroem fortissimum appellasset, superbum tamen agnoscit, ac dementem vocat. Ita Mezentium non minus fortem virum facta ostendunt: immanem tamen atque impium notat [sc. poeta].[36]
>
> (So the poet, although he has called Misenus a most brave hero, nevertheless recognizes his arrogance, and [therefore] calls him crazy. Mezentius' deeds show him to be a man not lacking in bravery: but [the poet] still describes him as cruel and impious.)

Scaliger's—and Virgil's—double takes are telling. Aeneas' trumpeter Misenus at first seems *fortissimus*: but, Scaliger reminds us, Virgil also calls him *superbus* and *demens* (arrogant and crazy). Similarly, Virgil corrects our strong impression of the evil Mezentius' bravery (he is *fortis*) with continual reminders of his ruthless impiety (he is also *impius*). When Scaliger amends his and Virgil's admiring description of these characters' courage, he betrays his nervousness that the appeal of heroic ambition may overcome the reader's proper concern for moral distinctions.

Both poet and critic, then, remain torn between heroic pathos and didactic moralizing. Mezentius, in particular, contributes to Scaliger's moralizing anxiety, and Virgil shares his critic's uneasiness. The poet tells us of Mezentius' hideous cruelty before he even appears in the poem (7.648–54.; 8.482–88.): Virgil seeks to defend us in advance against the powerful image of heroic energy that breaks on us when we finally see him in action. Mezentius' down-and-dirty *aristeia* in Book 10 perfectly expresses his Iliadic heroism, which is not easy to condemn in the warlike twelfth-century context Virgil invokes in his poem. Virgil's presentation and Scaliger's interpretation of Mezentius make him a living example of the gap between morality and the pathos of heroic decorum. The poet's and critic's warnings about his disreputable character try—unsuccessfully—to compensate for the undeniable epic glory of his *aristeia*.[37]

The pathos/moralism conflict appears in the *Aeneid*'s episodes of love as well as its depictions of heroic valor. Here, the reader's sympathy takes precedence over moral judgment. Most memorably, the Dido episode does not alienate us from her desire, proving its danger; instead, it draws us closer to her. Dante's Virgil shows one way of correcting love's disregard for public standards of morality when, in *Inferno* 5, he puts the Dido-like story of Paolo and Francesca in moral perspective by juxtaposing Francesca to two clearly bad examples, the lustful figures of Semiramis and Cleopatra. But the Virgil who wrote the *Aeneid* supplied no such didactic frame; Dido's distress, and her demand on us as readers, is interminable.

Scaliger's wish to distinguish good from bad emotion has its roots in Virgil's own ambivalence about the affair of Aeneas and Dido. There is a crucial difference, however, between the critic's and the poet's perspective. Virgil exploits his reader's similarly emotional responses to Dido's passion and Aeneas's piety, granting to each side its ethical weight. Virgil recognizes in the strife between piety and passion a worthy agon, and gives both impulses their due. Scaliger is more apprehensive than Virgil himself about the potentially corrupting effects of Dido's suffering; his moralizing anxiety leads in several places to reductive readings. Describing Dido's desperate pleas to her sister Anna to bring Aeneas back, Scaliger extracts a moral precept from the Dido story that violates the depth of its effect in the reader of the *Aeneid*:

> Liber enim nullus amans est: neque suus, sed sibi alienus. Iccirco addit [sc. Virgilius] odiosum verbum, supplex. Item quod minime decet hominem sui compotem, Animum summitere amori. [Aen. 4.414] [38]
>
> (Indeed, no lover is free, nor his own, but foreign to himself. Therefore [Virgil] attaches a hateful word, "begging." Likewise [he adds that] what least befits a human being who has mastery over himself [is] "to subject the spirit to love.")

To see the phrases that he cites ("animum summitere amori," "supplex") as evidence for a Virgilian condemnation of Dido's passion, Scaliger must violate the immediate emotional effect of the poem on the reader: he must choose moralism over pathos. In the passage from Book 4 that Scaliger discusses here, the reader, perhaps more than anywhere else in Virgil's poem, sees through Dido's eyes. She has realized that Aeneas' ships are ready to sail, that her fantasized future of marriage with him is over before it has properly begun. Virgil's shaken feeling for Dido is palpable in his intimate second-person address to her: "Quis tibi tunc, Dido, cernenti talia sensus?" (4.408: what did you feel, Dido, when you saw such things?). Augustine's famous account in the *Confessions* of his sorrow over Book 4 suggests a direct opposition between the reader's feeling for Dido, so powerfully elicited by the text at moments like this one, and his respect for Christian morality: Augustine, following Aeneas, came to Carthage. Scaliger, despite himself, bears witness to the accuracy of Augustine's feeling for Virgil. Such outright distortion of the text as Scaliger displays here proves necessary if we are to exile ourselves as readers of the *Aeneid* from subjective emotional identification with Dido's love.[39]

Though Scaliger, in his discussions of Dido's passion and Mezentius's and Misenus's heroism, warns against tragic or heroic pathos to ensure epic morality, such warnings are actually fairly unusual in his book. Like the other critics I examine in this chapter, Scaliger wants the poet's moral to be perceived through, not against, his emotional effects. Morality should be inherent in epic: it should not be necessary for the reader to correct his or her experience of the *Aeneid* with moral precepts forcibly read against the text, as in the case of the Book 4 passage on Dido. Scaliger's claim that a poetic character's moral nature (*mores*) produces his or her emotions (*affectus*) implies his wish to find an equally intimate relation between the reader's moral judgments and responses to poetic passion.[40]

In the same chapter in which he warns against readerly indulgence in Dido's passion, Scaliger demonstrates that he is not opposed to pathos as such: he praises Virgil's use of heroic emotion as an inherently moral force. The reader, Scaliger asserts, will respond to the *Aeneid* in moral terms by feeling its affective impact:

> Affectus sunt qualitates quae proficiscuntur a moribus, et antecedunt actiones....
>
> Nullis profecto Philosophorum praeceptis aut melior aut civilior evadere potes, quam ex Vergiliana lectione....
>
> Laocoontis verba audies, qui nihilo minore affectu inflammatus esse videbatur. Et mulieres Laurentes primaeque, mori pro moenibus ardent. Iisdem legibus hero servus, herus servo provisum curat. Rex pro populo, pro Rege populus audet extrema....[41]
>
> (Emotions are qualities which begin from personal character and pave the way for actions....
>
> Truly, from no precepts of the philosophers can you become better or more public-minded than from the reading of Virgil....
>
> You will hear the words of Laocoon, when he appeared inflamed with no little emotion, and the Laurentine women, "The first, who burn to die before the walls." The slave looks out for the master in the same way that the master looks out for the slave. The king for his people, the people for their king risk everything....)[42]

Scaliger here cites scenes in the *Aeneid* that express virtue as an excess of passion, not a tempering or restraining of it: Laocoon's striking of the Trojan horse (2.40–56.) and the frenzy of the Laurentine women. The latter, in Book 11, are reminiscent of the Trojan women who tried to burn the ships in Book 5. In their headlong passion, they resemble as well Turnus and Amata, the grief-stricken Dido turned bacchante, and Aeneas himself at his enraged moments in Books 2 (2.316: *ardent animi*) and 12. The Laurentine women are conspicuously unlike the example of female courage whom they immediately follow, the resolute Camilla; yet Scaliger chooses to applaud their uncontrolled rage rather than Camilla's discipline. We might also compare the Laurentine women to Laocoon, who, like them, is *ardens*, "burning" (2.41), as he fervently exhorts the Trojans not to accept the Greeks' ruinous *donum*.

Like Laocoon, the Laurentine women represent virtue as a feverish yielding to passion rather than a tempering of it. With this sudden disappearance of the role of temperance in virtuous pathos, Scaliger turns from the model of Aeneas, whose virtue resides in his self-controlled disciplining of his emotions. Now, pathos seems to embody morality, instead of requiring moral distancing or restraint. But how does one tell the difference between virtuous and morally risky enthusiasm— between Laocoon or the Laurentine women, on the one hand, and Turnus or Dido, on the other? Scaliger avoids this issue; he does not, for example, acknowledge the fact that Aeneas and Turnus present mirror images of each other when they are both burning with rage (*ardentes*).

The occasional likeness of Aeneas and Turnus presents perhaps the most trying case for the critic who wants a thoroughly didactic *Aeneid*. But even when Scaliger gives less ambiguous examples of friendly, filial, and paternal emotion, he is forced to confront the ways in which the poem's virtuous characters court comparison with its morally doubtful ones:

> Priamus in Politae caede omnia obliviscitur praeter filium, Regiam dignitatem, vitam. Idem pro filii cadavere castra hostium transmittit securus periculi, inermis, supplex, ad hostis pedes abiectus, prostratus. Laocoon manifesto in discrimine auxilium nato fert: contemnens potius mortem certam, quam sperans ultionem. Mezentius nato interfecto mori vult.[43]
>
> (Priam, when Polites is slaughtered, forgets his regal dignity, his life, everything except his son. Furthermore he travels through the enemy's camps for the sake of his son's body without care for danger, unarmed, a beggar throwing himself prostrate at the feet of his enemies. Laocoon in a clear moment of crisis brings help to his son: scornful of certain death rather than expecting to exact revenge. Mezentius, since his son has been killed, wishes to die.)

Significantly, Scaliger in this passage calls Priam's posture before Achilles (2.540–43) "supplex," a word he applies as a condemnation of Dido on the very next page, labeling it, as I have mentioned, "odiosum verbum."[44] The similarity between Priam's and Dido's pathos, their comparable emotional agitation, blurs the moral distinction between them that Scaliger wants to assert, though Scaliger refuses to recognize this sudden ethical uncertainty.

Another moral difficulty enters this passage when Scaliger mentions, alongside the emotions of two virtuous characters, Laocoon and Priam, the evil Mezentius' passionate regret on hearing of his son Lausus's death: "Mezentius nato interfecto mori vult." Comparing these three characters' emotional and extreme concern for their sons, Scaliger finds himself unable to assert the necessary moral distinctions among them. Mezentius is the cruelest character in the *Aeneid*; his place here alongside Priam and Laocoon enforces the impression that moral definitions become very hard to impose if one acknowledges the effects of emotion on the reader. Scaliger's reaction here duplicates Aeneas's own when he is spurred by Lausus's eager filial piety to thoughts of his own feeling for his father (10.822–24). The pathos of Lausus defending his father, along with Mezentius' final repentance and heroic death, which make him seem almost virtuous (10.846–72.), momentarily overwhelms the obvious moral difference between Anchises and Mezentius.[45]

The doomed Mezentius's tragic charm, when placed beside Lausus's pious responsibility, threatens the project of the moralizing critic. Epic's presentation of morally various but still intensely appealing characters argues against the selectivity that ethical choice demands. The resulting danger of moral relativity has been apparent since Plato, who writes in his *Laws* that the poet loses his "judgment" because he "must often contradict his own utterances in his presentations of contrasted characters, without knowing whether the truth is on the side of this speaker or that."[46] From Plato's *Ion* on, the critic needs a morally discriminating didacticism to set against his temptation to view epic as the wide-ranging, and morally neutral, exercise of decorum. Disturbingly, the epic's all-embracing sweep acts as a moral equalizer, militating against the triumph of good over evil. In epic, concerns of poetic justice risk being subordinated to the more pressing fact that evil is at least as fascinating as goodness. The moral difficulty that a protean, encyclopedic poetics presents persists in both *The Faerie Queene* and in Milton's monistic image of the unfallen cosmos as a variegated harmony that incorporates evil alongside goodness.

It is not easy for a reader to categorize the *Aeneid*'s characters, in their moments of passion, on a moral basis. Attracted by the intensity of pathos, we respond to Dido's grief as sympathetically as to Aeneas's and applaud Turnus's courage along with Pallas's. The reader does not feel the differences among these heroes as an ethical hierarchy. Scaliger's attempt to inject didactic point into passion by distinguishing between morally correct and morally dubious emotions ends in a confusion of distinctions and the strong implication that all Virgilian passions are somehow noble. Scaliger here stumbles against a basic problem in his Aristotelian ethics, whose habit of depicting virtue and vice within an endless variety of distinct situations tends toward a moral relativism that can feel very uncomfortable. The Aristotelian's generous acknowledgment of the world's variousness makes moral judgments difficult to justify.

In the first book of his *Discorsi del Poema Eroico* (1594), Torquato Tasso, like Scaliger, tries to incorporate didactic morality within emotion. Tasso emphasizes the Renaissance commonplace that the poet must induce virtue through pathos, through the reader's enjoyment of heroic representation, not the dry "usefulness" of moral advice.[47] But this hopeful union of the aesthetic and the moral fails at moments when Tasso reminds the poet to select only virtuous situations and characters, thereby subordinating pleasure to morality. Moral virtue suddenly becomes a "higher art" than poetic skill.[48]

In Tasso, as in Scaliger, a definition of good poetry as the panoramic pathos of decorum strives against a moral injunction that the poet represent the triumph of a good hero. In epic, Tasso writes,

> As in a little world, one may read here of armies assembling, here of battles on land or sea, here of conquests of cities, skirmishes and duels, here of jousts, here descriptions of hunger and thirst, here tempests, fires, prodigies, there of celestial and infernal councils, there seditions, there discord, wandering, adventures, enchantments, deeds of cruelty, daring, courtesy, generosity, there the fortunes of love, now happy, now sad, now joyous, now pitiful.[49]

In passages like this one, Tasso accepts the mimetic disinterestedness of encyclopedic epic. The poet, he writes, "is an imitator of human actions and habits . . . and if he is a good imitator, his poetry will be good."[50] Elsewhere, however, Tasso emphasizes that this kind of "good," mimetic skill decisively differs from virtue. And virtue, of course, is necessary to a "good"—in another sense—"poet":

> The poet is an imitator who could, as many have, use his art to delight without profiting. If he avoids that, he is a good poet, and in this perhaps like the orator, who is judged, as Aristotle held, not only for his skill but for his will [non solamente dalla scienza, ma dalla volontà].[51]

The morally, not merely technically, good poet plays his own censor. He chooses to represent virtue rather than vice in his poem, "since it is utterly unworthy of a good poet to give the pleasure of reading about base and dishonest deeds, but proper to give the pleasure of learning together with virtue."[52] As we have just seen, though, Tasso admits elsewhere that "base and dishonest deeds," as well as virtuous ones, provide poetic pleasure. Vice takes its place alongside virtue in the epic's "little world."

In Tasso, then, a gap opens between the poet's decorous "skill" and his moral "will." From the perspective of decorum, it is perfectly appropriate for the poet to depict evil actions instead of, or in addition to, the morally exemplary "action noble, great, and perfect."[53] In a similar vein, Tasso in the second book of the *Discorsi* applauds Achilles in strikingly amoral terms: "Wrath indeed strikes everyone as eminently suitable (*convenevolissima*) [to a hero]: Homer himself made the wrath of Achilles the subject of his supremely lofty poem."[54] Yet Tasso also nervously remarks that "Achilles... cannot be defended against Plato's objections to his avarice and cruelty in the dialogue on justice [that is, the *Republic*]."[55]

Tasso's ambivalence over the heroic anger of Achilles resembles his worry about the moral value of love, which the *Iliad* incarnates in the shape of Helen. On the same page of Book 2 that contains Tasso's praise of Achilles, we find his argument for love as a proper (*convenevole*) epic subject:[56]

> I cannot pass in silence over the love of Helen, which was decidedly noble, perhaps even decidedly beautiful, however wrong.... Isocrates held that all the grace and charm of Homer's poems springs from the beauty of Helen.[57]

Tasso begins his discussion of love by admitting an obvious case of passionate decorum winning out over morality: the rivalry for Helen. Paris's and Menelaus's love for Helen is "noble, perhaps even decidedly beautiful, however wrong." With this elevation of eros, Tasso implies that Homer's poem, like Helen herself, attains distinction first of all for its "grace and charm."[58] Tasso here chooses the amoral aesthetic allure of Helen's beauty, and Homer's poetry, over the moral obligation to curb one's attraction to such pleasures. But when, elsewhere in his text, he more characteristically claims Virgil's superiority over Homer, Tasso espouses a moralizing standard that praises the quality of the poet's text on the basis of the ethical worth of the character he depicts. Reiterating Plato's objection to Achilles' supposed avarice, Tasso writes,

> But Virgil, unless I am mistaken, had a better notion of general decorum: in Aeneas he gave shape to piety, religion, temperance, strength, magnanimity, justice, and every other knightly virtue; and in this particular he made him greater than the cruel Achilles, who sold the corpse of Hector to his pleading father, whereas Aeneas freely gave up the corpse of Lausus.[59]

As Tasso explains it, Virgil's "notion of general decorum" is "better" than Homer's, not because it is more appropriate but because it is more edifying—not for reasons of aesthetic decorum but for moral reasons.[60]

By contrast, Tasso asserts decorum, the pathos of impressive depiction, over morality when, earlier in Book 3 of the *Discorsi*, he criticizes Ariosto for showing his pagan heroes Rodomonte and Ruggiero as better than they probably were: "Often moral habit is good but inappropriate (*molti fiate i costumi sono buoni, ma non sono convenienti*), like strength in a woman."[61] In Book 2 of the *Discorsi*, Tasso stated epic's need to render its heroes as clearly virtuous as possible; tragedy, less concerned with moral persuasion, can rely on mixed characters.[62] But here, in his critique of Ariosto, Tasso makes morality yield to decorum. He acknowledges the aesthetic value of seeing characters as ethically mixed, regardless of the obstacles such realism may present to a poet's didactic intent.[63]

Philip Sidney, like Tasso and Scaliger, wants to resolve the conflict between the reader's emotional and his moral response into a coherent didacticism. Like them, however, he is afflicted by the division between pathos and the didactic, which stems from his own ambivalent relation to these two terms. In his *Apology for Poetry* (1583), Sidney's ambitious neo-Platonic critical project claims an effective connection between pathos and didactic morality in order to argue against Stoic and scholastic philosophy's separation of the two.[64] He defends epic poetry's incitement to passion, its "inflam[ing]" of the mind, as the most effective and desirable incarnation for a didactic project. Stirring up the reader with "desire to be worthy," Sidney claims, is the best way to "inform [him or her] with counsel how to be worthy." But when Sidney considers the actual form that moral decisions take in the *Aeneid*, he is compelled to recognize that Virgilian piety, whether the reader defines it in terms of Roman or of Christian morality, often requires a refusal of passion. Aeneas remains pious "in obeying the god's commandment to leave Dido, though not only all passionate kindness, but even the human consideration of virtuous gratefulness, would have craved other of him."

In a rhapsodic catalog of other classical heroes and heroines, Sidney tries to do what he could not manage in the case of Aeneas' affair with

Dido. From Achilles to Medea, he defends them as examples of the inherently moral quality of poetic pathos:

> Let us but hear old Anchises speaking in the midst of Troy's flames, or see Ulysses, in the fullness of all Calypso's delights, bewail his absence from barren and beggarly Ithaca. Anger, the Stoics said, was but a short madness. Let but Sophocles bring you Ajax on a stage, whipping and killing sheep and oxen, thinking them the army of Greeks, with their chieftains Agamemnon and Menelaus, and tell me if you have not a more familiar insight into anger, than finding in the schoolmen his genus and difference. See whether wisdom and temperance in Ulysses and Diomedes, valor in Achilles, friendship in Nisus and Euryalus, even to an ignorant man carry not an apparent shining. And, contrarily, the remorse of conscience in Oedipus; the soon-repenting pride of Agamemnon; the self-devouring cruelty in his father Atreus; the violence of ambition in the two Theban brothers; the sour sweetness of revenge in Medea; and, to fall lower, the Terentian Gnatho and our Chaucer's Pandar so expressed that we now use their names to signify their trades; and, finally, all virtues, vices, and passions so in their own natural states laid to the view, that we seem not to hear of them, but clearly to see through them.[65]

Trying for a clearly moralized decorum, Sidney points to what he considers the unequivocal virtue of Anchises and Ulysses, and the unequivocal vice of Gnatho and Pandarus. But some of the cases that Sidney cites as clear-cut are, in reality, rather confusing. Homer's Odysseus proves far from completely resistant to Calypso's charms, and Chaucer's Pandarus is far from contemptible. The central example of Ajax, which occupies the most space in Sidney's discussion, complicates the moral division considerably more. With the phrase "brief madness," Sidney alludes to Seneca's famous argument against anger in his *De Ira* (1.1.2: "Quidem itaque e sapientibus viris iram dixerunt brevem insaniam"). In Seneca as in Sophocles' *Ajax*, passionate uncontrol contaminates reasoned judgment.[66] Seneca's poetic depiction of anger warns against the infectious quality of passion in the name of reason. Yet, paradoxically, in the course of his warning he gives himself over to the passionate portrayal of anger in gasping, vehement style: "Flagrant emicant oculi, multus ore toto subor exaestuante ab imis praecordiis sanguine, labra quatiuntur, dentes comprimuntur, horrent ac surriguntur capilli, spiritus coactus ac stridens" (1.1.4: my eyes burn and spark, I am hot all over my face because of blood rushing from the heart, my lips are shaking, teeth grinding, hair bristling and rising, my breathing is a thick wheeze). As in Plato, in Seneca philosophy's rational program runs on the poetic feel of agitated enthusiasm. The extreme nature of Seneca's vivid image of gnashing teeth, flashing eyes, and hair standing on end, only one of many similarly thrilling moments in his text, undermines his radical distinction between reason and emotion.[67]

What kind of "insight into anger" does Ajax's madness offer an audience? The spectator responds sympathetically throughout Sophocles' play to Ajax's refusal to submit to authority and relinquish his desire for revenge, however frighteningly extreme this desire may be.[68] Similarly, the "sour sweetness" of Medea's revenge proves more sweet than sour for the sympathetic spectator compelled by her story.[69] The fury of Ajax and Medea really teaches us its own sublime intensity, instead of providing practical moral advice for avoiding such madness ourselves. Sidney, despite his claim for the educative value of tragic pathos, cannot finally convince us that our distressed, intense exposure to literary disasters might help us avoid them in real life.[70]

Sidney, nevertheless, still tries to moralize the effect of such pathos. He writes that the reader or spectator of tragedy knows the seductive danger of passions because he or she, instead of merely "hear[ing] of" them, "clearly see[s] through them." Sidney's rhetoric here covers a crucial ambiguity in his argument. Does seeing into the depth of passion mean "see[ing] through [it]," discerning a morality truer and more basic than passion's illusory heat? Or does morality exist within, as, passion—so that "through" signifies *by means of*? Sidney wants the union of emotion and morality, pathos and didacticism: "stirring" and "instructing" the reader should be perfectly congruent. Yet the idea of seeing beneath passion suggests the contradictory Stoic position that morality means the ability to distance oneself, as a reader or spectator of one's life, from a contagious involvement in pathos. For the Stoic, to stand back from emotion is to have insight into it.

Sidney's momentary Stoic posture is telling. Sidney, Scaliger, and Tasso, at certain crucial moments in their arguments, all follow Plato and the Stoics in making tacit allowance for the autonomy of emotion, the sense in which it, instead of a mere means to an ethical telos, remains a mysterious, stubbornly irreducible part of the individual—a power that we must distance or see through if we are to retain our hold on moral judgment. Plato calls this mystery the *thumos*, a psychic agency that deeply troubles his theory. Plato knows the nobility of the *thumos*, as the intense evocations of eros in the *Symposium*, the *Phaedrus*, and other dialogues attest. But, as we have seen, he also tries to discipline or avoid this rough, disruptive face of human desire, with its erratic and transgressive habits.

The conflicting, unreliably combined poles of moral judgment and poetic pathos are as explicit in Spenser as in Plato or the Renaissance critics I have been discussing. Spenser alludes to the risks of pathos when he evokes Burleigh's disapproval of his amorous subject matter at the beginning of his Book 4 —a reminder of official morality's demands that we might well expect after Book 3 of *The Faerie Queene*, with its rapt focus on erotic desire. Much of Spenser's third book, like the medieval and Renaissance romances that provide its major sources, marks a disjunction between love and honor, belying the poet's assertion that knightly courage flowers from the root of amorous devotion. A critical distance remains between Britomart's eros and the moral imperative toward honor that she is made to follow.[71] Love, no matter how faithful, does not moralize Spenser's song. In *The Faerie Queene*'s Book 2, as well, emotion threatens virtue, spurring Guyon's Stoic effort to refuse passion. From the very beginning of his poem, in Red Crosse's story, Spenser hints at the problem that looms full-blown in the specter of Burleigh: can the poet reconcile pathos with virtue?

# 2
# *The Faerie Queene,* **Book 1**

Red Crosse, writes James Nohrnberg in his *Analogy of The Faerie Queene,* "Was not popular at court . . . and his pride was hurt": thus the hero sets out on his quest. Red Crosse errs, according to Nohrnberg, because of excessive "self-reliance" and a corresponding lack of "self-knowledge." Nohrnberg is Spenser's best, most wonderfully encyclopedic reader, but his remarks are indicative of a general impulse in Spenser criticism that this chapter aims to criticize: its indiscriminate attraction to character psychology. As I will argue, Red Crosse is far less of a character in the psychological sense than Guyon or Britomart, and this difference provides a major key to the development of Spenser's poem.

Pathos plays a central role in *The Faerie Queene*'s progress from the book of Red Crosse to the book of Guyon, from plot to character. Unlike Books 2 and 3, Book 1 does not associate emotion with subjectivity. Instead, Book 1 uses both the strange, spectacular pathos of allegory and the emotional impact created by confusions of comedy and tragedy to subordinate character to narrative. For Red Crosse, emotion is an external force linked to plot rather than an inward aspect of personality, as the Despair and Contemplation episodes, especially, demonstrate. Guyon and Britomart, by contrast, prove their hidden awareness of the close relationship between pathos and individual consciousness.[1] Because of his subordination to providential narrative structure, Red Crosse lacks Guyon's and Britomart's subtly attuned attraction, and resistance, to the faults of our common nature. In Lacan's terms, Red Crosse's Symbolic agency proves hollow because he lacks the Imaginary desire that will provide the subjective center of heroic personality in Books 2 and 3.

The core of my case against totalizing readings of *The Faerie Queene,* which usually assert either that all the poem's characters are psychologically developed or that none is, is that a central shift in narrative mode occurs in Spenser's 1590 epic: from external in Book 1 to internal in Books 2 and 3. In 2 and 3, Guyon and Britomart suspect how their own desires impel the story, as Red Crosse does not.[2] Book 1 allegorizes romance to give plot—ultimately the plot of sacred history—a controlling didactic function; Books 2 and 3 carefully withdraw from this allegory's providential direction so that they can explore character as the site of moral truth.[3]

Guyon's subjective sensitivity to pathos reveals him as an exemplary knight, a figure with whom the reader identifies. Red Crosse's lack of consciousness, and his reading of pathos as an external trap, makes him all the more fitting as a different type of romance hero, the naive loser victimized by his author's plot twists. Una, the Dwarf, Arthur, and Contemplation continually rescue Red Crosse from the trouble his ignorance leads him into. Chrétien, with his bumbling Perceval, supplies a notable precursor for Red Crosse, as Nohrnberg remarks;[4] one also thinks of Malory's unlucky Balin and Ariosto's Ruggiero.[5] Red Crosse's unpropitious character in Book 1 remains a function of plot. A fuller vision would require from Red Crosse a self-reflexive sense of his person, the desire to direct himself, rather than what he actually has, the need to be well directed. Book 1 cannot present a hero who confronts his pride, only one who embodies it, largely unawares, and who therefore misses the pressing moral question that pride presents.

Many other critics have, like Nohrnberg, endowed Red Crosse with personal flaws, implying that he is a realistically motivated figure. But such analysis proves unsuited to this comically unreflective hero of Ariosto-influenced romance. As Patricia Parker writes of Book 1, "what seems more crucial" than the ethical question "'what did Red Crosse do wrong?'" is "the romance experience of not knowing where lines are until they have been violated or crossed"[6]—an experience that, I would add, refuses explanation in terms of the character psychology that grounds our usual notion of ethics. Red Crosse remains a creature of providential narrative structure, not a psychological hero. Nohrnberg is forced to admit, despite himself, that psychological assessments are really out of place in Book 1 when he writes, "It is not obvious why Redcrosse is so 'prone' to pride after escaping its House; the triumph of Orgoglio seems to follow on no great overweeningness, but merely on the return of Duessa."[7]

As readers we are continually tempted to psychologize Spenser's fiction, to make it make sense in terms of character. This temptation is a reasonable response to the poet's suggestion in his Letter to Ralegh that he will fashion an ethical exemplar for his reader. But in Book 1 the reader finds the psychologizing impulse impossible to sustain. If we translate allegory into heroic consciousness by claiming with Norman Maclean that "Red Crosse, rescued by Arthur [from Orgoglio, in Canto 8], now perceives Duessa's ugliness" and that this insight "indicates the restored capacity of Holiness to recognize falsehood,"[8] we must then ask why Red Crosse fails to see Despair's falsehood in the poem's very next canto. Red Crosse fails simply because he lacks Guyon's and Britomart's subjective consciousness. Unlike them, he cannot recognize moral choice as a force of self-definition.

Spenser's transition to realist character psychology in Books 2 and 3 is not a teleological progress. In later books, Spenser again puts aside psychic inwardness, emphasizing the externalized social patterns of heroic competition and amorous pursuit (in Books 4 and 6) and justice (in Book 5). Spenser's mixing of genres, one of the most noticeable aspects of his art, obstructs the potential for narrative teleology: the mixture renders providence as error, a wandering to and fro among kinds of literature. *The Faerie Queene* essentially concerns the differences of literary genres: chivalric romance and Christian quest, Ovidian and Petrarchan stories of love. By positioning himself both affectionately and critically toward these generic modes—for example, relishing Red Crosse's cartoonlike romance bravado while criticizing it as ethically inadequate—Spenser holds their differences in suspension, displaying their tensions instead of resolving them in favor of the "higher" genre or level of discourse.[9] Nothing could be more different from Milton's strenuous effort for a sacred poetry that will transcend the pagan modes it evokes.

Though Spenser in Books 2 and 3 will wander away from the impulse to providential design that Book 1 displays, this impulse still remains his starting point. Its importance is traditional: Book 1's plot-oriented, suprapersonal presentation of moral questions stems from the strain of Christian didacticism that follows classical modes of ethics, which in effect choose plot over character by trusting in the overarching cosmic structure that temporal destiny makes visible. Charles Taylor writes that for classical philosophers the soul, to attain wisdom, need only be turned in the direction of cosmic order. In other words, the soul's perception of order results immediately in the realization of order's truth. In Plato, for example, when one leaves the cave and moves toward the ideal, one achieves the wisdom that the ideal offers: truth persuades instantly. Classical ethics, in general, sees virtue as following automatically from the sage's awareness of the universe's good form. An important aspect of Christianity remains loyal to this classical idea: the Christian impulse to invoke providence, the temporally apparent fact of God's plan, as the source of goodness.

Augustinian ethics represents a contrasting, character-based side of Christianity, one that decisively departs from classical notions of virtue. Augustine deflects the emphasis of ethics from the perception of cosmic order to the individual soul's struggle to realize order within himself or herself. No longer, as in Plato, does knowledge of the good lead automatically to its pursuit. For Augustine perception of the truth remains subject to the soul's desire or will; it is even constituted by this will.[10] Pathos plays a key role here. Because the Augustinian will is symbiotic with the fallen emotion it strives against, emotion becomes in Augustine a central locus for moral belief.[11] The perception of pathos as proper to the particular individual, as a part of personality rather than an impersonal or natural force, marks Augustine's provocative alienation of the self from the orders of universal nature and divine design, his proof of an autonomous desire for salvation.[12]

Spenser's allegory in Book 1 testifies to Christianity's interest in the classical view of a suprapersonal plan, the counter to Augustinian individualism that Taylor describes. The book of Revelations, a major subtext for Book 1, participates in such a plan: its allegory enforces a monumental shift from earthly, experiential drama to cosmic schema in the service of didactic effect. The apocalyptic allegory of Book 1 secures the importance of its narrative by fixing it as an eternally valid, biblically authorized story, and reducing character to a merely local aspect or illustration of this story. Following Revelations, Spenser's allegorical representations in Book 1 emphasize the absolute fact of God's order and militate against the Augustinian emphasis on the difficulty, and the personal, inward nature, of the will to perceive this order.

Book 1's allegory stands for the possibility that Red Crosse might lose his status as character altogether and become a merely ornamental feature of the narrative. When Red Crosse comes upon emblematic allegorical figures like Despair or the Seven Deadly Sins, he risks being converted by the allegory into an even less subjective, more abstract embodiment of stereotypical qualities than he already is. Red Crosse's very first allegorical encounter, his meeting with Error, shapes the meaning of his entire career by threatening him with such reduction. Turning herself into one astonishing spectacle after another, Error exploits a manipulative pathos of the quasi-miraculous, in contrast to the pathos of subjectivity featured in later books of *The Faerie Queene*. In doing so, she renders Red Crosse a passive, abstracted victim of her plot. Error embodies the indecorous, tricky shifts of mood that endanger Red Crosse in this and subsequent encounters.

As befits her status as the symbolic representative of an errant knight's adventures, Error is multifarious, protean, and treacherously ambiguous. Most treacherous is the subtle parallel between the monster and the knight who faces her. In the case of both Error and Red Crosse, a deceptive mirroring of a virtuous exemplar occurs. Red Crosse's adventures bear some resemblance to those of St. George, a champion of God, but when he rejects Una, he divides himself from the saint's devotion to truth. Error presents a similarly distorted mirror of divine virtue. Like the offspring of the pelican, a familiar symbol of Christ, Error's brood feed on her dying blood. But then, surprisingly, they die themselves, frustrating the suggested parallel with Christ and his believers (sts. 16 –26).

The erroneous disproportion between Error and Red Crosse on the one hand, and their Christian models, on the other, runs even deeper: it infects the models themselves. St. George, Red Crosse's prototype, offers a dubious, skewed image of sainthood. More than any other, this saint resembles one of romance's pulp fictions. Similarly, Error, with her grotesque parody of charity (she suckles, swallows, and vomits her infant-like "yong ones" [st. 15]), presents an especially gruesome version of a virtue that is already, for Spenser, distorted by its central place in the Roman church.[13]

The fact that, despite these likenesses between them, Error is a hideous monster, whereas Red Crosse is an attractive, well-intentioned knight, speaks for Error's insidious capacity to cross the borders of decorum and readerly judgment. This is the point of the strangely serene pastoral simile in stanza 23 beginning "As gentle Shepheard in sweete even-tide . . ."—a strikingly inappropriate image for Red Crosse's clumsy, drastic battle with Error, until one remembers that she (mis)represents the inappropriate.

As Error's story continues, her rapid transformations produce an important shift of tone. Stanza 25 conveys an enigmatic and bizarre note of mystery: Error undergoes a Christ-like sacrifice for her brood, who "Mak[e] her death their life, and eke her hurt their good." In stanza 26, when the overstuffed corpse of Error is not, like Christ's, resurrected, but instead bursts open, the reader's fascination with Error's paradox turns to disgust. Our shift from wonder to nausea corresponds to a recognition that the pamphlets vomited by Error grotesquely mimic, instead of properly evoking, Christ's sacrifice and his Word. Such literature frustrates its own avowed purposes through its mockery of the proper, authoritative text, producing a captivating, but monstrously disproportionate, mass of mere words. Error's strange parody of Christian sacrifice pushes Christ's capacity to induce awe through miracles, an aspect of the savior especially celebrated by Rome, to a sickening extreme.

Error's spectacular pathos here tempts the hero to an easy didacticism. Spenser concludes his portrait of Error's self-destruction with a moralizing pronouncement that must represent Red Crosse's opinion rather than the author's: "Well worthy end / Of such as drunke her life, the which them nurst; / Now needeth him no lenger labour spend, / His foes have slaine themselves, with whom he should contend" (st. 26). The knight's facile didactic reading bears an uncanny similarity to the quick-fix moralism dispensed to readers by the heretical "bookes and papers" that Error vomits (st. 20). Red Crosse *should* still be contending with his foe, instead of complacently assuming Error's defeat.

Red Crosse's complacency shows itself in his assumption that he "s[ees] the vgly monster plaine" (1.1.14): Spenser argues against his own character's perception when he adds that "plaine none might her see, nor she see any plaine" (1.1.16).[14] By upsetting Red Crosse's confident definition of Error, the poet overturns the knight's brave self-image. While Red Crosse is the heroic victor in this encounter, appearing confidently serene as the gentle shepherd, he also ends up clumsily flapping his hands, "annoyed" (1.1.22) by the "gnat"-like "murmurings" of Errour's brood. By the end of stanza 23, Red Crosse has reverted from the "gentle" aristocrat in pastoral disguise to a rustic oaf: "With his clownish hands their tender wings / He brusheth oft, and oft doth mar their murmurings." Having a swarm of insects for an enemy—an enemy that finally and paradoxically self-destructs through no heroic action of his own—mars Red Crosse's self-assumed valor far more than he mars them. The blurry mirroring of subject and object in the poet's description of Error ("plaine none might her see, nor she see any plaine") implies an intertwining of Red Crosse and his opponents.[15] Error's insect young cluster around Red Crosse as they did around the monster herself (st. 23): Errour's mess rubs off on Red Crosse. As a result, he looks clownish, an example of boyish, backwoods enthusiasm rather than genteel solemnity.

In Canto 1, Red Crosse gets "wrapt in Errours endlesse traine" (st. 18) because the striking pathos of a poetic image, Error's hideous and confounding freak show, subverts any possibility of independent thought.[16] By incarnating the emotional authority of emblematic vision, Error shapes Red Crosse.[17] Red Crosse's most serious mistake, his acceptance of the false Una constructed by Archimago, follows from Error's sense of allegory as a duplicitous, shifting vision that fixes or fixates its victims: the sight of the seeming Una defines him just as the sight of Error did.

Spenser drives home the spectacular nature of allegorical sight when Red Crosse surrenders, not to the increased temptation of sexual desire which Archimago offers him in Canto 1, the seductive Una appearing to him in dream vision, but to Canto 2's more artificial, staged temptation of jealousy. In Canto 2 Archimago displays to the knight a false

Una cavorting with a lover analogous to Red Crosse himself. Here we get not a dream but a waking theatrical spectacle, as Archimago calls to Red Crosse "Rise rise unhappy Swaine . . . / Come see, where your false Lady doth her honour staine" (1.2.4). Red Crosse is ready, even eager, to see the real Una in the puppet creature constructed by Archimago. This magic, which remains outward rather than inward, a show not a fantasy, succeeds because it responds to Red Crosse's own permanently externalized, puppetlike nature, as expressed in his automatic reactions to what he sees. Red Crosse remains a literal, and therefore powerless, reader of scenes.[18]

As I will argue, Book 1 also preys on Red Crosse's literal-minded lack of agility when he mistakes kinds of pathos: he sees comedy where he should be seeing tragedy and vice versa. Such mistakes signal that we must perceive Red Crosse not as a self ripe for ethical evaluation but as a pawn of the good—so that his deeds alone, rescued from his faulty interpretations, may serve a virtuous plot. But, because Spenser (or is it Archimago?) is writing this romance, its plot partakes in the morally duplicitous character of encyclopedic epic, and therefore proves unreliable as didacticism. Contemplation offers arguments similar to Despair's; through this similarity, Spenser tacitly points out that we have no way of knowing the difference between good guys and bad guys without external authorial advice. And who, in this poem, can trust his author?

Red Crosse first appears unguided by any authorial guardian, in the midst of an uncertainty concerning the genre of *The Faerie Queene*'s pathos: will the poem be comic or tragically solemn? Spenser also expresses through Red Crosse doubts about his other generic bearings: is he headed for romance wandering or epic providence? The knight's mixed or ambiguous character signals his narrative's blurring of genre and mood. In the Letter to Ralegh, Spenser presented Red Crosse as a "tall clownishe younge man." Yet when the hero first appears in the poem proper, he is "Gentle" (1.1.1), that is, noble rather than clownish or rustic. Red Crosse even "seeme[s] too solemne sad" (1.1.2), a description in surprising contrast to his crude antics in the prefatory Letter, when "falling before the Queen of Faries . . . [Red Crosse] rested him on the floore, vnfitte through his rusticity for a better place." Even keeping in mind Spenser's frequent departures from his Letter in executing the poem itself, I suggest that this doubleness—Red Crosse appearing as both dignified gentleman and comic hayseed—is deliberate. The poet introduces a dissonance in our perception of his hero in order to foreshadow Red Crosse's crossed responses in the narrative of Book 1, the way that he confounds high and low matters, tragic and delightful pathos.

Spenser's indecorous, contradictory portrait of Red Crosse shows how the confused or mixed nature of *The Faerie Queene* interferes with the poem's didactic agenda. Spenser fractures the character of his hero, like that of his poem, so that it is hard to find moral virtue clearly presented in either. The sixteenth-century critical controversy over Ariosto's use of *mixta genera* in the *Orlando Furioso* is relevant here.[19] With the appearance of Ariosto's poem, the dogmatic Aristotelian separation of genres and the Horatian insistence on a schematic decorum suddenly confronts the full-blown maturity of a poetic form, Renaissance romance, that systematically (or, rather, unsystematically) confuses the boundaries of genre and "appropriate" action. Such mixing presents a threat to didacticism: significantly, some Renaissance critics object to Ariosto's interweaving of genres and types of characters because they see in the author's extravagant practice of *entrelacement* a labyrinthine arena of moral confusion. Pellegrino, for example, writes that Ariosto introduces so many characters, among them "most wicked, vile, and completely unworthy" persons, that the reader can discern no obvious ethical exemplar within the poem's bewildering and ornate network.[20] As Albert Ascoli has demonstrated, Ariosto uses the entanglements of his epic-romance format to cast doubt on the possibility of a straightforward didacticism even as he serves, and encourages, the reader's desire for the didactic.[21] Spenser, following Ariosto, tries to rescue a didactic sense for his narrative not by purifying it according to strict rules of decorum but by exploiting its confusions. The Protean nature of Spenser's romance dispels the unified truth of Pan just as Error deforms the Christian example she imitates, but the evidence of such deformation, like the disturbing connection between Red Crosse and Error, can serve a more mediated didactic purpose (as I will argue).

Spenser is not entirely at ease with his mixing of genres. Instead of allowing the moods of solemn chivalry and farcical knightly error to coexist peacefully, as in Northrop Frye's, Barbara Lewalski's and Bakhtin's (somewhat less calm) accounts of generic crossings, Spenser outlines the risks of such transgressions through Red Crosse's muddled responses.[22] These risks are fundamentally moral: they obstruct the Letter to Ralegh's goal, the creation of an exemplary Christian knight. Here Spenser's rather traditional aim prevents him from embracing the inclusive, freewheeling combinations of genre and tone, and the more innovative humanist morality, that is present, for example, in Rabelais.[23]

In Spenser, Christian romance's coupling of character and plot proves inherently uneven, forcing a reader to incline toward one or the other aspect of the text, and this unevenness obstructs the genre's didactic plans.[24] We can find an apt, if far less artful, parallel to Spenser's difficulty in approaching his moralizing goal in *Huon of Burdeux*. In this pious romance, which appeared in English in 1534, the hero's rapid switching between self-assertion and self-effacement, between the rule of character and the rule of plot, becomes a source of unintentional comedy. On the one hand, Huon submits himself to a divinely appointed narrative: he is continually preparing to die, bidding farewell to his wife and daughter before meeting whatever extraordinary danger he has been forced to face. When Huon, suddenly inspired with heroic energy, then fulfills the audience's expectations by vanquishing his foes, he equally routinely credits God, not his own prowess, for his success. But the ferocious power he displays in battle contradicts this assertion of plot over character, bearing witness to his self-willed trust in his own martial abilities. An example, from a scene in which Huon's ship is trapped next to an adamantine rock that guards a dragon-inhabited castle, will illustrate Huon's characteristic alternation between fatalistic passivity and frenetic bravado:

> Nowe I see well we be all but dede for we have no thynge to ete nor drynke, wherfore we shal dye for famyne and rage. But yf I maye enter in to the castell, I shall gyve that sarpent suche a stroke that he shall neuer more hurte enye man leuynge. Alas, what haue I sayde, my hardynesse nor prowes nor a wauntynge can not helpe me, for I se well that I and all you muste dye; for it is impossible for vs to departe hens.[25]

Not all heroes of Christian romance are subject to such drastic, hyperactive mood swings. But Huon's bipolar disorder, though an extreme case, is rather indicative of the genre's characteristic split between independent heroes and determining plots.[26] When romance foregrounds subjectivity, autonomous human emotion and desire, as it often does, it tends to avoid statements of providential direction.[27] The wandering boat or *barca aventurosa*, standing for the protagonist's errant desire, offers a chief emblem of romance.[28] Yet pious romances must have recourse to a directing authority in the person of God. The combination of the protagonist's self-directed, error-prone heroics with his dependence on an invisible, all-determining higher rule proves an uneasy one. *Huon* solves this difficulty by means of a simple oscillation between the hero's trust in his own forces and his periodic surrenders to the power of God, who accomplishes all things and in effect renders heroic human agency moot.

The St. George legend, more than any other saint's life, displays affinities with romance, and therefore presents a test case for the combination of character-based heroism with divine plotting.[29] George shares his central act of heroic self-definition, dragon killing, with many other popular protagonists of Renaissance romance, including Huon, Guy of Warwick, Valentine and Orson and, of course, Red Crosse.[30] George's defeat of the dragon, which epitomizes his legend's inclination toward heroic romance action, presents a problem for a narrative that also wants to assert his passive obedience to God. Most versions of St. George's career resolve the problem too easily. In Caxton's, Lydgate's, and Alexander Barclay's renditions of the legend, George first exhibits his capacity for action by killing the dragon; then, just as we are primed to expect another battle, George shows instead a greater ability than bravery in combat: he endures the passive suffering of martyrdom, which demonstrates his radical reliance on God's will more than dragon killing could.[31] The martryrdom that concludes the legend of St. George stands out as a hagiographical pathos produced by providential direction, a deliberate refusal of the exciting delights of romance combat exemplified by the earlier slaying of the dragon.

Chrêtien's Perceval and, later, Malory's, similarly desert heroic activity for piety, though Perceval chooses contemplation instead of George's martyrdom. Perceval ends his career as an anchorite who has refused the secular life of romance adventure. Orson also becomes a hermit after his adventures, as does Guy of Warwick, who is last seen living in a cave.[32] Spenser reevaluates the conflicts inherent in Christian romance when he refuses to extend the parallel with Perceval and Guy: he does not conclude Red Crosse's quest in the House of Holiness, despite Red Crosse's own claim that he wants to end there (1.10.63). Spenser's avoidance of contemplative religion as a means of closure indicates his commitment to paradox, to the difficulty of didactic reading instilled by the drama of romance form. He exposes, instead of covering over, the clash between the martyr's passive subjection to a divine narrative and the knight's heroic boastfulness.

Romance poetry like Ariosto's and Spenser's also resists closure through its use of interwoven narrative. Ariosto and Spenser give their readers a drama that inheres in momentary scenes rather than definitive conclusions. They achieve pyrotechnical heights of apparently random *entrelacement* in order to imply a skepticism about the order of the cosmos itself, thus obstructing the kind of providential structure that lends itself to moral point.[33] Yet Spenser, at least in Book 1, also wants providential plot as a didactic foundation. By the end of Book 1, Spenser knows the inadequacy of plot, even a providential one, for didactic purposes, and he therefore moves to a character-based didacticism in Books 2 and 3.

There is a connection between the Spenserian/Ariostan refusal to assert didactic closure through plot, their practice of *entrelacement*, and the mixed moods of their poetry. In the first canto of *The Faerie*

*Queene*, Spenser takes over Ariostan romance's habitual transformation of tragic or "solemne sad" pathos into light entertainment, even as he criticizes the consequences of this lightness for moral reading. The poet quickly qualifies his opening description of the solemn Red Crosse and the mournful Una (1.1.3–4) with the figure of the dwarf, who represents the return of a repressed triviality that first appeared in the Letter to Ralegh's cartoonlike forecast of the poem's story. The dwarf, an obviously comic character, deflates the sage and serious allegorical reading Spenser gives us in the first few stanzas of the poem. As *The Faerie Queene* begins we see the pious Red Crosse, bearing on his "brest a bloudie Crosse . . . / The deare remembrance of his dying Lord" (1.1.2) and the "inly mourn[ing]" and "sad" Una (1.1.4). Then comes the dwarf, who, Spenser tells us, "Lasie seemd in being euer last, / Or wearied with bearing of [Una's] bag" (1.1.6). At this point we are uncertain as to whether we should read the dwarf allegorically, as an emblem of "lasie," slothful inadequacy,[34] or whether he, like Sancho Panza, is just plain tired. This very ambiguity makes the dwarf a laughable case in contrast to Una's mournful and Red Crosse's noble dedication. The high pathos of Una's plight coincides with the moral meaning of the allegory; the everyday status of her harried servant names the mundane reality ready to puncture any allegorical pretension. There is a double authorial vision here, shifting between a genteel, chivalric dignity and the pragmatically base, that will reappear most prominently in Book 6, where Calidore's courteous ideals look from another angle like a rather grubby opportunism (see chapter 5).

We have yet to decide where Red Crosse should be placed—in the refined or the mundane. As I have noted, Spenser describes him in stanza 1 as a "gentle" and "solemne" hero; but this solemnity cannot hide a comic aspect.[35] The conflict of tones in Canto 1's opening stanzas has developed further by the end of stanza 6: when the storm arrives as the first event of the *Faerie Queene*'s plot, "this faire couple," Spenser writes, "eke to shroud themselves were faine" (1.1.6). The poet gives us a clear hint of irony in the adjective "faire," which implies the couple's literary-conventional good looks, their gentility, and thus their generic suitability to good weather: we wouldn't normally expect such a noble pair to be subject to an everyday calamity like a thunderstorm. Spenser attacks the artificiality of the separation between high and low more gently than Ariosto, but very much in Ariosto's vein. As when Ariosto makes his Ruggiero, who is preparing to ravish Angelica, struggle at length with his armor, Spenser here attends to the clumsy facts, like rainstorms, that so often upset decorum, in this case the staid chivalric dignity of Una and Red Crosse.

Spenser reverses his opening transformation of the solemn into the comically everyday when what looks like a trivial danger, the storm, turns out to be a grave one, as Una and Red Crosse seek shelter in Errour's wood.[36] Spenser juxtaposes Una's staid, expansive definition of the threats represented by "Errours den," the "wandring wood," with the trembling and frantic dwarf's "Fly fly" (1.1.13). Even though the dwarf counsels flight rather than attack, the rather ridiculous energy of the dwarf's tone matches Red Crosse's own adolescent gusto and contrasts with Una's mature sobriety. The "youthfull knight" reacts against the prudent Una's advice and, "full of fire and greedy hardiment," assaults Error (1.1.14). When he chooses action over Una's poised, reflective moral wisdom, Red Crosse encounters for the first time in the poem the risk entailed by his erroneous evaluation of moods, his failure to respond seriously to a serious danger.

Almost immediately after the encounter with Error, Red Crosse meets Archimago, who has disguised himself as a pious hermit. Here the knight again misevaluates distinct kinds of pathos. With Errour he misread a serious challenge as a trivial, easily defeated one. This time he does the opposite: he misrecognizes the comic as the sober or melancholy. Despite his "sober . . . and very sagely sad" appearance (1.1.29), Archimago's essential triviality should be (but isn't) evident to Red Crosse. His "litle lowly" hermitage is adorned with a charming, and to the reader suspiciously superficial, "Christyall streame," which "gently play[s]" (1.1.34) as Archimago peddles his "pleasing wordes" (1.1.35).[37] Playing the role of a "silly old man . . . / Bidding his beades all day" (1.1.30), Archimago represents the danger associated with the popish fetishism of icon and ritual that Jeffrey Knapp has called "trifling": taking the silly seriously, reading it as Christian simplicity rather than the romance deception and triviality it actually is.[38] Because of his assumption that Archimago is playing it straight, that his pose is a humbly admirable one, Red Crosse capitulates to Archimago's delusive games, becoming, like the phantom Una that visits him in his sleep, a victim of "Dame pleasures toy" (1.1.47).

Of course, the romance of St. George and the dragon is also a popish trifle, yet Spenser does not choose the legend for his theme in order to show it up as insufficiently sober. On the contrary, he is deeply invested in its delights. Spenser's critique of Archimago, then, is also a collaboration with him. He does not shadow his romance step by step with a continuously wary didactic lesson, as Harington did with his notes to his Englishing of the *Orlando Furioso* (1591). Romance trifles with Spenser and he with it. Like Archimago, the poet proves vulnerable to the charm of his own creations (1.2.1).

Spenser is not as worried as Harington about the moral risks of romance. But he does show, in a more subtle way, the threat his entertainment poses by diverting Red Crosse from the alertness necessary to virtue.[39] Red Crosse again misses an obvious danger by misreading a mood: he takes refuge in a pastoral locus frightening to the "fearefull Shepheard" who, "aghast," shuns it, but which looks to Red Crosse like a delightful "coole shade" (1.2.28–29).[40] This seeming locus amoenus, with its "calme shadow" (1.2.28), provides the counterpart to Archimago's restful hermitage in Canto 1. The reader looks over the hero's shoulder with a superior glance: Red Crosse in Canto 1 ought to have seen the lightweight nature of the popish pretense to sobriety, but here he interprets too lightly. He should take more seriously the moral danger posed by the delight of pastoral seclusion, which cannot be shrugged off as merely trivial.

Spenser quickly makes evident to the reader—though not to Red Crosse—the grounds for the sense of horror attached to the pastoral locus of Canto 2. When Red Crosse's trifling "falsed fancy" makes him "pluck a bough" as a "girlond" for Duessa, he raises the hideous cry of the human tree Fradubio. Fradubio's advice to Red Crosse, "Fly ... fly far hence away" (1.2.31), appropriates the dwarf's earlier comic words for a darkly tragic tone; Red Crosse misrecognizes Fradubio's tragedy by reading it in too distancing and defensive a way, as a fable not directly relevant to him. "Musing" he refers with arch puzzlement to Fradubio's laments as "these speeches rare" (1.2.31). Red Crosse's final horrified reaction to Fradubio as he buries the bough (he is "full of sad feare and ghastly dreriment" [1.2.44]) opts for avoidance of Fradubio's error—an example that, like Error herself, threatens to infect Red Crosse. Red Crosse's protective fright complements the detachment evident in his musing; both tones, because they try for escape from the event at hand, prevent him from understanding its meaning. Red Crosse is unknowingly subjected to Spenser's plot, unaware of its parallel between Fradubio and himself—a parallel abundantly clear to the careful reader (Fradubio "would haue kild" [1.2.39] his mistress Fraelissa as Red Crosse "would haue slaine" [1.2.5] Una after "seeing" her infidelity).[41]

Like Error, the Fradubio episode shows how, when Red Crosse encounters the pathos of other characters—passions that mirror his own—the meeting becomes a lesson in externalizing. In Spenser's allegorical mode one's emotions can appear as threatening figures fundamentally other than the self. So Red Crosse's sin of jealous, deceived rage appears in the figure of Fradubio. In Canto 2 Red Crosse is "still flying from his thoughts and gealous feare" (1.2.12) just as his counterpart seven cantos later, Trevisan, "fled, his eye ... backward cast,

/ As if his feare still followed him behind" (1.9.21). But the alienating allegory induced by a phenomenon like fear is actually an inward process that appears in outward form: Trevisan "of him selfe ... seemd to be afrayd" (1.9.23).[42]

The traditional allegorical presentation of dangerous forms of pathos—most memorably, the Seven Deadly Sins—exploits such externalization: the self is reified, and the person turned thing therefore appears separate from himself.[43] Commenting on Red Crosse's susceptibility to Duessa, a figure for the knight's own doubleness or self-contradiction, Spenser writes, "Forgetfull of his owne, that mindes anothers cares" (1.5.18). The House of Pride is full of characters who are similarly forgetful, who project their sins onto the external world of other persons or objects, and as a result, find themselves reduced to iconographic immobility. Lechery, for example, "joy[s] weake womens harts to tempt and prove" in order to discover his own lack of control and "new fanglenesse" in others (1.4.25–26). Avarice, who foreshadows Book 2's Mammon and Book 3's Malbecco, represents an even more drastic alienation of the self, not this time into other people, but rather into physical matter. Avarice, Spenser writes, "unto hell him selfe for money solde" (1.4.28), metamorphosing himself into what he possesses, "his owne."[44] Because of his "nightly feare to lose his owne," Avarice leads a wretched life "unto him selfe unknown" (1.4.28). With all the Seven Deadly Sins, the lack of inwardness entails a paralyzed exposure to the gaze of spectators like Red Crosse and the reader. They are fixed in place: like Gluttony, who is "unable once to stirre or go" (1.4.23), Avarice "could not touch, nor go, nor stand" (1.4.29).

For Spenser, the Sins' projection of emotional drives onto the world signals a lack of self-control, and therefore a lack of self. Only a stable, developed ego can discern and temper the insidious force of pathos. In the Sins' pageant, Spenser describes a surrender to drives that are not mediated by consciousness and that in fact destroy the possibility of a conscious, controlled life. The poet makes this point adroitly in his portrait of Wrath: "And on his dagger still his hand he held, / Trembling through hasty rage, when choler in him sweld" (1.4.33). Wrath's trembling is not the sign of fleeting self-restraint it initially appears to be, for he lacks the capacity (we learn in the next stanza) to hold back his rage even for a moment: "For of his hands he had no governement" (1.4.34). What may at first have seemed like an effort at discipline—reading Wrath's "still" hand as "quiet"—instead turns out to be a constant emotional overload, a "trembling" that blocks all possibility of conscious decision: "still" means "continually."

Red Crosse fits perfectly into the Sins' presentation of vice as a lack of self-possession induced by the loss of self to the other: he surrenders himself to his surroundings in the House of Pride, which form in turn a mirror or projection of his own error. Wrath's trembling hands will be echoed in Red Crosse's own reaction to Despair: holding the dagger, Red Crosse's "hand did quake, / And tremble like a leafe of Aspin greene" (1.9.51). Red Crosse is in danger of becoming a fixed, emblematic allegorical character like Despair himself, or like Wrath, a status that would obviate the need for a self and turn him into the mere function of an order of meaning directed from without: the plot of the "big Other."[45] Here Imaginary projection capitulates instantly to Symbolic scheming.

The more active or energetic his pride, the more Red Crosse becomes subject to Duessa's, Lucifera's, and Archimago's plotting. Red Crosse's lack of mastery in the House of Pride, his giving up of self, will be demonstrated even more tellingly in the Despair and Contemplation episodes. Contemplation comes as an answer in kind to Despair: he stakes his argument on Despair's plane of cosmic order rather than subjective response.

With Despair, as with Contemplation, Spenser departs from subjectivity in the service of a providential plot that will transcend the human. Canto 9, the episode of Despair, therefore exemplifies Stanley Fish's externalizing interpretation of Protestant poetics as an attempt to overcome the self's pathos in favor of God's providence. Fish argues that Protestantism requires the effacing of ordinary human nature, with its passionate reactions, in the name of God's supervenient mercy. According to Fish, Protestant authors want the higher reality of doctrine to replace its imperfect mortal "refraction"—our emotional lives—via the reader's discovery that his or her first responses to the text are incorrect because they are mortal or fallen.[46]

Fish correctly discerns this process of providential correction in Spenser's Despair scene. For the reader as well as Red Crosse, the seductive lure of Despair's rhetoric, his evocation of the pleasant security death can provide, represents an experiential danger that must be banished by a *dea ex machina*, Una, who has been sent from a doctrinal realm that lies beyond our human feelings. Una's reminder of God's grace, "In heauenly mercies hast thou not a part?" (1.9.53), comes "from a context outside the experience of the poem," Fish writes. In Fish's view, Spenser "lead[s] us beyond our perspective by making us feel its inadequacies and the necessity of accepting something which baldly contradicts it."[47] This "something" is grace, a higher perspective that cancels our (and Red Crosse's) felt but deceptive attraction to Despair. Fish suggests that grace must be accepted on faith, that it is not implied in our experience and, in fact, contradicts that experience's testimony—the evidence of Despair's affecting, and effective, seduction.

Fish is right imply that the gap between emotional experience and higher meaning is a Reformation phenomenon, one not present in medieval treatments of despair. Spenser's dramatic conflict between immediate reaction and doctrinal truth, in a case like the Despair episode, does not exist in late medieval and early Renaissance versions of temptation scenes—*Mankind*, the *Castle of Perseverance*, Skelton's *Magnyficence*. In these earlier texts, the psyche has been transformed into an allegorical arena of opposing forces. No clash occurs between the palpably felt and the abstractly moralized because doctrinal moralism is still experientially powerful for the reader. For the Middle Ages inward experience is not yet, as it will be for the Reformation, an alternative to abstract doctrinal truth.

Though he persuasively outlines the Reformation opposition between subjective pathos and providential doctrine, Fish goes wrong when he asserts that Protestant writers unhesitatingly choose doctrine over individual emotional consciousness. *The Faerie Queene*'s Despair episode does, as Fish claims, do its best to banish the truth of emotional subjectivity by showing an obviously demonic figure distorting and abusing emotional effects in a way that allows no chance for rational response. But other Protestant treatments of despair make it clear that an understanding of this spiritual state requires the sinner's reflection on his or her inward pathos, not just God's providential decisions.[48]

Spenser in Book 1, in contrast to these internalizing Protestant despair narratives, emphasizes outward plot over inward character. The episodes of Despair and Contemplation reflect Reformation theology's frequently voiced insistence on God's grace as an overpowering foreign agency that seizes the sinner, obliterating any merely human efforts in either the divine or the demonic direction. The sinner is given no time to "prepare" for, to respond affectively to, such efficient grace. It overwhelms him or her not as a unique individual but as another stereotypical example of sin that an inexplicable God has decided to save.[49] Insisting on the typicality and insignificance of the sinner in the hands of a merciful God—or an angry Satan—becomes a way of externalizing the self, turning the forces for good and evil that it possesses into invading allegorical agents that possess it. The psyche is subjected to pathos conceived as an alien, overpowering force. "The interior struggle of the human soul," Damrosch writes, "is made intelligible by translating it into the ultimate contest between good and evil."[50] In this allegorical scheme, God remains an external power who must not be assimilated or even made responsive to man's anxious yearning for him: "God's grace is bestowed quite apart from human merit, and even the most accurate understanding may find itself cut off utterly from grace."[51]

For the sinner gripped by the terrifying possibility that his guilt might be a lonely anomaly, that he could be a "chief of sinners" comparable with Satan himself, such allegorical externalization, like Lacan's Symbolic order, offers a comfort. The promise of Christ's ultimate triumph over Satan displaces responsibility from the uncertainty of private emotional life to the sure external truth of sacred history. As Damrosch remarks, describing the way Bunyan's allegorical tendency strains against, and often vanquishes, his competing attachment to practical, this-worldly life, "It was precisely the individuality of experience that these individualists feared."[52]

Fish precisely defines this externalizing version of puritanism: salvation means removing us from the trials of existence, correcting our emotional perceptions by replacing them with an abstract and predictable, and therefore reassuring, doctrine.[53] But Fish reads only one half of Protestant poetics: preferring the drive to escape from life's mutability into an otherworldly stasis, he fails to respond to Protestantism's internalizing, this-worldly aspect, its continued dwelling in the perilous instability of experience. Spenser's poem itself exemplifies the vicissitudes of the mutable world, even when, as at the very end of the Mutabilitie Cantos, it unfolds change to reveal the grace of harmonious "dilat[ion]."

Protestants who follow Paul and Augustine insist that we must accept the experiential struggle against the flesh and its works evident in sins like despair, instead of hoping that God's outside intervention will free us from struggle. William Perkins in *Of the Combat of the Flesh and the Spirit* commands us to recognize what he calls our "mixed" state, our continued inward susceptibility even as we strive for righteousness. "It is not as though I do not suffer wounds," Augustine exclaims in the *Confessions*, "but I rather feel that you [i.e., God] heal them over and over again."[54] Red Crosse's meeting with Despair ignores the inward significance of such vulnerability, turning it instead into evidence of narrative failure.[55]

With Despair, as with Contemplation, Spenser tries to resolve at the level of plot the clash between romance's chivalric deeds and the Reformation insistence that deeds by themselves will turn out to be insufficient for salvation. Despair's unraveling of knightly valor begins when he cites Red Crosse's heroism as evidence of his irremediable sin:[56]

> All those great battels, which thou boasts to win,
> Through strife, and bloud-shed, and auengement,
> Now praysd, hereafter deare thou shalt repent
> \* \* \*
> Is not the measure of thy sinfull hire

> High heaped vp with huge iniquitie,
> Against the day of wrath, to burden thee?
> (*FQ* 1.9.43,46)

Despair's accusation turns even Red Crosse's victories into failures, but his more obvious failures prove more obviously damning. Despair produces Duessa like a trump card, clinching his claim for the indelible nature of Red Crosse's sins (1.9.46). The hero responds immediately, and virtually automatically:

> The knight was much enmoued with his speach,
>     That as a swords point through his hart did perse,
>     And in his conscience made a secret breach,
>     Well knowing true all, that he did reherse,
>     And to his fresh remembrance did reuerse
>     The vgly vew of his deformed crimes,
>     That all his manly powres it did disperse,
>     As he were charmed with inchaunted rimes,
> That oftentimes he quakt, and fainted oftentimes.
> (*FQ* 1.9.48)

The facts of narrative here exert an instantly persuasive, even performative, force.[57] Spenser's "that," in the stanza's last line, deftly collapses Red Crosse's failures as a hero, the "sad feare" with which he buries the bough he has torn from Fradubio (1.2.44) and the "faintnesse" he feels upon drinking from the fountain (1.7.6), into his knowledge of these failures, which causes him to faint again now.[58] Pathos here becomes an effect of Despair's narrative, his convincing imitation of providential authority.

Red Crosse's instinctive surrender to Despair presents a mirror image of his earlier awkward, optimistic enthusiasm: there is something of the willing puppet in his response. Significantly, Arthur's description of the puller of the puppet's strings, an incomprehensible and manipulative heavenly destiny, occurs at the beginning of the Despair canto, as introduction to the scene of Red Crosse's temptation: "Full hard it is . . . to read aright / The course of heauenly cause, or understand / The secret meaning of th'eternal might, / That rules mens wayes, and rules the thoughts of liuing wight" (1.9.6). In the face of such mysterious direction, which governs not only human actions but also "thoughts," it becomes hard to tell the difference between God and Despair (or Archimago).

Of course, the danger of evoking a destiny that "rules mens wayes" lies in its reduction of God's will to the literal or visible evidence of events. Acknowledging divine direction in this manner means erasing the possibility of subjective, revisionary interpretation. As Despair says of God, "Is not his deed, what ever thing is donne[?]" (1.9.42). In such a world of sheer facts Red Crosse becomes the victim of whatever scene he happens upon, whether staged by friend or enemy. Despair's rhetoric does the same work as Archimago's magic. He pulls the narrative strings in a way that leaves no room for considered response: Despair's penetrating words "breach" or "perse" Red Crosse.

Red Crosse's visceral reaction to Despair, like his sight of the puppet Una in Canto 2, fails to acknowledge the way that evil inheres in subjective dream or desire. Instead, Red Crosse construes Despair as an alien and sinisterly effective agency. Red Crosse assumes that Despair is "the author of this fact" (1.9.37) of Terwin's death, wrongly supposing that Terwin himself bears no responsibility for his own ruin. Despair does not tempt Red Crosse in the familiar, subjective sense of temptation—by holding out an Imaginary invitation to inward desire, as with the dream Una of 1.1. Instead, Despair, like Archimago displaying the puppet Una to Red Crosse in 1.2, offers an unhappy inevitability, a plot that convinces through the sheer force of fact. As in that earlier scene, Red Crosse's acceptance of Despair's version means that he agrees to rule out any individual resistance to this narrative.

"Well knowing true all" means that Despair can rest his case on the errors that Red Crosse has committed—or, more accurately, fallen into—but which he is powerless to interpret. Despair need only point to the text, to the narrative mistakes that Red Crosse has no way of explaining now, as he had no way of understanding them at the time. (The messenger of Book 1's final canto, who is really Archimago in disguise, recounts Red Crosse's errors to Una's father to very similar effect [1.12.26 –27].)

The poet's handing over his hero to Despair in this way is a logical consequence, which Spenser faces fully and honestly, of Book 1's providential didactic narrative. In Book 1 Red Crosse can only succeed by entrusting himself to the hands of the right authority; the return of Eden relies on his passivity and the uninterpreted heroism that accompanies it. But Red Crosse has no way of telling the difference between a good "captain" and a bad one, between God and Despair.

At another moment of temptation as familiar as Spenser's Despair episode, Bunyan's Apollyon reminds Christian,

> Thou didst faint at first setting out, when thou wast almost choked in the Gulf of Despond. Thou didst attempt wrong ways to be rid of thy burden . . . Thou didst sinfully sleep, and lose thy choice thing: thou wast also almost persuaded to go back at the sight of the lions; and when thou talkest of thy journey, and of what thou hast heard and seen, thou art inwardly desirous of vainglory in all that thou sayest or doest.[59]

Despair, like Apollyon, will accuse his victim of vainglory, of relying solely on his own works—"All those great battels, which thou boasts to win." Despair rightly recognizes Red Crosse's dependence on his heroic deeds as sinful. As with Despair, Apollyon's mere displaying of narrative evidence, of the sinner's mistakes, produces an apparently damning case. But Christian, unlike Red Crosse, finds himself ready to reply to his tempter's accusations: "All this is true, and much more, which thou hast left out; but the Prince whom I serve and honour is merciful and ready to forgive."[60] Bunyan's pilgrim, in contrast to Spenser's knight, realizes that the possibility of God's grace stems from recognizing the sinfulness of his deeds and surrendering to the process of self-accusation that provides the defining marks of faith.[61] The power of this surrender lies in its openness to reinterpretation of the past and, with it, the generating of a newly subtle, and newly just, self-awareness.[62]

We can understand the difference between Red Crosse's passive and Christian's active meeting with temptation in the antithetical terms offered by Charles Taylor, which I have already described: the (Platonic) premise of automatic attunement to the cosmos vs. the (Augustinian) interrogation of the self's recalcitrant response to the divine. In the Augustinian tradition, which guides Bunyan's Christian, the grasping of God's order can only derive from our active perception of our own inmost nature. But in Spenser's Despair episode, as in most Platonic and some Christian versions of large-scale cosmic determinism, universal order itself, rather than the individual's reading of it, provides the source of authenticity that can override the fallen, everyday self.

In Book 1, Una frequently represents this universal order. Her cheerleading encouragement of Red Crosse against Despair and the dragon, her praise of him as "renowmed ... / Aboue all knights on earth," works as instinctively as Despair's discouragement. As Red Crosse listens to Una's praise, "So up he rose" (1.9.54).[63] Una's counsel is no more internal, no more psychically rooted, than Despair's manipulation. In the House of Holiness, as with Una's rescue of Red Crosse from Despair, the Old Law of providential determinism continues to eclipse the promised New Law of subjective response. The open narrative possibility of salvation usually marks the New Law's difference from the Old. But the power to resurrect that the poet ascribes to Fidelia's word (1.10.19) induces a mere echo of Red Crosse's despairing "death" in Canto 9, his renewed wish to expire, a victim of his plot's most conclusive moment.[64] Fidelia's book is written in blood, presumably the blood of the lamb that will wash away the "bloudy letters" of Moses' law (1.10.53), just as the "accurst hand-writing" cited by Despair will be blotted out by grace, according to Una (1.9.53). Yet it is surely significant that Canto 9's Old Law reappears in Canto 10, and in the numerically parallel stanza (53), along with the bloody writing of the Gospels. Alongside the fact that Fidelia's book induces despair just as Despair's Old Testament "hand-writing" did, this parallel compels us to recognize that the bleeding, self-sacrificial word of Jesus here offers merely a new version of the lawful Mosaic letter.

The hermit Contemplation also follows the Old Law when he emphasizes "the way . . . / That neuer leads the traveiler astray" (1.10.52), a route or plot that will guide and determine Red Crosse. This path promises to shield the knight from errors of the sort we have seen him commit. In his fervent response, Red Crosse accepts Contemplation's way, pleading,

> O let me not . . . then turne againe
> Backe to the world, whose ioyes so fruitlesse are;
> But let me here for aye in peace remaine,
> Or streight way on that last long voyage fare . . .
> (*FQ* 1.10.63)

Red Crosse's quick conversion to the "joyous rest and endlesse blis" (1.10.52) that Contemplation offers bears a suspicious resemblance to his surrender to the "eternall rest / And happie ease" held out by Despair in Canto 9 (st. 40). Red Crosse remains oriented toward passive security, "the man that would not live" (1.10.27) in the face of both Contemplation and Despair. Contemplation enforces this impression of the hero's passivity when he tells Red Crosse that as an infant, "all vnweeting," he was found "in a heaped furrow" by a "Ploughman" (1.10.66).[65] The sage hermit underlines the clownish, rustic nature of Red Crosse's character, imprisoning him in an earthbound passivity from which a higher power needs to rescue him. In Spenser's hands Red Crosse becomes raw material to be husbanded or cultivated by God-as-ploughman, put in the path that "never leads the traveiler astray."

Contemplation orders Red Crosse to return to his battles, but at the same moment the hermit also says that "bloud can nought but sin, & wars but sorrowes yield" (1.10.60). The dissonance that marks Contemplation's advice in this stanza indicates a larger conflict in Books 1 and 2 between the virtuous martial deeds that constitute a Christian romance and the Protestant charge that such deeds remain merely outward, and therefore insufficient for salvation, unless they are animated by faith. The Old Law logic of repayment offered by Despair—"For life must life, and bloud must bloud repay" (1.9.43)—persists here also, as Red Crosse asks, "But deeds of armes must I at last be faine, / And

60                           The Limits of Moralizing

Ladies love to leave *so dearely bought?*" (1.9.62; italics added).⁶⁶ The zero-sum game enacted by the Hebrew God's unbeatable plot bears a rather close resemblance to the sheer authorial manipulation that rules the baffled knight's errancy in Book 1.

    But Spenser's manipulative wiles do not prevent his plot from getting out of hand in a way that adulterates and frustrates moral point. In the transition from Canto 10's House of Holinesse to Red Crosse's battle with the dragon in Canto 11, the poet again, as in Canto 1, conveys the proliferating, unstable twists and turns of romance narrative through the juxtaposition of contrasting emotional tones. After the didactic sobriety of the House, the sardonic zest of the book's earlier romance combats returns in full, unaltered force: the dragon that faces Red Crosse bounces up and down "on the brused gras, / As for great ioyance of his newcome guest" (1.11.15). As in the *Shepheardes Calender*, with its alternation between moralism and recreative delight, Spenser in Book 1 remains saddled by a polarity: the seriousness associated with theologically loaded didacticism contrasts with the wry and jolly energy of the chivalric deeds that, for the most part, simply ignore such burdensome morality. The dragon-slaying of Canto 11, after the ploddingly wholesome lesson we have just heard in the House, offers a refreshing turn back to the easier delights of romance. Once again, the enactment of romance plot looks inadequate to the providential didactic meaning that Spenser attaches to it.

    Spenser here once again instills doubt about his own didactic project by drawing attention to *The Faerie Queene*'s clash between romance adventure and theological meaning. After Contemplation gives him his vision of the "new Hierusalem" (1.10.56), Red Crosse "adowne ... looked to the ground, / To have returnd, but dazed were his eyne, / Through passing brightnesse, which did quite confound / His feeble sense, and too exceeding shine. / So darke are earthly things compard to things divine" (1.10.67). Though a future saint, Red Crosse remains a "feeble," deficient mortal; he cannot properly comprehend a religious truth so incommensurable with his humble worldly status. The double image suggested by these lines persists: the poetic word cannot reconcile the earthly and the heavenly, romance and its Christian message.

    Critics have noted that Red Crosse with Contemplation wishes for the ease that comes from abandoning the quest. They have also mentioned the way this desire echoes the Despair episode. But Spenser's academic readers almost always claim that the difference between Despair and Contemplation is more important than the similarity. Jeffrey Knapp,⁶⁷ for example, asserts that Contemplation reveals Despair's offer of rest as a mere image, proposing in its place the reality symbolized by the Mount of Olives, which has strong apocalyptic connotations in Judaic and Christian tradition. But Spenser describes the Mount of Olives here in a startlingly secular way, juxtaposing it with Parnassus and thus compromising any claim that the Mount signals, in Miltonic fashion, a reality definitively greater than that of classical poetics. Spenser compares the Mount of Contemplation to

> ... that sacred hill, whose head full hie,
> Adornd with fruitfull Olives all arownd,
> Is, as it were for endlesse memory
> Of that deare Lord, who oft thereon was fownd,
> For ever with a flowring girlond crownd:
> Or like that pleasaunt Mount, that is for ay
> Through famous Poets verse each where renownd,
> On which the thrise three learned Ladies play
> Their heavenly notes, and make full many a lovely lay.
> (*FQ* 1.10.54)

This description pleasantly trifles with a pastoral locus amoenus, "flowring girlond"s and all, of exactly the type that Knapp claims Spenser here wants to reject for didactic purposes. The poet displays Christ as the reassuring genius enshrined in a landscape of pastoral innocence, in keeping with stanza 57's description of him as an "unspotted lam." We learned in Canto 1 to be wary of pastoral deception: can the wariness be so easily exorcised as Knapp suggests?[68] The sheer pleasure of place persuades us, as we read, to gloss over any difference between Parnassus and the Mount of Olives. But how could this harmonizing of classical and Christian serve Spenser's didactic intent?

It does not: instead, didacticism here fades away, lulled by the pleasantly indefinite mingling of pagan and Christian images. When Spenser conjures up the attachment to the spirit of place, and the memory of Christ associated with sites like the Mount of Olives, we may wonder whether Christ should really be sought so literally—whether the savior can be found in this site, as pagan spirit or gardener. Michael will rebuke Adam for such attachment to place in the final books of *Paradise Lost*, but Spenser suspends judgment on such questions. Because a shade of paganism suits the Spenserian quest—because he does not assert, as Milton does, the superiority of Christian over classical— Spenser continues to trifle with pastoral. But neither does he dismiss the risks of a classically sensuous locus. The cohabitation of classical and Christian is a natural mode for Spenser, but it may still deceive us, or diminish Red Crosse. Here, it is relevant that the Mount of Olives fails to provide a fully assured image of closure or final salvation: instead, it traditionally connotes Christ's warning to his disciples not to be certain about the arrival of the apocalypse, because it will come when they least expect it.[69] In light of this familiar meaning, the Spenser passage reads less like a statement of a secure heavenly, or earthly, rest than a continuing hesitation about attempting such a statement.[70] The reader, like the hero, must move on, roused to pursuit of the next adventure.

Book 1 ends by reiterating the force of adventures, emphasizing once again romance narrative's inclination to override subjective pathos. Duessa in Canto 12, playing the role of betrayed Dido, cites against Red Crosse the evidence provided by narrative facts, just as Despair did:[71]

> To me sad mayd, or rather widow sad,
>   He was affiaunced long time before,
>   And sacred pledges he both gave, and had,
>   False erraunt knight, infamous, and forswore:
>   Witnesse the burning Altars, which he swore,
>   And guiltie heauens of his bold periury,
>   Which though he hath polluted oft of yore,
>   Yet I to them for iudgement iust do fly,
> And them coniure t'auenge this shamefull iniury.
>                                   (*FQ* 1.12.27)

Facing Duessa's charge of unfaithfulness, Red Crosse stammers, "Vnwares I strayd / Out of my way" and "there did I find, or rather I was found / Of this false woman" (1.12.31–32). The knight suggests his relative innocence by introducing the same kind of evidence that Duessa has brought forward. He declares himself a mere pawn of the plot: "Vnwares" he "was found" by, instead of finding, Duessa.[72] Again, Book 1's romance entails a choice of plot over character. And romance energy, as the pure willful movement of plot, escapes providential closure when Red Crosse, at the end of Book 1, once again departs in search of chivalric excitement.

So Red Crosse, yet again the victim of the short attention span encouraged by a hyperactive questing mentality, pricks off into the sunset as Book 1 concludes. But his renewed wandering also fulfills Gloriana's, and God's, command. The conclusion of Book 1 demonstrates that providence's plot and the earthly deeds of romance adventure continue to sustain, and not merely upset, each other. During his fight with the dragon, Red Crosse must supplement his reliance on an extrapersonal agency of grace, the Well of Life, by what at first seems to be a contradictory reliance on heroic works.[73] "Ne let the man ascribe it to his skill, / That thorough grace hath gained victory," Spenser writes at the beginning of Canto 10, between Red Crosse's encounter with Despair and his battle against the dragon (1.10.1). But the energetically self-motivated defense of "his honour deare," his heroically self-reliant skill, seems just as necessary to Red Crosse's triumph over the dragon as the external intervention of grace in the form of the Well of Life (1.11.39).

The fact that Red Crosse at the end of Book 1 deserts the Eden ruled by Una's parents for more secular fights in Gloriana's service indicates that a disjunction persists between romance heroism and its enlistment by a moralizing narrative. In Book 2, Spenser remedies this disjunction by internalizing moral strife in Guyon. By the final canto of Book 2, a rigid Christian moralism incarnated in the Palmer has been left behind by Spenser's tense and subtle vision of his hero's contested virtue. In particular, the way that virtue tangles with sexuality in the Bower of Bliss makes the Palmer look rather moldy and obsolete: Guyon's own Palmer-like moralisms strike us as the flimsiest of defenses against Acrasia's voluptuous thrills. The perception of moralism's awkward distance from heroic passion will culminate in the openly erotic quest of Book 3.

Book 1 substitutes "knightly giusts and fierce encounters" (1.1.1), a stirring and confused story of heroic deeds, for the passions of subjectivity. Despair and Contemplation criticize knightly heroism as a faulty mode of narrative, not a faulty kind of self. In doing so, they persuasively substitute their tales of a restful telos for the endless "fierce warres" that Red Crosse has been following (Proem). Both Despair and Contemplation, I have argued, prove convincing in their (to be sure, differently motivated) attacks on Red Crosse's superficial errancy. In pursuing these critiques in my own analysis, I have not intended to deprecate the considerable poetic glories of Book 1, which, at Archimago's whim, bristles with both languid dreams and brittle, acrobatic showdowns. I want, instead, to bring Spenser's first quest into a dramatic confrontation with later parts of the poem. The confrontation is already implicit, for the reader, in key sections of Book 1. But Red Crosse himself, departing at the book's end to serve Gloriana, remains impervious to criticism. In Book 1, martial work serves an externalized version of sacred and political history. The knight's wars only show up as a bold, misguided diversion when we move on to the inward quest that begins in the psyche of Guyon.

# 3
# *The Faerie Queene,* Book 2

In Book 2, Spenser makes character rather than plot the focus of his interest. But plot still persists as a central factor in Spenser's poetics. Throughout the 1590 *Faerie Queene* Spenser remains ambivalently poised between externalizing and internalizing impulses, between antipsychological allegory, which he associates with plot, and an essentially contrasting concern for the inner emotions and motivated conduct of the self. Allegory and inwardness will be the two major poles of my discussion in this chapter, supplementing my earlier opposition between Symbolic moralizing schemes and the Imaginary pathos of subjectivity that continually disengages itself from moralizing. Guyon, in his desire for rigid self-definition, chooses subjectivity over submission to narrative; thus, he reacts against the plot-ruled style of Spenser's previous hero, Red Crosse. Guyon's obsession with control comes as a necessary answer to Red Crosse's occasional, nearly fatal tendency to let go or prematurely relax. Seduced by Duessa, Red Crosse tellingly finds himself "pourd out in loosness on the grassie ground." Despair's loose garments (1.9.36) and the image of furies "with their chaines *untied*" that he instills in his victims (1.9.24, italics added) drives home his role as the emblem of Red Crosse's slack incapacity to make an adequately motivated decision, one shaped by rational deliberation.[1] Book 2, by contrast, offers Guyon a version of subjectivity formed by his own choices. Guyon uses the category of temperance to organize and direct his experience in a way that Red Crosse cannot. But Guyon also, as I will argue, clings to the external enemies provided by allegory in order to shape his heroic image: he remains partially trapped in the narrative-oriented realm of Book 1.

Spenser's imagination of an inward, ethical self in Guyon results from his negotiation among three contrasting approaches to subjectivity: Stoicism, Aristotelian ethics, and Pauline-Augustinian theology.

I will argue that Book 2 poses Aristotelian and Stoic views of the self against the Pauline-Augustinian view.[2] For Augustine, as for the Greek tragic dramatists, emotion provides a sign of the weakness and contingency that unavoidably defines the human. Emotion, therefore, cannot be transcended through philosophical self-management of the Aristotelian or Stoic kind. Stoicism, by contrast, aims at organizing the self through the repression of pathos. In Book 2, Stoic ascesis is Guyon's goal, but Spenser clearly implies that Stoicism has its limits, that pathos cannot be successfully repressed.

Critics have argued for Spenser's affinity with a Protestantism that relies on the inwardness implicit in both the Christian-Stoic and the Pauline-Augustinian modes.[3] Of course, we must recognize other, less theologically oriented aspects of Spenser: he is a romance writer in the Mediterranean tradition and, as such, often cheerfully unconcerned with Christian theology. But the episodes of Book 2 in which Guyon's struggles reveal him most deeply as a character—Mordant and Amavia, the Bower, Pyrochles—bear a certain affinity to the writings of a Puritan like Milton, as Milton himself recognizes in *Areopagitica*. This is not to say that Spenser is a Puritan,[4] merely that his depiction of the self shares something with characteristic Puritan versions of it. On the basis of this similarity, I will note a central conflict in the Puritan self, between a Pauline focus on pathos and a Stoic resistance to it, that plays a central role in Spenser's Book 2.

For Puritanism, admitting the importance of emotional experience means considering the possibility that emotion might overrule the disciplined Stoic conscience that Puritans were deeply invested in. Even if Puritans were afraid to admit the full force of affect, they almost always returned to it as a focus of religious attention—along with its opposite, the Stoic discipline that tries to suppress affect. Some puritans emphasized the persistence and ungovernable strength of pathos; others, the need to restrain it in the service of Stoic self-control. Guyon, in his desire to become strict director of his emotions, champions the Stoic side.

Temperance, the characteristic virtue of Book 2, is an Aristotelian as well as a Stoic term, one important not only to the Reformation, but to Renaissance ethics in general.[5] Particularly relevant to Spenser is Renaissance Stoicism's argument over whether the wise man should aim at the destruction or the temperate management of affect.[6] Though Guyon usually aims for the control of affect, he is tempted by the idea of escaping from emotion altogether. Mammon's cave (2.7) presents to Guyon such an offer to do away with pathos to achieve a more efficient ethics. But the idea of destroying affect, annihilating one's emotional nature to secure one's virtue, proves dangerous in Book 2. Mammon's final test, the silver seat, offers Guyon the impervious assurance of a Socrates and, with it, the chance to absolve himself from passion. At this moment, Mammon threatens to turn Guyon into an allegorical figure of such absolute self-sufficiency that he would end in total immobility, just as Diana's nymph turns to stone as a result of her self-sufficient chastity in 2.2. Guyon refuses this temptation of radical Stoicism, avoiding immobility, and continues his career as a character subject to the desires that he means to control.[7]

If desire can only be uprooted by transforming the body into a monument of stony chastity, turning a person into a thing (and thus fulfilling a common Renaissance pun on "stock" and "Stoic"), then the Stoic impulse shares something with the allegorical one. Allegory, like Stoicism, wants to transcend the human by imaginatively transforming ideal human qualities into the stability of material nature: the Stoic is a rock beaten by the ocean's waves. Stoicism undertakes this escape from the human in an effort to ensure a moralism; however, such moralism reduces virtue to a rigid and inaccessible pattern.[8]

Guyon wants, at times, to be a radical Stoic: what Aristotle calls a *sôphrôn*, an untemptable, because unemotional, sage (EN 1146a). Mammon holds out the bait of the *sôphrôn*'s impervious, unbeatable character. But Guyon luckily veers away from the fixity promised by Mammon's nerve-wracked, obsessional pursuit of a rock-solid posture. As Aristotle's *enkratês*, a well-mixed or temperate type, he remains implicated in the emotional weakness epitomized by the badly mixed, intoxicating potions of Acrasia. Guyon's first major encounter in Book 2, the Mordant-Amavia episode, shows the crucial obstruction to his impulse to rise above pathos: the presence of what Spenser would call "original sin," an irresistible emotional weakness that defines the human.[9] Spenser makes this point largely through this scene's inquiry into the significance of baptism.

Here I will briefly review the debate over the meaning of baptism in Christian tradition, because this controversy is centrally relevant to the Mordant-Amavia episode. Since Augustine's and Origen's fourth-century discussions of baptism, Christians recognize that this sacrament, as Paul Ricoeur writes, "Makes us participate in the latent meaning and thus assimilates us to that which is symbolized."[10] When Guyon wrestles with the meaning of his attempt to baptize Amavia's bloodstained infant Ruddymane in 2.1, he engages in such inward action. By contrast, when Red Crosse's hands are "baptized" by the well of life (1.11.36), this is an external or allegorical rather than an inward event, and therefore an inadequate version of baptism. Guyon involves himself in what baptism means, not merely, as Red Crosse does, with its effects: Guyon senses the meaning of his deeds as Red Crosse does not.

This difference reflects the more general one between Red Crosse's victories and defeats, which are largely the work of external, magical influences, and Guyon's heroism, which stems from his struggle to achieve his characteristic virtue of temperance.[11]

But Guyon's interpretation of baptism, though it aims at the essence of the event as Red Crosse's does not, proves debatable in its bias toward the Stoic hope for an escape from pathos. To claim, as Guyon does, that Ruddymane's bloody stains can be scrubbed off is to follow Origen's Stoic inclination and whitewash the fact of original sin announced by Augustine. Guyon reads baptism as a symbolic commemoration of or "moniment" to ascesis. This is substantially the interpretation of baptism that Origen and Pelagius propounded. For them, baptism offers an emblem of successful moral discipline rather than a comment on the baptized person's continuing, inescapable sinfulness.

Guyon's interpretation of baptism as efficient, attainable ascesis looks doubtful not only because Ruddymane's hands remain bloody but also because of Guyon's own shortcomings as an ascetic. Book 2 casts doubt on the efficacy of Guyon's discipline, however strident his claims to moral superiority.[12] His trials derive from a conflict between the flesh and the spirit that his heroic self-control cannot overcome.[13]

Guyon denies the unmasterable nature of sin, refusing to acknowledge the Augustinian truth that heroic virtue cannot rise above human weakness.[14] His resistance to the vulnerability that sin implies comes into clearer view as Spenser shifts from Amavia's story to the next episode of Book 2, which focuses on Medina. Translating Mordant's fatal inward weakness into a disaster caused by his victimization at the hands of external powers, Guyon asks Medina that Mordant's son "might for memorie of that dayes ruth, / Be called Ruddymane, and thereby taught, / T'auenge his Parents death on them, that had it wrought" (2.3.2).[15] Guyon here presides over a swing back to Red Crosse's impetuous style of allegorical questing: his wish for a heroic avenger's destiny for Ruddymane, in its bluntly militant tone, courts a slightly silly overzealousness. Spenser's poem as a whole heartily participates in the realizing of allegory as drama that Guyon wants when he envisions a heroic plot for Ruddymane that will avenge his dead father (and make the babe's own hands even bloodier). But *The Faerie Queene* also consistently questions Guyon's heroic assumption that sin or vice can be vanquished through such direct confrontations with the other. As Book 2 continues, Guyon will seek out heroic encounters of the kind he imagines for Ruddymane, seeing in his own virtue the strength to succeed where the less self-knowing Red Crosse failed. Yet Guyon does not really know himself, for his championing of his inward strength causes him to repress the unavoidable fact that his true enemies lie within rather than without. Guyon shies away from the fact of his own entanglement in the bad desires he criticizes. Appropriately, these rejected desires then reappear in the fierce shapes of Guyon's allegorical enemies: Pyrochles, Cymochles, Phaedria, Furor.

The poem takes its revenge on Guyon's assumption that his foes must be alien to him by staging the Bower as a contest within its hero's own psyche. Guyon cannot know Acrasia's meaning by enacting it in his chosen terms, as outward conflict.[16] The fact that Guyon at the very end of Canto 12 construes Acrasia as the representative of other men's desires, not his own, is the inevitable extension of his wish to confront sensual weakness as something that appears before him rather than in him. Guyon wants to exempt himself from the way desire sabotages the possibility of any fully clear, articulated self-presentation.

So Guyon refuses to acknowledge his susceptibility to sinful impulses; however, unlike Red Crosse, he does suspect this truth, as I will argue in discussing his reaction to Mordant and Amavia. We can start to explain the difference between Red Crosse's naively confident courage and Guyon's more tenuous or wavering bravado by remembering that the work done by plot in Book 1 is done by Guyon's pressured and uncertain character in Book 2. Guyon's present-tense moral response does the work of Book 1's wandering, yet teleologically impelled, plot.[17] The hero's effort to take a straight, narrow course through the Bower mimes the definition of temperance as a thin line between too much and too little. Guyon's eyes are fixed on his own conduct; by contrast, Red Crosse gazes toward a purely external goal, an ultimate battle whose meaning occurs beyond him.[18]

Guyon's self-involvement also implies a claim to flexibility in reading pathos. As Book 2 begins, Guyon seems to master, as Red Crosse could not, the emotional meaning of his experience through revisionary retrospect. When Guyon narrates his first misadventure in Book 2, during which he, exactly like Red Crosse in Book 1, deceives himself through pity for the disguised Duessa, he makes light of his failure: "So can he turne his earnest unto game," the poet remarks, "Through goodly handling and wise temperance" (2.1.31). In contrast, Red Crosse attributes his adventures to God, not his own "handling"; he remarks to Guyon that "all I did, I did but as I ought" (2.1.33). Instead of revising his mistakes as Guyon does, Red Crosse is imprisoned by them, as in the somber revelations of his affair with Duessa at the end of Book 1.[19] By deliberately turning earnest into game, potential tragedy into comedy, Guyon shows a greater mastery of pathos than does Red Crosse, who (as I argued last chapter) remains consistently confused by the distinctions between emotional seriousness and triviality that Spenser presents in Book 1.[20] Guyon represents a good mix of moods, in place of Red Crosse's indecorous embodiment of two clashing qualities, boyish enthusiasm and solemn dedication: Spenser describes Guyon's "countenance demure and temperate, / But yet so sterne and terrible in sight" (2.1.4).

But Guyon's temperate mediation of such extremes, like his facility at manipulating the emotional meaning of the scenes he has lived through, displays a skilled avoidance of vulnerability, not a conquering of it. The evasive character of pathos embodies the insidious force of such weakness, which Guyon's will to interpretation can never correct. Guyon is affected by his mortal fragility; as we shall see, Britomart experiences even more closely than Guyon the intimate truth of pathos in the form of her weakness before her desire.

Anger and "ioyous pleasance" (2.6.1), Guyon's major temptations in Book 2, both play on his self-weakness. Pleasure melts the soul to a narcissistic, delightful excess; anger also contains a secret self-reflexive meaning, even as it takes the form of heroic action against an external other. Pyrochles bears a family resemblance to Guyon, who when he confronts his fiery enemy is full of fire (*pur*), "emboyling in his haughty heart" (2.5.9). Pyrochles, then, represents less an external than an internal danger, though because of the nature of allegory Spenser must present him as external, and Guyon must at least initially take him as such.

Guyon moves from an external to an internal orientation in his battle with Pyrochles. First, he trips himself up by assuming that Pyrochles is thoroughly alien to him. This assumption allows him to act in as furiously uncontrolled a way as his opponent, thus proving their similarity while himself remaining unaware of it. "To ouerthrow him strongly [Guyon] did assay, / But ouerthrew himselfe vnwares, and lower lay" (2.4.8). Spenser clearly suggests a mirroring of self and other in the combat between Guyon and Pyrochles. This mirroring frustrates Guyon because it reveals that his character is not proper to itself. Guyon is self-alienated, an Imaginary other to himself, because he sees his weakness only in the other, which is exactly where he does not want to be—he does not recognize his weakness as his own. Such alienation obstructs Guyon's ambition to become self-possessed, a proper, disciplined ego. As Mikkel Borch-Jacobsen writes, the ego is born out of the encounter with the other. Therefore, the ego can never be what it so desperately wishes to be: its own origin.[21] In this Imaginary doubling, the formative relation between self and other, the other looks dismayingly like the self. Pyrochles displays to Guyon a lack that afflicts Guyon himself, and it is this lack—of self-control—that prompts Guyon's rage.

Guyon's mimetic rivalry with his double Pyrochles drives home the role of visible competition and self-display in his ethic of temperance.

Guyon's reaction to his wound at the hands of Pyrochles in 2.5.7 is a significant moment:

> Exceeding wroth was *Guyon* at that blow,
>   And much ashamd, that stroke of liuing arme
>   Should him dismay, and make him stoup so low,
>   Though otherwise it did him litle harme

When Guyon takes his revenge for being forced to stoup at the hands of Pyrochles, he mirrors Pyrochles' blow: Guyon "made [Pyrochles] stoup perforce vnto his knee, / And do vnwilling worship to the Saint, / That on his shield depainted he did see" (2.5.11). The purely mimed or externalized nature of this "worship" makes it clear that Guyon's effort to differentiate himself from Pyrochles through physical combat makes a mockery of his supposed moral superiority: Guyon simply reflects his opponent's tactics. In this scene, the significance of Guyon's "saint" (an emblem of Gloriana) proves *merely* visible, just as Guyon's "harm" results from the evident shame of being seen to stoop before Pyrochles. The "worship" that Guyon forces on Pyrochles is apparent rather than inward. Guyon, then, begins his fight with Pyrochles by seeing victory in the display of his own brave appearance, not his inward self-restraint. His heroic show, in all its fiery splendor, bears a remarkable resemblance to Pyrochles'.

But Guyon rapidly progresses to a self-mastery intended to differentiate him from his enemy—and this progress toward inwardness shows how Book 2's rivalries differ from, for example, Red Crosse's battle with Sans-ioy in 1.5. "Maistering his might" and "tempering" his "cruell hand" (2.5.13), Guyon realizes what he did not just a few stanzas earlier: that self-control precedes and enables control over worldly circumstances. As he says to Pyrochles, exploiting a familiar Stoic topos, "Vaine others ouerthrowes, who selfe doth ouerthrowe" (2.5.15). Yet Guyon's criticism of Pyrochles' tendency to overthrow himself might just as readily apply to the "exceeding wroth" Guyon of a few moments ago:[22] despite the mature tone of his advice, he is a newcomer to self-government.

Allegory's fundamental investment in externalization, in the visible, complicates Guyon's effort to convey his internalizing point about the disciplining of pathos. Guyon supplements his inward-looking statement on self-overthrowing and self-mastery with a decidedly externalized version of how this self-mastery may be achieved:

> Fly, O Pyrochles, fly the dreadfull warre,
>   That in thy selfe thy lesser parts do moue,
>   Outrageous anger, and woe-working iarre,

> Direfull impatience, and hart murdring loue;
> Those, those thy foes, those warriours far remoue,
> Which thee to endlesse bale captiued lead.
>
> (*FQ* 2.5.16)

Pyrochles fails to understand Guyon's pushing of allegory toward the inward or symbolic. In his crudely literal attempt to follow Guyon's advice, he tries to flee his own flesh, to escape the enemy within by drowning himself (2.6.44–45). Pyrochles labors under the misconception that his passions are forces that inhabit, but remain foreign to, him. His attempt to wash off his desires (2.6.42) mistakes the elusive inner reality of corruption for its seemingly easier to handle, but illusory, visible signs. Pyrochles is finally forced to admit that "burning in flames, yet no flames can I see" (2.6.45): he cannot recognize the fact that his fire lies within.[23] Phedon turns in a similarly external direction with his very rapid transition from the thought of suicide to that of killing others (2.4.27–33.).

Spenser in Canto 5 cooperates with Pyrochles' externalizing impulses insofar as he tries to convey an antiallegorical, invisible truth within and through allegory. The poet cannot depict his conception of human mind and desire in anything but visible terms, even when, as in the case of Pyrochles, he points to such depiction as the source of a fatal error. Significantly, even as *The Faerie Queene* moves from Red Crosse to Guyon, from external to internal versions of character, allegory remains the poem's most important feature. The centrality of allegory cannot be grudged even when it strains against its own boundaries.

The matter of allegory remains a question for Spenser's readers as well as his characters. Guyon's meeting with Pyrochles, stationed at the midpoint of Book 2, bears crucial implications for the debate between those who would read Spenser allegorically and those who would read him psychologically. Berger, a psychologist, remarks that the voyage to the Bower that Guyon and the Palmer undertake in Canto 12 moves from external dangers, the easily recognized and avoided allegorical clichés like the Rock of Reproach, to a more inward threat, the *acrasia* or imbalance of body and spirit that lives in us.[24] Other readers, in an effort to make Book 2 thoroughly allegorical, have rejected the idea of such a movement toward the inward psyche. For example, Rosemond Tuve, in *Allegorical Imagery*, upholds an allegorical approach in order to combat critics' inattentive and anachronistic psychologizing of Spenser. Tuve's emphasis on allegory's realistic elements, the way in which it can faithfully represent experience, is acute and helpful. But this line of interpretation fails to account for the distance that Spenser's characters sometimes encounter between experience and its allegorical or proverbial explanation.[25] Allegory does not exactly fit experience, and this lack of fit makes Pyrochles suffer. As Berger suggests and Tuve denies, Book 2 clearly presents a tension between allegorical precept and lived example. As I have been arguing, Book 2 moves from an outward to an inward model. The motive for this development can only be Spenser's dissatisfaction with the purely outward or allegorical format of Book 1.

Guyon's encounter with the pumped-up, cloddish hulk Disdaine in Mammon's den further illustrates Book 2's development toward inwardness through the competitive mutual reflection of self and other. Just as with Pyrochles, Guyon here falls prey to a disdainful rivalry based on his infectious identification with Disdaine. Disdaine's

> harmefull club he gan to hurtle hye,
> And threaten batteill to the Faery knight;
> Who likewise gan himselfe to batteill dight,
> Till *Mammon* did his hasty hand withhold
> 
> (*FQ* 2.7.42)[26]

Unlike Guyon and Disdaine, Mammon focuses his desire on an object, wealth, that does not reflect the self. Money, a generic, impersonal commodity that can neither react to nor resist one's advances, attracts him precisely because it provides a means to avoid mimetic rivalry. Thus Mammon, a habitual solitary, reacts with shocked discomposure to the sudden appearance of a real live person, Guyon, at the beginning of Canto 7: "In great affright / And hast he rose" (2.7.6). In contrast to Mammon's reclusive impulse, Guyon finds himself intrigued by exactly such captivating reaction and resistance, the mirror play of self and other that temperance means to restrain. Guyon's relations to Disdaine, Furor, Pyrochles and the Bower's Verdant (whose position in Acrasia's lap Guyon is invited to occupy) all take this mirroring form.

A comparison between Book 1's Fradubio and the Mordant episode of Book 2 helps to define the role of pathos in the mixing of self and other that Guyon's temperate therapy tries to balance.[27] As I mentioned in the last chapter, the exemplary significance of Fradubio for Red Crosse, the way their cases present a parallel, is obvious to the reader but not to Red Crosse himself. Red Crosse's burying of Fradubio's bough-cum-arm defends him against Fradubio's example:[28]

> ... the good knight
> Full of sad feare and ghastly dreriment,
> When all this speech the liuing tree had spent,
> The bleeding bough did thrust into the ground,
> That from the bloud he might be innocent ...
> 
> (*FQ* 1.2.44)

Bewitched by Duessa (1.2.42), Fradubio is an innocent victim of magic, and Red Crosse believes he can be innocent too, despite Fradubio's reference to Red Crosse's "guilty hands" (1.2.31), if he can successfully remove himself from the tainted precinct. Spenser's determined evasion of an internal, moral explanation in favor of a topical, allegorical one leaves no room for reading Fradubio's fall as a self-generated error. Spenser here graphically figures Red Crosse's suffering at the hands of repetition, and of the power of place in romance.[29] Fradubio's fate represents entrapment by an external, visible snare: this is a place that Red Crosse can hope to avoid.

Red Crosse's reaction to Fradubio does look strikingly similar to Guyon's response to Mordant, as Nohrnberg notes. Red Crosse "astound . . . stood, and vp his haire did houe, / And with that suddein horror could no member moue" (1.2.31). Guyon is similarly paralyzed: "His hart gan wexe as starke, as marble stone" (2.1.42). But Spenser also, more significantly, draws a contrast between the magically predetermined nature of Fradubio's downfall and the motivated character of Mordant's. The latter represents a case of moral discipline for which Mordant himself must be responsible. Mordant's defeat derives from his own weakness, which sinks to its extreme when he "stoup[s] to drincke" from Acrasia's well. The mistake of Fradubio, by contrast, results only from one of Duessa's sticky lures.[30] Acrasia's manipulative talent, unlike Duessa's, is subtle enough to stand for self-induced sin. Mordant may have escaped Acrasia's visible bonds, but her influence remains within him. Fradubio is literally transformed into a tree; Mordant, internally "so transformed . . . / That [Amavia] he knew not, neither his owne ill" (2.1.54). Amavia temporarily cures Mordant by educating him in "wise handling and faire gouernance" (2.1.54), whereas Fradubio's fate cannot be amended, however strong his repentance.

The divergence between Fradubio and Mordant, and between the seductive techniques of Duessa and Acrasia, parallels the more central distinction, which I have already noted, between Red Crosse and Guyon. In contrast to Red Crosse's ignorance, Guyon distinguishes himself from his doubles with an enthusiasm that inadvertently reveals his unconscious sense of proximity to them. Guyon thus makes a statement about his own frail, precarious human status in the very act of trying to steel himself against this frailty. Here is the scene from 2.1 in which Guyon comes upon Mordant:[31]

> . . . vpon the soiled gras
> The dead corse of an armed knight was spred,
> Whose armour all with bloud besprinckled was;
> His ruddie lips did smile, and rosy red
> Did paint his chearefull cheekes, yet being ded,

> Seemd to haue beene a goodly personage,
> Now in his freshest flowre of lustie hed
> Fit to inflame faire Lady with loues rage,
> But that fiers fate did crop the blossome of his age.
> (*FQ* 2.1.41)

Guyon reacts to this "pitteous spectacle" with "ruth" and horror:

> His hart gan wexe as starke, as marble stone,
> And his fresh bloud did frieze with fearefull cold,
> That all his senses seemd bereft attone,
> At last his mightie ghost gan deepe to grone,
> As Lyon grudging in his great disdaine,
> Mournes inwardly, and makes to himselfe mone,
> Till ruth and fraile affection did constraine,
> His stout courage to stoupe, and shew his inward
>         paine.
> (*FQ* 2.1.42)

Guyon's reaction instantly proves the scene's relevance to him: he turns as cold as the corpse that hot blood has produced.[32] Even in its chill immediacy, Guyon's response is reflective. It depends on his intuitive act of comparison between Mordant and himself, suggested in his "inward" mourning and sympathetic "affection." The comparison stems from Guyon's sense of the relevance of Mordant's case to his own: Mordant offers a possible future that the self-disciplined Guyon must reject.[33]

It is true, as Berger claims, that Guyon compares himself to Mordant only to differentiate himself from the latter on the grounds of his greater virtue: Guyon avoids the knowledge of their true similarity. But he does have a subliminal sense of this likeness. Berger himself claims for Guyon in a later episode of Book 2, his encounter with Shamefastness (2.9.43–44), the kind of unconsciously knowing response that he denies to Guyon here. Guyon's turning away from Shamefastness in Alma's house, Berger writes, "is a self-conscious reaction" that "seems in part . . . a suppression of the fact that he is motivated by so uncontrollable a feeling . . . His complex gesture remains essentially an evasion. It is a turning away from the reality of his own krasis, from the recognition of human weakness."[34] I suggest that Guyon's encounter with Mordant much earlier in Book 2 involves a similarly telling evasion on his part.

In 2.1 Guyon tries to avoid self-abasement as he does later with Pyrochles when he "ma[kes Pyrochles] stoup perforce." In contrast to the case of Pyrochles, Guyon defends himself against Mordant not by humiliating him, but by warding off Mordant's message for him. The effort is not wholly successful, as Guyon's "inward pain" indicates. But Guyon's "stout courage," which "stoupe[s]" to empathy with Acrasia's victims as Mordant "stoupt to drincke" from her charmed well (2.1.55), soon reelevates itself via the moral pigeonholing of their tragedy. He turns the incident into a lesson about man's "feeble nature" (2.1.57), which only a temperate few, himself included, can transcend:

> The strong through pleasure soonest falles,
>   the weake through smart.
>
> But temperance (said he) with golden squire
>   Betwixt them both can measure out a meane....
>                       (*FQ* 2.1.57–58)

Guyon's moralism, based as it is in a defensive distinction between "the strong" and "the weake," proves unfeasible. There is an important sense in which Guyon's shamefast reluctance to "shew his inward paine" turns his leonine "disdeine" for inferiors into an acknowledgment, however hidden, of the common instinctual ground such a reaction tries to deny—a ground that Christianity calls original sin. Shame itself, with its telling attempt to hide the fact that the base is also the basis of human nature, participates in such an unwilling acknowledgment.[35] Guyon's analytic "be temperate" means less than the shock of his knocking knees, the gut feeling his dictum tries to evade ("How can anybody be temperate, given our sinful nature—aren't we all Mordants under the skin?"). The stooping comes before the asserted distinction: Guyon must yield to the implications of a common narrative situation, and to the affective entangling of self and other such commonality induces, in order to make the discriminating point that tries to repress his kinship with Mordant. Guyon tries to transform the Imaginary blurring of self and other, their empathic mutuality, into self-possessed autonomy—temperance's dream.[36]

Guyon tries to separate strength from weakness in the Mordant-Amavia episode. Unwilling to see that even Amavia's chastity can be touched by sin, he refuses to recognize her mortal fragility. Guyon wants Ruddymane's red hands to be "pledges" that Amavia has died "clere ... from blemish criminall," but the paradox of a bloody innocence, a weakness built into virtue from the start, proves too much for Guyon to bear.

With his moral advice, Guyon resists Amavia's and Ruddymane's paradox of guilty virtue. His sympathetic moralizing shows that he is already distancing himself from her sorrow, and from the risky example of Mordant.[37] Guyon's "Help never comes too late" (2.1.44) contests Amavia's reply, "All flesh doth frailtie breed" (2.1.52).[38] The bedside-manner aphorisms that Guyon speaks to Amavia, which in praising temperance steer a middle way between sentimental optimism and sententious aloofness, provide no help because they hold off from full engagement in a tragic scene of vulnerability and desire. But Guyon's pity for Amavia is not merely condescending: his sympathy implicates him in the passions of a "lower" nature.[39] Guyon's self-conscious, and self-congratulatory, virtue covers the faerie knight's suspicion of the secret wound he shares with his double Mordant, the other whose fleshly limitations he wants to transcend.[40]

Guyon claims, in effect, that temperance can eliminate the paradox embodied in Amavia's fountain, but by doing so he ignores the fact that temperance depends on a mixing of elements. In stark contrast to Book 1's unequivocal well of life, the fountain displays a shocking combination of chaste purity and gore. The babe himself indulges in a comparable incongruity of mood, playing in the midst of a "pitifull spectacle:" "And the cleane waues with purple gore did ray; / Als in her [i.e., Amavia's] lap a louely babe did play / His cruell sport, in stead of sorrow dew" (2.1.40). This clash of emotions corresponds to the description of passion presented in this episode, which emphasizes the way emotion confuses what we thought were reliable oppositions: "The strong it weakens with infirmitie, / And with bold furie armes the weakest hart" (2.1.57).

Passion, by confusing strong and weak, furious and infirm, frustrates the temperate effort to find a mean between extremes, to manipulate these emotional categories in a reasoned, directed way. Guyon attempts such direction not only through the Palmer-like aphorisms he offers to Amavia, but also through turning earnest into game as he does both at the beginning of his quest and at its end (with his final throwaway slur, "let *Grill* be *Grill*, and haue his hoggish mind" [2.12.87]). In contrast to the case of Red Crosse, who was assigned (and failed) the test of finding a single proper reading of events and characters (Archimago as dangerous, Fradubio as tragic), Spenser sets Guyon against a paradoxical reality that refuses all univocal readings: heroic strength is always also weakness. (Britomart, when she encounters the oxymoronic pleasant pain of love, runs up against a similarly stubborn ambiguity.) Guyon's revisionary ability to read tragedy as comedy, demonstrated at the beginning of Book 2, tries to exclude paradox by choosing one generic alternative over another, but his effort fails before the imposing enigma of original sin—the innocent babe sporting in the midst of bloody sorrow.

Canto 2 presents another attempt to surmount the paradox of sin with its story of Diana's nymph who, chased by "*Dan Faunus*," metamorphoses into a stone when she "set her downe to weepe for sore constraint, / And to *Diana* calling lowd for ayde, / Her deare besought, to let her dye a mayd" (2.2.7– 8). The tale's lesson seems to be that the successful avoidance of sin would require more than either heroic action or temperate self-control can offer. Instead, Diana gives a pure, passive resistance that finally makes her nymph less, not more, than human. The nymph, turned into a statue, naturally or inherently repels guilt. She represents perfect, unequivocal chastity as an unequivocal state, an escape from *The Faerie Queene*'s confusing indeterminacy of mixed moods and deceptive interpretation; however, the escape leads toward a paralytic alienation from narrative and therefore from the human condition itself. The statue's image of virtue as congealed purity argues against the feasibility of Guyon's effort to evade sin through temperance. If temperance means a mixing of elements, of passion and virtue, how can it attain to a virginal chasteness?[41]

Chastity as we see it in Diana's nymph can only exist as a perfect, hyper-Stoic removal of oneself from any pathos whatever, and the inevitable outcome of this removal is the transformation of the self into a stony monument to virtue.[42] Book 3 will turn the nymph's immobile chastity back into energetic flesh and blood. Britomart comes into her own here because she exemplifies a dramatic capability, and a vulnerability, far removed from the stunning but alienating perfection of figures like the nymph and Belphoebe.

Diana's nymph stands against Britomart's real, lived chastity as allegory stands against psychic inwardness. The contrast has significant implications for our practice of reading Spenser. Acknowledging that *The Faerie Queene* plays out a conflict between "inward" and allegorical readings means reflecting on current practice in Renaissance studies—in particular, on the unmet need for a heuristic method flexible enough to answer to the ambivalent stress in Renaissance literature on both the self and the structures that surround it. This ambivalence demands from Spenser's critics an ambidextrous handling of his poem. Many current analyses overlook the allegory-experience tension in Renaissance literature because critics often assume, as does Jameson in his treatment of romance, the need to de-emphasize subjective *Stimmung* and concentrate instead on the structural or narrative forms that promise a connection to historical structures. The critic loses sight of the ways that Renaissance texts themselves encode the choice between self and story as a debate between objective, abstract patterns of allegory and lived example, which is based on subjective mood. Jameson's version of romance submits subjectivity to structure. For him romance becomes an allegory of its own narrative form (and thus an allegory of history). As I argued in my introduction, this impoverishing of subjectivity accounts for the inability to deal with tragedy in Jameson and many of the new historicists—or their ability to deal with tragic fate only as the inexorable working of a system, a law that generates, rather than arguing with, the subject's desire.

I will go on to criticize Fish's version of reader response criticism as a similarly impoverished view of subjectivity, and suggest some ways to a better account of tragedy and epic as didactic genres. The basic tendency of readerly identification is to exceed any moral design: we sympathize with Milton's Satan before we think about whether he is good or evil. As Hans-Robert Jauss points out, moral judgment can never completely constrain the attraction that aesthetic examples exert. According to Jauss, Christian hermeneutics compensates for, and tries to overcome, the force of the reader's identification by means of its didactic thrust, which asserts that the reader should follow only virtuous examples.[43]

Fish seeks, as Jauss does not, to make aesthetics over into didactic moralizing by arguing the total efficacy of the text's effort to guide the reader's reactions. As Elizabeth Freund has shown, in Fish's version of reader response the text becomes a stand-in for the capacity of the reader's conscious will.[44] The reader's faith, according to Fish, resides in his or her eventual hope to absorb all didactic lessons permanently and completely. Fish's championing of moral will requires him to eliminate any suspicion of the split detected by critics like Pucci and Jauss between the reader's affective attraction to a text and his or her conscious, formulaic recognition of the text's message. In the case of tragedy, Fish will not recognize the gap between primary, uncontrolled affective response—fear or primal empathy—and the moralizing pity that distances the spectatorial self from the dangers of uncontrol that such affect represents.

In trauma as in tragedy, affect in its original form is repressed, even as it is shown. Fish's denial or repression of this repression leads him to reject psychoanalysis itself, because the Freudian model implies a failure of conscious mastery that Fish finds unacceptable. Citing Freud's statement that society "does not wish to be reminded of [the] precarious portion of its foundations," Fish comments, "I would go even further and say that neither society nor any member of society could be reminded of that precariousness, for to be so reminded would be to achieve what psychoanalysis itself declares to be unattainable, a distance on one's own concerns and obsessions.... When we are asked to state what we take to be the case about this or that, we will always respond in the context of what seems to us at the time to be indisputably true."[45] Fish's rough-and-ready pragmatic formula, "what seems to us at the time," enthrones consciousness as an omnipotent psychic agency, wholly rejecting the realm of ambivalence demarcated by the Freudian unconscious. (Note also Fish's conflating of "concerns" and "obsessions," as if the latter could be reduced to the former.) In Freud, as in Wittgenstein, we can never formulate the truth about ourselves to ourselves in a clear, controlled way, though the effort to do so provides Freud's humanistic, and heuristic, goal. The fact of the unconscious prevents such articulate satisfaction. Fish's remarks on Freud, in their pursuit of articulate explanation at any price, represent an unfortunate, and symptomatic, abandoning of a potentially fruitful model of reader response, the psychoanalytic process, in favor of a simpler and easier didactic therapy.

It is true, as Fish has demonstrated, that on the most overt level Milton's plan as an author sometimes coincides with this easy therapy: Milton wants to overcome his reader's empathic response to characters like Satan and turn this response into a moral warning against empathy. But Fish exaggerates Milton's desire for success in moralism when he implies that the empathic reaction is finally expendable, that we can deprive the resemblance between Satan and ourselves of its passionate, insinuating power once we become aware of Satanic fraudulence. Milton actually goes in the opposite direction to Fish's program, suggesting that to moralize is potentially to avoid a more difficult, truer experience—the fact of tragedy itself. *Samson*'s Manoa displays this avoidance of the tragic—Samson's monstrous encounter with the intertwining of strength and weakness, which we have already seen in Spenser's Book 2—in its most perfect, most blind, form.

Spenser does not test the relation between pathos and the drive to moralism with Milton's intense concern. As a result, our identification with Spenser's characters is less concentrated and emotive than with Milton's. The often bemused attitude toward the fiction of *The Faerie Queene* that we share with its author allows us a distance that Milton, who laments with us the fall of Eden as our common disaster, does not allow. In an episode like the Bower, we worry about Guyon's weakness in a way that assures us of our greater strength; we fear for Eve and Adam as for ourselves.

At certain moments in Book 2, Guyon attains strength by detaching himself from pathos, without giving in to the temptation that froze Diana's nymph, her total elimination of passion. With Mammon, he enacts a formulaic, proverbial assurance, "warie wise in all his way" (2.7.64). Doctrine here remains unconfused by the psychic drama that affects Guyon during the episodes of Mordant-Amavia and the Bower. Guyon keeps "another happinesse, another end" steadily in sight (2.7.33), and he knows exactly what to do to reach it.

At the very end of Book 2, Guyon wants to reject emotion.[46] When he finally judges Acrasia's victims, as when he refuses Mammon,

Guyon, pronouncing proverbial dicta, summarizes the chill assurance that empowers him: "Sad end (quoth he) of life intemperate, / And mournefull meed of ioyes delicious" (2.12.88). But Guyon's continuing susceptibility to the Bower's seductions proves the partial nature of his triumph.

Guyon overestimates his strength at the end of Book 2. The lack of convincing finality in Guyon's destruction of the Bower is apparent in the tentative, conditional character of this ending. Not only does Grylle remain his bestial self, but Guyon and the Palmer remain subject to navigational uncertainties: they depart from the charred ruins of the Bower "whilst wether serues and wind" (2.12.87). The note of hesitant contingency sounded by the Palmer in this line adds to the impression of a notably incomplete victory that the example of Grylle has just suggested. The fact that Grylle remains Grylle testifies to the frustration of Guyon's moralizing in the face of human weakness.

Unaided by the angel who, as God's grace personified, attended him after the ordeal in Mammon's cave, Guyon in the Bower relies for his strength on his refusal to recognize a psychic and emotional weakness that exists in him as in every human. Guyon cannot effectively separate himself from Acrasia. Despite his rejection of the flesh, the enticed hero finds his "courage" reared by the bathing maidens. He succeeds in asserting his noble exemption from faults, but the strain of his repression is visible in the violence with which he breaks Excesse's cup and defaces the Bower's elegant workmanship (2.12.57, 83). As a figure for moral incapacity, Acrasia remains inherent in Guyon as much as in Grylle; however, Guyon can misinterpret her as alien to him. This refusal of self-acknowledgment is the only way for him to continue his career beyond the Bower. Choosing doctrinal over existential truth, Guyon acts out the paradigm of Fish's (un)responsive reader and unwittingly demonstrates its limits, its repressive demands.

No higher authority can validate Guyon's position in Canto 12, as the angel does at the end of the Mammon episode; there is only his own power to disclaim his weakness. We might read this difference as a Spenserean self-critique: the poet renounces the angelic intervention of the earlier episode along with the clear statement of authorial moralism that went along with it ("And all for love, and nothing for reward" [2.8.2]). Any voice of virtue, Spenser now implies, must be an internal one. The guiding, comforting angel yields his moralizing role to the stern but—in the Bower, at least—ineffective Palmer.

The Maleger episode, which directly precedes the Bower, drives home the significance of Guyon's vulnerability, suggesting that Stoic strength cannot conquer the weakness that defines the human. Like Acrasia, Pyrochles, and Cymochles, Maleger is an internal, exemplary enemy:

> Flesh without bloud, a person without spright,
> Wounds without hurt, a bodie without might,
> That could doe harme, yet could not harmed bee,
> That could not die, yet seem'd a mortall wight,
> That was most strong in most infirmitie....
> 
> *(FQ* 2.11.40)

Woodhouse and A. C. Hamilton identify Maleger as the old Adam in fallen man, our integral remnant of original sin.[47] That Arthur's struggle in 2.11 is internal, a battle against his own mortal nature in the shape of Maleger, is suggested by the 1590 text that Spenser later amended: Arthur "thought his labour lost and trauell vaine, / Against his lifelesse shadow so to fight."[48]

Maleger, Arthur's mortality, cannot be vanquished by heroic virtue, only by grace. Here as in Pauline-Augustinian theology, a demonstration of the futility of trying to fight one's "lifeless shadow" or mortal weakness precedes grace. Even Arthur, the poem's strongest hero, must accept this weakness, discarding sword and armor and coming in direct contact with the old Adam "of the earth" (1 Cor. 15:47), the Antaeus-like Maleger. When Arthur's squire, Timias, rescues him, Spenser uses the occasion to assert the importance of Arthur's vulnerability for the doctrine of grace:[49]

> So greatest and most glorious thing on ground
> May often need the helpe of weaker hand;
> So feeble is mans state, and life vnsound,
> That in assurance it may neuer stand,
> Till it dissolued be from earthly band.
> Proofe be thou Prince, the prowest man aliue,
> And noblest borne of all in Briton land;
> Yet thee fierce Fortune did so nearely driue,
> That had not grace thee blest, thou shouldest not
>   survive.              *(FQ* 2.11.30)

Spenser presents Arthur's weakness during his wrestling with Maleger as the unravelling *en avant* of the moralizing strength that Guyon assumes before Acrasia's victims in the Bower. Appropriately, Canto 11 begins by reiterating the notion it is about to attack: Guyon's characteristic championing of the power that, he thinks, resides in the well-governed body.

> But in a body, which doth freely yeeld
> His partes to reasons rule obedient,
> And letteth her that ought the scepter weeld,
> All happy peace and goodly gouernment
> Is setled there in sure establishment....
> 
> *(FQ* 2.11.2)

Spenser will go on to undermine the feasibility of this ideal of proper governance in the Arthur-Maleger battle. As Canto 11 proceeds, it breaks down its opening analogy of virtue with "goodly gouernment," the parallel between bodily and political order. At first, though, the symbolism in Alma's house, like that of Elizabeth's Britain, reinforces Guyon's own ideology of temperance. The canto begins by stating the sure "setle[ment]" of the affections within a moral order associated with Alma, whom the poet compares to a "virgin Queene" like Elizabeth (st. 2). Spenser then contrasts such order with the "tyranny" that "strong affections" can exercise against the "fort of reason" when it is in a disordered state of "sinful vellenage" (st. 1).

It is important to notice the paradoxical nature of this disorderly emotional tyranny, which makes the flesh grow "fiercer through infirmity" (st. 1). Maleger, as the representative of death—a powerful though seemingly feeble enemy—will display a fierceness or strength within apparent infirmity that matches the infirmity concealed within Arthur's apparent strength. The oxymoronic character of Maleger also appears as an unexpected order or strategic lawfulness in his seemingly chaotic attack. Though Maleger's troops are described as "deformd," "monstrous" and "misshapen," and characterized by "straunge difference" (sts. 8, 10, 12), he is nevertheless able to manipulate them in programmatic, structured fashion:

> Them in twelue troupes their Captain did dispart
> And round about in fittest steades did place,
> Where each might best offend his proper part,
> And his contrary obiect most deface,
> As euery one seem'd meetest in that cace.
> 
> (*FQ* 2.11.6)

Maleger places his troops properly, "in fittest steades." In contradiction to his announced allegorical meaning, Maleger here represents a kind of decorum or good government: the ostensibly malformed demons that assail the fort of smell, for example, are actually "all shap't according their conditions" (2.11.11). The law of decorum applies as well to Maleger's arrows: "Those could he well direct and streight as line" (2.11.21).

The order within Maleger's disorder mirrors a disorder that thrives inside the orderly castle of virtue over which Alma presides. Even the well-run body proves helpless against the anarchic fact of death. Canto 11 asks how, and even whether, order can defend itself against the decay that death imposes. This question entails a further one: Is disorder really external to order, or might it instead be a hidden potential within order? Can Maleger's threat reasonably be represented, as it is here, in the allegorical, externalized form of attacking platoons? As in the case of Guyon's doubles Mordant and Pyrochles, the poem here questions the completeness—the orderliness—of its own allegorical method, even as it exploits allegory. Spenser does not permit heroic strength to stand as the clear contrary of weakness, as Guyon wants it to. Instead, strength participates in weakness. The oxymoronic character of human desire cannot be simplified into a choice between power or control, on the one hand, and impotent passivity, on the other. In place of the homogeneous law of temperance that Alma promises, the poet generates a more contradictory kind of structure as Maleger antithetically erodes the heroic role assigned to Arthur. A similarly riotous phenomenon occurs when Burleigh's detraction and the Blatant Beast's slander attack the poem's ethos and uncover its possibilities for narrative chaos.

Spenser questions his own allegory by undermining the oppositions that define it: light and darkness, strength and weakness. When Arthur first goes out to battle in Canto 11, he appears "with his gay Squire" Timias, bearing "glitterand armes" and "brandish[ing]" his "bright steele on hye" (st. 17). Similarly, in stanza 24 the poet shows Arthur "glistring in armes and warlike ornament."[50] The description of the morning setting, which "maketh euery creature glad" (st. 3), enforces the gaiety of Arthur's appearance. Significantly, it is Arthur's brightly festive energy that actually gives him away to the deathly Maleger, who sights him from afar and begins his assault (st. 24). To win the battle, Arthur must become Maleger-like: he abandons his usual radiant optimism for his enemy's morbid embrace. During his combat with the fiend, Arthur forsakes his premature assumption of a "happie end" to the battle (st. 35) and throws away his "bright shield" (st. 41) to grapple with his somber antagonist. Maleger's darkness magnetically attracts heroic joy, its antithetical partner, in order to erode it.[51]

To uncover the exact point of Arthur's vulnerability, we must look in more detail at his combat with Maleger. Arthur first encounters trouble in his fight with Maleger when he stops to restrain one of Maleger's companions, the old hag Impotence, whom Arthur assumes to be an easy target. When Impotence's counterpart Impatience overthrows Arthur, who is busy binding Impotence, it becomes apparent that Arthur has failed to appreciate the contradictory intimacy of these two characters. In allegorical terms, Arthur himself is impatient or maleager when he attacks Impotence, as he was not earlier in the battle (Arthur showed himself to be "warie" in stanzas 24 and 27). He underestimates the power of Impotence, thinking her an easy mark. As a character who is impatient for heroic victory, he ignores the possibility that his own passionate Impatience may be weak, that it may imply its seeming opposite, Impotence.

At this point, Arthur impatiently tries to defeat Maleger by means of unrestrained rage, in an attempt to eliminate the paradoxical relation of strength to weakness, impatience to impotence. In his effort to avoid his Imaginary relation to Maleger, Arthur reacts against the confusing nature of this "dead-living" figure for whom the dead earth furnishes a mothering "wombe" (sts. 44, 45) and who, in Parthian manner, attacks most effectively while fleeing (st. 26).

Arthur resists the enigmatic combination of opposites that Maleger strategically exploits.[52] Because Arthur rebels against, instead of recognizing, Maleger's maddeningly contradictory nature, the contradiction turns against him, frustrating his success.

Even Arthur's earlier success against Maleger's bands is questionable in context, again because of an elusive or riddling quality that escapes Arthur's grasp. Spenser compares the troops' arrows first to a snowfall, then to a flood, and finally to leaves (sts. 18–19: in epic tradition since Homer, this last image conveys the full weight of mortality). The poet's rapid shifting among these images indicates a delusive instability in the threat that Maleger represents. A leaf storm, like a blizzard or a heavy rainfall, infiltrates the arena; it cannot be conquered by the sword. Finally, Spenser emphasizes the bond that unites Arthur to Maleger when he likens Arthur, in his fight against this meteorological chaos, to a quasi-atmospheric phenomenon, a "fire" that "With murmurous disdaine doth inly raue" and "at last breakes forth with furious vnrest," with "rage and horror great" (st. 31). Arthur is himself *mal-aeger*, sickened by the disease that he combats in Canto 11—with the fire-storm image, he even, for a moment, figuratively becomes the disease.

The Arthur of Canto 11 at last faces his weakness instead of denying it as Guyon does when he claims "reasons rule."[53] Astonished by Maleger's persistence, Arthur at the canto's end sinks the demon in a "standing lake." Arthur's solution to his Maleger problem shows Maleger-like ingenuity rather than Stoic avoidance like Guyon's. Guyon shields himself against his enemies rather than actively exploiting their tactics as Arthur does here. The standing lake into which Arthur casts Maleger is, like Maleger himself, an emblem of deathlike, sluggish fixity.

Arthur now confronts Maleger explicitly in the form of his own mortality: he fights to "th'vtmoste meanes of victorie . . . / Or th'vtmoste issew of his owne decay" (2.11.41). Arthur at last defeats Maleger by "crush[ing] his carkasse . . . against his brest" (2.11.42), literally realizing the intimate nature of his antagonist. With this embrace, Arthur acknowledges the closeness of Maleger to his mortal self as Guyon will not acknowledge his opponent, Acrasia.[54] The "trembling terror" (2.11.39) Arthur feels when he fights Maleger gives proof of the mortal "infirmity" (2.11.49) that the very end of the canto emphasizes, a weakness that will continue to infect him even after he defeats his shadowy enemy. The canto's last two stanzas suggest the ineradicable nature of Arthur's malady. Spenser writes that Arthur's

>... feeble vaines
> Him failed.... and served not his need,
> Through losse of bloud, which from his wounds did bleed,
> That he began to faint, and life decay....
>   (*FQ* 2.11.48)

In the canto's final stanza, Timias leads Arthur to convalescence in Alma's house.

Book 2's Canto 11, then, enforces the Pauline-Augustinian claim for the permanent fact of human vulnerability, a claim that the poet represses in Canto 12. We must not forget that Spenser decides to end Book 2 with the Bower rather than Maleger: he chooses, with Guyon, to deny the pathos of the Imaginary double (Verdant) instead of admitting it with Arthur (Maleger). But the striking difference between Arthur's conflict in Canto 11 and Guyon's in Canto 12 reminds us that there are (at least) two opposing and irreconcileable ways of stating the question of Christian virtue, the Pauline-Augustinian acknowledging of human weakness and the Stoic resistance to it.[55]

If Maleger's death drive, in its uncanny, vampirish vigor, presents passion as the hideous energy of mortality, Acrasia's Bower, by contrast, chooses the relaxing thrill of sensual delight as the affect that most deeply defines us. Acrasia's pleasures, just as much as Maleger's horror, remain antithetical to moral rule. The luxurious beauty of the Bower leaves a far more persistent impression than Guyon's and the Palmer's terse, moralizing critiques of it. The Bower thus signifies Spenser's failure to achieve his avowed aim of uniting the sensual and the moral (expressed in, for example, Book 3's address to Burlegh).

In the Garden of Adonis episode of Book 3, Spenser tries to overcome the Bower's drastic separation of poetry and morality. The Garden, like Milton's Eden, does reconcile desire and virtue: but a moral severity that argues against pleasure exerts itself elsewhere in Book 3. Spenser's portrait of Britomart in Book 3, as we shall see, displays a division between a character's poetic emotion and his or her moral goal similar to that in Book 2. Britomart continues the paradigm established in Books 1 and 2: the argument between Imaginary and Symbolic, subjective pathos and didactic order.

# 4
# *The Faerie Queene,* Book 3

In Book 3, Spenserian pathos appears as a sexuality no longer reducible to the malady that Acrasia represents, the weakening of moral being. Spenser accomplishes this transformation by switching the gender of his protagonist. Because Book 3 centers on a female character, sexual pathos becomes a force that defines, and even coincides with, the psyche. By contrast, in Books 1 and 2, which featured male heroes, sexuality threatened the protagonist with loss of self-definition. Because she is a woman, Britomart's love for Arthegall is not a sign of our common mortality, like Guyon's desire in Book 2. Instead, it provides the source of her heroic sense of a unique self.

The fact that in Book 3 sexual pathos no longer has to be translated into original sin as it was in Books 1 and 2 means that Spenser has acknowledged the gap, most visible in the Bower, between the sensual impact of his poetry and the moral meaning he claims for it. In Book 3, Spenser tries to heal this division: he abandons the forcibly imposed teaching of the Palmer, which tries to obstruct desire instead of educating it. Glauce, who sympathizes with Britomart's love-pangs, plays the ancillary role to Britomart in Book 3, replacing Guyon's Palmer.

Glauce champions Britomart's amorous quest as a combination of duty and eros, not a simple choice of eros over duty: Britomart's emotion embodies a moral aspect. The moral transfiguration of desire that constitutes chastity in Book 3 differs markedly from Guyon's temperance, his use of moral reason against desire. Britomart, in decisive contrast to Guyon, must admit love as the center of her heroic education. But Spenser, I will argue, finally finds himself unable to harmonize Britomart's pathos with didacticism. Despite Glauce's reassurances, Britomart's character depends on a sense of risk derived from her suspicion that her desire remains permanently at odds with her honor. Full didactic reassurance would require an impossible transcendence of pathos, a movement beyond the complex implication of the self in gender identification. For Britomart in Book 3, discovering gender means encountering a fiercely passionate sympathy with the other that threatens to dissolve, even as it impels, the self's autonomy. In Book 3's Paridell episode, Spenser, in the name of didacticism, makes an effort to rise above the idiosyncratic pathos that marks Britomart's sexuality, but this Symbolic resolve means denying the Imaginary inwardness that constitutes poetic character.

There is a dangerous aspect to the pathos of erotic love in Book 3. Spenser announces that he will show how love can aid honor, making it unnecessary to avoid Venus as Guyon did at the end of Book 2: "For love does always bring forth bounteous deeds, / And in each gentle hart desire of honour breeds" (3.1.49; and 3.5.1, again on love: "In braue sprite it kindles goodly fire, / That to all high desert and honour doth aspire"). This harmony of desire and honor looks toward a firm, edifying separation of love from illicit desire or lust (3.3.1); however, Britomart's good passion proves in many ways continuous with the bad passion for which she is supposed to serve as a contrast. Insofar as it requires the delineation of a corrected or innocent version of passion, Spenser can only complete the didactic project of Book 3 in paradisal set pieces removed from human action in the world: the Garden of Adonis and the Amoret-Scudamour union.

Idealizing a companionate marriage is one way of trying to integrate erotic pathos into moral life, and Spenser's goal in Book 3, one never achieved within the poem, in fact turns out to be the marriage of Britomart and Arthegall. The effort for a coherence of the sensual and the moral within marriage achieves a special importance in the Reformation: in an important study, James G. Turner has traced the Protestant valorization of married sexuality.[1] But Spenser's book of chastity distances itself from this religious polemic. The kind of sexuality at issue in *The Faerie Queene* occurs outside marriage, though it may glimpse married love as its telos. Through most of Book 3, Britomart is still very unsure of Arthegall's status as her future spouse, and this lack of certainty lends her erotic trauma its explosive force. The link we have seen earlier between didacticism and narrative closure appears again. Because Spenser's story remains incomplete, moralism can never firmly anchor itself in the poem. When a permanent union does actually occur, coupling begins to seem overly conclusive. In the original 1590 ending of Book 3, Amoret and Scudamour look a little too firmly anchored in their snugly adhesive, hermaphroditic embrace. The marriage of Marinell and Florimell decks amorous union in a public, ceremonial landscape, deflecting our attention from the couple themselves to the pageantry that surrounds them. Strangely, in Book 3 we see erotic desire mainly in the context of marriages narrowly missed (Amoret) or not-yet-achieved (Britomart). Spenser is not interested in approving eros in the typical Protestant manner, by providing a generalized, morally acceptable picture of wedded love, and thus evading the specific troubles and lures of sexuality. Instead, he focuses on a love founded on the absence of Arthegall and Britomart's doubts about his reality. Her desire nourishes itself by struggling with an ontological qualm: What if Arthegall should turn out to be a mere fantasy? Despite the fact that Britomart's love is sanctioned by the goal of marriage, it achieves its power because of the shadowy, ungraspable nature of this goal, which cannot be realized within Spenser's poem.

Turner writes that Milton, unlike other Protestant apologists for wedded love, celebrates married sexuality in powerfully erotic, almost libertine terms. According to Turner, this sensual drive explains why Milton must also turn fiercely against sexuality in his divorce tracts. "Compared to the normal exponents of Protestant marriage doctrine, with their praise of moderate 'due benevolence,' Milton seems both an unbridled amorist and an embittered ascetic."[2] We can glimpse in Spenser's Bower something of Milton's odd, intense combination of licentiously overripe desire and severe moral constraint. This volatile argument between desire and moral restriction provides one of the key aspects of the kinship with Spenser that Milton recognized in himself. In the Garden of Adonis episode of Book 3, Spenser, like Milton in *Paradise Lost*'s Eden, tries to overcome the argument between constraint and license by internalizing moral limitation, so that we may see a joyous self-discipline as the truth of desire, even as happily indistinguishable from its fulfillment.

The intimate relation between love and moral discipline within Britomart indicates her immaturity. In Book 2 Guyon labors under a fully formed superego. Not so Britomart, whose career narrates the initial development of the psyche, rather than its consolidation under the rule of the superego that occurs as a result of the Oedipal crisis. In other words, Britomart's character is shaped by pre-Oedipal events as Guyon's is not.

The naive, intuitive amorous subjectivity represented by the headstrong, yet scared Britomart, who is in some ways a more militant version of Chloe or Psyche, stands in contrast to the often paralyzing self-consciousness of the masculine speaker in the Petrarchan tradition. The fact that Spenser in Book 3 has chosen to represent a woman as the subject of desire, rather than as its distanced, attenuated, and reified object, according to the almost invariable practice in the Petrarchan mode, signals his wish to reach a more intimate, originary context for love than the rather studied or brittle self-evaluation of a Petrarchan protagonist can provide.[3]

Britomart's childhood encounter with Venus's looking glass provides the origin of her desire, and thus of her self. Any reading of Book 3 must come to terms with this origin. Accordingly, I intend my use of psychoanalytic interpretation in this chapter to respond to the still-unformed psyche Britomart discerns in the glass, and to the fact that she remains an immature or incomplete self. Unlike Milton's Eve in *Paradise Lost*, who, as Mary Nyquist writes, yields in Book 4's reflecting pool episode to "h[im] whose image she really is, as opposed to the specular image in which her desire originated,"[4] Britomart stays preoccupied with her love's illusory or insubstantial origins. For Britomart, a development into heroic maturity would mean renouncing her feminine nature as well as her frequently expressed masculine impulses to project a castration or lack onto the other (her furious battles with Marinell and Paridell, for example). Maturity, in other words, demands an adoption of the desexualized posture of mastery, with its hypothesis of a definitive, hierarchical separation between self and other.[5] (In Milton, as I will argue, such mastery will show itself as an effort to prove the self by eliminating the other, definitively stealing the blessing.)

Desexualized mastery, which offers its own risks, depends on the positioning of the female subject as observer rather than actor. Britomart in part achieves such an observational, neutral position in the House of Busirane, where she sees rather than suffers through love's tortures and sees them without consciously understanding—having repressed her understanding of—their erotic nature. Mature control, like the moralism it enables, requires the third rather than the first person. However, I will argue that Britomart in this scene, despite her efforts at the maturity that a third-person stance offers, also slips back into first-person Imaginary desire, as she remains implicated in the more basic positions of erotic fear and attraction that have been present since her first look into Venus's glass. The one point in Book 3 at which Britomart does attain a securely desexualized mastery is the Paridell episode, 3.9–10; this new security enables her to claim, for the first time, her dynastic or historical role. In this scene, uniquely in Book 3, Britomart exiles pathos to make way for didactic moralism.

In the Paridell episode, Britomart momentarily achieves maturity through desexualization by assuming a distance from desire, her own and others', that can refuse polarities like active/passive and masculine/feminine. Britomart thus becomes the representative of a political morality that transcends the gendered self. Through most of Book 3, she has been unable to envision this transcendence; instead, as a feminine subject of desire, she has been torn between masculine aggression and feminine suffering or "griefe." As David Lee Miller remarks in another context,[6] to be such a feminine subject "is to internalize a double identification, both that of masculine agency and that of feminine object: it is, in effect, to internalize rather than project the gap between subject and object." Guyon tried to become the *Faerie Queene*'s hero of desexualization through masculine projection, continually transferring his weakness onto others. For Britomart, as a feminine self, the agenda that maturity requires will not be nearly so clear. We might contrast her diffident perplexity at the very end of the 1590 *Faerie Queene*, when she "half envies" the reunion of Amoret and Scudamour, to Guyon's efficient repression of anxiety by means of brutally decisive action at the end of his book.

Despite the major difference in the roles played by gendered identity and sexuality in Books 2 and 3, there are significant similarities between the two books. Britomart's vulnerability, like Guyon's, manifests itself as an overly sympathetic or like-minded reaction to her "doubles." Her sympathy stems from an intuitive knowledge of the human nature she has in common with characters like Malecasta and Amoret. Spenser does show us a key difference, however, between Guyon's and Britomart's respective ways of distinguishing themselves from the weak natures to which they respond. Guyon delivers moral dicta that allow him to oppose his temperate self to Acrasia's victims. The idea that passion is external to the self-disciplined hero, that it properly represents the weakness of others rather than oneself, provides the enabling force for Guyon's Christian-Stoic rhetoric. Unlike Guyon, Britomart is unable to articulate a vision of her own nature that would transfer her vulnerability onto her counterparts. Even in 3.9, she does not pronounce judgment on Hellenore and Paridell as Guyon does on (for example) Mordant, Amavia, and Grylle (2.1.57, 2.12.87). Britomart's chastity, like that of her allegorical analogue, Belphoebe, expresses itself as stunning, mostly tacit poise, rather than Guyon's sententious self-promotion.

Britomart's poise is far from placid, however; it is often disrupted by angry emotion. At the moments when she is horrified by her sympathy for her doubles, her sharing of Malecasta's or Amoret's wounds, she displays a martial fury that reacts fiercely against these potential alter egos. Because of this sympathetic impulse, the distanced posture of mastery that Britomart assumes during her final trial, the ordeal in Busirane's house, remains shadowed by a passionate knowledge that would implicate her as actor and victim rather than mere observer. Britomart's rage against Busirane, then, represents an attempt to ward off her own prevailing sympathy—or, rather, empathy—for both Amoret and Scudamour. The close relation to the double indicates the inwardness of desire, which Britomart tries to refuse by reading it in outward, physical terms. In this respect, what frustrates Britomart is the inaccuracy of the analogy between seduction and mortal combat that her wounds figure. Fighting Busirane does not mean protecting herself against the external threat of physical attack, but, more important, resisting her secret susceptibility to him: what Spenser calls "self-feeling" in 3.1.54. Because of the inward character of Busirane's threat, Britomart remains within contrary gender identifications—she cannot move beyond gender into neutral, third-person mastery.

The continuing presence of gender identification—specifically, masculine identification—plays a crucial role in Britomart's preference for the pose of combat. Through her masculine disguise, Britomart realizes her repression of "self-feeling" love's weakening power by engaging in outwardly directed, physical aggression against a martial enemy. The heroic Britomart stands before Busirane's flames invoking the glory of her "noble chevisaunce," the rescue of Amoret.

In the Busirane episode, the "languishing" Scudamour, a noticeably feminized figure, plays the counterpart to Britomart and her masculine strength. Scudamour compares Amoret's captive and powerless state to his own: " 'Faire Amoret must dwell in wicked chaines, / And Scudamore here die with sorrowing'" (3.11.24). Similarly, Scudamour "grone[s] as if his hart were peeces made" (3.11.8), a reflection of the extraction and "transfix[ing]" of Amoret's heart in the pageant of Canto 12 (3.12.21).[7]

Britomart still retains a feminine aspect: she feels "empassiond sore" by Scudamour's distress. Spenser emphasizes the severity of her sympathetic response, as "both with great ruth and terror she was smit, / Fearing least from her cage the wearie soule would flit" (3.11.12). In stanza 11, she offers this commentary on Scudamour's sad case:[8]

>... Sir knight, your cause is nothing lesse,
>Then is your sorrow, certes if not more;
>For nothing so much pity doth implore,
>As gentle Ladies helpless misery.
>But yet, if please ye listen to my lore,
>I will with proofe of last extremity,
>Deliver her fro thence, or with her for you die.
>
>(*FQ* 3.11.18)

Britomart's speech hints that she identifies with both Scudamour and the victimized Amoret. In this fascinating passage, Britomart casts herself in the role of the active, heroic knight aiming to "deliver" the oppressed damsel, the role that the suffering Scudamour should, but finds himself unable to, fill. Surprisingly, though, she also implicitly considers playing Amoret's part. On the one hand, Britomart proposes to undertake her heroic mission "for," in place of, Scudamour, a meaning reinforced by her "empassioned" sympathy for him. On the other, "*With her* for you die" suggests that Britomart might join Amoret's passive, suffering position in the House, where Amoret nearly dies "for" Scudamour, because she loves him and refuses to love Busirane. These two contrasting readings of "for," both of them present in the text, together drive home Britomart's double, contradictory gender identity. Amoret's "helpless misery" reminds us of Britomart's own troubled love for Arthegall, despite the far from helpless posture of knightly aggression she has here adopted.

Britomart's conflicting gender identifications dramatize how such role playing threatens to collapse self and other through an exploration of intense pathos. In this respect, Britomart's words about dying with Amoret and for Scudamour allude to the ultimate danger that Busirane's House offers, a dissolution of the boundaries of identity. Confronting Busirane, Britomart risks a loss of the distinctions between aggression and passivity, lover and beloved, that *amor* demands if it is to be heroic or noble. The indistinction that looms before Britomart has rendered Amoret and Scudamour immobile and helpless Imaginary mirror images of each other.[9]

The situation of sympathetic paralysis, too intimate in its dangerous mutuality, that the House imposes on Amoret and Scudamour helps us to understand Cupid's self-wounding, the most deliciously chilling scene depicted on Busirane's tapestries: "Ne did he spare sometime to pricke himselfe, / That he might tast the sweet consuming woe, / Which he had wrought to many others moe" (3.11.45). Cupid preys on himself because his gravest symbolic meaning is his threat to fix the amorous ego in a simultaneous rage against and feeling for an other who cannot be properly distinguished from the self. Erotic rage derives from the fact that the Imaginary I perpetually deludes itself into the belief that the other in whom it is implicated actually stands outside it, though it knows, to its intense frustration, the intimate depth of this bond. Lacan, by tracing the aggressivity inherent in the mirror stage back to this primal empathic relation, provides a useful key to Britomart's situation in Book 3. Alluding to the Freud essay I mentioned earlier, "A Child Is Being Beaten," Lacan writes, "The child who strikes another says that he has been struck; the child who sees another fall, cries. Similarly, it is by means of an identification with the other that he sees the whole gamut of reactions of bearing and display, whose structural ambivalence is clearly revealed in his behavior, the slave being identified with the despot, the actor with the spectator, the seduced with the seducer."[10]

Britomart's career dramatizes the link between narcissistic identification and anger that Lacan describes. She tries to wound Malecasta to protect herself from the passive "griefe" that attended her first sight of Arthegall in the mirror—an image of her own desire. Ironically, however, Britomart's striking out at Malecasta shows her complicity with the feeling she is trying to banish. For Britomart, wounding Malecasta means wounding herself, because she, like Malecasta, is a lover of fantasies. Her own shadowy, image-begotten nature frustrates and limits her: she is defined by her love of what seems to be a mere "shade and semblaunce of a knight."

Malecasta represents a kind of seduction that works more insidiously than Busirane's precisely because it does not realize itself in terms of external aggression, which would make an external defense possible, but instead depends on Britomart's inward susceptibility to sympathetic fantasy. Sneaking next to the sleeping Britomart, Malecasta gingerly attempts to display her heartsick desire. Her tender and surreptitious assault stands in contrast to the brutal transgressions of Busirane. As the battle with Malecasta's knights ensues and Britomart is wounded by the hand and eye of Gardante, it becomes apparent that Malecasta's use of erotic imagination is a more subtle weapon than Busirane's violent compulsion. Britomart cannot defeat Malecasta and her knights as she will defeat Busirane; she can only flee.[11] When Britomart assumes that Malecasta is a man as she slips into bed with her, as when she brandishes her sword in Busirane's House, she tries to gain control by transforming an internal sexual double into an external, aggressive enemy. But Malecasta unmistakably incarnates the danger of feminine sympathy, not masculine power.[12] And in her fear and attraction, Britomart has been susceptible, because sympathetic, to Malecasta, before the latter's breathless, hesitant entry into her bed.

The image of Venus and Adonis on display in Malecasta's house further illustrates the inward vulnerability that the crossing of masculine and feminine implies. Here, the feminine force of eros threatens to overpower its male victim. This theme recalls the scene of Acrasia and Verdant in the Bower, which shows how anger or heroic courage can be transformed into a helpless, overly relaxed vulnerability when these stalwart knightly emotions mix with sensual desire. The *carpe diem* song that accompanies Acrasia's victmization of her young knight "Gather the Rose of love, whilest yet is time" (2.12.75)—enacts a parody of heroic action. Tellingly, Acrasia seduces by presenting herself as prey to masculine assault: "Her snowy brest was bare to readie spoyle / Of hungry eies" (2.12.78). Yet the impression that Acrasia here gives of herself as a passive love object ready to be seized is obviously duplicitous: Acrasia masters Verdant as the latter lies limply "dispose[d]" in his mistress's "lap" (2.12.76). If one reads the "of" in the lines just quoted, "bare to readie spoyle / Of hungry eies," as an objective rather than subjective genitive, then it is the hungry eyes of the male voyeur-lover that are ruined, "spoyle[d]," by the "snowie brest" of Acrasia. This confusion, in which the seemingly passive and exposed breast turns out to be the secret master, crosses the conventional roles of male and female, as Verdant's heroic energy ebbs into sensual decadence.

Entering the Castle Joyeous, Britomart and Red Crosse gaze in wonder at the myth that provides the model for Acrasia and Verdant: Malecasta's tapestry of Venus hanging over the wounded Adonis and "bath[ing]" his sleeping eyes with "ambrosiall kisses" (3.1.36). Adonis's posture here is not so obviously corrupt or ruined as Verdant's comatose luxury in the lap of the Bower's witch, but as a symbolic encapsulation of the Castle Joyeous's continuous dalliance, the tapestry clearly represents a warning sign aimed at Britomart. Britomart, however, unlike Guyon, must confront the meaning of eros for her self-definition, instead of veering away from the erotic toward the warlike. Book 3 openly acknowledges that erotic pathos remains more fundamental than the knightly aggression that tries to defend against it.

The central aspect of the Venus-Adonis story for Britomart is the contamination of gender roles it suggests with its image of a Venus who has become a Diana-like huntress. Adonis is the hunted, the feminine object of desire, Venus the masculine pursuer. Yet this gender confusion does not prove incapacitating in Book 3, as it did in Book 2's Acrasia-Verdant scene; Spenser actually glorifies the union of Venus and Adonis as the central source of life in the Garden of Adonis. Implicitly, Britomart's status as a *Venus armata* or Dianesque Venus, a woman whose desire incorporates a masculine aspect, shows the strength of her character—whereas yielding to feminine pathos would imperil Guyon's selfhood in Book 2.

Malecasta suspects Britomart's doubly gendered nature, and is drawn to both her masculine and her feminine sides. Although we are told that Britomart's "amiable grace," her feminine aspect, renders her attractive to others, while her "manly terrour" holds them back (3.1.46), it seems to be Britomart's presumed male identity that first captivates Malecasta (3.1.47: "For she her weened a fresh and lusty knight"). Yet Malecasta's other first impression of Britomart in stanza 47 is that she is "so faire a wight." The adjective "faire" suggests Britomart's feminine nature, as does the quality that Malecasta seeks from her a few stanzas later, "comfort" or sympathy: "At last she told her briefe, / That but if she did lend her short reliefe, / And do her comfort, she mote algates die" (3.1.53). Clearly, Malecasta sees Britomart as implicitly similar to herself—one looks for comfort from like-minded (and, often, like-gendered) personalities—just as Britomart sees her double, the image of her own amorous "wound," in Malecasta's distress. This feminine dialogue is abruptly severed in the scene I have already mentioned: later that night, Malecasta climbs into bed with the sleeping Britomart and the latter, thinking Malecasta an anonymous male "loathed leachour" (3.1.62), leaps out, waving her sword.[13] Significantly, mirror images guide Britomart, suggesting her entrapment in Imaginary doubling. (Presumed) male attackers bring out her masculine prowess at combat, whereas female seducers elicit her affectionate pity.

On the one hand, Canto 1 warns Britomart not to indulge the feminine side of her personality represented by Malecasta but instead to keep her sword potentially erect at all times. On the other hand, the poet shows that such a choice is not possible for her. Britomart cannot avoid her feminine aspect, which figures her erotic susceptibility and therefore her essential self. Britomart's truest glory in combat, in the battle with Arthegall during which she rivals his masculine force, coincides with her vulnerability to love.

If Britomart, seemingly trapped between gendered positions, shifts from feminine to masculine identification during the Malecasta episode, for Red Crosse Malecasta serves the quite different function of warning against desire as such. This is another way of saying that Red Crosse's warning in the Malecasta episode is not internal, as Britomart's is. Malecasta has no relevance to Red Crosse's personality, neither when he defends her and allows her to disarm him [3.1.64], nor when he aids Britomart against her at the end of Canto 1 [st. 66]. Nohrnberg aptly compares Britomart's troubled sleep in Malecasta's house (2.1) to Red Crosse's nightmares under the spell of Archimago in 1.1.46–49: both characters start up in murderous "fierce despight" (1.1.50) at an attempted seduction that occurs while they are asleep. Yet the mental puppet show sent to Red Crosse, unlike Britomart's distress, requires Archimago's manipulation of him. The fact that Archimago directs the scene shows that Red Crosse's desire can be freely exploited, and even produced, by a higher power—an impression foreign to the case of Britomart, who produces her own feeling for Malecasta. The fact that, throughout her story, Britomart tempts herself, whether with love for Arthegall or sympathy for Malecasta or Scudamour, indicates the fundamental difference in narrative mode between Books 3 and 1. Red Crosse does not really belong in Book 3 because he does not tempt himself: the self-wounding Cupid of the Maske has meaning for Britomart as it does not for Red Crosse.

After her battle in the castle, Britomart continues to pretend to manliness with Red Crosse in Canto 2: she prefers to face "point of foemans speare" rather than "To finger the fine needle and nyce thread" (3.2.6)—a rejection of Malecasta's hypersensitive, and hyperfeminine, delicacy (Malecasta is, in a delicious phrase, "of every finest finger's touch affrayd," 3.1.61[14]). But at the same moment, Britomart, whose feminine identity has now been revealed to all, exhibits a powerless vulnerability that renders her similar to the emotionally "daintie" Malecasta. At the end of Canto 1 Malecasta moved her "fearfull feete" toward Britomart's bed while "panting soft, and trembling everie joynt" (3.1.60), and dissolved into helpless shrieks. Here is Britomart's Malecasta-like reaction to Red Crosse's report of Arthegall in the next canto:

> Theareat she sighing softly, had no powre
> To speake a while, ne ready answere make,
> But with hart-thrilling throbs and bitter stowre,
> As if she had a fever fit, did quake,
> And every daintie limb with horrour shake;
> And ever and anone the rosy red,
> Flasht through her face, as it had been a flake
> Of lightning, through bright heaven fulmined;
> At last the passion past she thus him answered.
> (*FQ* 3.2.5)

Britomart's "passion" (l.8) returns us to the Greek word *paskhein*, to experience, endure, or suffer. The etymology of passion connects it with passivity: emotion means being moved. In this scene, the sign of Britomart's love is her lack of "powre" (l.1), the abject victimization by her desire that marks her, like Malecasta, as a feminine subject.

To explain the significance of pathos in the Malecasta and Busirane episodes, I draw once again on Kenneth Burke's reading of tragic catharsis. According to Burke, the pity and fear that Aristotle defines as proper to tragedy are reassuring and compensatory, warding off the implicit dangers of a precathartic, sympathetic pathos that would implicate the spectator in what he or she sees. To exorcize the possibility of such intimate involvement with the spectacle, Aristotle construes pity, in particular, as the spectator's distanced, condescending judgment that the character on stage does not deserve his or her suffering.[15]

Burke's critique of the distance from tragic immediacy that Aristotelian pity strives for is akin to Pietro Pucci's, which I mentioned in my analysis of Renaissance criticism, though Pucci focuses on the distance ensured by cathartic fear rather than pity. Pucci celebrates the spectator's precathartic or pre-Aristotelian terror for the tragic protagonist, which is simultaneously the spectator's terror for himself or herself, as the essence of tragedy. Burke, similarly, treats precathartic sympathy with the characters onstage as the core of tragic experience that Aristotle's championing of pity tries to evade.

We can use Burke and Pucci to provide a scheme for the way passionate responses, with Britomart as with Guyon, first expose the common emotional basis of human life and then, by reacting against such exposure through Aristotelian catharsis, secure the hero's socialized individuality. Passion remains prior to didactic demand. To draw on Nietzsche's terms, a Dionysian pathos in which self and other, actor and audience, interpenetrate precedes the securing of self through the Apollonian distance and objective mastery that the audience's moral judgment makes possible. Or, as Lacan puts it, the Imaginary not only prepares the way for, but persists alongside, the Symbolic.

The predidactic nature of Britomart's responses is evident in the fact that she cannot articulate her claim to heroic superiority as Guyon did. Even more than Guyon, she remains subject to her own weakness. Like Belphoebe, Britomart in Busirane's house at times seems to transcend human vulnerability through the boldness of her innocence; until Amoret herself is unveiled, Britomart stalks Busirane with graceful impunity. But the combination of her wondering naïveté, reminiscent of Apuleius's Psyche, with her periodic bursts of rage, shows that her aloofness is really unlike Belphoebe's godlike poise; instead, it masks a still unformed, tentative personality. Britomart's chastity is tender and frightened rather than haughty: she participates in innocence as a way of resisting her own frustrated suspicion of her sexual sensitivity.[16]

Britomart's wrathful side also betrays her awkward immaturity, which remains more self-defensive than didactically attuned. In view of the intimate, involuted relation of Britomart's "exceeding wroth" anger, "horror" and amorous suffering in Busirane's House (3.12.33, 36), the House's seemingly temperate inscriptions advising her to "Be bold," and yet "Be not too bold," add up to a cruelly tantalizing parody of moralism. This bifurcated advice proves inadequate to Britomart's dilemma, the conflict within her of masculine and feminine, boldness and suffering—aspects of her personality that cannot be balanced. She cannot reduce the conflict to a harmonious mixture, as a morality of temperance requires. Instead, the mix remains volatile. Britomart's chastity is an extreme, angry reaction against her own desire.

This stanza, from Malecasta's house, gives a telling commentary on the way Britomart's split character, at once fierce and vulnerable, precedes any didactic lesson. Britomart's complex personality here shows itself to the reader's confused double-take:

> For she was full of amiable grace,
>   And manly terrour mixed therewithall,
>   That as the one stird vp affections bace,
>   So th'other did mens rash desires apall,

> And hold them backe, that would in errour fall;
> As he, that hath espide a vermeill Rose,
> To which sharpe thornes and breres the way forstall,
> Dare not for dread his hardy hand expose,
> But wishing it far off, his idle wish doth lose.
> (*FQ* 3.1.46)

Seemingly pleasant or "idle" amorous conventions strike a hidden, painfully receptive nerve in Britomart, who rages against them.[17] Britomart's character is a compound of masculine and feminine, aggression and amorous sensitivity, like the thorn and the rose pictured here. She "stir[s] up" a deep, unconscious terror in others because she is herself terrified and compelled by her affections. Britomart's aggression really has more to do with her own troubled project of self-discipline than with any external danger. The sanguine, impersonal precept "And hold them backe, that would in errour fall" implies that the drama of Britomart's actions translates easily into a moral meaning directed at her audience; however, despite the implication, that drama remains intrapsychic and its relation to didactic goals is still unclear. In 3.1 Britomart's anger does not provide a way for her to master her pitying affection. Instead, it presents a vulnerable rather than a masterful defense, an expression of affection in the form of a fiercely affective denial. A more wistful or bemused version of the same emotional confusion prevails in Britomart as she looks on at Amoret and Scudamour at the end of 1590's Book 3.

Britomart's "manly terrour," then, is no merely utilitarian disguise, but a psychic defense astonishing in the tenacity of its emotional grip, as we see from the uncontrolled, "enraged" ferocity of her attack on the knights at the end of Canto 1 ("she fiercely at them flew, / And with her flaming sword about her layd" [3.1.66]), which is followed by the "fever fit" already discussed (3.2.5). Britomart's involvement in her original trauma, her passion for Arthegall, prevents her from consciously formulating the principles of her own discipline and thus becoming an example for an audience. Her anger acts out something dynamic and inchoate, which cannot be reduced to the condescension toward others required in a moral lesson: "Huge sea of sorrow, and tempestuous griefe" (3.4.8).

Before showing how Canto 9 departs from the usual image of Britomart, I will briefly review her career. Britomart's emotional experience stems from the fact that, despite her posture as a self-contained Diana or Minerva, she has always been vulnerable to an(other's) image and look—first her own image, which she glimpses in Merlin's glass, and then the shadowy form of Arthegall. Significantly, Britomart compares herself to Narcissus when she explains her grief to Glauce (3.2.44). Britomart, like Narcissus, has experienced the mirror stage, in which the self is constituted as an other. In Venus looking glass she sees first her self, then the beloved, still nameless Arthegall, who exists as a perplexing confirmation of this self's essential incompletion. Britomart's sexual identity is founded in a moment that makes her passive in relation to the fantasy that inhabits her. The cinematic dissolve from Britomart's vision of her own body in the glass to the picture of the strange knight marks the engendering of this fantasy image in her: "When she had espyde that mirrhour fayre, / Her selfe a while therein she vewd in vaine / . . . Eftsoones there was presented to her eye / A comely knight, all arm'd in complet wize . . ." (3.2.22–24). The dissolve suggests that Britomart's self-reflexive consciousness, her picture of herself, depends on her sight of, and subjection to, the picture of Arthegall. Her sense of herself as subject provides the object of her desire; in turn, her subjectivity bases itself on her fantasy of Arthegall.

Malecasta's self-indulgent desire, which depends on her vision of Britomart, echoes Britomart's own dependence on the sight of the other. Malecasta's tender nature finally prompts Britomart's anger because Britomart senses that it figures her own tenderness as well—and because it suggests the possibility that Britomart's desire, like Malecasta's, may really be an indulgence of weak incompletion, rather than a striving for the solid strength of the completed quest. The frustration or lack suggested by the looking-glass scene and the Malecasta episode returns in the Amoret-Scudamour union of the 1590 ending. Britomart must shy away from this kind of closure, because its seeming wholeness is really based, like Malecasta's fantasies, on fragmented dependency.

Britomart's self-assertion in the opening cantos of Book 3 comes when she desperately, passionately appropriates otherness. Most memorable, perhaps, is her soliloquy when, after rushing furiously at Marinell, she addresses the ocean itself as her own "huge sea of sorrow."[18] This scene bears witness to Britomart's attempt to compensate for her weakness through an impulsive Imaginary seizing of the world. She also tries for mastery in a different way, however: seeing herself as an other in the Symbolic, rather than the Imaginary, sense.[19] While riding with Red Crosse, she depicts herself as "a simple mayd" (3.2.12) who has been done "foule dishonour" (3.2.8) by Arthegall. In this fantasy of a fully developed social relation between herself and Arthegall, Britomart, in order to master her secret wound, diagnoses it as the result of the customary aggressions present in the Symbolic order of knighthood. Constructing a fictional image of herself as a stereotypical injured damsel, Britomart creates a character definitively separated from herself as real characters like Malecasta, Marinell, Amoret, and Scudamour are not—but as Paridell will be. She aims at mastery through the distance between the complicated self that observes and the hapless cliché she portrays, the "simple mayd." Such self-alienation, which, to achieve a definitive identity, separates the I and the alien image that have been so confused, was an impossibility in Britomart's original looking-glass episode and in Malecasta's House. In those scenes, the gaze was Britomart's master; now, she rules the conversation as she sees fit.

The Symbolic mode that Britomart indulges in with Red Crosse, though it offers possibilities for mastery through a third-person distancing of the self's travails—the simple maid is adroitly but superficially disguised as a first person—cannot, because of this very distance, embody her desire as the true first person of the Imaginary can. The relation of loving antagonism between herself and Arthegall that Britomart will enact in Books 4 and 5 provides a return to her earlier self-absorbed passion, an emotion that far exceeds the reach of a typical figure in the chivalric game like the distressed, ladylike waif she plays with Red Crosse.

Even in the scene with Red Crosse, Britomart is no mere player. Pricked by a trace of her original passion for Arthegall, she softens, despite her Symbolic armor. Her "inly" pleasure at hearing the praise of Arthegall from Red Crosse's "curteous tongue" (3.2.11–12) is reminiscent of the poisonous, alluring effect of courtly dissimulation and second-guessing recently dramatized in Malecasta's house. Here is Spenser's description of Red Crosse's courteous praise of Arthegall, along with Britomart's response:

> His feeling words her feeble sence much pleased,
>   And softly sunck into her molten hart,
>   Hart that is inly hurt, is greatly eased
> With hope of thing, that may allegge his smart;
> For pleasing words are like to Magick art,
> That doth the charmed snake in slomber lay:
> Such secret ease felt gentle Britomart,
>   Yet list the same efforce with faind gainesay;
> So dischord oft in Musick makes the sweeter lay.
>         (*FQ* 3.2.15) [20]

Britomart's amorous injury responds more to the courtly compliments that Red Crosse applies to Arthegall than to the edifying plan, the knowledge Merlin has given her of the historical role her marriage will play. The pun on fain/feign in line 8 of stanza 15, Britomart's "faind gainesay," suggests the connection between love and her courtly flirtation with fakery.[21]

Britomart's feigning with Red Crosse in 3.2 does not heal, but rather exacerbates her loving distress over the potentially absent or fantastic status of Arthegall. Courtesy here becomes a vehicle for Britomart's complicity in her own amorous torment. The devious way she elicits Red Crosse's praise of Arthegall, like the curiously raised eyebrow she offers the wincing Malecasta in the preceding canto (3.1.54–55), suggests Britomart's awareness of dissimulation's pleasures—even her amenability to the self-indulgence feigning can provide. The suspicious terms Spenser uses in his description of Britomart's conversation with Red Crosse—specifically, the passage's invocation of "Magick art," an art so dangerous throughout *The Faerie Queene*—indicates that Britomart is drifting, here, toward a confusion of virtue and vice that would make their exemplary contrast impossible.

In Canto 2's feigning with Red Crosse, courtly rhetoric's blurring of ethical definitions in the service of a sensibility receptive to paradox abets Britomart's careful indulgence in pathos. She is not overwhelmed by feeling; instead, she stays master of it. But this mastery will not last. She soon yields, again, to a passionate uncontrol during her ensuing scene with Marinell (3.4.12). Her delight in the disharmony brought on by Red Crosse's accusation against her future lover, the "dischord" that "makes the sweeter lay," foreshadows the fiercer "love and despight attonce" that provides the motive for her attack on the unfortunate Marinell. Britomart's fight with Marinell, a hapless mama's boy, is a blind attempt to find a release for her passion. As she confronts Marinell, she converts "sorrow into suddein wrath" (3.4.12), but without knowing the import of either emotion.

Here Spenser takes a definitive, if brief, turn toward a moralized destiny. Britomart finally steels herself against her indulgence in courtly pathos only by transfiguring her emotion into something higher: the vision of epic-historical duty. In Canto 9, posed against Paridell, Britomart becomes an example for readers. She makes pathos didactic by transforming it in the way suggested by Burke's scheme, turning it from a personal "grief" into a public duty: pity for the fallen Troy that gave birth to the England that will flower under Elizabeth.[22] This metamorphosis from private to public passion argues against the symbiosis of love and honor that Book 3 so frequently claims for itself.[23]

Though Britomart's destiny has appeared earlier in the book, it has not yet taken effect in her; therefore, 3.9 is necessary. Merlin's speech in Canto 3, which ends with a shining view of the "royall virgin" Elizabeth (3.3.49), should have dispelled her worries about Arthegall's insubstantiality, her suspicion that he might be the mere "shade and semblant of a knight" (3.2.38)—but it did not. Merlin's briefing of Britomart for her historical mission failed to make her pangs of desire yield to the solid reality of an ideological obligation more important than amorous doubt. During most of Book 3, Merlin's prophecy seems less present to Britomart than her desire for Arthegall.

In Canto 9, Britomart lets history direct her; as a result she assumes, at least for the moment, a didactic voice. Spenser here significantly invokes the admonishing sight of Minerva and her "*Gorgonian* shield" (3.9.22). Like the formidable Britomart, Minerva/Athena with her Medusa emblem is able to impose a dreadful, immobilizing wound on men. Minerva might be considered a civilized or sublated version of the Medusa whose image she bears; she, therefore, provides an appropriate symbol of Britomart's morally persuasive aura in this scene. Medusa's terror, like Britomart's felling of Marinell, hits too close to home to convey a didactic lesson we could handle. But Minerva offers a desexualized mastery, and therefore a moralizing power, in place of the monster's blunt horror.[24] The substitution of Minerva for Medusa explains why, in 3.9, the knights around Malbecco's table can be taken with "delight," rather than fear, as they are (figuratively, not literally) "smitten . . . / With great amazement of so wondrous sight" (3.9.23): the unveiled Britomart-as-Minerva.[25] Interestingly, in 4.6 Scudamour looks on "sore terrified" at Britomart's brilliant countenance but then rapidly "turn[s] his feare to faire deuotion" (4.6.24). "Though terror be in love and beauty," as Satan observes in *Paradise Lost*, Britomart's grace mellows her beauty's chilling sublimity.

Canto 9 announces an escape, in the service of didacticism, from the courtly emotional ambiguity that defines Britomart's personality in the scenes with Red Crosse and Marinell.[26] Here, a simplified exemplary mode stands as a corrective to the cruel paradoxes of courtly love that Malecasta and Busirane also represent: "Good by paragone / Of euill, may more notably be rad," writes Spenser, "As white seems fairer, matcht with blacke attone" (3.9.2).[27] The black-and-white contrast of Britomart to both Paridell and Hellenore allows her to rise above her Amoret-like vulnerability. By refusing, in Canto 9, the kind of courteous dissembling she indulged in earlier with Red Crosse, she finally claims the precedence of her weighty historical role over the amorous doubts that seek relief in courtly flirtation.

To explain this movement away from private pathos and toward history in more detail, I now turn to the specifics of the Paridell episode's plot. As Canto 9 begins, Satyrane and the faerie knight Paridell seek lodging at the home of a miserly old man, Malbecco. Because Malbecco denies them his hospitality, Paridell and Satyrane are forced to sleep in a sty. There they are joined by Britomart, who, still disguised as a man, again flexes her knightly muscle, clobbering the awakened and furious Paridell.[28] Finally, all three knights force their way into Malbecco's castle by threatening to set fire to it.[29]

Malbecco is married to a beautiful young woman, Hellenore, whom he keeps hidden in "close bowre . . . from all mens sight" (3.9.5). Spenser's description of Hellenore, who "does ioy to play emongst her peares" (3.9.4), but is instead closeted away by Malbecco, is reminiscent of Canto 2's statement that Britomart's love for Arthegall makes her "inclose" herself "in dull corners" instead of playing with her "equall peares" (3.2.31). The verbal echo suggests that Hellenore, like Malecasta, represents a potential alter ego that Britomart must reject. The fact that Hellenore is so much more distinct from Britomart than Malecasta was—so much less emotionally and psychologically complex, and therefore so much easier for Britomart to spurn—shows the distance between the clear exemplary contrasts of Canto 9 and the amorous confusion that has already preoccupied Britomart during her encounters with Malecasta and Red Crosse. Britomart finds it easier to distinguish herself from Hellenore, and Paridell, than from Malecasta because the stakes are now social and political rather than personal. Britomart is divided from Hellenore and Paridell not by a private sensibility but its public consequences, not by feelings but manners. In her conversation with Paridell, Britomart will bluntly assert a didactic point by announcing her clear difference from a historically corrupt character. This confrontation proves exemplary because it occurs in the Symbolic realm: it concerns competing social identities rather than, as with Malecasta, the fierce resistance to and inclination toward the Imaginary other. Chastity has become a public issue, to be acted out in a vigorous debate over courtly morality.

Strangely, Canto 9 begins with an apparent similarity between the methods of virtue and those of vice—a similarity that the poet will refuse later in the episode so that he may produce a sharp exemplary contrast. Making their entry into Malbecco's "comely bowre" (3.9.19), the knights provide their own "curtesy," "welcom[ing] themselves" (3.9.25, 19). Spenser here prefigures the corrupt and intrusive courtliness that Paridell, in his pushy, overblown egotism, will embody. The poet begins, then, by making the issue hard, before going on to celebrate the ease of telling a virtuous from a degenerate knight. Satyrane's criticism of Malbecco inadvertently foreshadows the triumph of Paridell's method of male domination over Malbecco's: Satyrane says that only "gentle curtesyes," not physical "restraint" like Malbecco's, can "perhaps containe" a woman (3.9.6); however, ironically, the knights' own entry into the castle is backed by a crude rather than noble or "gentle" use of physical force. Such force provides the necessary support for chivalric persuasion at the outset of Canto 9. In the manner of Book 6, Spenser here blurs the distinction between courtesy and discourtesy that the rest of the canto will uphold in the strongest terms.

Britomart's and Satyrane's rather mundane and discourteous use of macho force against Paridell for the comically practical purpose of securing a place to sleep yields to high seriousness during the knights' dinner with Malbecco and Hellenore. After Britomart has removed her helmet and revealed her feminine identity, she seems the perfect agent of concord, a *Venus armata* harmoniously blending honor with charitable grace:

> And *Paridell* though partly discontent
>   With his late fall, and fowle indignity,
> Yet was soone wonne his malice to relent,
>   Through gracious regard of her faire eye,
>   And knightly worth, which he too late did try,
> Yet tried did adore. . . .
> 
> (*FQ* 3.9.25)

Spenser poses the chaste "love" that the unveiled Britomart inspires in Paridell and the others against the lust incited by Hellenore (st. 24). Britomart reveals herself here with staid self-possession:

> Tho whenas vailed was her lofty crest,
>   Her golden locks, that were in tramels gay
>   Vpbounden, did them selues adowne display,
> And raught unto her heeles; like sunny beames,
> That in a cloud their light did long time stay,
> Their vapour vaded, shew their golden gleames,
> And through the persant aire shoote forth
>                          their azure streames.
> 
> (*FQ* 3.9.20)

The passage harks back to a earlier unveiling, when Britomart refuses to disarm in Malecasta's house but "vent[s] up her vmbriere" instead (3.1.42):

> As when faire *Cynthia*, in darkesome night,
>   Is in a noyous cloud enueloped,
>   Where she may find the substaunce thin and light,
> Breakes forth her siluer beames, and her bright hed
> Discouers to the world discomfited;
> Of the poore traueller, that went astray,
> With thousand blessings she is heried;
> Such was the beautie and the shining ray,
> With which faire *Britomart* gaue light unto the day.
> 
> (*FQ* 3.1.43)

The appearance of brilliant self-definition Britomart gives in the first canto of Book 3 turns out to be a deceptive one: her emotions actually obscure her, in contrast to the straightforward clarity of her uncovering in Malbecco's house. With Malecasta she is unable even to guide herself accurately, much less the "poore traueller," the reader for whose sake she ostensibly provides a didactic example. Cynthia's brightness seems awkwardly out of place without its nebulous shield; her discovery discomfits more than it reassures. Britomart's tormented, cloudy self-consciousness becomes even more fuzzily evident a few cantos later, as Spenser exploits another meteorological image. During her fight with Marinell, Spenser does not depict Britomart as he did in Canto 1, as a resplendent Cynthia illuminating her surroundings. Instead, she becomes a stormy sky. Obscured by passionate confusion, she vents impulses she cannot understand:[30]

>As when a foggy mist hath ouercast
>   The face of heauen, and the cleare aire engrost,
>   The world in darkenesse dwels, till that at last
>   The watry Southwinde from the seabord cost
>   Vpblowing, doth disperse the vapour lo'st,
>   And poures it selfe forth in a stormy showre;
>   So the faire *Britomart* hauing disclo'st
>   Her clowdy care into a wrathfull stowre,
> The mist of griefe dissolu'd, did into vengeance powre.
>                    (*FQ* 3.4.13)[31]

Britomart's wrath expresses the turbulence of her desire, instead of the dignified devotion to honor that Spenser claims for her in his programmatic statements of didactic purpose. What catapults her into the fight with Marinell is an emotional outpouring, for the moment angry rather than amorous, but still fervent and confused. But 3.9 will define Britomart clearly and, by doing so, transform her from a figure of emotional perplexity into one of calm strength. Paridell makes this transformation possible by dramatizing the difference between his perverted courtesy and Britomart's grace. In Canto 9, Paridell seduces Hellenore, whom the *senex amans* has reluctantly unveiled, with "that art he learned had of yore," the "lewd lore" of flirtation (3.9.28). The details of the flirtatious game that Paridell plays with Hellenore (their deliberate spilling of the wine, for example) are drawn from Ovid's *mores* and, more important in this context, from the letters of Paris and Helen in Ovid's *Heroides*.[32] Hellenore "re[a]d[s]" Paridell's "meaning" and "answer[s]" with "the like":

> She sent at him one firie dart, whose hed
> Empoisned was with privy lust, and gealous dred.
>
> (*FQ* 3.9.28)

And Paridell "open[s]" his "weake hart" to the "wound['s]" "false influence" (3.9.29). At first glance, Paridell seems to suffer from a wound like Britomart's, Amoret's, or Malecasta's. The scene clearly echoes Malecasta's "guilfull mesage" to Britomart at Castle Joyeous's supper table: "And aye betweene the cups, she did prepare / Way to her love, and secret darts did throw" (3.1.51). But Spenser, by depicting the love of Paridell and Hellenore as a vain travesty, clarifies its essential difference from the passionate emotions of a character like Malecasta. Despite the addictive, habitual nature of Malecasta's desire, it is authentic as Paridell's is not. Paridell's feigning turns the amorous trial that is achingly authentic, and alluring, earlier and later in Book 3 into an easily resisted sham. Both Paridell and Hellenore, in singles-bar fashion, know the "learned line" (3.9.30) too well to generate any real passion from it. The learning behind this love is empty; it is a "lewd," or ignorant, as well as lascivious, "lore" (3.9.28). Mihoko Suzuki notes Castiglione's suggestion that courting techniques like writing one's love in spilled wine have, by the sixteenth century, become obsolete—and therefore ridiculous, adds John Harington in the preface to his Ariosto (1591).[33] Paridell's seductive *modus operandi* is both archaic and clichéd.

Instead of resembling Britomart's "inly" pangs of desire, Paridell's superficial, phony pain merely complements Malbecco's miserly lust:

> But nothing new to him was that same paine,
> Ne paine at all; for he so oft had tryde
> The powre thereof, and lou'd so oft in vaine,
> That thing of course he counted, loue to entertaine.
>
> (*FQ* 3.9.29)

The "inward griefe" (3.9.30) that Paridell feels in his as-yet-unconsummated desire is patently false, an outward show or "entertain[ment]" based on merely rhetorical "intimat[ion]" (3.9.30), not the truly intimate. Paridell's "gracious speech" and dissembler's "skill" (3.9.32) inhabits a different world from that of the revealed Britomart's "gracious regard." She has really been hurt by love, whereas he only feigns such a hurt. The clear-cut nature of this distinction between true and false desire, so different from the state of affairs in Malecasta's house, enables Britomart to rise above her previous amorous trials as she finally claims the connection to historical providence that Merlin has offered her.

When Britomart counters Paridell's flirtatious feigning, as she is about to do, by engaging a higher level of the poem—epic history—she demonstrates that Spenser has established her in her role of national heroine by freeing her from the courtly amours that have so intimately absorbed her. The historical claim allows her to assume a manner whose assurance and confidence contrast sharply with her earlier love-stricken one. Most readers, however, themselves rapt in the precious and intoxicating world of Spenserian eros, wisely prefer the private to the public Britomart. Britomart's rich, puzzling amours in the early cantos of Book 3 will not yield their appeal to a rather prosaic politics. But Spenser, the rather calculating national poet, the author who will be prodded by Burleigh's angry brow, wants to cash out pathos for moralizing, and political, ends. Evidently, Spenser felt a rebuke in the mere fifty pounds—no small change by courtly standards—he received for the 1590 *Faerie Queene*.[34]

Yet Spenser is no mere opportunist, however politically canny and cautious he steps. Morality also serves the perfection of the self, as Britomart's newly integral, confident persona, charged with a dynastic destiny, shines far beyond the stunted, trivial perversions of her companions. Paridell, Malbecco, and Hellenore together stand for the conspiracy of parody and vain desire that we also see in False Florimell's hackneyed Petrarchan cosmetics (3.8.6–7). By drawing a contrast between these characters, on the one hand, and Britomart, on the other, Spenser, as Nohrnberg writes, distinguishes between two forms of *imitatio*: a chaste self-modeling directed inward, represented by Britomart, and a delusive, scattered fantasy life that finds its object in False Florimell.[35] Championing Britomart, Spenser asserts the need for a heroic self that can suppress the pathos that will otherwise, powered by reckless eros, drive the self to fragmented distraction. The discipline that allows Britomart access to historical providence proves the danger of the elusive, addictive desire embodied in False Florimell—the impulsiveness that makes Paridell a slave to the transitory.

Paridell's habitual shallowness is obvious first of all in the stale, clichéd character of his amorous game, but his place in dynastic history is equally vacuous. Spenser here invokes the theme of the repetitive, historically vapid "secondhand romance" described by Nohrnberg, Angus Fletcher, and Berger.[36] As Berger has noted, the archaized Hellenore can mean "Helen-o'er," a parodic repetition of the original Helen.[37] Hellenore is abducted (but then, unlike Helen, rapidly abandoned), by Paris's descendant Paridell in Canto 10. Malbecco conveys an analogous hint of repetitive simulation: his transformation into the one-dimensional personification Gealousy, a character locked within the stasis of a fixed place, suggests the single-track, vain "echo" hidden in his name. While Paridell embodies a cartoonlike compulsion, obsession rules Malbecco. Spenser finally metamorphoses Malbecco into a physical rather than a mental tendency to dwell on the same subject, a sterile mimicry of Adonis's undying fertility: "Yet can he never dye, but dying lives" (3.10.60). Paridell's future is similarly static, a hackneyed, second-hand version of his ancestral past—and of the poem's previous quests. When first introduced, Paridell is "pricking on the plaine" in flatly literal simulation of Red Crosse's first appearance (3.8.44, 1.1.1).[38]

Paridell tells Britomart that

> From him [i.e., Paris] my linage I derive aright,
>   Who long before the ten yeares siege of *Troy*,
>   Whiles yet on *Ida* he a shepheard hight,
> On faire *Oenone* got a louely boy,
>   Whom for remembraunce of her passed ioy,
>   She of his Father *Parius* did name;
>   Who, after *Greekes* did *Priams* realme destroy,
>   Gathred the *Troian* reliques sau'd from flame,
> And with them sayling thence, to th'isle of *Paros* came.
>
> That was by him called *Paros*, which before
>   Hight *Nausa*, there he many yeares did raine,
>   And built *Nausicle* by the *Pontick* shore
>   The which he dying left next in remaine
>   To *Paridas* his sonne.
>   From whom I *Paridell* by kin descend;
>   But for faire Ladies loue, and glories gaine,
>   My natiue soile haue left, my dayes to spend
> In sewing deeds of armes, my liues and labours end.
>                                     (*FQ* 3.9.36–37)

Paridell's magnification of Helen's abductor into "Most famous Worthy of the world" (3.9.34) implies an inflated pride in his ancestry: most Renaissance treatments of Paris condemn his choice of Venus as a capitulation to pleasure.[39] Via a Latinate pun, Parius might suggest "more than" Paris, but the succession Paridell describes offers only more (or, more accurately, less) of the same. (*Pares* and *parvus*, along with *pario*, are other puns that come to mind.[40]) The Homeric and tragic word *paros* means "before," suggesting the repetitive, past-centered character of Paridell's ancestry: "That was by him called *Paros*, which before...."

The faerie Paridell's boastfulness looks especially misplaced when one considers his status as a permanently reduced version of Paris, stuck outside the central tradition represented by Britomart's future marriage to Arthegall: Troy-Rome-Troynovant. Vaunting his own directness, Paridell claims an ancestry "derive[d] aright," but his line has diverged from the mainstream of Virgilian history. As Lawrence Manley notes, the isle of Paros, with its "Troian reliques" (3.9.36), echoes the miniature Troy in Book 3 of the *Aeneid*: Buthrotum, whose carefully arranged picture of the past will have no part in the future founding of Rome.[41]

Spenser may also be punning, here, on the Greek prefix *para-*, which can denote a turning aside or deviation, a perverse twist. Paridell presents a classic, and colloquial, example of vice, as a paroemia (*para* + *oimos*, "way" or "road") is literally a by-the-way expression. Paridell becomes a bad example or byword when he strays from the steady course of Roman, and therefore British, history, tracing his "linage" from Paris rather than Aeneas.[42] His wandering marks his vision of human experience as transient and expendable. Paridell cites Oenone's naming of Paris's son, his grandfather, Parius, not as a properly Virgilian instance of cultural duty devolving from father to son but as a mere "remembraunce of . . . passed ioy," a lasting emblem for the most disposable kind of sexuality. The momentary nature of the familial relationships here is conveyed by the artificiality of the names repeatedly and monotonously derived from Paris's: as if repetition were continuity.

Paridell's speech contains an important suggestion about his role in Spenser's epic, one that reinforces his status as a small, negative, but necessary example. Paros is an island in the Aegean famous in antiquity for its white marble, and *Parius lapis* is a Renaissance term meaning "touchstone," the black stone used to test gold.[43] Spenser exploits this latter-day meaning of *Parius lapis* to define the black-and-white exemplary mode of 3.9: in 3.9 it is Paridell, grandson of Parius, who provides the touchstone for Britomart's emerging historical consciousness. In keeping with the canto's opening lines, the "black" Paridell, unconscious of history and symbolic of its decay, offers the bad example by which the "white" Britomart and her destiny may "more notably be rad." Spenser may also be playing on the changing appearance of *Parius lapis*, which in his day meant a black stone, rather than a white one, as in antiquity; the play would be related to the theme of second-hand romance and the decline of heroism. In any case, the poet renders Paridell's lust as a touchstone, an object of vulgar parody instead of an inward experience, with its pathos reduced to played-out simulation, so that a higher judgment can appear, Britomart's cathartic pity over the fall of Troy.[44]

The elevated, ceremonial character of Britomart's emotion here recalls Burke's and Pucci's remarks on the distance that Aristotelian catharsis provides. "Whenas the noble Britomart heard tell / Of Troian warres, and Priams Citie sackt, / The ruefull story of Sir Paridell," Spenser writes, "She was empassiond at that piteous act" (3.9.38):

> Then sighing soft awhile, at last she thus:
> O lamentable fall of famous towne,
> Which raignd so many yeares victorious,
> And of all Asie bore the soueraigne crowne,
> In one sad night consumd, and throwne downe:
> What stony hart, that heares thy haplesse fate,
> Is not empierst with deepe compassiowne,
> And makes ensample of mans wretched state,
> That floures so fresh at morne, and fades at euening late?
> (FQ 3.9.39)

There is no question of a sympathetic or identificatory twinge here: unlike Malecasta and Busirane, Paridell does not impinge on Britomart's emotional life. Britomart's reaction is not personal but historical, a lament for the mutability that afflicts even the brilliant glare of earthly kingdoms. For Britomart, Paridell offers a mere reminder of Troy's fate; he is not a tragic figure in his own right. In the lines that follow, accordingly, Britomart firmly subordinates Paridell's personal fortune to that of Troy, foreshadowing her own national concern:

> Behold, Sir, how your pitifull complaint
> Hath found another partner of your payne:
> For nothing may impresse so deare constraint,
> As countries cause, and commune foes disdayne.
> (FQ 3.9.40)

Prodding Paridell to tell of Aeneas's fates, Britomart lets him know where her own interests lie—in his historical "complaint" rather than Paridell himself. The providential plot of national history here becomes a didactic source, just as the plot of sacred history was in Book 1. Undaunted by Britomart's didactic lesson, however, Paridell skews national history to personal ends, depicting Aeneas as an irresponsible suitor like himself whose courting of Lavinia brought catastrophic consequences:[45]

> At last in *Latium* he [i.e., Aeneas] did arrive,
> Where he with cruell warre was entertaind
> Of th'inland folke, which sought him backe to driue,
> Till he with old *Latinus* was constraind,
> To contract wedlock: (so the fates ordaind.)
> Wedlock contract in bloud, and eke in bloud

> Accomplishd, that many deare complaind:
> The riuall slaine, the victour through the flood
> Escaped hardly, hardly praisd his wedlock good.
> (*FQ* 3.9.42)

Britomart then takes over the account, correcting Paridell's emphasis on the disastrous costs of Rome's founding (the "cruell warre" between Italian and Trojan, the bloody wedlock of Aeneas and Lavinia). She reminds him of this cruel history's glorious fruit: the incomparable city of Troynovant (London) founded by "the Troian *Brute*" (46):

> But a third kingdom yet is to arise,
> Out of the *Troians* scattered of-spring,
> That in all glory and great enterprise,
> Both first and second *Troy* shall dare to equalise.
>
> It *Troynovant* is hight, that with the waues
> Of wealthy *Thamis* washed is along,
> Vpon whose stubborne neck, whereat he raues
> With roring rage, and sore him selfe does throng,
> That all men feare to tempt his billowes strong,
> She fastned hath her foot, which standes so hy,
> That it a wonder of the world is song
> In forreine landes, and all which passen by,
> Beholding it from far, do thinke it threates the skye.
> (*FQ* 3.9.44–45)

Paridell's wandering account, which stops with Troy's "scattered offspring" and ignores their Roman and British destiny, is itself the "fatal errour" he attributes to Aeneas's Trojans (3.9.41). It gives way to Britomart's evocation of the ambitious glory of British rule, a dynastic celebration attuned to Elizabethan culture's imperial self-image.[46] The repetitive emptiness of the family descent that Paridell lauds stands in unambiguous contrast to Britomart's insistence on a progressive or emulative history. As even Paridell is forced to admit after being upbraided by Britomart, British history "far did passe" "all the antique Worthies" (3.9.50). Like Paridell's earlier admiration of the revealed Britomart, this moment offers her a clear didactic victory. Yet Britomart's triumph is only momentary: Paridell almost immediately returns to his casually ahistorical adulteries in Canto 10.

The Britomart-Paridell episode, then, grounds the poem's pathos in a historical context, making it over into an emblem of the poet's official function as celebrant of Elizabethan order and its historical claims. In this canto as elsewhere in the poem, *The Faerie Queene* effectively becomes (to use Andrew Fichter's phrase) a "dynastic epic."[47] Given the importance of Spenser's dynastic vision, emphasized by Fichter, Quint, Yates, and others,[48] why does the poet depart from history and end Book 3 with Busirane's torture of Amoret, an episode in which courtly convention is seen, as it was earlier in Book 3, as the arena of private travail, a language of personal desire rather than historical promise? The reversion to private amours at the end of Book 3 is, in fact, characteristically Spenserian in its choice of narrative diversion over teleological progress. Britomart's speech against Paridell is an exceptional moment for her, not the sign of any permanent development into epic-historical, dynastic consciousness. Obsessed by Arthegall's shadowy romantic status, Britomart cannot follow Merlin's historical direction for long.[49] At the very end of Book 1, Spenser opts for the heroic pathos of continued knightly errancy over the providential conclusion that Red Crosse's marriage to Una would secure. Here, in Book 3, the poet once again chooses digression and the nondialectical over a linear or progressive poetics.

The real center of Book 3 is Britomart's desire, which remains disjoined from any public moral purpose. Spenser's transition from Guyon, a male protagonist who sees sexuality as a foreign presence, to a female protagonist who can be identified with her sexuality, signals the poet's increasingly open investment in such desire as the defining pleasure of his poetry, what Hazlitt called Spenser's "voluptuous pathos." As the Paridell episode demonstrates, however, poetic voluptuousness is still a source of worry for Spenser. The poet continues to moralize against his own poetry's affect, though now the ground of moralism is national rather than theological, as in Book 2.

As Spenser's poem continues, the reader wonders more and more whether the poet can reconcile his aesthetic effects, both tragic pathos and voluptuous delight, to his moralizing program. Writing on Book 6, a section of the poem even more preoccupied than Book 3 with courtesy and increasingly concerned over the risk of pleasurable amorality that courteous dissimulation implies, Daniel Javitch suggests a dichotomy between the "recreative" rapture of Mount Acidale and the "responsible" activity, the quest for the Blatant Beast, from which Acidale distracts Calidore.[50] Here as in Book 3's Red Crosse–Britomart dialogue with its "pleasing words ... like to Magick art," Spenser figures the marvelous effect of poetry as a courtly grace delightful for its own sake. By enveloping characters in an enchantment that seems beyond both moralizing summary and practical use, such affect militates against the civic duty that would impel the poet and his heroes to glorify queen and country. At Acidale, the hero momentarily forgets his will to glory; he loses his quest. Moralism appears just as irrelevant as knightly honor. Calidore demands from Colin Clout a didactic gloss on the graces' dance, but, as Clare Kinney suggests, he then seems to ignore Colin's lesson completely. The knight succumbs to a "ravished" stupor, what Kinney calls a "purely sensuous delight in the landscape":[51] Calidore "with greedy delight his fancy fed / Both of [Colin's] words . . . / And also of the place, whose pleasures rare / With such regard his sences ravished, / That thence he had no will away to fare" (6.10.30).

Daniel Javitch writes that Spenser in Book 6 "beckons the reader to take back and make use of poetic images in his actual life,"[52] to turn the wonder of Acidale into a tool for moral improvement. But Javitch's pessimism about the possibility of such a project's success suggests a persisting gap between poetic affect and the moral meaning the poet wants to draw from it, between the impact of the aesthetic moment and the requirements of social use. In chapter 1, I described the difficulty attendant on Sidney's attempt to assert that poetic pathos conveys an immediate moral function, that Ajax's frenzy proves not merely the power of poetry's spectacular *ekplêxis* or astonishment, but also the dangers of the madness it depicts. The spectator's absorption in Ajax's passion must remain separate from, and more powerful than, the distanced, and distancing, admonition against such passion that Sidney wants tragedy to convey. In Spenser we see a similar precedence of sensual immediacy over didactic lessons. The passionate spectatorship of Calidore at Acidale cannot incorporate moral direction. A permanent division remains between the moments of affect that Spenser's poetry creates in its reader and the poet's project for an epic order that will mediate a political demand, the celebration of British *imperium*. As I suggested in my introduction, we must confront this division, not by choosing psychology or politics as the ruling term, but by asking how the two terms speak to—and against—each other, both in the Renaissance and in our own time.

# 5
# From Spenser to Milton

I have concentrated my discussion of Spenser on the three books of the 1590 *Faerie Queene* because the 1596 version, which adds Books 4 to 6, almost always turns pathos into a public matter of scandal or honor rather than a private, psychological question. In Book 4, in particular, "private loues" become the matter of "publicke praise" (4.9.36), or blame; pathos no longer defines inward personality as it did for Guyon and Britomart.[1]

*The Faerie Queene* moves from the inward pathos of Guyon and Britomart to the more externalized, theatrical passion displayed in Arthegall's wrath and Calidore's love. Neither Arthegall nor Calidore are shaped as personalities by their emotions as the heroes of the 1590 poem were; for the most part, they use emotion strategically, as an instrument of policy—whether the policy is in the interest of the state or of the individual's already constituted desire.

In the worldly arena of Books 4 to 6, emotion takes the form either of an anger associated with violent rivalry or a generous pity that can heal such violence. Yet this curative, didactic function of pity is not fully assured, because the inwardness associated with Books 2 and 3 continues to threaten Spenser's new world of public competition and reconciliation. Pity in Books 5 and 6 continually threatens to regress to a more intimate force, empathy, which cannot be used for moral purposes because, unlike pity, the conscious self cannot manipulate it.

The Blatant Beast, who comes into his own in Books 4 to 6, suggests that emotion has become a tyrannical law, resistant to any project of self-management. The Beast's random rage epitomizes the way that the Spenserian contest between pathos and morality now appears under the aegis of harsh, unavoidable necessity. Spenser still hopes to discover an efficacious practice of virtue to defend against this threat: accordingly, the hermit suggests that the remedy for "the stubborne rage of passion blinde" caused by the Blatant Beast can be found in self-discipline (6.6.7). But the unmotivated nature of the Blatant Beast's attacks suggests a spreading contagion that, instead of responding to the victim's character, is haphazardly sprayed at all. Like Sclaunder's attacks (4.8.48), the Beast's targeting of innocent bystanders renders irrelevant the hermit's attempt at an inward, character-based defense against it.

In Book 5 virtue, to stay viable, must prove itself capable of warding off the corrupting sway of passion—but also of domesticating and exploiting passion for public purposes. Book 5 enacts a nearly continuous debate over whether pity has a place in the rigorous justice dispensed by Arthegall. Arthegall seems clearly correct not to "pitty" Munera (5.2.26), and clearly mistaken in pitying Radigund (5.5.13)—an error that leads to his captivity. Yet sympathy is a positive force, rather than a danger, when Arthegall recognizes Arthur: after almost engaging in furious combat, Arthegall stops short, "touched with intire affection" (5.8.12). Sympathetic pity here removes Arthegall from the dangerously wrath-obsessed context of knightly misrecognition.

The value of pity shifts in the course of Book 5. Early in Book 5 wrath, personified by Talus, excludes pity in the interest of strict justice. In cantos 1 to 5, Talus's anger protects justice against the weakening force of sympathetic affection.[2] The reversal enacted in the latter half of Book 5, in which pity becomes a positive force, results from the tempering of justice by equity that occurs at Isis church (Canto 6). In other words, equity yokes pity to justice, making the wrath of Talus look more than usually clumsy and brutal. Accordingly, Spenser bars Talus from the precincts of equity because he lacks "sence / And sorrowes feeling" (5.6.9). By 5.6, pathos has become a just, humanizing force. Whirling his murderous "yron flayle," Talus does recur often enough in the latter half of Book 5. But his search and destroy tactics no longer serve the admonitory function of counteracting pity.

It is no surprise, then, that in the scene of Duessa's trial (5.9), Spenser praises Mercilla's conjoining of justice and pity, her "piteous ruth" for her condemned opponent.[3] Pity here provides the guarantee of justice's authenticity, its definitive separation of itself from tyranny. Mercilla displays her compassion for Duessa, her "more than needful naturall remorse" (5.10.4), at the very moment that she delivers her "doome" against her. Mercilla's rule, we are led to believe, is morally justified by her feeling for its victims.

Even after the validation of pity that occurs at Isis church, however, Spenser remains ambivalent about its value, and he embodies his doubts in the figure of Arthegall. During Duessa's trial at Mercilla's court, Arthegall refuses to pity the defendant: justice must still suspect compassion. Arthegall's "zeale," his "constant firme intent," hints at the danger of Arthur's pity for poor Duessa (5.9.45–51: Arthur "for great ruth his courage gan relent" [5.9. 46]). Suddenly realizing the full scope of Duessa's evil, Arthur "repents" of "his former fancies ruth." In general, Arthegall succeeds in his quest for justice by avoiding sympathetic affect. In one of the rare cases in which he does not steer clear of sympathy, his meeting with Radigund, his masculine strength drains away, and justice becomes impotent. Spenser's wariness over combining pity with just judgment means that he senses pity's tendency to backslide, regressing to an instinctive empathy that loses the self in the plight of the other. Such emotional receptiveness weakens the ego and dissolves its capacity for conscious command: the primal danger for Book 5, which demands a stiff vigilance from those, like Arthegall, who would serve and protect.[4]

Yet pity, despite the dangers that Book 5 illustrates, becomes an emblem of virtuous moral decision in Book 6. The Salvage Man, "much emmoued" by the sight of Calepine being chased by Turpine (6.4.3), finds himself transformed by his new sense of compassion; Calidore is "deepe[ly] . . . moue[d]" to knightly charity by Aldine's story of his unfortunate love for Priscilla (6.3.15); and Calepine feels "tender ruth" for Matilda (6.4.34). Later, Mirabella's capacity for sympathetic pathos signifies the genuineness of her repentance: she is "touched with compassion entire" when she sees Timias persecuted by Scorne and Disdaine (6.8.3). By contrast, the hardened criminal Turpin "did counterfeit kind pittie, where was none: / For wheres no courage, theres no ruth nor mone" (6.7.18).

Book 6 persistently links the question of pity to courtesy, the book's titular virtue. The poet's most important argument for the necessary place of didactic pity within courtesy occurs in Book 6's first canto, when Briana, "all overcome with infinite affect" as a result of Calidore's "exceeding courtesy" (6.1.45), finds herself converted to virtue. But we must juxtapose this example of Calidore's courtly persuasion, which induces virtue by evoking a gentle affective response, to his aforementioned "salvage" ferocity in combat when he slays Maleffort. In Calidore, courtesy and rage uneasily coexist. The contrast within him may lead us to suspect that Spenser is attempting a premature harmony of conflicting forces when he claims, through Calepine, that only very rarely do "curtesie and manhood euer disagree" (6.3.40). Calidore, like Calepine later on, seems to share the Salvage Man's fierce rage for battle to such a degree that one thinks twice about the didactic efficacy of his morally wholesome moments, like the sparing of Crudor (6.1).[5] Calidore's courteous pity counterbalances the severe "manhood" embodied in his anger but cannot make us forget its destructiveness.

Calidore's courtliness relies on the public exploitation of pathos. Tellingly, the fact that courtesy comes under considerable moral scrutiny in Book 6 indicates that pathos in its newly public form may be at odds with moralizing. Spenser's suspicion of courtesy culminates with a pointed parallel that harks back to Paridell, the corrupt lover courting Hellenore under the suspicious eye of Malbecco. Here is the oddly analogous scene of Calidore wooing Pastorella at dinner, while the paternal voice of Melibee drones wholesome sententiae:

> Whylest thus he talkt, the knight with greedy care
>   Hong still vpon his melting mouth attent;
>   Whose sensefull words empierst his hart so neare,
>   That he was rapt with double rauishment,
>   Both of his speach that wrought him great content,
>   And also of the obiect of his vew,
>   On which his hungry eye was always bent;
>   That twixt his pleasing tongue, and her faire hew,
> He lost himselfe, and like one halfe entraunced grew.
>
> Yet to occasion meanes, to worke his mind,
>   And to insinuate his harts desire,
>   He thus replyde. . . .
>                              (*FQ* 6.9.26–27)

As he will be at the sight of Acidale, Calidore finds himself "rapt with . . . rauishment." Yet here the rapture proves "double" or duplicitous, because Calidore's real focus is the beautiful Pastorella, whose "faire hew" he devours so eagerly that he almost—but not quite—forgets to practice his seductive wiles. Obsessed with amorous pursuit, the knight "los[es] himselfe." In this instance of Calidore's courtesy, pathos does not lend force to morality, as it did in his conversion of Briana. Instead, it exemplifies the amoral erotic interest that distracts him from Melibee's sage advice. Calidore appreciates Melibee as a superficial, "sensefull" rhetorical gloss for his morally risky sensuality. Clearly, Calidore's desire for the wise man's daughter overrides his supposed pleasure in this *senex*'s virtuous autobiographical advice: the opening lines of stanza 27, with their reference to Calidore's "greedy care,"[6] tip us off to Calidore's thirsty opportunism, his canny use of "occasion."[7]

The general situation—the seduction of a beautiful young woman at the table of an old man, whether husband (Malbecco) or father (the similarly named Melibee)—as well as the cunning skill that the lover applies in each case, implies a similarity between Paridell and Calidore. But Spenser suggests the Paridell-Calidore analogy even more strongly with a sly structural hint. At 6.9.36 he compares Calidore in shepherd's guise to the shepherd Paris who "the loue of fayre *Oenone* sought, / What time the golden apple was vnto him brought"; in the numerically equivalent 3.9.36 occurs Paridell's citation of his forefather's affair with "faire Oenone."

In both Book's 3 and 6, Spenser points to Paris's character as an abandoner of women, specifically Oenone, as well as a seducer of them. The ethical dubiousness of Paris rubs off both on Paridell and, in a more subtle or disguised way, on Calidore.[8] We remind ourselves that, because of the "golden apple," a symbol of competition appropriate to Calidore's rivalry with Coridon in Canto 9, Paris will forsake Oenone for Helen (see 6.9.40: "Old loue is litle worth when new is more prefard"). The poet declares, if only in a stage whisper, that the competitive streak that motivates Calidore's, like Paris's, chivalry will result in the dangerous moral ambiguity of quests for love as well as war.

Spenser follows up his suggestion of the Paris-Calidore analogy in a more covert manner in the next canto of Book 6, Canto 10. Calidore's wondering gaze at Moun Acidale implicitly alludes to the Judgment of Paris that Spenser mentioned more directly in Canto 9, but here the poet eliminates the element of competition or strife in favor of a rhapsodic spell that transcends decision. Spenser will substitute three graces ("Venus damzels," as Colin Clout explains [6.10.21]) for the three goddesses in the Greek judgment, with Calidore, like Paris, as observer/judge. The fourth "mayd," Colin says, is "but a countrey lasse" (6.10.25)—a local grace who evidently stands in for Colin's beloved Rosalind (from *The Shepheardes Calender*).[9]

Spenser here, in contrast to the 6.9 scene, distinguishes Calidore from the likes of Paris and his descendant Paridell. Acidale's combination of the graces, who are associated with Venus and thus suggest the Judgment of Paris, with the Oenone / Rosalind figure of the "countrey lasse" accomplishes a kind of imaginary solution to the real danger in Calidore's skill as a Paridell-like amorous operator, the potential for wholesale immorality that goes along with a career devoted to the rivalrous conquest of women. The four figures on Mount Acidale remain inseparable: Calidore cannot choose among them. Because Acidale suspends choice, he does not forsake the country lass, and the rural setting she represents, for Venus's damsels, the Graces. Spenser thus sharply differentiates Calidore from Paris, who chose the divine glamour of Venus over the countrified Oenone. The poet reverses the situation of the Judgment. Along with this reversal, a move from public to private pathos occurs that is unusual in Books 4 to 6. The move is made all the more notable by Spenser's submerged allusion to the April eclogue of the *Calender*, with Colin's official serenading of "fayre *Eliza*, Queene of shepheardes all" (aka Gloriana, aka Elizabeth). As the unnamed fourth Grace takes over Eliza's position, Calidore's self-absorbed aesthetic delight frees him from the worldly obligations and choices associated with political life; for the moment, both national and moral quests are forgotten. Yet, strangely, the very strenuousness of this wish for an aesthetic liberation from pragmatic demands indicates that Calidore's rapture will prove fragile,[10] that it must yield to a reasserting of bluntly realistic courtly contests.

When Calidore returns to earth after the sparkling and inexplicable delight of the Acidale scene, he encounters the "rancl[ing]" "wound" (6.10.31) of love, a low-down distress that contrasts sharply with Acidale's serene ecstasy. As Calidore, afflicted by love, returns to Pastorella, it seems at first that the passionate epiphany of Acidale may have had a morally purifying effect. His desire looks, for the moment, like moral virtue: "All dewfull seruice voide of thoughts impure / Ne any paines ne perill did he shonne, / By which he might her to his loue allure, / And liking in her yet vntamed heart procure" (6.10.32). But Spenser's word "procure" here lets us know that Calidore's care remains pragmatically exploitative. The knight's flamboyant behavior during his ensuing rescue of Pastorella from a tiger, a symbolic replacement for the Blatant Beast of his appointed quest, smacks of a self-satisfied bravura that is rather less than pure.[11]

Calidore is not a gentle but a calculating heart. Even as he remains faithful to his desire for Pastorella, he takes pains to behave "wisely well" (6.10.38). In the case of both Paridell's and Calidore's desire, the satisfaction of passion contradicts the standards of duty (Calidore's quest for the Beast) and moral philosophy (Britomart in 3.9, the Palmer-like figure of Melibee in 6.9). Though Calidore is a far more attractive, graceful character than Paridell, for both amor has become a cunning means to nourish a habitually performing self thrilled by victory and worldly reward. No longer does desire point to the need to find one's center or true self, as it did with Britomart.

In light of the movement from private to public pathos in Books 4 to 6, I now want to examine the way that Spenser transforms amorous passion at the beginning of Book 4 from an inward aspect of the self, represented primarily by Britomart, to a fully externalized law of desire governed by masculine competition. Spenser already heralded this change by replacing Britomart with Florimell, the quintessential object of masculine pursuit, for a long stretch of Book 3 (Cantos 4 to 8). The ancillary female characters in Book 3, Amoret and Belphoebe, augment Britomart's significance like loyal understudies by reflecting various aspects of her, whereas Florimell replaces and even travesties the star. We can only appreciate Florimell as an example of helpless, passive virginity; she offers a limp antithesis to Britomart's bold virtue.

Florimell's passivity, which comes into its own in Book 4, represents something necessarily relevant, if only by exclusion, to Britomart: the role of woman as passive object of desire, a role Britomart would be forced to play were she not a gendered anomaly, a masculine female clad in armor. Normally, there are only two gendered positions available in the chivalric system: male knight and female beloved (or other female figure auxiliary to the knight's quest, like Perceval's sister). Britomart, a desiring, questing woman knight, represents in her confused person the radical confounding of this conventional chivalric opposition.[12]

Book 4's presentation of desire as "senselesse," impersonal, and mechanical outweighs the presence of Britomart, with her peculiarly memorable gender identity. Here, love is fueled by a masculine game-playing that obliterates any distinctive characteristics of the knightly competitors as well as the individuality of their shared beloved.[13] The robotlike rivalry of Book 4, with its effacing of individual subjectivity, stems from the generic context of chivalric romance as well as the related historical matter of Renaissance courtliness.[14] Both literary and political versions of knighthood submerge individual identity in a Symbolic equalizing. Each romance knight, notes Jameson, must face "the perplexing question of how my enemy can be thought of as being evil (that is, as other than myself and marked by some absolute difference) when what is responsible for his being so characterized is quite simply the identity of his own conduct with mine."[15]

Books 2 and 3 subordinated the stereotypical or programmed heroism of chivalric romance to the poet's characteristic humanist obsession with the fashioning of a noble self through "vertuous and gentle discipline." In Book 4, the public world of chivalric competition returns with a vengeance. I have noted how Spenser's pursuit of the discipline of virtuous character moves him away from Book 1's adherence to plot. With Book 4 we return to Book 1's choice of plot over character, though here plot is tangled and unredemptive, in contrast to the scriptural overtones of Book 1.

Spenser in Book 4 makes Britomart an exception to the rule of chivalry, which in the course of the book's bewildering plot subjects nearly all its characters, in decisively impersonal fashion, to the twin laws of love and anger. In contrast to the other knights' encounters, her trials remain strikingly inward and reckless in the passions they incite. In an astonishing, breathless scene, which strongly echoes Tancredi's recognition of Clorinda in Canto 3 of Tasso's *Gerusalemme Liberata*, Britomart, now battling against Arthegall, fights her way to the sudden incarnate sight of her beloved. As Arthegall strikes her with savage power,

> The wicked stroke vpon her helmet chaunst,
>     And with the force, which in it selfe it bore,
>     Her ventayle shard away, and thence forth glaunst
>     A downe in vaine, ne harm'd her any more.
>     With that her angel's face, vnseene afore,
>     Like to the ruddie morne appeared in sight,
>     Deawed with siluer drops, through sweating sore,
>     But somewhat redder, than beseemed aright,
> Through toylesome heate and labour of her weary fight.
> (*FQ* 4.6.19)

The gentle comic touches in the final lines of the stanza decorously mix the familiar Petrarchan cosmetology of desire with Britomart's well-earned perspiration. As before, we see the unveiling of Spenser's heroine in her full, delicate strength, but this time Britomart's epiphanic star turn is accompanied by a fierce shock. Now, uniquely, Britomart's self-disclosure is involuntary, a fact that makes it all the more revealing of an angelic intimacy "vnseene afore." This scene also differs from Britomart's other self-unveilings in the reciprocity of the encounter it depicts. (The episode's mutual character marks its signal difference from Tasso's scene, which preserves Clorinda's chastity at the cost of her humanity by denying her a recognition of Tancredi.) Britomart realizes that Arthegall has come to her, that he is *here*, not just in vague prediction, and he responds with radiant, inward desire: "Thereat full inly blushed *Britomart*; / But *Artegall* close smyling ioy'd in secret hart" (4.6.32). The reciprocal quality of this *anagnorisis* sets it apart from the myopic, irrational strife of the other contests in Book 4. This meeting, unlike the battles that occur among Paridell, Braggadocchio, Satyrane, Ferraugh, and Pria/Dia/Triamond, and unlike Scudamour's theft of Amoret from the Temple of Venus, rejects the standardized misrecognitions of knightly battle in favor of a self-knowledge based in the complex emotions of Britomart's past history, which is summed up by its origin in Venus's looking glass:

> When Britomart with sharpe auizefull eye
>     Beheld the louely face of Artegall,
>     Tempred with sternesse and stout maiestie,
>     She gan eftsoones it to her mind to call,
>     To be the same which in her fathers hall
>     Long since in that enchaunted glasse she saw.
>     Therewith her wrathfull courage gan appall,
>     And haughtie spirits meekely to adaw,
> That her enhaunced hand she downe can soft withdraw.
>
> Yet she it forst to haue againe vpheld,
>     As fayning choler, which was turn'd to cold:

> But euer when his visage she beheld,
> Her hand fell downe, and would no longer hold
> The wrathfull weapon gainst his countnance bold....
> (*FQ* 4.6.26–27)

The affecting, hesitant tact that appears in Britomart's effort to feign martial solidity lifts her far above the rote overboldness of the other knights in Book 4. Here as in Book 3, Britomart's manner figures a subtle and tricky debate with her desire. Arthegall's response, his attempt at self-control, mirrors Britomart's inwardness, as her "modest countenance," "so goodly graue, and full of princely aw," reins in— and at the same time spurs on—Arthegall's "ranging fancie," in allusion to the chariot of Plato's *Phaedrus*:

> And looser thoughts to lawfull bounds withdraw;
> Whereby the passion grew more fierce and faine,
> Like to a stubborne steede
> whom strong hand would restraine.
> (*FQ* 4.6.33)

As in the Platonic subtext, the allure of the "stubborne," obstreperous horse works with, not just against, the aspiration toward a beautiful telos. Now, Britomart glimpses this goal, the prospect of a complete love, with its promise of union, as she has not before. Unlike the astonishment of Paridell at Britomart's appearance in 3.9, Arthegall's "fancie" matches Britomart's own struggles with her desire.

But Arthegall must once again be the man that got away. The Imaginary mirroring of Arthegall and Britomart will end, and Britomart will disappear from the poem, when their mutual recognition recurs in Book 5 as a severe instance of Symbolic law, in the form of Arthegall's perverse embrace of the Amazonian dominatrix Radigund (*raidê*, "harsh" ; and *gunê*, "woman"[16]). Arthegall unveils Radigund in the course of his heated combat with her just as he uncovered Britomart in Book 4. Arthegall, on the brink of victory, tries to disarm the Amazon, but it is really he who is disarmed:

> But when as he discouered had her face,
> He saw his senses straunge astonishment,
> A miracle of natures goodly grace,
> In her faire visage voide of ornament,
> But bath'd in bloud and sweat together ment....
> (*FQ* 5.5.12)

One might compare this becoming "bloud and sweat" not only to the drops that bedew Britomart in the Book 4 recognition of Arthegall discussed earlier but also to the delicate, diaphanous perspiration that bathes Acrasia in the Bower "through languour of her late sweet toyle" (2.12.78). Here blood flows as it does not in the two other scenes, a sign that Radigund represents the brute-force version of Acrasia's gentle seduction.

The fact that Radigund cannot bring herself to acknowledge Arthegall as her "souerayn Lord," an acknowledgment that, we are told, would ease her "loue-sick hart," points to the poem's uneasiness about Britomart's refusal until now to submit herself to Arthegall. Britomart has not, any more than Radigund, conceded Arthegall's political advantage over her. In fact, ensuing events might more plausibly support a claim to Britomart's superiority or sovereignty over Arthegall. In Canto 7 Britomart plays a cameo role, rescuing Arthegall from Radigund's dungeon, in a scene that clearly echoes Guyon's freeing of Acrasia's victims (5.7.38: forced to cross-dress, Arthegall has been "deformed" like Acrasia's men-beasts).

Spenser overturns Britomart's priority over Arthegall in order to safeguard patriarchal authority. Canto 7 ends, contrary to all readerly expectation, with the abrupt reduction of Britomart to "womanish complaints" over Arthegall's return to manly adventure and her subordination to his sense of masculine "honor" (5.7.44). This is Britomart's last appearance in the poem, as the wondrous, and exclusively male, meeting of Arthur and Arthegall supersedes the union of Britomart and Arthegall that it echoes (5.8.12). At this moment, Britomart's immersion in feminized pathos of the most stereotypical sort, disturbingly like that of the many other sobbing, desperate maidens who populate the pages of *The Faerie Queene* (Una, Amavia, Florimell, Serena, Pastorella, and so on.), means that Spenser has done away with the central question of Book 3, the subjective function of pathos in Britomart's construction of her identity. Her grief-stricken passion becomes merely a common feminine feature, like Una's or Florimell's fair "blubbred face" (1.6.9, 3.8.32). The earlier Britomart's androgynous grace stemmed from her complex, emotional bewilderment, which Spenser now rejects in favor of a monotonous, purely functional pathos, Radigund's rude masculine force. Radigund's victory responds fittingly to Arthegall's harsh, violent rage for order, which espouses the unequivocal. In Book 5, rough justice has the upper hand; however, grace will return as the crucial value of Book 6.

The combination of sexual desire and uncontrolled rage that Spenser's moralism characteristically stigmatizes (in Argante, for example) achieves its bluntest form with the appearance of Radigund. For once in *The Faerie Queene*, pathos and moralism are firmly aligned. The

Radigund episode's straightforward use of pathos to enforce a pejorative moral point eliminates the unsure, seductive contact between desire and heroic obligation that animated Spenser's poem in the Bower of Bliss and during much of Book 3.[17]

The Garden of Adonis presents a different kind of attempt to resolve the gap between pathos and moralism, not as in the Radigund episode through the brutal caricaturing of emotion, but through the refining of morality so that it may attune itself to, and simultaneously temper, the pathos of desire. Although I have been discussing Books 4 to 6, I want to turn back to the Garden of Book 3 to illuminate its conjunction of pathos and moralism, which provides the best segue to Milton's sense of this issue in *Paradise Lost*. In the Garden Spenser aims to develop a new morality that will guide and foster, instead of devaluing, the sensual aspect of his poetics. The Garden, the locus amoenus that corresponds to Book 2's Bower, generates its moral meaning intrinsically (that is, sensually), not as a correction to what it delusively seems to be. The Garden *is* the true innocent pleasure that the Bower masqueraded as. As A. Bartlett Giamatti writes, "The Garden of Adonis binds up and reconciles the fundamental conflicts of the poem in overtly sexual, ultimately Christian, terms."[18]

Yet Spenser frames even the Garden of Adonis with a suggestive uncertainty as to whether its pleasures are really innocent or not. In doing so, he indicates that desire depends on a disjunction, however lightly drawn, between its own force and that of moral obligation. Spenser embodies this disjunction in the figure of Chrysogonee.[19] Despite the prevailing impression of Edenic naïveté in the Garden, Spenser strangely echoes Ovid's account in the *Metamorphoses* of the incestuous Myrrha,[20] who is like Chrysogonee a pregnant fugitive, but a guilty rather than a pure one. Also counting against the atmosphere of innocence is a strangely heated, even lascivious, depiction of Chrysogonee bathing her "chast bodie" (3.6.5):

> farre from all mens vew,
> She bath'd her brest, the boyling heat t'allay;
> She bath'd with roses red, and violets blew,
> And all the sweetest flowers, that in the forrest grew.
> (*FQ* 3.6.6)

This picture of Chrysogonee "all naked bare displayd" (3.6.7) surely means that she is not "farre from all mens vew." The reader here becomes the voyeur, equivalent to Guyon spying on the maidens in the Bower, Actaeon in the Mutabilitie Cantos, or, most immediately, the Venus who surprises Diana a few stanzas later in this same canto (st.

18). Significantly, the Garden of Adonis, unlike the Bower or the Temple of Venus, does not constitute an object of vision for one of the narrative's protagonists. Spenser presents it to the eyes of author and reader alone, and the reader here clearly occupies the place of spectator or voyeur usually reserved for the Spenserian hero.

This spectatorship has a moral dimension. Diana is "sham'd" (st. 19) by Venus's interruption of her bathing in the Garden episode, just as Chrysogonee feels "shame" and "disgrace," despite her "guiltlesse" pregnancy (st. 10). Clearly, the embarrassment evoked here figures the reader's partial or erroneous viewing of Chrysogonee the Diana-figure in Venus's sensual terms, now that the author has exposed her to desirous eyes.[21]

The power of place, so familiar in romance, is at work in Spenser's conjuring of voyeuristic sensuality: the Garden of Adonis, of course, devotes itself to Venus, and Chrysogonee and Belphoebe must therefore be read through Venus's eyes, which are now also ours. Even the chaste Belphoebe becomes a Venus-figure when she nurtures Timias's wound in Canto 5, just as Venus nurtures Adonis's. The reader cannot disjoin chastity from eroticism: in Book 3, Venus inevitably guides Diana. Britomart's only route to her honorable destiny lies through the love she spies in Venus's looking-glass, and it is difficult for both Britomart and the reader to separate her quest for Arthegall from the less pure desires of a Venus or a Malecasta.

The contrast between Venus's playful point of view and that of the heartbroken Satan spying on Eve in Book 4 of *Paradise Lost* tells us something about the enormous difference between Spenser's and Milton's respective ways of guiding their readers' responses. The reader's voyeuristic interest in Chrysogonee or Diana is not potentially Satanic. Spenser presents such spectatorship not as a desperate, seductive evil but as the response to a fresh marvel, as healthy in its sensuality as the amorous vicissitudes of Britomart herself.

Arguing that Spenser uses the Garden of Adonis to condemn voyeurism, C. S. Lewis brings Spenser too close to Milton: he injects a Miltonic morality of decision into the Protean nuances of *The Faerie Queene*. Spenser, far from rejecting voyeurism, here knows himself enticed by it.[22] Contrary to Lewis's assumption, the Garden does not provide a definitive correction of what is amiss in the Bower—mirroring the Bower's luxurious heat only to depict an unearthly innocence sharply distinct from it. The Garden does not strengthen the distinction between virtue and pleasure; it further confuses this distinction, just as Malecasta, offering a contrast to Britomart, is incorporated within her. For the reader who responds empathically to Britomart's unsure desire, Book 3 perplexes the opposition of chaste and unchaste into a lively uncertainty. Spenser does not pose Venus against Diana; instead, with Britomart, he makes Diana ask after the Venus in herself.

Despite Milton's strikingly un-Spenserian drive to choose between his paradise and the world we know, the Eden of *Paradise Lost* resembles the Garden of Adonis in its attempt to integrate morality and the experience of desire—desire being the internal face of what Spenser, when he looks from an external, cosmic perspective, calls mutability. In his Eden, Milton incorporates into sex itself the rule of temperance that *Comus*'s Lady (like Guyon) uses to withstand the body's passions, just as Spenser's Garden conquers mutability by incarnating it in the landscape in the form of the continually dying, yet still viable Adonis.[23] Like Spenser's Garden of Adonis, Milton's Eden tempers temporal decay and renders it harmless by making it the embodying of pleasure. The inevitable absence of the beloved that means desire-as-death in the fallen world is, before the Fall, merely a means of flirtation,[24] "sweet reluctant amorous delay" (4.311).

Milton's Eden, then, like the Garden of Adonis, is about nuances, the finessing of the relation between desire and morals. But Milton's insistence on separation of terms as a means to truth—his interest in an overriding, decisive contrast between innocence and fallenness—still marks his difference from Spenser. We must move on to the fallen world, with its radical division between pathos and social moralism, to understand how this split produces Miltonic individuation. This understanding requires a move, as well, from a sexual to a religious way of defining the self, a transition embodied in the Lady. In Milton's poetic career, from the Lady to Samson, religious pathos means confronting the extreme of conscience in solipsistic trial. But Milton, after this estranged, lonely moment, hopes to correct conscience's heroic isolation through socially structured authority. Throughout his writing, he rebels against and tries to amend the division between private pathos and public moralism. In *Areopagitica*, for example, Milton proposes the authority of the good teacher, like Spenser's Palmer, as an escape from the radical solitude imposed by spiritual crisis, as well as the chaotic free-for-all of Reformation polemics.

Milton's idea of a public, didactic role for pathos develops in the course of the 1640s, as emotional response and moral teaching become increasingly interdependent in his work. Milton already implies that pathos can convey a Palmer-like didacticism when, in his 1642 *Reason of Church Government,* he records his ambition to write a "true poem." But, at this early point, he sees the relation between poetic emotion and moralism as a relatively external or instrumental one. As a religious author, Milton writes, he will exploit pathos as a device to further his moral message:

> Whatsoever in religion is holy and sublime, in virtu amiable, or grave, whatsoever hath passion or admiration in all the changes of that which is call'd fortune from without, or the wily suttleties and refluxes of man's thoughts from within, all these things with a solid and treatable smoothnesse to paint out and describe. Teaching over the whole book of sanctity and virtue through all the instances of example, with such delight to those especially of soft and delicious temper who will not so much as look upon Truth herself, unless they see her elegantly drest, that whereas the paths of honesty and good life appear now rugged and difficult, though they be indeed easy and pleasant, they would then appear to all men both easy and pleasant, though they were rugged and difficult indeed.[25]

Milton's plan to define moral doctrine "with a solid and treatable smoothness" that will appeal to his audience is reminiscent of Spenser's Letter to Ralegh. Spenser claims in his Letter that his era's taste has forced him to write a poem filled with sensational effects. The poet is interested in the high moral goal suggested by his stated intent, "to fashion a gentleman or noble person," but his audience is not. According to Spenser, his readers have compelled him to disguise his moral project with what he describes as the "delightfull and pleasing" stylistic surface of *The Faerie Queene*—the equivalent of Milton's "smoothness" in his *Reason of Church Government* passage.

Spenser's Letter asserts that the purpose of his poetic refinement is the alluring of readers who normally measure literature only by its yield of pleasant "outward showes."[26] By giving them their pleasures, Spenser will convince his audience to accept as well the nonpleasurable moral beneath the surface. By alluding, like Spenser, to this common "sugar-coating" version of the *dulce et utile* formula, in which poetic delight tricks the reader into swallowing the poet's moral, Milton implies that he too uses delight as a convenient hook, a way of warming up or drawing in his audience.

Despite what he claims in his Letter, Spenser's use of *movere* and *delectare*, pathos and delight, is not extrinsic or ornamental but, as we have seen, an integral part of his poetry. For Milton the same is true: both the unfallen pleasure of Eden and the tragedy of the Fall are too central to his poetic project to be reduced to the status of rhetorical tools.[27] Milton commits himself to a poetics that makes Christian conscience live in his hero's and his reader's affective responses—a work that, he hopes, will make pathos and morality cohere as body and soul. The Pauline notion of a "way through weakness to the greatest strength," which Milton applies to himself in his *Second Defense* (1654),[28] suggests a justification for the poet's presentation of affect in tragic cases like those of Adam and Samson. The catastrophic tests these characters face are, like Milton's own blindness, necessary to the truths they achieve, not just dramatic ways of describing truth to an audience.

The *Reason of Church Government* implies that pathos and delight are rhetorical devices, able to make an inward truth palatable and publicly available without falsifying it. This scheme necessarily assumes the audience's inadequacy, its need to be comforted by easy didactic schemes. At least from the early 1640s, the time of *Areopagitica*, Milton refuses to accept such limitations in his readers. As Milton moves away from the conventionally classicized epic aspiration described in *The Reason of Church Government* toward his ambitious desire to make epic itself a "godly" form divorced from pagan deception, such rhetorical manipulation must reveal itself as antithetical to his poetry's Christian intent. Milton in his major poems rejects *The Reason of Church Government*'s instrumental, outward definition of poetic affect. Milton's desire to transform his readers into the author's spiritual counterparts, as righteous in their understanding as the poet himself is, requires the abandonment of this conventional poetics, which assumes the author's condescension to his audience.

The *Reason of Church Government* already presents some evidence for Milton's wish to incorporate authorial inspiration and spiritual reading. In one important passage, Milton rejects mere rhetorical-persuasive poetics, whose patron muses are "Dame Memory and her Siren daughters," in favor of "that Eternall Spirit who can enrich with all utterance and knowledge."[29] Milton here proposes a wedding of "utterance" and inner "knowledge," of what the *Reason of Church Government* elsewhere calls "solidity" and "art," that transfigures both terms, implying his ambition to define style as the substantial form of his faith. Milton's autobiographical emphasis in 1641's *Apology for Smectymnuus* aims at a similar embodiment of verbal style. "When good and faire in one person meet," as in the ideal author who is "himself a true poem," it seems possible to overcome the dichotomy between fair rhetorical surfaces and private, inward virtue that I have been discussing.[30] (In the following chapter on *Paradise Lost*, I will go on to consider the difficulties that Milton encounters in his desire for the realization or embodiment of virtue.)

As the pathos of Milton's private religious searching becomes public in the work of his polemical imagination, he hopes that such a harmony of internal and external will triumph. In 1644's *Areopagitica*, Milton identifies his audience with himself, implying that his faith is shared by all English believers, here described as an incipient "nation of prophets."[31] Milton's desire for such a fit and prophetic audience attests to his need to imagine readers as strong as himself, as willing to face historical experience without seeking comfort in the "excremental" superficiality of doctrine.

Milton writes in the preface to his *Doctrine and Discipline of Divorce*, "The *Jews* . . . were neither won with the austerity of *John the Baptist*, and thought it too much licence to follow freely the charming pipe of him who sounded and proclaim'd liberty and relief to all distresses."[32] But the Miltonic word often shuns the ecumenical Christian's "charming pipe," instead withdrawing into the strength of a self-containment that needs no wider audience. The exemplary author forms his own text, and his integrity remains proof against any reliance on a public's embraces. In the divorce tracts, this autobiographical strain shows Milton's desire for internal justification through private impulse. Only the married person himself—or perhaps very occasionally herself—can know whether a divorce is necessary. A knowledgeable defense of divorce can only stem from the personal experience of a ruinous marriage. Yet Milton cannot finally rest with such first-person, potentially anarchic self-justification. His plea for divorce rests on his concept of true marriage, which concept in turn depends on his ability to depict and argue for it via certain customary and acceptable rhetorical forms. The weird torsions of Milton's prose style as it is suffused by the energies of his personal case underline his resistance to the need for such public argument, even as he engages vociferously in it. This author's syntax, under the pressures of excitement, sometimes goes beyond the Latinate to Jackson Pollock–style splatter, with glowering bursts of polemic hurled impatiently onto the page.

The split between Milton's desire to separate the self, whether from its audience or from the God it worships, in order to ensure the authority of the self, and his contrary desire for a self in continuity with others, is the key to my discussion. In his major poems, Milton continues to question, even as he clings to, his desire to incorporate pathos and moral message as an indissoluble whole that will join the author to his audience. Milton in these works confronts a problem not encountered by Spenser: how can the inwardness of religious experience be communicated to the public without falsifying and reducing it?[33] When *Paradise Lost* in its final books faces the fallen world's seemingly endless cruelty, it courts the temptation to avoid public, worldly experience. Here, as in *Samson*, Milton reacts to the inexplicable failure of the revolution to produce a "Godly rule," a failure that cast doubt, for many English Non-Conformists, on the justice of God's providence. Some radical Protestants responded by withdrawing from politics altogether, others by emphasizing the afterlife rather than earthly events.[34]

Such a withdrawal from history attests to the failure of puritanism to answer publicly to the difficult reality of the postrevolutionary era. Exactly because of the severity of such historical disaster, a didactic "smoothness" that evades history may be attractive to Milton. In parts of *Paradise Lost* and *Paradise Regained*, Milton tries to convince himself of the reasonableness of Christian doctrine by avoiding the drama of earthly emotion and adhering to the same official, and superficial, standards that he tests so severely at other moments in these same poems. But at the end of *Paradise Regained* and, even more, of *Samson*, Milton moves away from the unrealistic facility of doctrine and toward a religious mystery that cannot be fully encompassed by the terms of either didacticism or public chronicle. The enigmatic endings of 1671's major poems reject the possibility that a readily intelligible truth will appear when it is clarified by worldly trial—a hope endorsed by Milton in *Areopagitica*—just as they reject the abstractly philosophical, cloistered doctrine that would avoid trial.

Didacticism now comes into real question. The idea of emulating or learning from the careers of Samson or the Son in *Paradise Regained* proves far more dubious than it did with respect to Adam and Eve in *Paradise Lost*. Accordingly, Samson and the Son are not subject to the exemplary analogy, nor the intense sympathy, between reader and characters that comes into focus in the tableau of Adam and Eve at the very end of *Paradise Lost*. The final books of *Paradise Lost* present us first with Michael's clear but facile moralism, then with the conclusive image that supersedes moralism: an irresistible invitation to identify with our first parents as they leave Eden. No such sympathetic identification will be available to us in *Paradise Regained* and *Samson Agonistes*. Instead, at the end of both poems, we are left in silent surprise, staring at the permanent and unapproachable site of a paradox.[35]

# 6
# *Paradise Lost*

## I. Discontinuous Creation

Milton's poetry places tragic loss at the center of self-definition. In this chapter, I emphasize first of all how the emotional discontinuity or fall that any tragedy exposes provides the essential basis for Milton's creation of a self and a world. My subject in the second half of the chapter, on the final books of *Paradise Lost*, is Milton's reflection on the link between tragic pathos and the poetic image, which proves formative for an isolated subjectivity, the individual of conscience that Milton fashions as his exemplary self. In the final books, the lonely pathos that afflicts, and forms, Adam's fallen self may seem overshadowed by Michael's doctrine of continuity, of sacred history as a coherent process. But the poem as a whole, including the final books, perceives through the falls of Adam, Eve, and Satan the fatal gaps in God's ostensibly unified universe.

Here Milton departs from the epic model provided by Spenser, his major precursor in English poetic tradition. In Books 2 and 3 of *The Faerie Queene*, Spenser defines the pathos of discontinuity or separation as the basis for selfhood. But Spenser finally places the trials of the separated self in the reconciliatory context of a mutable yet harmonious cosmos. By the end of the Mutabilitie Cantos, we discover that "all things stedfastnes doe hate / And changed be: yet being rightly wayd / They are not changed from their first estate; / But by their change their being doe dilate" (7.7.58). *The Faerie Queene* discloses a phantasmically expansive, "dilate[d]" universe whose final stability, composed of endless change, takes precedence over the ascetic, self-reforming quests of characters like Guyon and Britomart. Spenser's strategy has an important hermeneutic implication: his poetic harmony means acceptance of ambiguity, in contrast to Milton's drive to resolve the conflict between subjective pathos and law by reducing the ambiguous to the unequivocal. Self and world cohere as Spenser recognizes in the pathos that poetic wonder elicits the meeting of subjectivity and cosmic order. *The Faerie Queene*, distilling pure moments of embowered calm, concentrates the expanse of epic into the rapt security of *multum in parvo*. Milton, in the first two books of *Paradise Lost*, and again in his depiction of Eden, exploits the attractions of Spenser's centripetal locus amoenus, with its lulling, morally dubious ambience: the pastoral otium that, as in the case of Calidore, means surrendering the dutiful impulse to the quest. After the Fall, however, Milton shatters Spenserian enchantment to assert a clear didactic message. Milton's inheritance of Spenser's seductively doubtful, microcosmic spots of time finds its exemplification in passages like the bee simile that closes Book 1 of *Paradise Lost*—an image so alluring in its blurring of Virgilian grandeur and magically diminutive fairyland:

> As bees
> In spring time, when the Sun with Taurus rides,
> Pour forth thir populous youth about the Hive
> In clusters; they among fresh dews and flowers
> Fly to and fro . . .
> . . . . . . . . . . . . . . . . . . . . . . . . . . . .
>             till the Signal given,
> Behold a wonder! they but now who seem'd
> In bigness to surpass Earth's Giant Sons
> Now less than smallest Dwarfs, in narrow room
> Throng numberless, like that Pigmean Race
> Beyond the Indian Mount, or Faery Elves. . . .
>                                     (*PL* 1.768–81)

Here, the poet plays with perspectives to enforce a sense of ambiguous, hazy magic: is Satan's band tiny or enormous, or both at once? We wonder what kinds of creatures these are, to what degree still angelic, and our admiration happily coincides with our uncertainty. But as fallen readers, we cannot remain in this marvelous landscape. Our fascination must be resolved into a judgment against evil, as Milton, beginning in Book 3, unmasks the Satanic sublime as a rather shoddy fraud, not the brave self-deception it seemed to be. After the Fall, most noticeably in the final books of *Paradise Lost*, Milton withdraws from the vertiginous ambiguity that the fallen angels exploit in Books 1 and 2, hinting that the seductive wonder of our gaze, in its mortal fragility, cannot fully realize or embody itself, "and wing'd ascend / Ethereal, as wee. . . ." (*PL* 5.497–99). In Spenser's world of protean fantasy, no such failure of realization can occur. Faerieland incorporates wonder in the continuous, seemingly infinite expanse of its poetics. Milton, by contrast, organizes his universe around a fault that interrupts the infinite continuity of creation. Imagination falls short of reality, and the pathos of this failing, because it means a confrontation with the real, allows the poet to find a way to compensatory strength through weakness. Once our vision has failed, once fallen images have been broken and revealed as deceptive, Milton's desire for visible authority remains. The desire can only find answerable expression by discovering power in tragically imperfect figures like Adam, Eve, Samson, and the poet himself.

Milton's refusal of Spenser's seamless, endlessly mutable textuality means a new consciousness of loss that leads to a newly severe and capable poetic authority.[1] For Milton such authority demands narrative choice: the decision to award the blessing to a younger brother (figured as Christ) rather than an elder one (Satan). Miltonic rivalry between brothers, most prominent in *Paradise Regained*, departs from the Spenserian bonding between Imaginary doubles, who tend to remain in blurred symbiosis. The confusion that occurs between Red Crosse and Sans-ioy, Guyon and Pyrochles, and Britomart and Malecasta culminates in the hermaphroditic union at the end of the 1590 *Faerie Queene*. Milton, in contrast to Spenser, aims at not union but decision. Instead of Spenser's mutuality, Milton insists on the powers of displacement and—to draw again on Lacan's terms—Symbolic judgment.

For Milton, unlike Spenser, literary representation must discover that it is not the ambiguous, emotive fullness it seems to be but instead remains dependent, like the poet himself in his mortal blindness, on higher authority. In its practice of re-presentation, the Miltonic text is tempted by a rich, and richly delusive, sense of its own self-sufficiency. Yet the author's awareness of his text's trusting, but still equivocal and secondary, connection to God's word rescues him from Satanic arrogance by compelling him to find his work lacking in comparison with the original labor of divine creation. This Miltonic curtailing of imagination culminates in the dull and repetitive violence that populates the final books, which depict the mere letter of history as if all fallen humanity, including the poet, must remain mired in reductive tableaux. As I will suggest, Milton remains worried over, even as he binds himself to, the diminishing of the poetic and the human that such a conclusive reduction imposes.

In Spenser, the poetic image occurs as a wondrous, recreative moment, fragile and tenuous but not, as in Milton, risky in its reliance on a merely human word that will finally prove inadequate. The supreme example of sudden Spenserian illumination occurs at Acidale, where the poet distills delight with an intensity that encapsulates poem and world together. Acidale's "pleasures rare / With such regard [Calidore's] sences rauished, / That thence, he had no will away to fare, / But wisht, that with that shepheard he mote dwelling share" (*FQ* 6.10.30). In Milton, such encapsulation remains suspect—as in Satan's first "sudden view / Of all this World at once" (*PL* 3.542–43). The singular, vast suddenness of this "at once," the fresh sublime that Satan's—and the reader's—gaze astonishes itself with, must yield to the more abstract survey of the Father who "ben[ds] down his eye" "his own works and their works at once to view" (*PL* 3.59), or Raphael's equally theoretical presentation of the synoptic universe as "one first matter all" (*PL* 5.472). Miltonic ascesis, in shying away from the drama of the moment, becomes an abstract scheme. Divine sight in *Paradise Lost* provides the infinite mathematization of space that Galileo bestows on the Renaissance mind, eliminating the uneven, revelatory twists and turns of a mythographic cosmos.[2] For God the Father, all things are immediately available to a vision that, as a result, denies the precipitous sting of the Satanic, and human, sublime. Milton will go on to expose an unresolvable conflict between such abstraction and the more immediate and momentary individual experience of pathos—a conflict that Spenser's mythography recasts as polymorphous harmony.

The Miltonic confrontation between schema and the moment of pathos takes center stage in Book 3 of *Paradise Lost*. The Father's gaze, which marks his first appearance in the poem, directs itself, of course, toward the event of Satan's fall. Milton thus implicitly phrases the debate between the fallen self and the authority it opposes as a question of temporal priority. Which came first, Satanic loss or the Father's assertion of his power? At the very beginning of *Paradise Lost*, Milton hints at an answer when he presents himself as the poet of the Fall, in opposition to Moses, the poet of creation.[3]

> Of Man's First Disobedience
> . . . . . . . . . . . . . . . .
> Sing Heavenly Muse, that on the secret top
> Of Oreb, or of Sinai, didst inspire
> That Shepherd, who first taught the chosen Seed,
> In the beginning how the Heavns and Earth
> Rose out of Chaos. . . .
>
> (*PL* 1.1–10)

Milton's interruptive "in the beginning" situates his own work before the Mosaic text: loss takes precedence over genesis. This priority, the fact that Milton begins from the unexplainable and unavoidable fact of a Fall, means that the goodness of God's creation gets located as compensation for a loss that precedes and motivates it. Though Milton in *Paradise Lost* images God's creation as an extravagant plenitude that overflows all reason or occasion—"wild above rule or art, enormous bliss" (5.297)—he also, crucially, suggests the contrary, that creation stems from an originary instance of lack. The poet indicates that the source of creation lies in a limited, specific motive: compensation for the angels' fall.[4] God supplants fallen angels with human beings in order "good out of evil to create" (7.190). The official argument of *Paradise Lost* asserts the exact reverse: that evil is parasitic on goodness, because God's creative must be prior to Satan's destructive power. In this programmatic or orthodox version, the fallen angels' rebellion really turns out to be dependency—a secondariness dramatically apparent when Beelzebub in Book 2 lowers himself to hoping that "Heav'n's fair Light" may eventually ameliorate the darkness of hell and "purge off this gloom" (2.397–402). But Milton's doctrinal assurances about the impossibility of fallen autonomy, which usually rely on the fact that rebellion borrows its terms from the authority it has tried to refuse, cannot conceal the fact that a real, historical discontinuity *has* occurred.

The hidden presence of a historical fault or gap that both instigates creation's plenitude and accounts for its fallenness shows up, not only in Satan's revolt, but (more surprisingly) also in Milton's paradise. But the fault appears only gradually: Book 4 first presents unfallen creation as a harmonious collection of delights. Adam's opening speech in Book 4 glorifies a free-flowing, heterogeneous variety that encompasses even the tree of knowledge, the sign of death. Adam reports to Eve that God has left them "this easy charge,"

> of all the Trees
> In Paradise that bear delicious fruit
> So various, not to taste that only Tree
> Of Knowledge, planted by the Tree of Life,
> So near grows Death to Life, whate'er Death is. . . .
> (*PL* 4.421–25)

"So near grows death to life": Adam's wonder signifies a perceptive, poetically discriminating reluctance to cross the border from the "delicious" difference of a world "so various" into the fallen realm of antithesis. His hesitation suggests an identification of unfallen life with the retaining of the potential for an infinite, monistic spectrum of good things. But is it really possible, even in Eden, to stay on this side of the border, to remain a monist? A few lines later Adam enters the realm of oppositions. He turns the pleasurable differentiation he has just described into the harsh sign of hierarchical power. Adam reads the features of paradise in quasi-fallen fashion as marks of authority *qua* separation:

> ... for well thou knows't
> God hath pronounc't it death to taste that Tree,
> The only sign of our obedience left
> Among so many signs of power and rule
> Conferr'd upon us, and Dominion given
> Over all other Creatures that possess
> Earth, Air, and Sea.
> (*PL* 4.426–32)

The implications of categorical possession and power that Adam voices here—as Eden becomes a compilation of "so many signs of power and rule"—ill suit the seductive lure of Milton's paradise, which presents itself as a beautifully attuned "blissful bower" (*PL* 4.690) that, like the Spenserian earthly paradise, ostensibly precedes all claims to authority through hierarchical separation. But authoritative separation does, in fact, come first: God's dominion, expressed in his status as source of creation, depends on his power to distinguish earth from sea, human from animal. And God requires the forbidden tree, which as the one absurd element in an otherwise reasonable, justifiable Eden, fractures the harmony of paradise, to make his power explicit.

Miltonic creation, then, relies on a break between the source and what that source creates—a break that inevitably widens into creation's rebellion against its author. In Adam's memory of his origin, the delighted gaze that assumes the harmony of "shady Woods, and sunny Plains, / And liquid Lapse of murmuring Streams" (*PL* 8.262–63) soon metamorphoses into his consciousness that a power must have generated him and his world as subordinate to and different from itself: "How came I thus, how here? / Not of myself; by some great Maker then, / In goodness and in power preeminent" (*PL* 8.278–80). Similarly, in the reflecting pool scene of Book 4, Eve's source, Adam, interrupts and usurps an already established cohesion between Eve and the "clear / Smooth Lake" of her landscape, unmasking such continuity as faulty or delusive (*PL* 4.459–60). In contrast to Adam's interventionist posture, Eve's experience of the landscape as womblike context lacks the power to divide and name that gives authority to God's creation—his "divorcing command," as Milton calls it in the *Doctrine and Discipline of Divorce*.[5] As Geoffrey Hartman remarks in a related Wordsworthian context, "This is the voice of waters"—a maternal continuity—"rather than of the spirit hovering over the face of the waters," which sets itself apart from, and thereby masters, what it names.[6] The spirit of origins must intervene and shatter what appears to be a primal unity, revealing it as narcissistic illusion. Together, the divine voice and Adam himself remind Eve that he is her source, prior to her, and that she must therefore tear herself away from her natural setting in order to cleave to him:

> Whom fli'st thou? Whom thou fli'st, of him thou art,
> His flesh, his bone; to give thee being I lent
> Out of my side to thee, nearest my heart
> Substantial Life, to have thee by my side
> Henceforth an individual solace dear. . . .
> (*PL* 4.482–87)

Ironically, Adam's case for the priority of man over woman relies on the very image that, born of the first woman's experience, argues against the power of such hierarchical thinking: the individuum or undivided self that Eve just felt when she melded with her image in the landscape. Only now, in Adam's words, such harmony appears as a nostalgic "solace" for a difference or fault that has ineluctably occurred rather than the primal fact it was for Eve. The traditional image of "one flesh" offers our most resonant, memorable picture of marriage; in *Paradise Lost*, however, married union becomes, not a seamless harmony, but a drama of distinction and distance between Eve and her original, Adam. As a result, Adam cannot effectively assert Eve's closeness to, her oneness with, him. He cannot make his claim stick. From the time she parts from Adam's side—the parting that originates desire—the pair will not be "individual," that is, undivided but separate. Eve flees, but Adam pursues and "claims" her: such distance proves necessary not only to the beginning of desire but to the hierarchical power, summed up by Adam's assertion of priority, that begins along with it. Adam precedes and gives birth to Eve. But as in the case of the creator-God who provides his model, for Adam this act of generation makes up for, and therefore recalls, an originary lack.

Adam's impulse toward a primal wholeness reminds him, to his simultaneous pain and delight, that he gave up "substantial life" to gain an elusive supplement, a partner "joined" to him only by the blessed human artifice called marriage. Reunion can never enact the perfect fit it seems to promise, because such perfection never *literally* existed. Yet the figurative perfection of relationship, in the form of attunement or sympathy, remains a Miltonic ideal, powerful exactly because it is wishful or desirous rather than fully realizable.

Lack insinuates itself into the very notion of an infinite creation, which is central to *Paradise Lost*.[7] In Book 8, Adam tells God,

> No need that thou
> Shouldst propagate, already infinite;
> And through all numbers absolute, though One;
> But Man by number is to manifest
> His single imperfection, and beget
> Like of his like, his image multipli'd,
> In unity defective, which requires
> Collateral love, and dearest amity.
>
> (*PL* 8.419–26)

The "single imperfection" Adam mentions in line 423 means that the multiplication of the human image, however extenuated or progressive it becomes, can never, by definition, reach totality. God requires fruitfulness from his creation because man, unlike his Father, remains "in unity defective"—he needs more. But, however much it happens, fruitfulness cannot asymptotically make up a whole. Man's "single imperfection" signifies, not just the lack attached to him because he starts out defective—only one, and needing more. More than this, his imperfection constitutes a singular fault that cannot be overcome but instead becomes only more explicit when he starts to multiply himself. Inscribed into the human origin or source itself is a definitive, at first delightful but finally tragic, distance between this source and its secondary companion: the pathos of Imaginary separation that defines subjectivity, even in Eden, as incipient fallenness. Adam's phrase "collateral love, and dearest amity" reminds us that Eve, though she begins from Adam's side (*latus*), attracts him exactly because she does not remain there—because she flees, distances herself, defers desire and thus reveals desire as difference.

In the case of the latecomer Eve's resistance to her fathers, Adam and God, the transferring of power to secondary hands becomes a full-blown usurpation. In her fall, Eve claims priority over the authority that generated her. This claim is indicative of Milton's general emphasis on the displacement of the earlier by the later. At least in Satan's version of the story, the Son supplants him as Jacob did Esau. Spenser's Mutabilitie Cantos, by contrast, encompass early and late together under the aegis of Nature. Spenser thereby provides a solution to the threat of rebellion that has occupied him during Books 5 and 6 of *The Faerie Queene*. Milton's belated figures—Satan, Eve, and the Son—want to appropriate their origins rather than glossing or unveiling the way that origins generate a world, as Spenser's Mutabilitie, her rebelliousness quelled, ends up doing.[8]

With its emphasis on the pathos of substitution, Milton's poetics reveals the monotheistic drive to eliminate its background in monolatry. From the Nativity Ode on, the poet makes it clear that the authority of the one God, his elimination of rivals, begins in the preference of one deity over others (as the Mosaic commandment puts it, "thou shalt have no other gods *before* me"). But such competitive monolatry remains too invested in the instability of the Imaginary. Milton's choice of monotheism over monolatry, his drive to decide in favor of the one true God, rather than merely to prefer that God to his rivals, means an overgoing of *The Faerie Queene*, with its pagan attachment to the continuing strife of deities, and its merely relative subordination of Mutabilitie to Jove's stable rule.

To sum up: the way that the secondary supplements or completes the primary in Milton—Eve is necessary and second to Adam just as both the Son and Satan are to the Father—ends in the actual fact of the first's displacement by the second. An Imaginary bond based on indefinable mutuality gives way to the harsh Symbolic imposing of definition through hierarchical power: this is the story of the fall familiar to all Milton's readers. This second stage of active displacement sets the impact of poetic pathos, which is impelled by the tragic struggles of belated characters, against doctrinal assertions of the source's necessary priority, that is, the Father's self-announcement as author of the terms of history. The latecomer's claiming of self appears more intensely felt, and therefore more powerful, than the schematic, doctrinal structure of an authority that would precede this claim and diminish it by determining its place in a larger order. Milton cannot, finally, subordinate the tragedy of a belated self to any greater sense, though he tries to do so in the final books of *Paradise Lost*. Here, in Milton's dark epic, the pathos of subjectivity coincides with the severest losses known to history: Eve's eating of death, the Son's sacrifice.

From almost the beginning of his career, in the harsh trump sounded by the Nativity Ode, Milton recognizes the importance of discontinuity to the birth of a true self. Truth means, not seamless integrity—since the pursuit of virginal wholeness might well lead to an idolatrous attachment to the image of one's own purity—but instead a history of encountering the decisive tests imposed by enemies who have cut the self off from its familiar, protective world. In the Nativity Ode, Milton attacks the pagan religious impulse that, by dispersing itself in its objects, forestalls the development of a self conscious of its separated status, and therefore of the potential for autonomy that conscience provides. As Christopher Kendrick writes, Milton's Protestantism charges a paganistic Catholicism with "multiplying false object-ties . . . sating desire by sticking it everywhere," and thereby impeding the focus necessary to the achievement of conscience. In answer to such fragmentation, Milton in subsequent works will offer models, beginning with *Comus*'s Lady, of a self-directed and therefore pious desire, one that precedes its objects. Faith must be prior to the symbols it invokes, so that these symbols will become signs of its inward power. But, as the case of the Lady shows, such inwardness courts a much more radical kind of idolatry, the danger of narcissistic self-absorption—becoming one's own idol. There is no opportunity for the test that proves authenticity, the dramatic encounter with a threatening other, if you already, presumptively, own yourself. Insulating itself from attack, chastity may end up as an icon that entraps the ascetic imagination in its self-concern. In the Lady as in Britomart, Kendrick remarks, "Chastely virtuous acts seem to spring from a spontaneous self-regard . . . and thus emit a curiously amoral effect . . . [chastity is] peculiarly threatened by its own intense flow, by formlessness and fixation."[9]

The Lady's chastity in its volatile, anxious energy, with her "rapt spirits" brimming on the edge of "sacred vehemence" (*Comus* 795–96), risks the possibility that it may lack form, the stability or solidity needed for faith. But, by pursuing a guarded self-assurance, chastity also risks an excess of stability—the fixation that ends in immobility, with the Lady's flesh stuck to Comus's stony chair. Milton opts for stasis over kinetic energy. The Lady's fixity, her untouchable and immovable virgin state, presents a youthfully extreme version of the embodiment of faith that Milton strives after.

In *Comus*, the issue of the image and the subjective pathos it elicits intertwines with the question of a spiritually achieved body. For Milton, conscience must embody itself—a grasp of lived, incarnate existence in its essential truth becomes the means for the soul's self-definition. As Stanley Cavell remarks, Wittgenstein's statement, "the human body is the best picture of the human soul," suggests that the body offers the *only* truly answerable expression of the soul.[10] Virtue or vice must be, not merely have, a bodily state. The soul, realized in this way, derives its authority from its vision of itself as a just body. Yet we strain against this realization; we think of the body as a representation of self sadly bound to the inevitable limits of the reified, an object that will not quite measure up to the soul that sees itself in it. When the argument between soul and body truly takes hold, it can turn us dangerously against ourselves, making us think that, because we are embodied, we are necessarily infected by a poisonous incapacity for spiritual expression. Spurned in this way, the body becomes mere dead matter, the earthly clog or clod so vividly present in the rhetoric of the Divorce

Tracts and *Comus's* Attendant Spirit, who sees the world's physicality as a "sin-worn mold."

There is a kind of desperation here that turns against the flesh, as if embodiment inherently opens up the possibility of its own defectiveness. How is it possible that the body might prove inadequate to the soul, and therefore not a true body? "As if unless the responses I reveal are the responses of the body that is me, I am not expressed. But why," Cavell asks, "should I want this, want it perhaps enough to die for it by leaving this body?"[11] We can never completely eliminate the idea of the body as representation, as an object to be accepted or rejected, in favor of the body as necessary and adequate expression. Even when we embrace the body's image as the definitive picture of the self, as Milton does in *Paradise Lost*'s Eden, this image remains an image, a representation rather than one flesh with the soul. The suspicion persists, therefore, that the body may turn out to be an empty idol, a mere Narcissus-like image projected by an alien spirit whose desires we then want to disown as not truly ours. At such a moment, when we panic over our fantasy that the sin-worn mold shackles us irredeemably, the body seems fatally other than the soul, corrupting rather than reflecting it. The soul can guard against this risk of alienation from embodiment only by seeing itself as a rarified entity accompanied by spiritual forces. In their palpability to the reader's imagination, though, these forces in their turn become embodied and therefore subject to delusive possibilities. When the Lady says of her guardian figures Faith, Hope, and Chastity "I see ye visibly" (*Comus* 216), she inadvertently reminds us that their shapes are not visible on stage—her effort to conjure assistance must fail because it still relies on the work of imagination, rather than a reality independent of and more powerful than poetic wishfulness.[12] Paradoxically, here imagination remains too *outside* the self. The Lady's career of virtue is not yet internal; she still wants to place her faith in the outward, alien characters her invention summons, and her faith therefore unmasks itself as fantasy. A few lines after the vision of Faith, Hope, and Chastity, the guide she seeks appears in the form of a wandering, deceptive cloud into which the Lady reads a silver lining:

> Was I deceiv'd, or did a sable cloud
> Turn forth her silver lining on the night?
> I did not err, there does a sable cloud
> Turn forth her silver lining on the night,
> And casts a gleam over this tufted Grove.
> (*Comus* 222–26)

Here the Lady *is* deceived. Her cloud is not a fortunate omen, as she assumes; instead, it heralds the appearance of Comus and the real beginning of her trouble. When the Lady echoes herself in describing the cloud, she exposes the hollowness or falling short that afflicts the nymph Echo, to whom she is about to sing—and who also figures the tricky fading of imagination into illusion. The Lady cannot predict or control the meaning of the shapes she draws on. When she hauntingly announces the onset of her temptation scene—"A thousand fantasies / Begin to throng into my memory, / Of calling shapes and beck'ning shadows dire" (205–7)—she reminds us that there is little difference between the shadowy fancies she feels invading her, forces that might be identified with poetry itself in its powerful insinuation of a pagan eros, and the protective figures that she summons (Hope, Faith, Chastity, Echo, the cloud).

When Comus, instead of Echo, answers the lady's song, the possibility suggests itself that this pair may somehow recapitulate the situation of Narcissus and Echo, that their seeming mismatch—with Comus now playing Echo to the Lady's Narcissus—may be apt. Comus, exclaiming, "Can any mortal mixture of earth's mold / Breathe such Divine enchanting ravishment?" (244–45), falls in love with the Lady's voice just as Echo does with Narcissus's. He gives himself away, surrendering his usual will to mastery to an Imaginary allure.

How is the Lady like Narcissus? The point of the Narcissus myth is that Narcissus is made to recognize himself as the image that masters him: "Iste ego sum," he finally cries in Ovid, "Quod cupio mecum est: inopem me copia fecit" (Met. 3.463, 466). At this moment of recognition, the beautiful self-sufficiency that Narcissus has assumed proves impossible: seeming *copia* turns to *inopia*, poverty. His self is revealed as radically lacking, forced to remain wedded to its shallow, equally defective double—his bodily image. Through his use of the Narcissus story, Milton instills a fear that the virtuous self, when it invokes its own embodied power, may turn out to be relying on the insubstantial. This fear, in turn, causes the Lady to withdraw altogether from her imagination; during her final showdown with Comus, she cannot risk the poetic power entailed by her Orphic threats. She reacts against the unreliable phantasms that earlier led her astray, into fantasy, by refusing to conjure *any* image. But the result of such iconoclasm is that she cannot move; locked in conflict with Comus, she becomes a Medusa imprisoned in aggressive fixity rather than a Diana, the "fair silver-shafted queen for ever chaste" (442) whose graceful autonomy eludes her opponents. The "Gorgon shield" and its "rigid looks of Chaste austerity" (448–51) redound on the Lady herself.

In Milton, Diana stands for chastity as the fluid potentiality of grace; Medusa represents a contrasting model of chastity as frozen violence. In the self's effort to move beyond the awkwardness of adolescent virginity, Diana provides an attractive model for avoiding an either/or decision between Il Penseroso's silent stasis and headlong flight, the allegro moves of a Britomart. The former alternative may mean getting trapped in a defensive, and therefore indefensible or cornered, assertion of autonomy. The latter may mean courting a self-delusive fantasy in which the happy wish to inhabit one's symbols outruns their answerability, as in the case of Spenser's Britomart.

But the Lady, trapped in her defensive, Medusa-like pose, cannot attain Diana's energy. She will not speak to Comus because she might ruin her voice's potential by realizing it in action. In this respect she resembles Milton, who sometimes fears that the integrity of his creative promise might be dissipated by too quick a passage into the actual deed of poetic invention. Diana's noble grace resolves this problem by slowing youthful, overeager ambition into an assured, tacitly coherent poise: Diana promises to mediate between repose and active risk by incorporating both staid permanence (she is "for ever chaste") and the swift exercise of power (her "silver-shafted" arrows). But we are still too early in Milton's career for Diana's erotic purity, and the fully mobile, yet integral, heroic self it implies, to come into its own.

In *Paradise Lost*, Diana appears full-blown in the shape of Eden's chaste married love, which avoids the Lady's aspiration to a frigid austerity while also avoiding libertine looseness. The encounter with the other as an event of continuous harmony sums up the poet's vision of unfallen relationship. Milton's pursuit of this vision of marriage as continuity begins in the divorce tracts, which precede *Paradise Lost*. Here, Milton's image of marriage tries to heal the division between an idealizing imagination and the tests of practical reality. Milton attempts this therapy by depicting marriage as a mirroring or reciprocity. But perfect harmony proves unreal and therefore ineffectual: the divorce tracts' ideal of reciprocal love fails to confront the actual facts of distance and sexual difference. (In a more mature fashion, *Paradise Lost*'s Eden will confront and try to overcome the defect of imagination in the face of the real, thus marrying reality and desire). As in the case of Narcissus's empty reciprocity, an ideal union risks merely conjuring an idolatrous picture of itself, to be undermined by the brutal reality of miserable marriages like Milton's own to Mary Powell.

*The Doctrine and Discipline of Divorce* couples self and other in wishful and rapturous union when it alludes to the figure of Anteros in Plato's *Phaedrus*. In Renaissance mythography, Anteros is the twin brother of Eros, his rival, counterpart and mirror image. Drawing on the Eros-Anteros image, Milton in *The Doctrine and Discipline of Divorce* explores its quest for the true double as a fable of "matrimonial love":

> Love, if he be not twin-born, yet hath a brother wondrous like him, called Anteros; whom while he seeks all about, his chance is to meet with many false and feigning desires that wander singly up and down in his likeness. ... Love. ... often deceived, embraces and consorts him with these obvious and suborned striplings, as if they were his mother's own sons, for so he thinks them. ... But after a while, as his manner is, when soaring up into the high tower of his Apogaeum, above the shadow of the earth, he darts out the direct rays of his then most piercing eyesight upon the impostures and trim disguises that were used with him. ... till finding Anteros at last, he kindles and repairs the almost faded ammunition of his deity by the reflection of a coequal and homogeneal fire.[13]

This passage from an unreliable, feigning fancy to a solid, answerable truth did not occur in the case of the Lady, though the end of *Comus* does image a mutual recovery from doubtful misadventure similar to the one that Plato depicts—the union of Cupid and Psyche after her wanderings. What enables the Platonic discovery of truth through a happy eros, as the subtext from the *Phaedrus* makes clear, is the reciprocal character of this love. But, tellingly, the reciprocity also entails illusion and imaginative projection:

> The springs of that stream which Zeus as lover of Ganymede named "desire" (*himeron ... ônomase*) flow in abundance upon the lover, some sinking within him, and some flowing off outside him as he brims over; and as a breath of wind or an echo rebounds from smooth hard surfaces and returns to the source from which it issued, so the stream of beauty passes back into its possessor through his eyes. ... like a man who has caught an eye-disease from someone he can give no account of it, and is unaware that he is seeing himself in his lover as if in a mirror. And when his lover is with him, like him he ceases from his anguish; when he is absent, again like him he longs and is longed for, because his return of love is a reflection of love (*kata tauta au pothei kai potheitai, eidôlon erôtos anterôta ekhôn*), though he calls what he has and thinks of it as friendly affection (*philian*) rather than love.[14]

Plato's apparent neologism "anteros" exploits the Greek prefix *anti* to suggest both a counter to or substitute for eros and a reflection of love in the form of the beloved's image of the absent lover. But as desire rebounds in this way, it deceives. In the myth of Anteros, the lover's ignorance of his love object provides the unstable basis for desire. The echo boomerangs, returning to its source, and the source is affected exactly because it does not know this desire is its own: "he ... is unaware that he is seeing himself in his lover." Like Narcissus, the lover can give no account of what he suffers (*kai outh' hoti peponthein ... eipein oud ekhei*) because he becomes the victim of a tricky mirroring of which he is unaware; he turns out to be the object rather than the subject of desire. The apparent mirroring, then, is really an asymmetry. Like Britomart in Malecasta's house, Plato's lover is subject to a sympathetic, unbalancing Imaginary passion.

Renaissance mythography reads Plato's Anteros in several conflicting ways—as a bad form of love analogous to the earthly Venus; as a figure who takes vengeance on behalf of spurned lovers; as Amor Lethaeus, who, as his name indicates, turns desire to oblivion. But Milton rejects all these options for a more truly reciprocal one that also stems from mythographic sources. Milton defines Anteros as a fitting and "coequal" "reflection," the summing of an erotic pair that provides answerable companionship rather than wishful illusion and the loss that attends it. By means of this revision, Milton offers a fragile, hopeful ideal of symmetry. Eros and Anteros are sometimes seen, as in Cartari's emblem book, facing each other and struggling over a palm frond; in Milton's reading, the struggle becomes complementary rather than destructive. The equality of this encounter repairs the misfiring inherent in Narcissus's, and the Platonic lover's, uneven mirroring. Here Milton opts for harmony over fallen, tragic separation.

The exact mirroring of Eros and Anteros in MIlton's revisionary myth makes up for the unevenness that the *Symposium* images when it refers Eros's ancestry to the union of Poros and Penia, want and plenty. Milton cites Plato's myth of love's genealogy in *The Doctrine and Discipline of Divorce*. But Milton revises Plato's citation of Poros and Penia, which appears in the divorce tract shortly before the figures of Eros and Anteros, to repair its problematic asymmetry. Plato's Socrates reports that "Love was the son of Penury, begot of Plenty," Milton says, because "the dignity and blessing of marriage is placed rather in the mutual enjoyment of that which the wanting soul needfully seeks than of that which the plenteous body would joyfully give away." Here Milton shies away from the principle of genesis, of giving, embodied in love's mother Poros and her spokeswoman Diotima; for him marriage is the encounter of two equally needful souls under the noble aegis of the father, Penia or want. Milton's passage reads more like Agathon's openly narcissistic vision of love in the *Symposium* than like Socrates'. For Agathon, as Joyce puts it in *Ulysses*, "love loves to love love." In Socrates' account, eros desires its opposite; its want can therefore never be filled by a happy "mutual enjoyment." Platonic eros stays productive because, perpetually different from itself, it gives and gives a future: it displaces itself in favor of an alien, yet unknown object. But like Agathon's, what Milton's eros wants is not Socratic difference but similarity: the flattering picture of itself, young, beautiful and virtuous, that it enjoys as partner in a true marriage.

But if Milton wants a perfectly sealed symmetry, he also (and more fundamentally, as we discover by the time of *Paradise Lost*) feels impelled toward a disjunctive and unpredictably chosen future, the gift basic to desire. Because of the risk of narcissism that symmetry suggests, *Paradise Lost* must turn away from the divorce tracts' figuring of marriage as an equal mirroring, for the epic insists on sexual difference, the fact that we desire an other who does not look like the self. The realization of difference happens at a specific moment: in Book 4's reflecting pool scene, Adam's distinction, his otherness to Eve, surfaces as the revealed moment of her decision to accept him. The duplicate syntax of Eve at the lake—"I started back, / It started back"— yields to a duplicitous mirroring that actually claims Adam's precedence rather than the first couple's symmetry: "Whom fliest thou? / Whom thou fliest, / Of him thou art."

The voice that leads Eve on to acceptance of Adam collaborates in her choice. Milton thus reveals the need for authority's nudging, and with it the possibility of diverging from authority that propels choice in the first place. Choice appears when Eve invokes a possible alternative path: "There had I fixed mine eyes till now." As the Fall nears, such potential for the alternative, for difference, will widen into the false prospect of autonomy, then into the displacement that stands at the source of Satanic envy. Poetic imagination's discovery of its own power—its at once chastening and enticing faculty of invention—here becomes synonymous with its realization that it is impossible to fix the distinction between autonomy and envious displacement. The heavenly voice promises Eve a safe, coherent fulfillment of self; however, actual fulfillment comes when she endangers this offer of Symbolic coherence, falling away from authority's exact truth through an extreme claim to subjectivity. Eve's real embodiment, her move from mere mirror image to autonomous flesh, arrives not in the promised xerox copies that the voice offers her ("multitudes like thyself" [4.474]) but in her palpable love-strife with Adam—and also, alas, in the vertigo, both exhilarating and terrifying, of Book 5's dream, which cannot compete with Adam's abstract explanation of how fancy's "wild work" (5.113) produces dream images. Eve's thrilling nausea during the dream offers a bodily proof that overtakes the doctrinal theory that Adam presents. A trangressive Imaginary pathos convulses the self more decisively than Eve could have foreseen. The danger of subjective pathos is its inclination to move beyond the limits set by the Symbolic authority that explains it; it tends to exceed that limit and remain inexplicably resistant to explanation.

In retrospect, Eve's lake looks to her "pure as th'expanse of heav'n" (4.456)—she revises her original exulting in her own impression so she can gesture toward the divine source it *prevented* her from seeing. Perhaps Milton's address to light in his Book 3 invocation similarly fixes him in an illusory hope of bringing heaven before his blind eyes, a glory shown, as to Tantalus, by a divine source that will evade, and punish, the ambitious author grasping for it. The prospect of imagination overstepping its bounds, encroaching on God's territory by narcissistically indulging in a projection of human fantasy onto him, provides Milton's own greatest temptation.

At times in *Paradise Lost*, Milton defends against the risks of the subjective pathos that imagination relies on by insisting that, in the fallen world, imagistic realization can only occur as reduction, not as the imaginative expansion that Satan hopes for. One thinks of Ithuriel's spear, whose touch deflates Satan, making him "return / Of force to [his] own likeness," "his own shape" (4.812–13, 819). As if he has internalized the spear's effect, Satan's drive to realize his own rebellion culminates in the irresistible compulsion to reduce his quest. Laughing, he boasts to his troops in Book 10 that he has seduced Eve "the more to increase / Your wonder, with an apple" (10.486 – 87). Satan here means to ruin the most important of *Paradise Lost*'s moods, wonder—a feeling first elicited in our response to the fallen angels of Books 1 and 2—by trivializing the object of admiration. Book 10 shows the wages of such reduction: Satan himself gets reduced to a snaky caricature. The mechanism of this metamorphosis is particularly interesting for my purposes because it reveals a continuity that fatally confuses a heroic self's attempt at autonomous meaning. God turns Satan's claim of success into its antithesis, as the applause of his troops becomes a hiss. The transformation reveals, in answer to Satan's desire to keep himself separate from the divine, that God can change seeming opposites into each other and reveal the basic, underlying homogeneity of his universe. (Of course, this was already the unwitting implication of Satan's "evil be thou my good," which inadvertently discloses the dependence of evil, in its wish to become a Burkean "God-term," on good.) In Adam's Satan-like speech of despair in Book 10, he predicts a similar collapsing of opposites when he imagines his descendants saying, "for this [that is, death and misery] we may thank *Adam*" (10.736). In this line, a blessing or word of thanks becomes an "execration" or curse (10.737).[15]

Milton links such reversal of meaning, which exposes the underlying ironic continuity of the world, to the parodic or distorting capacity of repetition. Though the inspired poet will claim that he faithfully increases and multiplies the words of his biblical source, for Adam after the Fall, the mere image or re-presentation of these words mocks his, and our, desire for a now unavailable original. As Adam, in his

Book 10 speech, cites scripture, he perverts the original sense of the text:

> O voice once heard
> Delightfully, *Increase and multiply*,
> Now death to hear! for what can I increase
> Or multiply, but curses on my head?
> (*PL* 10.729–32)

We have moved from Echo in Comus, to the partnering echo of Eros and Anteros in the *Doctrine and Discipline of Divorce*, to Adam's resounding of God's word: a cry bereft of any destination but his newly hollow self. All that will be increased are curses on Adam's head; he will generate sterility rather than fruitfulness, death over and over instead of Eden's ever-differentiated life. Milton's irony sums up the anxious, heated involvement of fallen desire in empty or destructive repetition. So Adam after the fall wishes that "For this one Tree had been forbidden ten" (9.1026),[16] and Eve in Book 9 fears the multiple copies, the "multitudes like thyself," that God promised her at Book 4's reflecting pool. Along with Eve, we see the birth of rivalry: it comes home to her that she might be replaced, rather than augmented, by a new version of woman ("I shall be no more, / And *Adam* wedded to another *Eve*" [9.827–28]). Already, the poet foreshadows the repetitious history of Books 11 and 12, with its multiple, echoing falls. Eve's consciousness that she is replaceable is allied to the cold self-estrangement present in this new rhetorical form, soliloquy, which does not occur before the Fall.

To Adam's horror, God's word has taken on a suddenly foreign meaning: he has been chosen, but for what terrible task? Why has God made him, "mould[ed him] man," in the first place (10.744)?[17] The presence of an alien but authoritative text in one's mouth defeats the basic Miltonic notions of inspiration and faith, which mean aligning oneself with the authority that stands behind one's statements. (Recovering, Adam in Book 11 will confidently name his spouse as she was named by God: "Hail to thee, Eve rightly call'd, / Mother of all Mankind" [11.158–59].) Nor can the cornered Adam here attempt the brave yet deferential equivocation of the poet's voice rising like the sun in Book 3: "May I express thee unblam'd?" (3.3). He has lost power.

Loss leads to another experiential reduction. Because authority, after the fall, now shows itself as foreign, as elsewhere, Adam and Eve generate standards based on their newly fallen experience—constraining, rigid measures. Fallen alienation requires a new model of severe comparison, of substitution and exchange: Eve says that unfallen pleasure "flat seems to this, and harsh" (9.987); Adam worries that "much pleasure we have lost" by falling so late (9.1022); and Eve fears that she falls "short / Of" Adam's "perfection" (9.963–64). Yet after the Fall, but before such drastic reduction to a strict economy of fallenness, Milton allows a brief space of opportunity for the discovery of a human invention that freely profits in the absence of a visible God. Eve, liberated by the fall, for a brief but immensely powerful moment breaks the dichotomy that Milton usually claims between idolatrous reliance on one's own imagination and submission to a superior authority. Immediately after eating the apple, she muses:

> And I perhaps am secret; Heav'n is high,
> High and remote to see from thence distinct
> Each thing on Earth, and other care perhaps
> May have diverted from continual watch
> Our great Forbidder, safe with all his Spies
> About him.
>
> (*PL* 9.811–16)

"Our great Forbidder!" As I read her, Eve is neither naively hopeful nor self-deluded here. Instead, she shocks herself with her sudden capacity to create an imaginative possibility. Now a free subjectivity, Eve discovers the power of fiction, which resides somewhat covertly at the center of Milton's own text—but with rather less than Milton's own anxiety at the discovery. The thought that she is "perhaps . . . secret" is not a shrinking before a higher power, as when she and Adam later sew fig leaves and hide from God. It is, rather, a wild, surprising surmise, with the air of a new beginning. (Eve's "early care" "each morning" will be to nourish the fantasy that sprang from the tree [9.799].) Picking up on Raphael's statement to Adam at 8.172–73— "Heav'n is for thee too high / To know what passes there"—Eve does not parodically reduce it. Instead, she inverts and elaborates Raphael's lines by imagining God as a paranoid intelligence, a comically negative "great Forbidder" so surrounded by "all his spies" that he cannot see what passes on earth. If Eve really were secret, the poem's categories would fall apart. But the "perhaps" is important here: Eve narrates a bizarre, attractive potentiality, not a fact. This is a new phenomenon. Before the Fall, wild imagination was merely introduced into Eve, as in the Book 5 dream. Here, she actively imagines, making her words her own instead of letting herself be victimized by authority's word. The depressed and fearful Adam, by contrast, will soon become a victim, mouthing scripture's curse with his "increase and multiply" speech.

At this point in *Paradise Lost*, Eve's crazy invention amounts to an escape from the authority of doctrine in favor of heightened "Experience" (a term she invokes at 9.807). As Wallace Stevens writes in "On the Road Home," a dialogue spoken by "two figures in a wood":

> It was when I said,
> "There is no such thing as the truth,"
> That the grapes seemed fatter.
> You ... you said,
> "There are many truths,
> But they are not parts of a truth."
> . . . . . . . . . . . . . . . . .
> It was at that time, that the silence was largest
> And longest, the night was roundest,
> The fragrance of the autumn warmest,
> Closest and strongest.[18]

By making her own fiction rival God's, Eve in her strong autumn or fall suggests that there really are many truths, and therefore no standing hierarchical distinction between sacred words and human ones. Nietzsche remarks in *Beyond Good and Evil* that, when we find ourselves in an aestheticizing rather than a moralizing mood, all religions seem beautiful fabrications. "The will to knowledge," Nietzsche writes, arises "on the basis of a far more powerful will, the will to non-knowledge, to the uncertain, to the untrue! Not as its antithesis but—as its refinement! ... here and there ... we laugh at how it is precisely the best knowledge that wants most to hold us in this simplified, altogether artificial, fabricated, falsified world, how it is willy-nilly in love with error because, as a living being, it is—in love with life!"[19] Eve's new knowledge is in love with its own error, because it is (desperately and fearfully, it's true) in love with life. She defeats the crude moralistic antithesis between the authoritative Word and humanity's willful deviations from it.

At the moment of Eve's speech, Milton suggests a protoromantic recuperation of the Lady's fantasy as free imagination, careless of any guardian's moral authority. But after Eve has spoken, as Michael begins to take over the narrative, a far more constrained universe appears. The rest of Milton's poem offers an account of fallenness as the fixation on, rather than the free play with, an image; as past rather than future directed.

## II. The Final Books

In recent years the final books of *Paradise Lost* have enjoyed a series of distinguished readings from some of Milton's best critics: Stanley Fish, Mary Ann Radzinowicz, George Williamson, Barbara Lewalski, and others.[20] Why then, yet once more, the final books? A partial answer is suggested by a look back at the list of critics I have mentioned.

Most of them belong to the school of interpretation that presents a picture of Milton as a successful and calmly assured didactic poet. This is exactly where I believe that Milton criticism has gone wrong: not, to be sure, in underestimating Milton's desire to instruct his readers but in attributing to him an overoptimism about his hopes of didactic success. In the final books fallen education faces its hardest test. Despite their persuasive brilliance, and the lasting illumination they have brought to the difficult question of Miltonic teaching, we may still ask whether Milton's neo-Christian readers (to revive Empson's derogatory appellation) might be claiming too unequivocal a clarity for this poetry, preventing them from really taking the measure of the trial to which Milton subjects Michael's teaching. I argue against Fish's interpretation as representative of the critical line that prizes Milton's didactic efficiency above his testing of this didacticism.

Fish asserts that Michael's didactic plan wins out over experience: in effect, that Milton fully endorses Michael's abstract, transcendent version of truth rather than Adam's passionate reactions to the history he sees.[21] In Fish's view, Milton rejects the palpable, and therefore false, reactions of the first fallen reader, Adam, in favor of otherworldly abstractions that may more accurately convey doctrinal truth. The divine, in this reading, shows itself superior to human pathos; it cannot be grasped through our emotional responses, which distort truth by submitting it to a subjective bias.[22] According to Fish, then, Milton makes Michael's speeches less emotionally impressive than Adam's reactions for the same reason that he makes Book 3's God the Father a less exciting speaker than Book 2's Satan: to demonstrate the dispassionate quality that marks God's truth as more than merely human.

The considerable eloquence and sophistication of Fish's reading has had a revolutionary impact on Milton studies. But it fails to take Milton's own implicit questioning of Michael into account. As a result, Fish misses the double-edged character of Milton's reflection on didacticism in the final books. The poet himself argues at times against Michael and his neo-Christian partisans Fish and Lewalski. By making the immediate pathos of a separated self, Adam's reactions to the shock of historical evil, overshadow Michael's comforting didactic abstractions, Milton casts doubt on Michael's charge that Adam's emotions are delusive and superficial, inferior to the invisible clarity of moral truth. Milton thus brings into question the truth of the morality Michael expounds, with its discovery of a justification for divine judgment founded in the clear but too distant pattern of sacred history.

The issue of Christian iconoclasm is central here, given the close connection that the iconoclast assumes between emotions and visual images.[23] In Books 11 and 12, Milton, wary of the insidious pathos of the visual, tries to flatten the images of fallen history in order to make them less risky, less promising for a rebellious or freely questioning imagination. But even though Michael attempts to cast his tableaux as merely instrumental or expendable bearers of a doctrinal message, Adam wrestles with Michael's doctrine through subtle, sophisticated acts of interpretation that will prove more familiar and true to us than the angel's abstract definitions of God's order.

Milton, then, reduces his images of history in the final books to the dully sensational in an unsuccessful effort to diminish their profound connection with Adam's emotional subjectivity, which guides his readings of the fallen world. The poet tries to make the image shallow in an effort to ward off the possibility that pictorial expression, by incarnating the divine in forms amenable to human fantasy, may nourish our interpretative power at the expense of God's authority. But Milton knows his own ambivalence in this matter, and he ends by brilliantly privileging Adamic subjectivity over Michael's dual interest in the abstract and the bluntly spectacular.

Michael's use of spectacle has something in common with a Christian didacticism that turns the pathos instilled by images to immediate moralizing effect. For example, Thomas Beard's *Theatre of God's Judgments* (1598) avidly exploits emotionally powerful visions for moralizing ends.[24] Beard represents a tradition in Christian historiography of bending history to didactic purpose by graphically depicting, in tableau or "theatrical" form, the more gruesome of God's judgments, from the plagues on Egypt and the burning of Sodom to contemporary disasters.[25] Beard in his history particularly delights in showing the "most strange and horrible death[s]" of the ungodly, whether tyrants, rebels, or persecuting Catholics. As he points out happily, "generally few persecutors escaped without some evident and markable destruction."[26] God's power, for Beard, lies in the prediscursive, instantaneous nature of his miracles, and his audience's astonishment at them. The "evident and markable" shock of the miraculous is supposed to persuade by the sheer force of the image, moving our recognition of divine judgment before the intervention of verbal argument. Such theatrical moralism as Beard's provides a powerful weapon in the pulpit: the preacher relies on his ability to discourage sin by vividly describing the monstrous horrors that will inevitably repay the sinner.

Michael exploits, but also draws back from, such an intense conflation of the visual image and its moral point. Many Reformation iconoclasts, like Michael, differ from Beard and others in their worry about presenting divine authority as "evident and markable." To show God's power as spectacle is to run the serious risk of turning him into a Satanic magician, a figure who would elicit fascinated desire rather than faith.[27] Reformation iconoclasm and antitheatricalism, in acute consciousness of this risk, often oppose the idea of displaying Christian doctrine in *any* visual form.

Milton himself remains divided over whether intelligible traces of God's historical judgment exist. In 1660's *Readie and Easie Way*, published on the eve of the Restoration, Milton presents the palpable evidence of natural disasters in London during the reign of Charles I, "the frequent plagues and pestilences that then wasted this citie," as proof of God's disapproval.[28] But in his last pamphlet, *Of True Religion* (1673), Milton explicitly rejects this method of estimating God's will through the apparent evidence of famine, flood or plague. Here Milton insists that the true signs of sin are invisible. The plague of 1665 and fire of 1666 had been widely taken as indications of the coming apocalypse,[29] but in Milton's view God had by the 1670s become far too disappointed by mankind's sinfulness to employ any longer such visible signs of his judgment:

> For God, when men sin outragiously, and will not be admonisht, gives over chastizing them, perhaps by Pestilence, Fire, Sword, or Famin, which may all turn to their good, and takes up his severest punishments, hardness, besottedness of heart, and Idolatry, to their final perdition.[30]

Like his contemporaries Richard Baxter and Thomas Goodwin, Milton in *Of True Religion* draws a distinction between the "carnal," superstitious fear of God prompted by the tangible threats of "Pestilence, Fire, Sword, or Famin" and the authentic, internalized religion of the sinner "working out his salvation with fear and trembling," "the trouble and melancholy . . . of true religion and amendment."[31] But like them, Milton remains dedicated to his own very palpable, and in some strange sense carnal, imagination of things divine.

Here and elsewhere in his work, Milton's iconoclasm addresses not just his anxiety about what Calvin calls the "heathenish" superficiality of images but also his intense concern with their capacity to elicit narcissistic fantasy, the "human ingenuity" that, intoxicated with its own imaginative power, substitutes human for divine work. Milton in his early prose pamphlet, *Of Reformation* (1641), seems to have agreed with the Edwardian humanists' reading of icons as merely vulgar rather than seductively inward vehicles of imagination. The humanists who surrounded the Lord Protector Somerset in Edward's reign opposed religious images not because they represented the dangerous transformation of the divine into the human, but because they were symbols of superstitious folly, the "gross" aspect of popular worship.[32] In *Of*

*Reformation*, accordingly, the "costly and deare-bought . . . snares of Images, Pictures, rich Coaps, gorgeous Altar-Clothes" that the Prelates exploit feebly ape the divine. Milton argues that the grotesquely defective character of such images will be easily evident to the educated Protestant. *Of Reformation* claims that the idolatrous Prelates "justly fear that the quick-sighted *Protestants* eye clear'd in great part from the mist of Superstition, may at one time or other looke with a good judgement into these their deceitful Pedlaries."[33] In effect, this view denies to idolatry a large part of its enticing Satanic power, its fascinating offer to fulfill our desire for godhead, by implying that it can sway only the uneducated, "superstitious" masses.

But the poet's imagination, in its dramatizing of the divine, poses a danger, and a promise, to himself and his fit audience far more serious than that of the facile Catholic icons derided by the Edwardians and by the early Milton. Because images provoke passionate and complex responses—the responses of a free individual subject—they may present a threatening antithesis to religious truth even when they offer themselves as its vehicles.

In response to his realization of the way that images offer opportunity to our free thinking, Milton, fairly often in the final books, transforms their complexity into the straightforwardly lurid. Defending against the force of the image by exploiting his God-given power to reduce it to the simply horrifying, Michael provides an overwhelming picture of death in Book 11. Michael invokes death's force as a devastating monotony reechoing to the end of time. There are, he reports,

> many shapes
> Of Death, and many are the ways that lead
> To his grim Cave, all dismal. . . .
> (*PL* 11.467–70)

Michael also asserts that the invisible ethical meaning of mortality signifies more powerfully than its grotesque and alarming shapes: death is, he says, "to sense / More terrible at the entrance than within" (11.469–70). This is a clear example of doctrinal abstraction taking the stage. Strangely, though, Michael makes an exceedingly dismal image the basis for his anti-imagistic point when he describes Cain's brutal murder of Abel:

> [Cain] inly rag'd, and as they talk'd,
> Smote him into the Midriff with a Stone
> That beat out life; he fell, and deadly pale
> Groan'd out his soul with gushing blood effus'd.
> (*PL* 11.444–47)

The fervent immediacy of Michael's description deserves to be pondered. Though he shows Adam these scenes of history in order to speak against the power of the visible "shapes" they present, Michael's lesson still relies on the encapsulating impact of the visible. Michael's "Death thou hast seen / In his first shape on man" (11.466 – 67) defines death as a figure literally present to our sight. The "first" shape is the authoritative, primal one: *this* tableau will forever, over and over, be implanted in Adam's and the reader's memory. Like an inhumanly tenacious, imprisoning mask, death casts "his first shape *on* man." As in the case of Ithuriel's spear, which turns Satan back to his trivial "real" form, it seems here that the poetic image can only be realized as gruesome caricature, definitively imprisoning human existence in bodily form. Similarly, the Lady's virgin body traps her in *Comus:* she can only be released when she metamorphoses into her antitype, Eve. But in Michael's version, pathos and its sensory embodiment assume a blunter, cruder shape than Eve's paradise knew.

The stark imagistic force that Milton offers in the final books stands in contrast to the landscape of unfallen Eden. Adam and Eve in Eden share in a hospitable experiential subtlety, a "sacred and homefelt delight" (to cite Comus's reaction to the Lady's song) far removed from the rather stiff and programmatic shock effects of these fallen scenes. The striking visuals make it difficult for Adam to pursue a sensitive reading of the Abel-Cain episode—but he does. First, we must set Adam's reading in a Reformation context critical of Catholic sacramental practice. Luther speaks for anticeremonial Protestants, including Michael, when he reminds us that "what justified Abel was by no means his sacrifice, but his faith; for by this he gave himself up to God, and of this his sacrifice was only the outward figure."[34] Similarly, Calvin's commentary on the Cain and Abel story interprets Cain as external ceremony, Abel as internal faith.[35] Luther and Calvin provide ammunition for Fish's pro-Michael reading, and Michael himself helps out the Fish argument when he makes his anticeremonial criticism of Adam clear elsewhere in the final books by arguing against Adam's desire to raise "grateful Altars" to God (11.323, 335–54.). In Michael's typically Protestant view, Adam, despondent because Abel's "due rites" (11.440) seem to have failed to convince God of his dutifulness, remains too fixated on the palpable aspect of such "rites," on visible rewards like Eden's "sweet / Recess" (11.303–4) and visible punishments like Abel's murder. Michael offers instead a more rarified justice, the undefined compensation that he cites as God's gift to the virtuous (11.459).[36] With the Reformers, and in opposition to Adam's apparently superficial reaction, Michael suggests that the injustice done to Abel's character, not the horrible manner of his death or its incongruity with the Old Law correctness of his sacrifice, remains the essential fact about his death.

But Michael's interpretation of Adam's reaction underestimates his pupil. Adam is shocked first of all by the idea that "great mischief hath befall'n / ... that meek man, who well had sacrificed" (11.450–51): he intuitively discerns Abel's goodness or "meek"ness in the manner of his sacrifice. Instead of stopping at the sacrifice's outward appearance, he uses it as an index to moral character. Abel's faith appears in his gesture, with an integrity perhaps no longer current in our vastly fallen existence. Only after Michael's emphatic revelation of Abel's identity as his son does Adam react to the sheer sight of Abel's death. Adam's first reaction is ethical, reinforced by his sheer horror at what he sees: the sacrifice of the wrong man (which, unknown to him, will be repeated and transcended in Christ's death). Adam is not solely or primarily invested in appearances.[37]

In truth, it is Michael, not Adam, who avoids the central problem of the Cain-Abel episode: the invisibility of the blessing awarded to Abel. Michael, himself "moved" and challenged by the killing of Abel (11.453), cannot justify God's universe by depicting historical events, only by invoking an abstract notion that Abel's faith will "lose no reward" (11.459). Michael's inability to reward Abel's faith in visible terms leads him to denigrate the substantial reality of history altogether—and therefore, as we have seen, to reduce it to lurid pictorial form—in favor of an easier moralism based on invisible spiritual compensation. Adam, by contrast, when he takes the scenes of history as profound matter for ethical judgment, returns our attention to the problem of divine (in)justice presented in its most concrete, palpable shape.

Milton's apocalyptic forecast in Book 12, the scene of the Son's triumph over Satan, emphasizes Michael's exploitation of the visual rather than Adam's shaken, tentative responses. Michael finally does promise historical compensation for fallen evil when he suggests that the world after the Second Coming "shall all be paradise, far happier place / Than this of Eden" (12.464–65). But the hope that finally sustains Adam and Eve, the achievement of what Michael calls a "paradise within thee, happier far" (12.587), means that they must counter their yearning for a literally present new Eden by internalizing it. As Eve beautifully tells Adam, "With thee to go / Is to stay here" (12.616–17).

In his tense and vivid depiction of the crucifixion in Book 12, which directly precedes the passage on the Second Coming I have cited, Michael poses the miraculous new Eden that the Son promises against the internalized law he also represents, the ethical message of the paradise within. Both the outward and the inward answer to evil somewhat awkwardly address the violent gap between Christian teaching and reality that afflicts fallen history:

> For this he shall live hated, be blasphem'd,
> Seiz'd on by force, judg'd, and to death condemn'd
> A shameful and accurst, nail'd to the Cross
> By his own Nation, slain for bringing Life;
> But to the Cross he nails thy Enemies,
> The Law that is against thee, and the sins
> Of all mankind, with him there crucifi'd,
> Never to hurt them more who rightly trust
> In this his satisfaction; so he dies,
> But soon revives, Death over him no power
> Shall long usurp; ere the third dawning light
> Return, the Stars of Morn shall see him rise
> Out of his grave, fresh as the dawning light
>
> ... this act
> Shall bruise the head of Satan, crush his strength
> Defeating Sin and Death, his two main arms....
> (*PL* 12.411–35)

This passage enacts a tension between the abstract statement of a law of "faith not void of works" and the palpable image of one sublime work, the "God-like act" that "annuls" Adam's "doom." These lines begin with a vengeful chiasmus, a furious depiction of Christ the judge nailing man's "Enemies" to the cross as the savior has himself been nailed, "shameful and accurst." But as the passage continues Milton softens the energetic reality of Christ's enemies into an abstraction. Christ crucifies the "Law" and the "sins / Of all mankind," not Satan. The quality of rarified, detached moral definition here means to remind us that "enemy" is a bodiless term, not a dramatic reality. Yet the dramatic force of the passage remains, in somewhat ungainly linkage with its insistence that the combat is really an abstract one. "But to the cross he nails thy Enemies / The Law that is against thee": the first line thrusts forward into drama; the second draws back into the merely abstract. The afterimage of a dramatic situation, Christ's vengeful anti-crucifixion of Satan and his followers, persists, despite the doctrinal abstraction of "the Law."

By staging the crucifixion in direct proximity to the Second Coming—the rather significant intervening period is swallowed by a line break ("So he dies, / But soon revives")—Milton at once provides an apocalyptic optimism and finds it lacking. This cannot be the conclusion of *Paradise Lost* exactly because it depends on such an enormously willful elision of the world we know. In an important sense, apocalypse will not work here because, in addition to being determinedly wishful and therefore finally unrealistic, it is also too unregenerately real. The crucifixion and resurrection present an evident, and strident, revenge on Cain's descendants, but the blunt visibility of this outcome entraps Milton and his readers in a drive to caricature and simplify like Satan's own. With his depiction of the crucifixion, the poet resurrects an image that Michael has, just a few lines earlier, denied to Adam: the picture of Christ's triumph over Satan as a "local wound" or "duel." "Dream not of thir fight," Michael told Adam, "As of a Duel, or the local wounds / Of head or heel": Christ will "recure" human mortality "Not by destroying Satan, but his works / In thee and in thy seed" (12.386–95). But the picture of Christ dragging Satan in chains "through all his Realm" that Michael now presents is far from abstract or "invisible" (12.455). This is exactly the kind of local, visible "duel" that the angel has warned Adam against imagining.

It is important to add that *Paradise Lost* finally detaches itself from such rancorous, apocalyptic pathos, conscious that apocalypse may be merely an escapist strategy designed to ward off the demands of the mortal present. Wary of this escapist tendency, Milton withdraws from his reliance on Michael's aggressively visible proofs of providential judgment. The end of Book 12 removes its readers from both Michael's spectacle and his doctrine when Adam shifts away from the extremes of joy and lamentation and gains an even, steadfast realism. The last lines of *Paradise Lost* are, then, in a real sense, the return of Eden's nuanced world, after Michael's too sharply drawn agons of good and evil in the final books.

Book 11 rescued Adam from his solitary despair in Book 10, his feeling that he was "beyond all past example and future / To Satan only like both crime and doom," only to submerge his example in the more desperate and massive reality of history. But the final self-sufficiency of Eve and Adam depends on their distance from this history. The sublime grandeur of universal narrative, along with the melodramatic emotion of Adam as isolated sinner, departs to ensure a space for the separated yet reconciled self, a "solitary way." At the conclusion of Milton's epic we remark a new sense of domestic intimacy that, because it has passed through tragic loss, is both at home in the world and poised in defensive anticipation of worldly disasters. We take in the exhilarating and melancholy shock of knowing that our fallen life begins with Adam and Eve. They dwell "on even ground now with [their] sons" (11.348).

# 7
# *Paradise Regained* and *Samson Agonistes*

> Thence what the lofty grave tragedians taught
> In chorus or iambic, teachers best
> Of moral prudence, with delight received
> In brief sententious precepts, while they treat
> Of fate, and chance, and change in human life;
> High actions, and high passions best describing....
> —Satan in *Paradise Regained*, 4.261–66

The final books of *Paradise Lost* show Milton's ambivalence, his attachment to both Michael's abstract moralism and Adam's experiential emotion. Experience, arguing against moralism's practice of easy closure, claims that moralism merely reduces the human world. But Michael's didactic speeches, as we have seen, also offer a guiding authority that tries to clarify and render schematic the meaning of worldly commitments by adopting an alienating distance from them. In *Paradise Lost* the poet, attached to both moralizing authority and its subjectivist antithesis, cannot resolve this debate, though he does, briefly and resonantly, move beyond it at the very end of *Paradise Lost*, with its haunting glimpse of exiled domesticity. The companion poems of Milton's 1671 volume, *Paradise Regained* and *Samson Agonistes*, display markedly more skepticism than *Paradise Lost* does about the capacity of a didactic project like Michael's to answer adequately to experience.

In this chapter, I focus on Milton's demonstration that moralism, by relying on a predictable narrative goal, proves itself inadequate to the contingencies embodied in individual lives. In *Samson Agonistes*, Manoah and the Chorus stand for such interest in a foreseeable future, in violation of Samson's unique and mysterious destiny. In *Paradise*

*Regained*, the Son counters Satan's dependence on historical prediction, first through withholding discourse about his future, then through actively, unpredictably changing the terms of his contest with Satan on the pinnacle. The Son asserts his future by detaching himself from his audience's, as well as Satan's, worldly expectations. Here, as in *Paradise Lost*, Milton establishes himself as a poet of discontinuity, of authoritative separation: the Son exemplifies our cherished and unrealizable hope to free the self from the uncontrollable influence of a history that has already occurred, the Satanic fall that situates the Son's rise. The Son's hope for autonomy falls at the end of *Paradise Regained*, but so does Satan's plan to manage and control the Son's future.

For most of *Paradise Regained*, the Son's cool, Stoic posture provides him with the needed distance from Satan's controlling narrative. But at the poem's end, as at the end of *Samson*, the pathos of an astonished audience—both Satan and we who witness his fall—becomes the necessary means to remove the hero from the Satanic reading that has threatened to entrap him. At the end of *Paradise Regained*, the Son departs sharply from his usual taut, plain style. In the course of the poem, he has repeatedly refused the temptation to use emotion to make his didactic point, to accompany "sententious precepts" with "high passions," as Satan puts it in the passage I quote as epigraph for this chapter. Milton's wariness of pathos during most of *Paradise Regained* goes hand in hand with the poem's vision of the Son's identity. At 1.260–67. the Son begins to discover who he is by reading about himself in the Bible; at the beginning of Book 2 Milton asserts this theoretical or textualized form of discovery over more experiential, passionate versions of self-feeling. Even Mary's speech, which like the disciples' laments begins in melodramatic pathos, ends by subordinating the mother's emotional torment to the father's impassive word: "I to wait with patience am inur'd; / My heart hath been a store-house long of things / And sayings laid up, portending strange events" (2.103–4). Mary removes herself from her "afflictions" (92) by adopting the mode of her son in Book 1, searching the text of the Bible for evidence of her role ("as old Simeon plain foretold," 87).[1] But such calm taking stock of oneself on the basis of established textual hints cannot, finally, form the foundation for the Son's power. Instead, he must rely on the original dramatic force of his argument with Satan.

The conclusion of *Paradise Regained*, like that of *Samson Agonistes*, uses the reader's emotional response to turn from the providential to the enigmatic. At the end of *Samson*, Samson forsakes his earlier efforts to define history as a lawful pattern and turns to unpredictability instead, in the form of his shocking victory over the Philistines. Like Samson, the Son must make history unexpected and dramatically surprising—

"dark / Ambiguous and with double sense deluding," to borrow his own characterization of pagan oracles (1.435). In both poems, the hero turns from a view of the future as repetition of the past and opens himself to a future that is more obscure and therefore more answerable to the mysterious relation between the divine and the human.

Such pathos of the unexpected, I will suggest, binds the Son to an encounter with Satan, though the Son, with unprecedented definitiveness, wants to refuse any such dependence on his adversary. The Son tries to detach himself from his double, Satan, in to assert a pure self-sufficiency. As in *Paradise Lost*'s crucifixion scene, the most tempting form of pathos in *Paradise Regained* is anger, which promises to overcome the dangerously similar other, Satan, by annihilating him. In *Paradise Lost*, the Son's rage revealed him locked in static conflict with Satan; here, Milton hopes more boldly that the Son's redemptive power may achieve a freeing turn of narrative. *Paradise Regained* cannot prove the autonomy of goodness; the Son remains implicated in an Imaginary rivalry with Satan even as he breaks from his antagonist.

Samson, like the Son, will end his career with a shocking spectacle. And in *Samson Agonistes*, as in *Paradise Regained,* the pathos elicited by this destructive show, the ruin of the Philistines and their temple, finally suggests the continuity of good and evil rather than their independence. Samson comes into his own only by uniting himself to the force he has resisted, his Philistine opponents—by "d[ying] with the Philistines," as the Biblical account puts it. In *Samson*, Milton reveals the pathos of continuity as a Dionysian force capable of generating a future inexplicably different from the past. This future resists any assimilation of Samson into history: as at the puzzling conclusion of *Paradise Regained*, where we wonder about the significance of the Son's "private" and "unobserv'd" return to his mother's house, Samson's audience remains distant and uncomprehending. Both heroes, finally, stay secret, hidden from our understanding.

During most of its narrative, *Paradise Regained* renounces the spectacular, or, more accurately, stigmatizes and diminishes spectacle by associating it with Satan's tawdry theatricality. After the Father's baptismal blessing of his son early in the poem (1.276–79), miraculous voices cease. This ascesis corresponds to the subdued discipline of the poem's style: Milton tries to give his readers only what is necessary. The poet's laconic, even tacit mode responds to need rather than desire.[2] Need can be answered with a specific, concrete object—perhaps a biblical passage like "man does not live by bread alone"; need wants a definitive answer as desire, which really wants its own persistence in unsatisfaction, does not. Yet need as such, prior to both the Imaginary and the Symbolic, cannot in its impoverished literalism generate an identity for the young Messiah. He must move beyond the search for a father's Word that would supply a simple and simply available resolution to Satan's testing. In place of his earlier, too precocious insistence on an easily available scriptural identity—when, perusing the Bible, he "soon found of whom they [i.e., the prophets] spake/I am" (1.262–63)—the Son must achieve a more sophisticated and inventive Symbolic mastery over the Word and therefore over Satan. The Symbolic occurs at the site of Imaginary desire, even as it attempts to supersede it by discarding the presence of Satan. The latter, as the Son's Imaginary partner, remains necessary to his character even as the Son tries to rise above him through the Symbolic. Milton's readers, like Satan, still inhabit the world of earthly desire; the Son himself wants a puzzling, alluring conclusion that will outdo Satan's magic—he too remains implicated in the Imaginary.

Like *Samson*, *Paradise Regained* exploits the resistance of pathos and its Imaginary impulse to the moral legibility of Symbolic plot. By means of this resistance, Milton questions the feasibility of the public didactic goals that he espoused in early texts like *Of Reformation* and *The Reason of Church Government*, as well as the final books of *Paradise Lost*. In *Paradise Regained*, the Son avoids future certainty, the glory he knows will be his, in the name of a darker divine destiny that can evade the criterion of foreseeable narrative results that Satan has appropriated. Just as Samson learns to resist the urge to explain his failures as a clear, "legal" pattern, the Son in *Paradise Regained* forswears the temptation to interpret his victory in terms of the established cycles of secular history—a temptation that Christian theology has warned against from Augustine on. Such predictive foresight would mean defining success in the terms commanded by Satan,[3] who stakes his case on his talent for forecasting the Messiah's reactions, motives, and future career.

The Son restrains himself from overtly battling Satan's emphasis on prediction until the very end of Book 3. Up to this point, he rebuts with calculated silence Satan's persistent references to worldly fortune as a threat that can be tamed through a Machiavellian (or Satanic) faculty of pragmatic, political calculation. In response, the Son is careful not to prophesy his assurance of his future dominion. Even Book 3's prophecy ends with the Son's retraction of his stated future: henceforth oracles are ceased. In Book 4, similarly, the Son answers Satan's temptations to secular empire not by voicing his assurance of the divine outcome, eager though he is to display his knowledge, but by suppressing his voice and claiming the necessary opacity of God's plan. The hermetic quality of the Son's power, like that of the Gospels' mysterious parables, resists interpretation in order to defend the faith against simplifying didacticism—the Pharisaic need for a palpable proof or "sign" (Mark 8:12) that would authenticate the Messiah's identity by making narrative sense of his actions.[4]

The question of narrative pattern also involves the Son's own development: a precocious rabbinical scholar (1.210–15) or *Gaon,* he claims to have always already been what he is. But this claim is, in the end, not enough: the Son must enter into his father's dominion, must authenticate himself, through a dramatic action that creates his maturity. Even though he synopsizes his future early in the poem (2.111–12), the Son must still come upon or discover it. His desire to create a shocking break in the narrative, to realize prematurely his future status as apocalyptic victor over Satan, proves to be his only means of achieving his office, though it represents the aspect of the Son that is too close to the Satan who rebelled—too much like the enemy in its edgy impatience, and too responsive to his angry stimulus.[5]

Pathos, then, stands here as in *Paradise Lost* for the potential for radical difference, for a discontinuity in plot realized first of all in Satan's revolt and continued in the Son's victory over him. But not even Satan's wish for a melodramatic newness can avoid emulating the paternal authority it shocks, most notably the Father's impulse to hierarchical order. The Son as well, in his rebellion against Satan, sometimes mimes those aspects of his precursor, the Father's older, disobedient heir, that he most loudly protests. For example, the Son's reliance on pathos for a time actually enforces the predictability that Satan invokes, the need for security that he leans on so heavily after his fall. The Son's desire to show his divinity courts the ironic danger that the fulfillment of divine will may be a mere repetition of the Old Law that Satan cites so often, rather than the prophesied superseding of the Old by the New. For example, in answer to Satan's temptation of worldly kingdoms in Book 3, the Son describes the conversion and ensuing repatriation of the Jews. He envisions the Israelites' return, which is traditionally seen as a sign that the Second Coming is imminent, as a repetition of their crossing of the Red Sea. His Father, says the Son,

> ... at length, time to himself best known,
> Rememb'ring *Abraham,* by some wond'rous call
> May bring them back repentant and sincere,
> And at their passing cleave the *Assyrian* flood,
> While to their native land with joy they haste,
> As the Red Sea and *Jordan* once he cleft,
> When to the promis'd land thir Fathers pass'd;
> To his due time and providence I leave them.
> (*PR* 3.430–37)

The Son here expresses not the desire for a liberating antitype, for the qualitatively different fulfillment that he elsewhere promises but rather the wish for a replay of the historical exodus.[6] The Son's fervent literalism as he pictures the Israelites returning to their homeland—"to their native land with joy they haste"—shows that he is indulging in an impulse for graphic, and geographic, prophetic fulfillment that has something in common with Satan's thirst for power. The Son now seems swayed by the urgent zeal with which Satan, earlier in this book, tried to tempt him (3.172–73: "Zeal and Duty are not slow, / But on Occasion's forelock watchful wait")—as well as by Satan's predilection for historical repetition (1.104–5: "The way found prosperous once / Induces best to hope of like success").

In Book 3, the Son, by defining the apocalyptic future in literal, overtly topographical terms, as a return to Israel, seems to be making assumptions close to Satan's own about the power of the brute facts of history and geography. (For example, when Satan gives his literalistic military advice in the next book he tells the future Messiah to enlist the Parthians rather than the Romans as allies, because Parthia is nearer and more dangerous to Israel [3.360–70.].)

But the Son tempers the prophecy's blunt reliance on a conclusive image by stating that God "may bring [the Israelites] back repentant and sincere," at some "time to himself best known." His zealous wish for a visible conclusion to history that will outdo Satan's fantasies, a "wond'rous call" to rouse mankind, yields to a patience that is willing to let the certain appear uncertain. In this passage, then, the Son cautiously withdraws from his desire for historical fulfillment, refusing to let Satan coax him into tipping his hand. Just after the reference to the redeemed hasting with joy to their native land, the Son adds, "To his [i.e., his father's] time and providence I leave them." Once again, the Son patiently and deliberately withholds an expression of his plot's future.[7] Similarly, early in Book 4 the Son, after aggressively offering Satan the image of his kingdom as "a stone that shall to pieces dash / All Monarchies besides throughout the world" (4.149–50), draws back from the image of inevitability his aggression implies. These lines hint at the poem's revelation of the Son's spectacular power in its final episode, when he crushes Satan while being dramatically saved by angels from dashing his own foot against a stone. But that moment is not yet: the Son pauses and withholds his realization of the apocalyptic image. "Means there shall be to this, but what the means, / Is not for thee to know, nor me to tell" (4.152–53).

The Son's characteristic insistence that redemption is an internal transformation of the soul and therefore cannot be pictured—that it dwells "in pious hearts, an inward oracle" (1.463)—also argues against his Old Law picture of the Israelites' conversion as a reminder of exodus, a return rather than a transformation.[8] But Satan disputes this emphasis, exploiting the Son's characteristic internalizing inclination in the interest of worldly, predictable results. In Book 4 Satan responds to the Son's strategy of withdrawal from spectacular fulfillment by offering him an inward or character-based definition of heroism. Significantly, this definition is a Stoic one, revealing Stoicism's impulse to attain security over the future. By tempting the Son with the characteristically internalized rhetoric of Stoic morality, rather than material success, Satan tries to expand his domain from the world and the flesh to the inward self-discipline that the Son has claimed as his own. Yet worldly dominion remains the real telos. "These rules will render thee a King complete / Within thyself," Satan says, "much more with Empire join'd" (4.1283–84). Successful inwardness here entails outward victory as well: according to Satan's crude literalization of the Stoic image of self-rule, metaphorical empire over one's passions is a worthwhile goal because it implies a sure potential for real, political empire.[9]

Satan's outward turn, his offering of kingdoms, gives away the tempter's this-worldly bias. It also, somewhat surprisingly, responds to a similar inclination in the Son, his desire to exercise power or rhetorical "empire" over an audience through what the Father calls "his great warfare" (1.158).[10] The Son is not immune to the impulse to seize power over his listeners; Satan's offer of rhetorical persuasion touches a nerve. Milton here associates rhetorical with military force. "Politic maxims" have a seductive impact on the Son in *Paradise Regained* because rhetorical aggression provides a displaced form of the martial activity that he once planned as a means to his victory. This earlier, overtly warlike strategy surfaces during the Son's opening meditative soliloquy in Book 1, when he reveals that he has been tempted by the idea of military feats. The Son makes it clear that he has chosen words rather than violence as his mature means of conquest, but he states his choice in a way that reveals a lingering attachment to violence:

>     Victorious deeds
> Flamed in my heart, heroic acts, one while
> To rescue Israel from the Roman yoke . . .
> . . . . . . . . . . . . . . . . . . . . . . . . . .
> . . . Yet [I] held it more humane, more heavenly first
> By winning words to conquer willing hearts,
> And make persuasion do the work of fear;
> At least to try, and teach the erring soul
> Not willfully misdoing, but unware
> Misled; the stubborn only to subdue.
> 
> (*PR* 1.216–26)

"The stubborn only to subdue": so Augustine in his preface to the *City of God* adapted Virgil's idealized description of Roman political morality and turned it into a Christian motto (Aen. 6.853: "Parcere subiectis et debellare superbos"). The Son's *Aeneid* allusion implies that martial conquest may still be necessary if and when verbal persuasion fails—though Augustine, unlike the more militant Son, reads the "war" that rescues the Christian from Rome as a purely figurative conflict of the soul, not the body. The Son has muted his desire to "subdu[e]" his enemies by force; he will now exploit the force of rhetoric, not arms, but his taste for combat lingers.[11] Satan is not so far off the mark, then, when he proffers the triumphs available through conquest, and with them the exhilarating *aristeiai* of classical strategy. The phrase "inflamed / With glory," which Satan uses to describe Caesar at 2.41–42, even echoes the Son's "Victorious deeds / Flamed in my heart" here.

Does the Son of *Paradise Regained* give in to this militant impulse on the pinnacle, courting the risk of assuming demonic talent by proving himself better at Satan's own game rather than essentially different from him? Does he surrender to the temptation that the Lady of *Comus* refuses, fulfilling an impulse toward dramatic triumph, toward conquering the other through the force of heroic words and deeds—an impulse that has appeared, and been stifled, earlier in his dialogue with Satan?[12] Our first inclination is to answer "no." After all, Milton depicts the Son in definitive contrast to human heroes like the Lady, or Adam and Eve: they face a transition from Imaginary to Symbolic selfhood that the Son claims to have bypassed. His alienated lucidity about his plight in the wilderness, for example, at 2.252–53 ("But now I feel / I hunger"), suggests that his experiences have already been translated into a prophetic, rather than a purely personal, lexicon. The Son's third-person articulation of his career veers away from the first person of idiosyncratic desire. Yet, as I have been arguing, the Son remains subject to a tense will to enter into his obligation, not merely a distant, assured consciousness of it: he *is* subject to the Imaginary.

In their interpretations of *Paradise Regained*, three eminent readers of the poem, A. S. P. Woodhouse, Northrop Frye, and Arnold Stein, agree that the Son is a hero of Symbolic knowledge rather than Imaginary desire; in other words, that his self-revelation on the pinnacle is not, as Stein puts it, an "act of will." According to this reading, the Son at the end engages in, not a fall into humanness, but a temporary condescension to the human, an "act[ing of] transcendence in the world."[13] Stein claims that the Son perfectly maintains the distance between God and man while "acting out the perfection of God in man."[14] I suggest, to the contrary, that the Son's apotheosis is not just an act but a commitment to the human. To put it another way: the doctrinal paradox of a God who becomes divine by becoming man undermines this doctrine when it is acted out, when it becomes drama instead of mere abstraction. The Son turns—so it seems—fully human, or even Satanic, in his anger. Woodhouse, Frye, and Stein all espouse what Empson would call the "neo-Christian" claim that Milton's translation of doctrine into drama fulfills, rather than compromises, doctrine.[15]

Kerrigan and Tayler refine Stein's argument when they suggest that Milton's Son at the end of *Paradise Regained* succeeds in vanquishing the similarity of good and evil by acknowledging it. According to this interpretation, the Son claims his difference from Satan on the basis of the autonomy of the one who knows. *What* he knows is his potential affinity to his demonic counterpart, the capacity for independence and oedipal rebellion against the father that he must transcend in order to identify himself with his father's will. Fish, in an analysis that sees Milton as yielding less to ambiguity than the variously Freudian readings of Tayler and Kerrigan, similarly asserts the poet's success as a triumph of the unequivocal.[16]

But can the Son, or his author, know so clearly and authoritatively? Against all of these readings the sting of Empson's interpretation remains, with its implication that Milton cannot fully control the split between his doctrinal and his poetic desires. Doctrine fails to guide Milton's poetry in an assured or reliable way, despite his effort to identify poetic sublimity with doctrinal truth. The Son, when he shows "Godlike force" in his vanquishing of temptation (4.602), dares to fall into human form and human dramatic conflict—just where Satan has fallen. The Son is more than his father's Word; he is also Satan's rival.

Early in the poem, the Son points to his impulse toward the spectacular when he hints at a similarity between his own powers and Satan's. In Book 2, the Son answers Satan's offer of food by extravagantly proclaiming

> I can at will, doubt not, as soon as thou,
> Command a table in the Wilderness,
> And call swift flights of Angels ministrant
> Array'd in Glory on my cup to attend
>
> (*PR* 2.383–86)

"As soon as thou": the Son here seems to want to compete with Satan in miraculous gesture, to act as quickly and effectively as his enemy, and thus to recognize their secret kinship. "The Son of God I also am, or was," Satan slyly announces in Book 4: "Relation stands" (4.518–19). We might see *Paradise Regained* as a competition between these two sons of God, two candidates for dominion over humanity.

Perhaps, then, the Son proves himself the younger brother with his superior cleverness, his interpretative skill—and his adroit theft of the blessing, accomplished by disguising himself in ingenious, rhetorically adept figures, dark and ambiguous like Satan's oracles.[17] Augustine, speaking of Jacob's triumph over Esau, evokes "the guile of the man without guile," the honest deception that reveals "a profound mystery of the truth."[18] The Son's true mystery, like Jacob's, cannot easily be distinguished from its cunning, demonic antithesis. Seeing the action of *Paradise Regained* as a contest over the blessing means attributing a shared desire to the Son and Satan that Christian myth intends to, but cannot fully, eliminate with its emphasis on the Messiah's unrivaled Symbolic office.

At the end of *Paradise Regained* it is Satan who falls in earnest, not the Son. But the Son's precarious stance, his "uneasy station" (4.583) on the pinnacle, hints at the substance of Satan's hope that the Son might fall instead. The interchangeability of roles implied here proves potentially damaging to the Son's claim of unique status. When angels rescue the Son from his pinnacle, Milton's syntax makes us think that it is Satan, not the Son, who has been saved: "So Satan fell; and straight a fiery Globe / Of Angels on full sail of wing flew nigh, / Who on their plumy Vans receiv'd him soft / From his uneasy station...." (4.580–83).[19] With this decidedly ambiguous "him"—does the poet mean Satan or the Son?—Milton tempts us to see from Satan's point of view. At this moment, it is the "relation" conveyed by a syntactical ambiguity that "stands," not the Son in his attempt to establish his difference from his adversary. Milton does divide the Son definitively from Satan but only by making him court the Satanic thrill of an eleventh-hour denouement.

Yet the Son does take an interpretative stand during his final temptation. To the extent that he can accomplish the differentiation of himself from Satan, he does so through his attitude toward pathos. When the Son refuses to fall from the pinnacle, he refuses as well Satan's recent insinuation that the exercise of persuasive power means submitting oneself to one's desire for, and vulnerability to, the things of this world (4.166–67). In Book 3, Satan depicts a conqueror's enslavement to emotion: Caesar "inflam'd" with glory, weeping because his empire did not begin soon enough (3.40). Satan here implies that an interest in moving an audience through the wondrous spectacle of one's own glory goes along with a surrender of power to a feeble passion like his own, and like Caesar's (3.23–24). The Son, Satan suggests, should give in to his wish for empire, and for the rhetorical sway over an audience essential to imperial power, as Caesar and Satan himself have. If the Son were to yield to Satan here, his power would be expressed as, reduced to, the mere vulnerability of human passion—the Satanic level. Guarding himself against this appeal, the Son responds not with mercy but with steadfast anger.

Milton in *Paradise Regained* stands alone, defending himself and the Son against the insidious force of Satanic pathos, by reducing it, reading it as a shallow, trivial characteristic. Satan's passion in most of *Paradise Regained* is superficial, a thin pretense that he exploits for argumentative effect, in contrast to the sublime drive of *Paradise Lost*'s king of hell. But Satanic emotion becomes a serious, if momentary, threat to *Paradise Regained*'s agenda in Book 3, when it suddenly acquires the startling authenticity of self-conscious desperation. "Worst is my Port," asserts Satan in response to the Son's argument that he is only seeking what will amount to more damnation for himself:

> I would be at the worst; worst is my Port,
> My harbor and my ultimate repose,
> The end I would attain, my final good.
> My error was my error, and my crime
> My crime; whatever, for itself condemn'd,
> And will alike be punish'd; whether thou
> Reign or reign not; though to that gentle brow
> Willingly I could fly, and hope thy reign,
> From that placid aspect and meek regard,
> Rather than aggravate my evil state,
> Would stand between me and thy father's ire
> (Whose ire I dread more than the fire of Hell)
> A shelter and a kind of shading cool
> Interposition, as a summer's cloud.
> If I then to the worst that can be haste,
> Why move thy feet so slow to what is best?
> (*PR* 3.209–24)[20]

Satan's hopeless need to corrupt, even to corrupt himself, is palpable. Here as in *Paradise Lost*'s voyage toward Eden, he is "glad now that his sea should find a shore" (*PL* 2.1011): some port, no matter which, for his destructive impulse. Satan's emotion, at this moment if nowhere else in *Paradise Regained*, overshadows the Son's dispassionate doctrine. As in his Mount Niphates speech in *Paradise Lost*, Satan even sarcastically co-opts that doctrine in a shockingly self-conscious elaboration of what he knows his desperation must mean: "Worst is my port, / My harbor and my ultimate repose, / The end I would attain, my final good."

Oddly, in these lines Satan's self-awareness does not corrode his pretense to authenticity as it usually does in *Paradise Regained*. Instead,

Christian definitions of the "final good" suddenly look superficial in comparison with the Satanic death drive. We feel the force of Satan's point: if one has lived the experience of evil as he has, the theoretical moralism that speaks in such terms as "final good" becomes mere raw material for bitter parody.

But Satan betrays his own passionate confession, one of the few places in *Paradise Regained* where he ruffles his steady rhetorical course,[21] with a smooth and obviously specious argument. First, he asks for the Son's mercy, a transparent attempt to persuade the Son to make himself vulnerable (3.217: "that placid aspect and meek regard"). Satan then too skillfully returns to his major theme, the imperial temptation, telling the Son, "If I then to the worst that can be haste, / Why move thy feet so slow to what is best?" (3.223–24). Here, along with the stylistic polish of the internal half-rhyme "worst" and "haste," and the slick invocation of an easy contrast between Satan and the Son, Satan's despair recurs like a twitch, a habitual reflex that he exploits for rhetorical purposes. His feeble attempt to trick the future messiah into first mercy, then zeal, shows him glib, rather than tortured, in his self-consciousness. The subtlety of Satan the contriver obliterates the frank self-assessment that directly preceded, with its autobiographical pathos ("My error was my error, and my crime / My crime"). In these final lines of Satan's speech Milton directs his poem away from the deep, despairing fixation on the past that he has briefly allowed to Satan.

Yet Satan did, for one moment, override the Son's calm terms: the enemy's "worst is my port" elicited an intensity of readerly response that the Son has so far refused to provoke. When Milton suddenly lets Satan puncture *Paradise Regained*'s studied, unemotional poetics with the force of his despair, he risks investing his poetic energy in Satan rather than the Son. So Milton withdraws his investment as he does after Satan's Mount Niphates speech: he insists that the tempter's sublime hopelessness must be a fraud.[22]

In depicting the Son's use of emotion, which will more than rival Satan's own, Milton turns from providence as steady predictability, as if to recuperate for God's purposes Satan's praise of "zeal and occasion," his turbulent drive toward extreme, critical moments.[23] The Son gives divine will an anticipatory character that exploits the pathos of surprise. This aspect of the Son's power appears most clearly as the angelic choirs who have received the Messiah, after directing their hymn of praise to him as "True Image of the Father," now address a threat to Satan:[24]

> ... hereafter learn with awe
> To dread the Son of God: hee all unarm'd
> Shall chase thee with the terror of his voice

> From thy Demoniac holds, possession foul,
> Thee and thy legions, yelling they shall fly,
> And beg to hide them in a herd of Swine,
> Lest he command them down into the deep,
> Bound, and to torment sent before their time.
> (*PR* 4.626–32)[25]

In this shocking use of the Gospels' Gadarene swine episode, Milton associates the Son's wrath with a magic that can transform his enemies into bestial victims by anticipating their evil desires. This theme of anticipation signals a turning point in Milton's narrative: the Son can now precede his antagonist, instead of waiting for Satan's taunts. The Messiah need no longer hold back his desire to act prematurely, to punish his enemies "before their time." His conclusive routing of Satan from the pinnacle resembles in its anticipatory character his transformation of the rebel angels into swine: it takes such stunning effect because it occurs surprisingly early in the encounter, which is by far the shortest of Satan's three temptations. Unlike Caesar, whose empire arrives belated, and unlike Satan, who preys on second chances, the Son has a jump on his enemy's schemes—he turns his own belatedness into priority.

The Son's use of his position as latecomer indicates that he depends on his opponent. He needs to elicit a dramatic response from Satan, to make Satan unveil his true character, in order to demonstrate his victory over him. But the Son's argumentative practice claims, paradoxically, his autonomy from Satan. And Satan, shockingly enough, similarly asserts his independence of the Son's example. In Book 1, Satan tries to attenuate the Son's exemplary force when he draws a distinction between admiring virtue and following it: "Most men admire / Virtue, who follow not her lore" (482–83). Here, Satan asserts that he can appreciate the Son's moral self-definition without allowing himself to be conquered or compelled by it. The distance that Satan here assumes from the Son goes along with his definition of pathos as an isolated, individual possession: "Fellowship in pain divides not smart, / Nor lightens aught each man's peculiar load" (1.401–12.). But Satan's narrowing of pathos's sphere to a hidden space within the self turns out to be a mere defensive maneuver against his emotional identification with the Son, his drive to occupy his rival's place. Satan does follow, passionately cathected as he is onto the Son's rising career, which could have been his own; he cannot stand back and merely admire. Nor can the Son's audience, finally, hold themselves back from intimate relation to him, though they cannot grasp this relation in cognitive terms.

The Son reminds us, against Satan, that his pathos asks us to identify with, to take part in, his suffering. The Messiah's office dramatizes pathos as not a "peculiar" but a shared burden with this crucial speech in Book 2:

> What if with like aversion I reject
> Riches and Realms; yet not for that a Crown,
> Golden in show, is but a wreath of thorns,
> Brings dangers, troubles, cares and sleepless nights
> To him who wears the Regal Diadem,
> When on his shoulders each man's burden lies;
> For therein stands the office of a King,
> His Honour, Virtue, Merit and chief Praise,
> That for the Public all this weight he bears.
> (*PR* 2.457–65)

The vague, circumlocutory reticence of the Son's reference to "the Public" cannot disguise the intense forecast of his crucifixion in the phrase "wreath of thorns." Milton reminds us that the pathos of suffering, and the sympathetic reaction it draws from an audience, gives the only available proof of the Son's identity as God in man.

We must also take the Son's anxious disciples seriously as witnesses of the Son's suffering, an audience analogous to Milton's readers. The disciples, too, act as protagonists parallel to the Son himself, ruled by a similar rhythm of anticipation and withholding. At 2.37–49, they bracket the memory of their enthusiastic reaction to the Son's appearance ("thus we rejoic'd") by "But let us wait," a shying away from fully passionate conviction. They hold back their emotional response, just as the Son restrains his desire to give the sign that elicits emotion.

Impatience, the tense desire for a sign promising tangible outcome, is common to the Son, the disciples, the poem's readers—and Satan. When the Son finally does give a sign, at the poem's end, this gesture seals his victory even as it indicates his need to leap beyond the patient terms he has set for himself.

> There on the highest Pinnacle he set
> The Son of God, and added thus in scorn.
> There stand, if thou wilt stand; to stand upright
> Will ask thee skill; I to thy Father's house
> Have brought thee, and highest plac't, highest is best,
> Now show thy Progeny; if not to stand,
> Cast thyself down; safely if Son of God:
> For it is written, He will give command
> Concerning thee to his Angels, in thir hands
> They shall up lift thee, lest at any time
> Thou chance to dash thy foot against a stone.

> To whom thus Jesus. Also it is written,
> Tempt not the Lord thy God; he said and stood.
> *(PR* 4.551– 62)

Here, finally, the Son refuses to choose between falling (which is associated with reliance on his father's angels and therefore trust in his authority) and standing (which Satan links to the Son's own presumed desire: "If thou wilt stand"). By citing his father's words as his own, the Son rejects the conflict between autonomy and obedience that Satan wants to impose on him. He stands but not (just) because he *wants* to. The Son thus refuses the kind of willing that derives its force from a conflict with the law, claiming instead a coincidence between the law and his will. In his act of standing the Son expresses the Father in and as himself.

But, despite the assertions of most commentators, this scene is not just about the Son and his Father; there is a third party present to complicate, and even contaminate, the Son's achievement of a mature identity. The Son's self-expression demands an audience to work: Satan the spectator falls when he is "smitten with amazement" at the sight of God in man. He must be made to see, and in a spectacular, theatrical way—as Samson makes the Philistines see. The Son needs the acknowledgment of his Other, in this case not his father but his opponent, Satan, to assume his Symbolic office. Like Freud's grandson Ernst with his *fort-da* game, the Son makes Satan magically disappear. He demonstrates Symbolic maturity by stage managing a scene in which he can control the Other's presence by making him absent.[26] This control means attaining, through the manipulation of knowledge, a victory over the precognitive entrapment in another's image—which is also one's own image—that the Imaginary offers. The Son tears himself away from the influence of Satan, a character whose evil profile supports his own goodness, to claim instead an autonomous identity. The Son's Symbolic assertion overcomes Satan's boast of a confusion between the Son's career and his own. But the poet cannot fully exorcize this confusion because the energy of the Son's victory derives from his struggle with it. We are unable, finally, to separate the Son's superior knowledge from the presence of the competitor who impels his desire for superiority.

*Paradise Regained*, like *Paradise Lost*, ends with a quiet declining of apocalyptic show as the Son draws back from spectacle one last time, retreating into the unseen. The Son returns "private" and "unobserv'd" to his mother's house. He reverts from his public encounter, which Milton compares to Hercules' with Antaeus and Oedipus' with the Sphinx, to his enigmatic human origins. In doing so, he dramatizes a respect for hiddenness, for the riddle's secret power, that Oedipus did not show; Milton somehow associates this obscure feeling with Mary, whose private sympathy for her son reveals his most humbly affecting aspect.

The Son's dependence on maternal protection, then, appears only when it can safely be exposed: after his triumph over Satan, which exploits an aggressive rather than a vulnerable pathos because of the shield against the other that aggression offers. As usual in his work, Milton veers away from the suffering of the crucifixion to a more militant image of the Son's powers. The Son must refuse emotional weakness because of Satan's ability to claim such vulnerability as his own, whether in his description of the weeping Caesar or in his voicing of his own despair. *Paradise Regained* reminds its audience that only the savior's cold, inflexible anger can successfully resist, and outperform, the pathos of Satanic tragedy.

*Paradise Regained* can conclude only after the Son substitutes Satan for himself: Satan "fell whence he stood to see his Victor fall" (4.571). By means of this substitution, the Son rewrites history, undoing the sacrifice of the innocent son, himself, and sacrificing Satan instead. In contrast to the Son, Samson ends by indulging, instead of refusing, the ironic wrongness of his victimization. The Symbolic mastery embodied in the Son's redemptive knowing remains alien to Samson, who at the poem's climactic moment surrenders to his desire, his "intimate impulse," and feels himself driven toward an uncontrollable fate. If the pathos of Imaginary fixation survives alongside Symbolic knowledge in *Paradise Regained*, *Samson* will repudiate Symbolic or cognitive justification altogether in favor of the primal Imaginary relation between Samson and the Philistines. *Samson*, unlike *Paradise Regained*, makes its hero confront his weakness—not repress or rise above it—so that he can achieve his victory, which is also his defeat.

> Between the security confessed by the recitation of the founding events and the menace announced by the prophet there is no rational synthesis, no triumphant dialectic, but only a double confession, never completely appeased; a double confession that only hope can hold together.... No *Aufhebung* can suppress this deadly fault. This is why the double relation to history is profoundly betrayed when we apply the Stoic idea of providence to it and when the tension between narration and prophecy is assuaged in some teleological representation of the course of history.
> —Paul Ricoeur[27]

*Samson Agonistes,* like *Paradise Regained,* exploits pathos to overturn the possibility of a predictable, clearly instructive providential narrative. In both works, the lack of predictability means the absence of a sure didactic lesson, as an enigmatic, astonishing conclusion wins out against moralism by undermining the rational narrative structure that moralism requires (what Ricoeur calls the "rational synthesis"). The end of *Samson Agonistes* leaves us in doubt whether Samson is really inspired by God, whether his revenge is a divine or a human one. Milton encourages the reader to choose this unresolveable mystery over the easily moralizing reading of Samson's ending produced for public consumption in the Chorus's final "all is best." Samson's physical union with his Philistine enemies proves more profound than the message that his Israelite audience draws from his fate. In other words, the bodily presence of his deeds surpasses communicative understanding. At the end of *Samson*, as a result, Milton gives up thinking history insofar as history involves the facts of discursive persuasion and learning. Yet this abandonment of the historical signifies not the poet's retreat but rather his conviction about the singularity of a human individual like Samson, who proves essentially unassimilable to the grand structure of the sacred plot. A similar refusal of monumentality occurs at the endings of *Paradise Lost* and *Paradise Regained*; in these two poems, however, the refusal relies on the intimacy of family romance. By contrast, *Samson* emphasizes the sheer material reality of death, which unites the hero to, not his family's or his nation's, but his enemies' alien presence. ("Dire necessity . . ." the Chorus tells the dead Samson, "conjoin'd / Thee with thy slaughter'd foes in number more / Than all thy life had slain before" [1666 – 68].) This is a radical, ironic coherence, immediate and conclusive in contrast to the reiterative cosmic scale of the final books of *Paradise Lost* (or, for that matter, Spenser's Mutabilitie Cantos).

*Samson* draws on what David Damrosch, writing on Psalm 78, describes as the "anti-epic" aspect of the Bible, its sense of human history as "a riddle or parable." Often in the Hebrew scriptures, God's will expresses itself in "'dark sayings'" that subvert the reader's wish for a straightforward, optimistic story of redemption.[28] Almost from the beginning of the Samson story in Judges, the text drives home the impossibility of reducing the riddle of Samson's character and his connection to the divine to a clear, communicable message. When the angel of the Lord tells Manoah and his wife of the special character of the hero who is about to be born to them, Manoah tries to detain this heavenly messenger, demanding his identity. The angel replies, "Why ask my name, seeing it surpasses understanding [or: is wonderful, *pil' î]*?" (Judges 13:18). In *Samson*, Milton's vision is even darker and more riddling than the Bible's. As in the biblical story, the sublimity of Milton's Samson will be bound together with incommunicability, against Manoa's (and, often, Samson's own) wishes for clear meaning.[29] The

Philistine shout that "tore the sky," disrupting a fluent dialogue between Manoa and the Chorus (1472), echoes the interruptive character of Samson's last act, an amazing break in discourse that resists explanation to the end.

Samson's irreparable mistake is, on one level, an obvious one: he has violated the sacredness of divine mysteries by committing an act of clear communication. In divulging to Dalila the secret of his strength, he "profan[es] / The mystery of God" (377–78).[30] But, after further consideration, this clarity also darkens. Samson betrays "the sacred trust of silence" (428) by "presumptuously ... publish[ing]" his "holy secret" (497–98), making it a meaning available even to Philistines; however, *why* he does so remains an impenetrable riddle. Samson's lack of reticence with Dalila, his astounding willingness to speak in response to her seduction, has always been a stumbling block for readers of the Samson story, a moment defiantly insistent in its obscurity. Does Samson think he is favored beyond any visible or evident law—that he will be protected by God even after breaking the prohibition against revealing his secret, just as he was favored after breaking another, equally explicit prohibition, against marrying with the Philistines? Is he testing God (to cite one of Johannes de Silentio's definitions of faith in *Fear and Trembling*)? We, Samson's audience, will never know.

The Chorus shares our desire for a reliable interpretation of Samson's actions, a lawful, predictable reading, even as they worry that their eyes may misperceive the hero (115–26), that his light within darkness may remain inaccessible to their black-and-white definitions. They try to make Samson's career accord with an evident or apparent law by separating the woman of Timna's "stain" from Samson: "unchaste was subsequent, her stain not his" (324–25).[31] The Chorus misses the point that Samson sought marriage to a Philistine precisely in order to court such a stain—he transgresses communal commands so that he may succeed. Samson never sticks to his own: he seeks the alien. His strength is his phoenix-like uniqueness or exceptionality, which makes him a paradox-exploiting adversary to the norms of Hebrew law. Samson's status as a Nazarite "separate to God" implies an exposure to otherness—the only way for him to enforce his singularity is to confront the passions of his counterparts Dalila and Harapha. He therefore himself refutes the Stoic assumption he voiced in an earlier soliloquy: that heroic individuality can prove itself independent of others, and that such independence provides security against the disruptive power of pathos. Emotion, Samson realizes, transgresses the boundary between self and other—it is the same Imaginary force that proved so essential, and essentially risky, for the Son at the end of *Paradise Regained*. As Jean-Luc Nancy writes, "The presence of the other does not constitute a boundary that would limit the unleashing of 'my' passions: on the contrary, only exposition to the other unleashes my passions."[32]

One exposure that crucially affects Samson is his subjection to the power of the state, which informs Samson's character as it does Dalila's by mixing private desire and public obligation. The commands of the state shape desire in Dalila's betrayal of Samson and in Samson's own choice of the woman of Timna, through whom he "sought an occasion" against the Philistines. Here the issue of gender enters, inseparable from questions of emotion and interpretation: Samson's private need for, and later his intense repudiation of, Dalila combines with her public role as another Philistine woman, another "occasion" for his military career. To defeat the Philistines, Samson must return to his attraction for them as his counterparts, whose warlike obligations rival his own. Instead of subordinating Imaginary desire to Symbolic duty, Samson crosses the two. Finally, he gives vent to his desire in destroying the Philistines, an action that may also fulfill a divine command. In tearing down the temple, Samson, like the Son, expresses a violent desire that, it seems, paradoxically serves the law. But Milton, departing from the vision of steadfast conscience in *Paradise Regained*, describes a more brutal kind of superego in Samson, one that even more radically contaminates the Symbolic mandate with Imaginary aggression. Samson draws drastically and self-destructively on the primitive energy of the id as the Son does not.

The potential for such Imaginary violence terrifies Samson as it does his audience; he can avoid it only through interpretations that give his career an artificial consistency or reliability. Samson himself often tries to escape from his confusion by proposing reasonable explanations for his case. He first names God's endowing him with a disproportion of strength and wisdom as the definitive clue to his failure (208–9). But is this an explanation? It seems, instead, merely the positing of a self-contradictory God behind the self-contradictory Samson—tortoises all the way down.

Samson's next rationalization for his fall relies on gender as an explanatory key: he blames his weakness, his attraction to an "object more enticing" (558) than strong drink—that is, Philistine women. In *Samson*, Milton gives Samson's weakness, his susceptibility to pathos, a gendered form. Giving in to Dalila means becoming feminized. As Kerrigan has noted, the poet images "Philistia" in feminine terms, as a woman like Dalila.[33] In the course of the play, Samson projects his own "feminine" vulnerability onto Dalila. But his rhetoric indicates that the sins he charges her with are in fact internal to him (the classic frustration of the Imaginary). As such, they refute Samson's hope that he is not touched or "defiled" by his outward state, that his mind remains free. As I will argue, at the play's conclusion Samson acknowledges the weakness within him by turning from this championing of the mind and decisively confusing mind and body.

Before this realization of the fundamentally internal status of pathos, Samson's antifeminist projection entangles him in his enemy's values by giving him the dangerous profile of a Philistine idol worshiper. As Samson describes it, Dalila's "fair enchanted cup" (934) has the power of the magical Philistine deities; by arguing that her sorcery has entrapped him, Samson concedes miraculous force to "Philistia."[34] The Chorus implicitly recognizes the way that Philistine visual splendor has infected Samson when it describes Samson and Dalila in similar terms: both are gloriously ornamented. The Chorus sees Samson as a hero "with gifts and graces eminently adorned" (679), and Dalila as a "thing / ... bedecked, ornate, and gay" (710–12).[35] As Dalila says, she and Samson are "near related, or the same of kind" (786).[36] This similarity implies that Dalila somehow participates in Samson's character, that she is a constitutive Imaginary being for him. She is within him, not the insidious outside force he defensively construes her as. Samson and Dalila's dangerous mutuality is like that of Britomart and Malecasta, or Guyon and Pyrochles. These characters remain irreparably and intensely occupied with an Imaginary desire that threatens to dissolve the boundaries between self and other, man and woman, strength and weakness.

Defending against such an effacement of autonomy, Samson pictures Dalila as a mere external appearance who allures him by threatening to reduce him to her own feminized state. Samson tries to ward off this threat, as he refuses Harapha's "bulk without spirit vast," by choosing mind over body. Similarly, he interprets his Philistine bondage as a matter of merely outward, bodily condition: "Can they think me so broken, so debas'd / With corporal servitude, that my mind ever / Will condescend to such absurd commands?" (1335–37). But Samson's "foul effeminacy" (410) is internal to him, a product of the fact that he is a body, and therefore vulnerable. This internality appears in the figures of Samson's discourse. At 607–15, Samson creates an image of spirit as flesh, lamenting the fact that "torments" are not "confin'd / To the body's wounds and sores ... But must secret passage find / To th'inmost mind ... And on her purest spirits prey, / As on entrails, joints, and limbs." A few lines later, he says, similarly crossing images of mind and body, "Thoughts my Tormentors arm'd with deadly stings / Mangle my apprehensive tenderest parts" (623–24). On the level of poetic language as on that of plot, Samson, despite himself, identifies his inward mind with his body. As Dalila points out, Samson, in giving out his secret, shows in himself the weakness of "woman" (and reveals his strength as located in a vulnerable bodily part, his hair): "Ere I to thee, thou to thyself wast cruel" (778).

Samson gives in to the similarity between himself and Dalila at the play's end by being in the same place twice (to cite a popular Renaissance etymology of "Samson"): in effect, he remarries Philistia. There is a crucial relation between the "ornate, and gay" spectacle associated with Dalila and the spectacular conclusion produced by Samson at the temple of Dagon. By surrendering to the Philistines' invitation to perform at their rites, Samson yields to the dreaded effeminacy or impotence enforced by his earlier capitulation to Dalila—a failure he was determined not to repeat. Suddenly, he appears to lose his resistance, accepting his status as a passive object for the eyes of his Philistine audience: "Made of [his] enemies the scorn and gaze." This very loss of power turns out to be Samson's means to power. Samson thus joins his militant strength to the vulnerability that the Son of *Paradise Regained* refuses. Samson openly embraces the paradoxical nature of pathos, its confusion of strength and weakness, as the Son does not.

When he goes to Dagon's temple, Samson accepts the enigmatic truth that overcoming the Philistines and their "unclean" rites (1362) also means accepting their secret meaning for his own fate. Samson's violent victory entails a susceptibility previously associated with his sexual relation to Dalila. Mieke Bal notes how closely the Samson story intertwines sex and violence. As his riddle of the lion carcass turned honeycomb hints, Samson's lion strength, his masculine power, depends on his mixing with the honey sweetness of desire.[37]

The connection between sex and violence arises most bluntly in Milton's drama when Samson warns Dalila that she must not come close to him "lest fierce remembrance wake / My sudden rage to tear thee joint by joint" (952–53). This explosive tearing, suggesting orgasm, finally occurs, of course, at the Philistine temple. But Samson, to break his enemies in pieces, must first tangle or "ravel" himself in Dalila's Philistine snare. Samson's strength stems from his being reduced to an exposed, feminine position; his violent energy depends on his subjection to sexual desire. His pathos of suffering, which feminizes him, has its mirror in Dalila's Jael-like appropriation of a masculine talent for martial strategy. A warrior as well as a wife, Dalila incarnates the symbiosis of sex and violence also entailed by Samson's pursuit of military success through marriage. The Chorus presents Dalila as the definitive example of "woman's love" as paradox (1010–17), "much like thy riddle, Samson" (1016), or the complex tangle of God's plan.

*Samson* proposes an even more radical interpretative puzzle than its hero's attainment of strength through contamination by Philistine sexuality: how can Samson be both a "petty God" in his own right and an instrument of God's will? As J. A. Wittreich has recently demonstrated, it is by no means evident that Samson's final action is divinely inspired, especially given Samson's frequently dubious reputation in the Renaissance as a suicide and thus a defier of God.[38] The suicide sins by substituting his own will for God's. So does the murderous avenger: Samson may be dedicated to his own aggression rather than to God's plan when he destroys the Philistines. This obscurity also raises the question of whether Samson's heroic character or God's plot rules the play's conclusion. Does Samson grow into heroic maturity, or does he, like Spenser's Red Crosse, remain immature, a pawn in God's hands?[39] Assuming that this alternative can be resolved means failing to grasp the riddling character of *Samson*'s conclusion: we must stay with the alternative in order to capture the riddle's true force.

Samson displays a marked inclination toward self-motivated, heroic autonomy in the boast he delivers just before he pulls down the Philistine temple. Here, Samson explicitly claims his status as a free agent. "Hitherto, Lords," says Samson (as reported by the Messenger),

> ... what your commands imposed
> I have perform'd, as reason was, obeying,
> Not without wonder or delight beheld.
> Now of my own accord such other trial
> I mean to show you of my strength, yet greater;
> As with amaze shall strike all who behold.
> (*Samson* 1640–45)

With "of my own accord," Samson suggests that he himself is the source of his own strength; such self-reliance must negate the obedience to God for which Manoa and the Chorus praise him. But perhaps this is Samson's display of irony, since he knows the contradiction between his current image of autonomy and his earlier hint that God may encourage his attendance at the Philistine rites "for some important cause" (1377–79). The idea that this coming strength is "greater" may imply a sense of supernatural guidance—or it may not. Here, the poem poses an undecidable choice between divine will and self-will, inviting a permanent conflict of interpretations. This is not to say that autonomous human action and divine providence are necessarily irreconcilable, merely that *Samson*, unlike most Protestant texts, sets them in stark opposition, forcing the reader to search for an unavailable narrative resolution.

Most critics of *Samson* have wanted to demonstrate that Samson's final act of pathos relies on God, that he here rejects his earlier arrogant heroics, when he strutted like Achilles over the Philistine dead. But we cannot prove such a development. It is not at all certain that

Samson abandons his heroic pride and yields to God's direction. Like the Son, Samson relies on a surprising, transfiguring turn of events to become what he is. But no visible divine sanction accompanies Samson's defeat of the Philistines, in contrast to the Son's triumph over Satan in *Paradise Regained* with its attendant angelic chorus—so perhaps it is his own human work.

Milton conveys such uncertainties by using *Samson*'s dramatic form to create a proliferation of points of view. Every character in the play has a different reading of the hero, and every reading remains in some sense lacking. No one, including Samson himself, is a reliable judge of events. Samson even contradicts himself, alternately blaming God, Dalila, and his own weakness for his fall. The final Semi-Chorus perhaps comes closest to accuracy in emphasizing the enigmatic nature of Samson, whom they describe as "vigorous most / When most unactive deem'd" (1704 –5). Samson, like his counterpart Dalila, resists interpretation to the end.[40]

In the case of Samson as in that of *Paradise Lost*'s Eve, whose motives for separating from Adam remain tantalizingly obscure, this resistance to interpretation marks the heroic desire for a hidden, and perhaps forbidden, truth. But Samson's choice of isolation, his turning from his wife, differs from Eve's turning from Adam when she eats the apple: until the very end of *Samson Agonistes*, Samson wants to reach knowledge by overcoming pathos, whereas Eve aspires by directly embracing the passionate inquiry offered to her. Eve pursues a solitary passion, as Satan seduces her by eliciting the emotion of astonishment—a talking snake!—and hinting at the promise of a knowledge that she can exercise independently of Adam. Samson's trial is in a sense an inversion of Eve's. He associates independence from his spouse with the hope to be free from passion, rather than to indulge in it. Eve's ambitious intelligence is bound to her emotions, and this relation, though it leads to disaster, remains a crucial sign of what is permanently valuable about Eden; whereas Samson, the hero of a very fallen world, hopes to understand himself and God by warding off the emotional vulnerability associated with sin. Samson assumes for much of the play that his self-reliant resistence to pathos proves his virtue: returning to his wife would be a fatal display of weakness.[41]

We can account for much of the difference between *Samson*'s and *Paradise Lost*'s scenes of temptation by remembering the role of gender in Milton. The divorce tracts argue that women are to submit themselves to the marriage relation; men, on the contrary, must be able to stand apart from and evaluate this relation if they are to remain strong. The *Doctrine and Discipline of Divorce* (1643) depicts the male divorcer as a man "who after sober and coole experience, and long debate within himselfe, puts away" his wife.[42] The thoughtfully objective, decisive autonomy Milton attributes to the (ex-)husband here is countered by the tortured, almost crazed suffering he credits him with elsewhere in the divorce tracts. But such autonomy, which Milton hopes will make possible the husband's distance from pathos, still remains the ideal of masculine behavior within an unhappy marriage.[43]

The divorce tracts are haunted by the spectre of a "God-forbidden loneliness" instilled by bad marriage, worse than the solitude a man may experience outside the marriage bond.[44] Milton tries desperately to make such estrangement, whether it occurs inside or outside marriage, into an occasion for calm, assured self-interpretation. But *Samson*, after testing this aspiration to autonomy, finally rejects the "sober and coole" hermeneutic faith the divorce tracts wish to give the husband. Samson, unlike Milton's ideal divorcer, cannot achieve a detached, accurate reading of his marriage: it remains a riddle to him, and himself with it. At the play's end, Samson must revert to the Philistia represented by his wife and yield to the pathos of tragic crisis, in a turn that obscures the possibility of the clear, independent grasp of self he has wanted.

Exposure to an audience plays a central role in Samson's final departure from his hope for autonomy. In his career as political and theological polemicist, Milton suffered a similar vulnerability to audience. Because of his embattled history as a frequently attacked Puritan apologist, Milton dwells on the possibility that his audience will misunderstand the man of faith. The interpretative uncertainty that propelled the Interregnum's turbulent process of social and religious change, and its effect on Milton the political pamphleteer and man of conscience, is directly relevant to *Samson Agonistes*. Through its allusions to Milton's role in the revolutionary conflict, *Samson*, even more than Milton's other works, generates its didactic moments in the friction between social and personal history. The rough intersection of private conscience and the public politics of religion is present in Milton's later prose works as well. The *Treatise of Civil Power* (1659) concludes, as Barbara Lewalski writes, that "the Spirit's mysterious action makes any human judgment of another's religion wholly impossible."[45] Private faith splits off from the realm of public opinion in which earlier, optimistic tracts like *Areopagitica* struggled to place it.

The *Treatise of Civil Power* goes further by doubting the solidity of even private belief. In a shocking moment that has important ramifications for the conclusion of *Samson*, Milton suggests that faith, or what seems to be faith, may unknowingly misjudge itself. To "interpret [the Scriptures] convincingly to his own conscience," Milton writes in the *Treatise*, "none is able but himself guided by the Holy Spirit; and not so guided, none than he himself can be a worse deceiver."[46] Inwardness might well mistake itself, even in the absence of an audience. If it is indeed possible to deceive oneself within the private relation of self to Scripture, the relation that Milton here argues for as the sole basis of faith, how can the believer be assured that what he thinks is the Spirit's guidance is not really his own self-deceiving fantasy? How can Samson know he is truly inspired by God? Milton in his *First Defense* (1651) writes of Samson's victory "whether prompted by God or by his own valor."[47] This "or" is echoed in *Samson Agonistes*'s description of Samson the hero during his *kairos*, leaning in preparation on Dagon's temple "as one who pray'd, / Or some great matter in his mind revolv'd" (1638–39).

Such subjective uncertainty makes one wish for a publicly demonstrable structure of belief, a sure, rationally explicable providence. But the providential pattern that Milton alludes to in *Samson*, the "dire necessity" of God's historical justice, looks disturbingly like a series of predetermined disasters. Samson's bondage, like Job's sufferings, displays a sheer, repetitive cruelty.[48] As Michael tells Adam in Book 12 of *Paradise Lost*, "So shall the World go on, / To good malignant, to bad men benign" (12.537–38). Passages like this one suggest a paranoiac vision of God's narrative as lawfully, pointedly perverse or destructive, the necessary, programmatic progress of evil. This grim possibility tempts one to incline once again toward the side of subjective pathos: to envision an escape from history by finding a redeemer who will break the pattern with a surprising, liberating act of passion.

For most of the play, we remain unsure whether Samson's willed victory will require such a drama of pathos. The Chorus shares our uncertainty as it reflects on the hero's subjective options, opposing the image of a passion-inspiring redeemer to an alternative, sharply contrasting potential identity for Samson, that of calm moral exemplar:

> Oh how comely it is and how reviving
> To the Spirits of just men long opprest!
> When God into the hands of thir deliverer
> Puts invincible might
> To quell the mighty of the Earth, th'oppressor,
> The brute and boist'rous force of violent men
> Hardy and industrious to support
> Tyrannic power, but raging to pursue
> The righteous and all such as honor Truth;
> Hee all thir Ammunition
> And feats of War defeats
> With plain Heroic magnitude of mind
> And celestial vigor arm'd,

> Thir Armories and Magazines contemns,
> Renders them useless, while
> With winged expedition
> Swift as the lightning glance he executes
> His errand on the wicked, who surpris'd
> Lose thir defense, distracted and amaz'd.
> But patience is more oft the exercise
> Of Saints, the trial of thir fortitude,
> Making them each his own Deliverer,
> And Victor over all
> That tyranny or fortune can inflict.
> Either of these is in thy lot,
> *Samson*. . . .
>
> (*Samson* 1268–93)

History demands a choice of response from the hero: the sublime wreaking of vengeance on a "distracted and amaz'd" Philistine audience or a quiet, exemplary "patience." The Chorus's moralizing impulse is to subordinate sublimity to Samson's lesson of internal fortitude. Because exposure as a shocking spectacle appears less reliable for didactic purposes than patient inwardness, they attach temperate adjectives ("plain," "comely") to Samson's martial-heroic greatness. The final Semi-Chorus, in a similar attempt to soften the violence of external military action, contrasts Samson's instantaneous, ethereal sweep to the grinding rage of the Philistines, transforming his aggression into grace: Samson's "dragon"-like flamboyance is really the triumph of an eagle wielding "cloudless thunder," we are told (1692–96). The patient Samson who is "his own Deliverer" could become the agent of his audience's disciplined moral imitation, a didactic example of cool, resolute strength. But the course of the play will oppose patience to spectacle. The spectacular Samson finally wins out over the exemplary one, the intensity of his immolation preventing him from occupying the role of moral guide.

The contrast between catastrophe and patient inwardness, the pathos of spectacle and moral point, remains a radical one in *Samson*. (And, as we have seen, even inwardness provides no guarantee of a reliable didacticism.) An analysis of the Messenger's reaction to Samson's triumph indicates how the visible miracle that Samson produces will win out over his solitary, introspective example. The Messenger tells the Chorus that he "sorrow'd at [Samson's] captive state, but minded / Not to be absent at that spectacle" in the "spacious Theater" where Samson is to perform (1603–5). Though the Messenger feels for Samson's captive solitude, he is more interested in his status as a miraculous, commanding sight, one necessarily alien to his awestruck audience.[49]

Samson, for most of the play, reverses the Messenger's priorities, prizing his pure and dignified despondency over the superficial, entertaining "feats" the Philistines demand of him. "And in my midst of sorrow and heart-grief / To show them feats, and play before thir god" (1340–41): the hero disparages the external sight of himself as a humiliation, preferring to guard his internalized self-obsession.[50] Until the play's end, he dwells "in [his] midst," denying the possibility that he might again use his external, physical strength.

Samson's insistence during much of his trial that the true meaning of his case must be internal amounts to a refusal of the worldly pathos that he will finally embrace and exploit. Thus, Samson in his iconoclastic mood opposes two types of "bondage," his former moral or psychological subjection to Dalila and his current physical slavery for the Philistines, asserting that moral captivity is more degrading than physical: "These rags, this grinding, is not yet so base / As was my former servitude" (415–16).

Manoa, in contrast to Samson's inclination toward internal or moral meaning, chooses the external. He identifies Samson's strength with his hair, an external feature, rather than his capacity for inner endurance. Manoa's superficial interpretations divide him from Samson and place him on the side of the letter rather than the spirit—a favored contrast in Milton. In pursuing a ransom for Samson, a purely external solution for his misery, Manoa ignores the sickness of internal doubt that afflicts his son. Manoa's adherence to the letter of the law denies the play's crucial paradox: when Samson shifts toward external, public history by tearing down the Philistines' temple, inward and outward are together *and* in opposition in a way that the didactic demands of Manoa and the Chorus cannot accept. The end of *Samson* represents not the harmony of history's public letter and conscience's private spirit but the impossibility of such reconciliation, even in the actual collision of private and public. We, Samson's audience, are confounded by the appearance of his strength's inner meaning in the form of an outward, historical event.[51] Samson's truth finally breaks the private/public division that provides so much of the play's antithetical structure.

During most of the play, Samson, like Manoa, tries to deny the paradoxical conjunction of inward and outward. He wants to master his history by rendering it as lawful narrative, making an inward, unpredictable pathos accord with the outward rule of publicly available results. For example, he says he thought his second marriage, to Dalila, "lawful from [his] former act" (231), his previous marriage to the woman of Timna. Associating his first marriage with his martial victories and thinking that such worldly success proves the divinely motivated status of his "intimate impulse," Samson hopes his second marriage will follow the same pattern.[52] Samson's original decision to marry a Philistine woman was a flagrant breach of Hebrew law. By construing his marriage to Dalila as "lawful," however, Samson invents his own legalism as a means to predict experience. He inverts his earlier reading of his career, in effect reasserting the validity of the communal law he broke when he married a Philistine woman. But this new reading is as legalistic as the old: now contact with the Philistines becomes the invariable sign of failure, rather than, as earlier, success. Samson's about-face shift in interpretation only reveals the inadequacy of predictive, legal form.[53]

When, at the Chorus's first approach, Samson summarizes what he thinks he has learned from his failure, he indulges in a moralizing similar to his defense of his marriage to Dalila in its attempt to make events regular or transparently "lawful." "I learn / Now of my own experience, not by talk, / How counterfeit a coin they are who friends / Bear in their superscription" (187–90). Samson himself, in capitulating to the Israelites' betrayal, has been "proverb'd for a Fool," he says (203). Samson's attempts to comfort himself by providing proverbial interpretations of his suffering fall short. The convenient maxim that tries to regulate providence and reduce it to a plausible and foreseeable narrative also reduces, in Pharisaical manner, the divine authority it means to serve. Proverbial legalism distorts the mysterious character of divine will into a simulacrum of human justice, which is less adequate to human experience than God's mysterious law exactly because it tries to simplify experience.

The economic image suggested by "counterfeit coin" is significant in *Samson*. Instead of providing a return on the "passion" his audience has "spent" (1758), Samson at the play's end offers a profligate, destructive self-sacrifice in which God "may dispense with" him (1371). We now have, in Bataille's terms, a general rather than a restricted economy, one centered on the seemingly impossible fact that Samson's useless body can generate a monstrous strength.[54]

In its attempt to return to a restricted economy, Manoa's legalistic reading of Samson as a national hero remains complacently euphemistic. The ceremonies commemorating Samson's death, Manoa says, will celebrate his great deeds and lament his failures, "Only bewailing / His lot unfortunate in nuptial choice, / From whence captivity and loss of eyes" (1743–45). Thus Manoa tries to separate Samson's victories from his defeats in a way that violates the doubtfulness and complexity of his son's career.[55] Similarly, the Chorus's judgment that "all is best, *though* we oft doubt" (1746; italics added) ignores the integral role that doubting plays in *Samson*'s conclusion. Unknown to Manoa and the Chorus, Samson's defeats provide the means to his success.

Without the "nuptial choice" of Dalila, Samson would not have ruined the Philistine temple; without the woman of Timna he would not have achieved his earlier victories. Yet the play goes even further, casting doubt on the very notion of success. After Samson's final action, Israel will again fall under Philistine domination, and will again forget its true God as it repeatedly does in the Judges narrative (see Judges 2:10, 1 Samuel 4:2–11). From the point of view of historical results, Samson dies in vain.

The Book of Judges fully illustrates the ironic, transgressively violent character of the Hebrew God, whose punishment of Israel for its forgetfulness of true religion seems unjustifiable because it aims at the sheer exercise of divine retribution rather than didactic effect (apostasy appears to be an incorrigible fact of the human condition in the Hebrew Bible). Earlier in the play, Samson himself euphemized the ways of God, defending himself by indulging his resistance to paradox, when he derided the Philistine divinities, asserting that "Gods unable / To acquit themselves and prosecute their foes / But by ungodly deeds, the contradiction / Of their own deity, Gods cannot be" (896 – 99). But the God of *Samson* likes to contradict his own deity: the power of the divine relies on the confusion that stems from humans' inability to understand his will.

When God, or Samson, punishes the Philistines with catastrophe, pathos becomes pathological, an indulgence in the excitement of disaster. This terrible work seems "ungodly": why such bloodshed? Slavoj Žižek emphasizes Freud's point that the superego feeds off the forces of the id.[56] The superego is an agency of severe enjoyment as well as duty: it can envision duty in the form of desperate, and often gruesomely violent, pleasure. The thrill of triumphing over evil, which Satan in *Paradise Regained* continually and unsuccessfully holds out to the Son, is as surely evoked at the end of *Samson* as it is in the more secular terms of *The Faerie Queene*'s Book 5.

In the end, Manoa and the Chorus resolutely ignore the ruthless, barbaric character of Samson's superego. Neither Manoa nor the Chorus achieves the realization that Samson's career transcends the staid providential ceremonies designed to commemorate Israel's national victory. This is a form of public forgetting more radical than the one depicted in Judges, because it produces a false continuity where history actually exhibits the gaps of apostasy and betrayal.[57] Nor do the Israelites sense that there may be anything dubious about seeing Samson as a symbol of disciplined, Stoic patience. These characters' inability to grasp the uneasy, provoking character, the sheer excess, of Samson's triumph suggests the impossibility of seeing this hero as a conventionally inspiring Christian symbol without simplifying him beyond recognition. Samson proves to be less a model for heroic action leading his audience to virtue than a "mirror of our fickle state, / Since man on earth unparallel'd" (164–65), a phenomenon as unique and inimitable as the course of dire necessity itself. Even though Manoa and the Chorus finally display Samson's triumph as a historical lesson, its real, "unparallel'd" meaning lies buried with the hero himself under the uninterpretable rubble of catastrophe.

The conclusion of *Samson Agonistes* goes beyond *Paradise Regained* by taking pathos past subjectivity into the realm of radically impersonal communion: Samson among the Philistine dead. Milton moves past the individuating power of conscience to the terrain of the primitive superego, an undifferentiated necessity that overwhelms the self's capacity for judgement. The move toward an unknown future that *Paradise Lost* and *Paradise Regained* inaugurate finds its consummation here in a realm altogether beyond historical edification and moral exemplarity—though the presence of the Chorus at the end tells us that the bodily immediacy of Samson's fate will inevitably be translated, across an unbridgeable gap, to such uses. Didactic rhetoric springs, phoenixlike, from the ashes of the hero's trauma.

# Conclusion

One of current criticism's significant inheritances from tradition is the assumption of a division between literary language and the language of social morality.[1] Despite the recent emphasis on history, we often still read the poetry of Spenser and Milton in terms of a supposed polarity between aesthetic and public intent. Though I, too, am suggesting in this book that poetic pathos implies a radical demand that exceeds religious or political programs, I have argued against assuming any easy division between poetry and public moralism by showing that these poets' moralizing impulses remain implicated with their aesthetic interest in pathos. Symbolic social law relies on, even as it resists, the Imaginary of literary creation.

Recent criticism of Milton usually subordinates aesthetics to morals. Fish and Radzinowicz, for example, assert that Milton's didactic goals firmly and invariably guide his art. In this conclusion, I will take a critical look at the didactic critics' choice of moralizing over aesthetics as well as the Romantic tradition they react against, which prizes aesthetic pathos over didactic agenda.

I begin with the Romantic privileging of art and passion. In his choice of the aesthetic as a favored critical category, Milton's great successor, John Dryden, presages Romantic criticism and signals a departure from the Reformation's rather more moralistic ways of evaluating literature. As I remarked in my first chapter, Renaissance and Reformation criticism of epic suffers from a gap between the pathos of amoral decorum and didactic morality, though Scaliger, Tasso and Sidney try, in different ways, to conceal or overcome this difference. In the more secular age of Dryden, the disjunction between poetic affect and moral rule becomes an explicit opposition, and poetry's aesthetic worth takes priority over the occasions for moralizing it provides. With Dryden, the vision of epic as aesthetic panorama achieves unequivocal victory over moralism.[2] In his Preface to *Fables* (1700), for example, Dryden admits his own preference for Homer's fiery Achilles, "hot, impatient, revengeful," over Virgil's pious and proto-Christian Aeneas, who is "patient, considerate, careful of his people, and merciful to his enemies."[3] In his "Discourse Concerning the Original and Progress of Satire".(1693) Dryden demonstrates even more markedly the dominion of classical decorum over Christian morality in his criticism. In the "Discourse," Dryden praises Milton on the grounds that "no man has so happily copied the manner of Homer; or so copiously translated his Grecisms, and the Latin elegancies of Virgil." After applauding Milton's classical poetics, Dryden goes on to criticize the tedious effects of Milton's Christian theme on his classical standards: "'Tis true, he runs into a flat of thought, sometimes for a hundred lines together, but 'tis when he is got into a track of scripture.'"[4] In the same essay, Dryden agrees with Boileau "that the machines of our Christian religion in heroic poetry, are much more feeble to support th[e] weight" of heroic sublimity "than those of heathenism."[5] Dryden, like Empson, accuses Christianity of being unpoetic.

In his *Aeneis* preface (1697), Dryden transforms Milton into a romance writer in order to deny the success of his Christian-didactic project. In effect, Dryden claims that *Paradise Lost* can be reduced to the "long and tedious havoc" of romance that Milton derides in the invocation to Book 9 (9.30) as poetically and theologically insufficient. Dryden openly spurns Milton's scriptural project by placing him as a writer of romance rather than a sacred poet. Milton would have ranked with Homer and Virgil, Dryden writes in his preface, "If the Devil had not been his hero, instead of Adam; if the giant had not foiled the knight, and driven him out of his stronghold, to wander through the world with his lady errant."[6] Dryden turns *Paradise Lost* into romance so that he can turn down Milton's appeal to a divine source, and thus diminish his precursor's poetic powers.

Dryden's ignoring of Milton's didactic goals, his restriction of epic to the aesthetic sphere, shows his distance from Milton's overtly moralizing intentions, which guard his identity as Protestant poet.[7] Dryden stands near the beginning of a critical tradition that will, in the twentieth century, assert the need for poetry to preserve its integrity by rejecting the straightforward espousal of any ideological content including—especially—Christian morality.[8] He thus defines a new distance between aesthetic and religious modes, between poetry and the sacred.

Romanticism adopts and extends Dryden's legacy of aesthetic reading. Hazlitt, in particular, champions Spenser as an amoral poet devoted to sumptuous and refined artistic effects. Hazlitt's brilliant appreciation of *The Faerie Queene*'s "voluptuous pathos" celebrates the

Spenserian style as "the perfection of melting harmony, dissolving the soul in pleasure, or holding it captive in the chains of suspense."[9] Hazlitt forgets Spenser's Protestant moralism as he absorbs the stylistic delights of *The Faerie Queene*. "Dissolving the soul in pleasure"—the threat that Acrasia's Bower poses to Guyon—becomes a poetic delight rather than an immoral lure. As Hazlitt praises the gently sensual surface of Spenser's poetry in language associated with the Bower and Phaedria's lilies of the field, he casts aside the negative moral significance that Spenser attaches to this sensuality: "The undulations [of Spenser's poetry] are infinite, like those of the waves of the sea," Hazlitt writes, "but the effect is still the same, lulling the senses into a deep oblivion of the jarring noises of the world, from which we have no wish to be ever recalled."[10] For Spenser, such pleasure is a dangerous drug, though it also constitutes the exquisite essence of his poetry; Hazlitt loses the sense of danger. Though Hazlitt strongly hints at an association between Spenser's poetic power and his evil characters, he decides not to articulate the moral risk this association conveys: "The poet takes and lays us in the lap of a lovelier nature [i.e., like Duessa and Acrasia]. . . . He waves his wand of enchantment [i.e., like Archimago]."[11]

Milton undergoes a similar aestheticizing transformation in the hands of Keats, who in his annotations of *Paradise Lost* concentrates on the moments of sympathetic, lyrical passion in Milton as if they were independent of the poet's moral project, which Keats clearly wishes to avoid. Keats's reading of Milton emphasizes the passages in *Paradise Lost* that embody what Geoffrey Hartman has called Milton's "counterplot,"[12] the poet's time-stopping lyrical suspensions of his drive toward narrative conclusions. As I have suggested in this book, such easing of the pressure for narrative closure also means a veering away from didactic agenda and toward the potential for a different, morally unverifiable future. Though Hartman sees the counterplot as a stalling of temporal movement, it also signals the pressure of a kairos that, more powerful than any predictive "warning voice," will interrupt and transform the smooth expanse of history.

Despite their general lack of interest in Miltonic moralism, the Romantics retain a committed, if unorthodox, sense of the religious aura of his (and their own) poetry. Empson, by contrast, though he is also an aestheticizing reader, refuses to recognize the possibility of a religious affect distinct from summary or reductive moral doctrine. For Empson, all Miltonic religion is abstractly moralizing in a way that obstructs the truly poetic.

I have argued against Empson's reading in this book. But one need not embrace all of Empson's secularizing assumptions to see him as a useful corrective to the critical tendency, most notably present in Radzinowicz and the "neo-Christian" tradition she represents, to claim that Milton writes a completely integral, successfully moralizing religious narrative—a perfectly formed linear progress toward individual regeneration that also expresses a clear realization of God's will. Radzinowicz writes that, in *Samson Agonistes*, "Milton seeks to change the minds of readers by showing them a mind being itself changed in the characteristic way in which the mind can be changed, by dialectic leading to resolution, internal drama leading to integration, conflict leading to harmony."[13] Against Radzinowicz, I claim that Milton presents a far more radical and disturbing picture of the process of change, one that acknowledges the conscious mind's sense of inadequacy when it finds itself called toward the obscurity of an unknown future. Such acknowledgment of unpredictable and possibly incomprehensible transformation must necessarily call in question the drive toward didactic resolution that Radzinowicz prizes.

In a recent, characteristically perceptive essay on *Samson*, John Guillory's emphasis on a rigidly patterned secular historical narrative, like Radzinowicz's emphasis on a religious one, works to recontain Samson's disruptive revolutionary force. Guillory claims that he wants to resist giving "an illusion of narrative intelligibility" to Samson's fate, but he finally asserts such intelligibility, which he calls Samson's "exchange-value" within the social structure, as the condition of the hero's meaning. Though he cites Bataille in elucidating the effect of Samson's "useless" self-sacrifice, Guillory goes on to explain Samson's violence, against Bataille and for Marx, by construing it as a symptom of (what he sees as) capital's drive toward interpretable narrative. Guillory admits that Samson's death offers a protest against the ideas of profit and loss that drive capital (and, I would add, Christian didacticism). Destroying himself, the hero stakes his proud identity against "the very law of rational calculation." But the critic still wants to calculate this incalculable sacrifice. Guillory reduces Samson to a function of the socioeconomic system when he claims that capital produces and determines the realm of excessive expenditure, the aesthetic, that it sets off against rationality. Poetry, then, in this reading, proves to be merely capital in disguise, a secret source of profit. But Guillory remains silent on the question of what this profit amounts to: how can *Samson* be persuasively converted to a lesson about the uses of art, and in particular tragic pathos, for capitalism? Moreover, do these uses really succeed in consuming the aesthetic realm without remainder? Guillory's Marxist historicism simply represses the independent force of pathos by trying to bring it under the rule of doctrine: in this case, a law of historical development that offers comfort to the critic who seeks the ease of legal explanations.[14]

Empson recognizes the gap between drama and doctrine, poetic and didactic success, that much current Milton criticism, from neo-Christ-

## Conclusion 193

ian to new historicist, dedicates itself to resolving (that is, repressing).[15] Most Miltonists are more confident than Milton himself was in claiming that the poet fulfills his doctrinal goals in his poems, reconciling the demands of the self's narrative adventures with those of prescriptive Christianity. Milton's doctrinal admonitions necessarily contradict the dramatic reality of the poem. Satan's resistant and Eve's independent mind appeal to the sympathetic reader even as the authoritative voice of the poet labels them wrong.

Milton criticism has failed to acknowledge fully the extent to which, for this poet, the tempering of human affect must engage in a doctrinal violation of it, an intrusion from outside the reader's experience of the poem. The problem with Radzinowicz's moralism, like Fish's reader response criticism, is that it sees this doctrinal action as a fulfillment, a reconciliation of reader and author to text rather than the author's painful wounding of his own text's power. When Milton's reader reacts against the author's moralizing intrusion, this reaction is also, at least in part, Milton's own. Milton cannot, finally, accept such doctrinal judgments against his poetry, even as he realizes and exploits their necessity.

Milton's doctrine must betray his aesthetics in this way because he knows that his sublime sacred drama, if left to stand without doctrine's explicit admonitions, might turn into a merely poetic rather than a religious text. Doctrinal abstraction, unlike the passionate dramatizing of scripture, explicitly refuses to be read in secular terms. *Paradise Regained* and *Samson Agonistes,* in moving away from the unequivocal doctrinal strain embodied in *Paradise Lost*'s Michael, assert a sacred and profane ambiguity, the Janus face of earthly experience. In his last major poems, Milton does not simply use earthly drama to embody a religious message so that he can make the message more palpable, as the neo-Christians claim. Instead, he makes the status and direction of the message itself doubtful.[16] Is Samson inspired when he pulls down the temple, or does he engage in a self-motivated act of violence? Does the Son definitively distance himself from Satan at the end of *Paradise Regained*, or does he come dangerously close to Satan, testing faith in a manner as theatrical as Satan's own—so that we, like his audience in the Gospels, are tempted to accuse him of doing Beelzebub's work (Matt. 12:24 –25)?

In *Paradise Regained*, Milton wants both to avoid and to indulge in the confrontational resemblance between good and evil.[17] The poet's avoidance of the confrontation is undoubtedly more noticeable than the ways he yields to it. *Paradise Regained* stars the Messiah rather than a human hero exactly so that Milton may avoid a dramatic battle between virtue and vice, with its entanglement in Imaginary desire. Many readers have remarked on the tepid quality of Satan's temptations, particularly at the poem's beginning. The Son knows good by knowing good, not evil: for much of *Paradise Regained* he tries to face Satan without facing him, without doing anything that might mirror Satan's own tactics. But the Son finally proves his power, as I argued in my discussion of the poem, by raising the possibility of such a mirroring—by considering that the younger brother's triumph might conceal a family resemblance.

The angelic chorus at the end of *Paradise Regained*, with its celebration of the Son as his father's "true Image," carefully wards off the poem's suggestion of a kinship between the Son and Satan. *Samson* renders impossible any similarly corrective moment: the tactful moralizations of Manoa and the final Chorus prove manifestly inadequate to the scope of Samson's pathos. *Samson*'s ending attains its force through its proximity to the barbaric, but the commentary of Samson's father and his people must deny this brutality in its effort to make Samson unequivocally saintly.

The violence of *Samson*, which in its ruthless evidence of the hero's will may appear ambitious and worldly rather than submissive to God, bears witness to a disruption in cultural history. Milton writes at the beginning of an era for which sacred poetry will become increasingly difficult and religious enthusiasm increasingly suspect. As David Quint remarks, Milton in creating *Paradise Lost* as a poem with a literal claim to prophetic truth "may be behind the prevailing taste of his own time which . . . valorized the literary text's innovation and individuality to the relative disregard of its claims to truth."[18] Milton's prophetic ambition to unfold truth through the pathos of inspired religious drama, a difficult quest even for him, becomes less and less feasible in the increasingly secular age that follows.

In this transitional historical context, Milton worries about the possibility that his sublime drama may overwhelm its moral paradigms, and this worry forces him to circumscribe sublimity by means of moralism. Like Spenser with his Mammon, Milton sometimes makes evil ironically and obviously self-frustrating in an effort to evade the full force of its insinuation into our lives. He occasionally casts Satan as an allegorical bogey or caricature, "th'infernal Serpent" (1.34). But there are many astonishing counterexamples in which Milton does give Satan's pathos its due. Satan's Mount Niphates speech provides one memorable instance. At the end of the speech, Milton adds this authorial aside:

> Thus while he spake, each passion dimmed his face
> Thrice changed with pale, ire, envy and despair,
> Which marred his borrowed visage, and betrayed
> Him counterfeit, if any eye beheld. . . .
> (*PL* 4.114 –17)

# Conclusion

Satan's *real* despair unmasks him as a counterfeit angel. "If any eye beheld": whose eye? To angels, Satan is nothing more or less than a counterfeit; but to our sight, which observes him more closely than Uriel's, he conveys the pathos of his fall, and therefore proves himself real. When Satan's true character shows through his disguise as a "stripling Cherub" (3.636), Uriel discovers him to be a mere hoax; but for our eyes only, he is a sublimely fallen angel, subject to an appallingly genuine grief. Here, the gap between holy pretense and infernal desire expresses a descent from the angelic into a lower and more familiar realm, the human, a fall that unveils the desire and desperation we know best. Satan is real to us not despite but because of his self-contradictory status as fallen divinity; such contradiction also defines human heroism in its aspiration to godlike privilege. Satan in despair is not really "alone, / As he suppos'd, all unobserv'd, unseen" (129–30). He remains on stage, playing to us along with his own self-consciousness. Since such theatricality unavoidably marks our own fallenness, Satan's melodramatic nature speaks for, not against, his truth as a counterpart to us. Satan is, therefore, authentic, not counterfeit; and his pathos, foreshadowing Adam's, provides the most indelible lesson of *Paradise Lost*.

This trial by contraries, then, makes up Milton's teaching. If didacticism tries to censor the self's potentially Satanic impulses by assuming a voice larger and truer than the self, then poetic pathos implicitly acknowledges, against this moral project, that all truly compelling voices are internal, and therefore suspect: that Satan speaks for author and reader, who are bound together by the Imaginary movement of sympathy. For Spenser as well as Milton, there are risks in this acknowledgment, as these authors well know; but they also know the price one pays for moralizing reduction. Centuries later, our desires remain divided between the comforts of the reductive and the disorienting afflictions of subjective pathos. But, in a true poem, it is pathos that transports us, shaking us into new perception. Like Adam in Eden, we can say of Spenser and Milton,

> here
> Far otherwise, transported I behold,
> Transported touch; here passion first I felt,
> Commotion strange, in all enjoyments else
> Superior and unmoved, here only weak
> Against the charm of beauty's powerful glance.
> (*PL* 8.528–33)

# Notes

## Introduction

1. The self's distance from the typological pattern of history, according to Damrosch's analysis, takes on a radical quality in Bunyan's Protestantism, in the gap between the externalized, allegorical mode of *The Holy War* and the internalized self-searching of *Grace Abounding*, that it does not possess in medieval Catholicism. See Leopold Damrosch, *God's Plot and Man's Stories* (Chicago: University of Chicago Press, 1986).

2. See Norbrook, *Poetry and Politics in the English Renaissance* (London: Routledge and Kegan Paul, 1984). I should also mention here the recently revived controversy over the importance of Spenser's influence on Milton, which Annabel Patterson has brought into question: see her "Couples, Canons and the Uncouth: Spenser-and-Milton in Educational Theory," *Critical Inquiry* 16, no. 4 (Summer 1990): 773–93.

3. Spenser's Protean flexibility in moving from one term to the other may overwhelm the sharp focus on specific scenes usually necessary to what we call the dramatic, but it does so only to restate the poem's interests in the larger theater of genre and tradition. For a statement of Spenser's supposed nondramatic quality, see *Renaissance Self-Fashioning* (Chicago: University of Chicago Press, 1980), 192; for the seminal statements in the debate, see Roger Sale, "Spenser's Undramatic Poetry," in *Elizabethan Poetry*, ed. Paul Alpers (New York: Oxford University Press, 1967), and Alpers, *The Poetry of the Faerie Queene* (Princeton: Princeton University Press, 1967). Goldberg's *Endlesse Worke* is in some ways a refinement of Sale's description of *The Faerie Queene* as an undifferentiated and bewildering mass—though Sale sees in the mass an emblem of narrative certainty, whereas Goldberg sees narrative undecidability (Jonathan Goldberg, *Endlesse Worke* [Baltimore: Johns Hopkins University Press, 1981]).

4. See Leonard Trinterud, ed., *Elizabethan Puritanism* (New York: Oxford University Press, 1971), 11, 135, and the selections from Foxe and John a Lasso in Trinterud that outline the difference between "visible" and the "invisible" religion (58–65., 112).

5. See Peter Lake, *Moderate Puritans and the Elizabethan Church* (Cambridge: Cambridge University Press, 1982) and Patrick Collinson, *The Religion of Protestants* (Oxford: Clarendon Press, 1982), 251, 281–82. See also Derek Hirst, *Authority and Conflict in England, 1603–58* (Cambridge: Harvard University Press, 1986), 60–89.

6. Northrop Frye, *The Great Code* (New York: Harcourt Brace Jovanovich, 1982), 130 (see also 100 –101). For a specific application of Pauline-Augustinian individualism, and its argument against institutional goals, to the epic tradition, see Andrew Fichter, *Poets Historicall* (New Haven: Yale University Press, 1982), 64. For an analysis of the limited extent to which Calvin admitted the idea of personal, inward "preparation" for God's gift of grace, and the contrast between Bullinger and Calvin in this regard (a contrast that survived in English Puritanism), see Norman Pettit, *The Heart Prepared* (New Haven: Yale University Press, 1966), 41– 60. The internalizing tendencies in Protestant literature are theorized by Barbara Lewalski in *Protestant Poetics and the Seventeenth Century Religious Lyric* (Princeton: Princeton University Press, 1979). A recent important interpretation along these lines is Richard Strier's *Love Known* (Chicago: University of Chicago Press, 1983). See also Wilbur Sanders, *John Donne's Poetry* (Cambridge: Cambridge University Press, 1971).

7. Lacan calls society's moralizing powers the Symbolic, in contrast to the inward, inchoate desire of the Imaginary. In my opinion, Lacan pays too little attention to the maturation process, implying that the struggle between Imaginary and Symbolic must end in an ironic submission to the Symbolic rather than a more liberal or reciprocal relation that would foster individual development. Here I would confront the partiality of Lacan, who emphasizes Freud's statements of Symbolic mastery, with the partiality of the objects-relation model proposed by Jonathan Lear, which comes close to eliminating the Symbolic altogether. See Lear, *Love and its Place in Nature* (New York: Farrar, Straus and Giroux, 1990).

8. William Kerrigan, *The Sacred Complex* (Cambridge: Harvard University Press, 1983), 8.

9. On the subject of the primitive superego, see Slavoj Žižek, *Looking Awry* (Cambridge: MIT Press, 1991), 23–26.

10. The core of heroic subjectivity in Homer, the reckless and self-centered arrogance that Homer sometimes calls *atê*, may be considered as a "subjecting to" the rule of competitive heroism that generates a social necessity, martial victory. But even in Homer it cannot be rationalized in this manner. Most prominently (but not exclusively) in the figure of Achilles, heroic arrogance takes on an extreme life of its own that, as I argue in chapter 1, cannot be understood as a mere symptom of functional social power, the "results culture" of archaic Greece (to use A. W. H. Adkins's term; see Adkins, *Merit and Responsibility* [Oxford: Clarendon Press, 1960]).

11. See Jonathan Dollimore, *Radical Tragedy* (Brighton: Harvester Press, 1984).

12. On this issue see Joan Copjec's "The Orthopsychic Subject," *October* 49 (1989): 53–72. Copjec identifies a pivotal moment in Althusser's misreading of Lacan: according to Althusser the Imaginary is the means of Symbolic inscription rather than the subjectivity that the Symbolic must repress to found social order.

13. For such a political argument, see Emmanuel Levinas, *Totality and Infinity*, trans. Alphonso Lingis (Pittsburgh: Duquesne University Press, 1969 [1st French ed., 1961]), along with much of Jacques Derrida's work in the 1970s and 1980s, and Daniel Price's *Without a Woman to Read* (unpublished manuscript).

14. Jameson's idealist move, which makes his book the mere effect rather than the ingenious invention of a transcendent imperative to historize, is reminiscent of Kojève's claim that Hegel's *Phenomenology* was in fact written by history in the shape of the man Hegel (who "is somehow Napoleon's self-consciousness")—though Jameson lacks Kojève's self-mocking ironies. See Alexandre Kojève, *Introduction to the Reading of Hegel* (Ithaca: Cornell University Press, 1969), 69–70.

15. A Marxist dialectical treatment of romance enables us, writes Jameson, to "escap[e] from the purely individualizing categories of ethics," to "transcend the cat-

egories into which our existence as individual subjects necessarily locks us and open up the radically distinct transindividual perspectives of collective life or historical process." Predictably, then, romance finds its fulfillment in the utopian telos of Hegelian Marxism. Jameson, *The Political Unconscious* (Ithaca: Cornell University Press, 1981), 116.

16. Jameson, 116. Contrast Jameson's reflections on individual action on 49–50. An even greater problem is Jameson's assumption that Nietzsche's phrase "beyond good and evil" must connote postindividualism; as Jameson well knows, his reading turns Nietzsche's anticollective bias upside down in the service of his own antiindividualism.

17. I am here following Stanley Cavell, "The Avoidance of Love: A Reading of King Lear" (in *Must We Mean What We Say?* [New York: Scribner's, 1969] and *Disowning Knowledge* [New York: Cambridge University Press, 1987]).

18. See Stephen Greenblatt, "Psychoanalysis and Renaissance Culture," in *Literary Theory/Renaissance Texts*, ed. Patricia Parker and David Quint (Baltimore: Johns Hopkins University Press, 1986). Greenblatt suggests that the early modern period precedes and makes possible modern subjective psychology, but his essay focuses on excluding, rather than explaining the genesis of, this subjectivity. A similar treatment of the subject is offered in Greenblatt's essay "Fiction and Friction" in *Reconstructing Individualism*, ed. Thomas Heller et. al. (Stanford, Calif.: Stanford University Press, 1986), esp. 33–35.

19. Greenblatt, "Psychoanalysis and Renaissance Culture," 223.

20. Jameson, 113.

21. See Patricia Parker, *Inescapable Romance* (Princeton: Princeton University Press, 1979), 75.

22. See Burckhardt's citation of Petrarch's praise for the systematic oppression of the ruler of Padua: Jakob Burckhardt, *The Civilization of the Renaissance in Italy*, trans. S. G. C. Middlemore (London: Phaidon, 1950), 5; also Gordon Braden and William Kerrigan, *The Idea of the Renaissance* (Baltimore: Johns Hopkins University Press, 1989), 12.

23. Burckhardt, 81.

24. See Burckhardt, 44. Burckhardt, like his inheritor Nietzsche, also recognized the power of the state to stifle culture and individuality, especially in the wake of the Franco-Prussian war of 1870–71. An interesting formulation of this opinion can be found in Burckhardt's *Force and Freedom*, ed. J. H. Nichols (1943; reprint, New York: Pantheon, 1964), 117–18; see also 170, 229–30, 149–51. See also Hayden White, *Metahistory* (Baltimore: Johns Hopkins University Press, 1973), 230–64.

25. I should note that the considerable influence of Burckhardt's description of state power on the new historicism is almost never acknowledged.

26. See Jonathan Goldberg, *James I and the Politics of Literature* (Baltimore: Johns Hopkins University Press, 1983), 148.

27. Greenblatt, *Renaissance Self-Fashioning*, 257 (italics added). See also 111, with its suggestion that the apparently personal is really impersonal or institutional.

28. Ibid., 9.

29. Ibid., 85; see also 81–82.

30. To claim that the subject is institutionally produced, Greenblatt must distort historical chronology. Greenblatt finds an intense inwardness in Wyatt, who is writing during the same Henrician era as Tyndale; yet he claims that Tyndale's emphasis on external authority precedes and engenders the later [*sic*] development of Protestant subjectivity like Wyatt's. Moreover, if it is true that, as Greenblatt claims, Wyatt, like Tyndale, is "governed by the essential values of dominance and submission," that

he sees "no privileged sphere of individuality" but only external power, how then does one account for what Greenblatt himself describes as Wyatt's intense personal emotion in his penitential psalms (117, 119–20)—a confessional pathos that Tyndale lacks?

31. Foucault intended this viewpoint as a demystifying, Nietzschean reduction to origins. But Nietzsche's *Genealogy of Morals* emphasizes, in an analysis incomparably severer and more searching than anything in Foucault, that institutional discipline is a cruel, empowering means for the individual to invent himself. Nietzsche sees asceticism as the self's most extreme, intent strategy, and therefore asceticism begins in the priestly individual's desire for meaning, power, and survival, not in an external force's commands. Foucault evidently realized that he had neglected the individual; see his statement in *Technologies of the Self: A Seminar with Michel Foucault*, eds. Luther Martin, Huck Gutman, and Patrick Hutton (Amherst, Mass.: University of Massachusetts Press, 1988), 19: "Perhaps I've insisted too much on the technology of domination and power . . . I am more and more interested in . . . the history of how an individual acts upon himself." Accordingly, the volumes on ancient ethics in the *History of Sexuality* emphasize self-fashioning over institutional determination.

32. See, in particular, Greenblatt, *Renaissance Self-Fashioning*, 119. Greenblatt here asserts both the conflict and the interrelation between the institutional "penitential system" and the sinner's (Wyatt's) private penance.

33. Greenblatt, *Renaissance Self-Fashioning*, 119–20.

34. See Goldberg, "Shakespearean Inscriptions: the Voicing of Power," in *Shakespeare and the Question of Theory*, eds. Patricia Parker and Geoffrey Hartman (New York: Methuen, 1985); Dollimore's *Radical Tragedy*, 204–17; and, for the critique of Enobarbus, Janet Adelman's *The Common Liar* (New Haven: Yale University Press, 1973), 24.

35. The issue of the new historicist and Foucauldian interest in marginal or eccentric phenomena—the anecdotal—is a complex one (see Hayden White, "The New Historicism," in *The New Historicism*, ed. H. Aram Veeser [New York: Routledge, 1988]). Foucault's emphasis on the weird or freakish, the unpredictable interstices of power, does not argue against totalizing of the kind I am referring to here. Foucault chooses the marginal or eccentric because it cannot be seen as an effectual historical force that might disrupt totality. See "Truth and Power," in Michel Foucault, *Power/Knowledge*, trans. and ed. Colin Gordon (New York: Pantheon, 1980). Paul Smith, *Discerning the Subject* (Minneapolis: University of Minnesota Press, 1988), is an important study of the issue of Marxist and Foucauldian subjectivity. Smith criticizes both Marx and Foucault for wanting to construe the subject in too close harmony with social discourse—a point that is, I believe, complementary to my own.

# Chapter 1. Pathos and Moralizing in Classical and Renaissance Tradition

1. For the identification of Milton's Fall as an Aristotelian *peripeteia*, see John Steadman, *Epic and Tragic Structure in Paradise Lost* (Chicago: University of Chicago Press, 1976) and Barbara K. Lewalski, *Paradise Lost and the Rhetoric of Literary Forms* (Princeton: Princeton University Press, 1985), 228. We might compare Adam's pathos in Book 10 to his surrender to the pathos of the Flood, which, as Neil Hertz points out (in his "Wordsworth and the Tears of Adam," in *The End of the Line* [New York: Columbia University Press, 1985]) cements an intense identification between

the poet, Adam, and the reader by localizing history in a moment, and overriding the larger structure of humanity's survival and redemption.

2. Martha Nussbaum has made this point eloquently regarding Stoicism's effort to extirpate the passions: Nussbaum, "The Stoics on the Extirpation of the Passions," *Apeiron* 20 (1987): 128–77. Giovanni Ferrari, in *Listening to the Cicadas* (Cambridge: Cambridge University Press, 1987), 112, argues that Plato does not regard emotion as an enemy; though he is tempted by the attitude, he is determined to ward it off. In the *Republic*, at least, I would argue against Ferrari, Plato yields more than slightly to the temptation; in the *Phaedrus* (Ferrari's focus) he pursues a different strategy, attempting to transmute the turbulent emotion of the lustful horse into a means to philosophical ecstasy.

3. See Lear, *Love and Its Place in Nature*, 58. I will return to Aristotle and the theory of tragedy in discussions of *The Faerie Queene*.

4. For analogous Stoic examples, see Cicero, *Tusculan Disputations* 3.26, or Seneca's Epistle 98.5: "Sic autem componetur, si, quid humanarum rerum varietas possit, cogitaverit, antequam senserit, si et liberos et coniugem et patrimonium sic habuerit tamquam non utique semper habiturus et tamquam non futurus ob hoc miserior, si habere desierit."

An extended treatment of Greek Stoicism's views of pathos is given by Brad Inwood, *Ethics and Human Action in Early Stoicism* (Oxford: Clarendon Press, 1985), 127–81.

Many Stoics are careful to moderate the philosophical extreme that would deny all emotions as the insidious beginnings of vice. Lipsius, for example, welcomes the socially responsible feeling of sympathy or mercy while prohibiting the indulgent vice of pity. Lipsius, *Two Bookes of Constancie*, trans. Sir John Stradling [1594] (New Brunswick, N.J.: Rutgers University Press, 1939), 99; for the Roman version, see Seneca, *De Clementia* 2.7. For the Renaissance distinction between mercy, which is valuable, and pity, which is often seen as a disease of the mind, see Nohrnberg, 383. Ancient Greek attitudes toward the expression of grief are described in Kenneth Dover, *Greek Popular Morality* (Oxford: Basil Blackwell, 1974), 167–69. For a later Stoic version, see Seneca's Cons. Helv. 16. Thomas Gould helpfully defines pathos in terms of human vulnerability to the unforeseeable and unexplainable—an emphasis that I believe complements my own opposition between, on the one hand, the pathos of a human subjectivity cut off from rationalizable narrative or social structures and, on the other, a sense of guiding, explicable providential narrative (Gould, *The Ancient Quarrel Between Poetry and Philosophy* [Princeton: Princeton University Press, 1991]).

5. Plato insists that the *arkhôn*, who is comparable with the captain (*kubernêtês*) of a ship, should have in him no part of his sailors' emotional nature. The nautical image is important. In a passage from Book 3 of the *Republic*: Socrates says that it will be necessary for the rulers of the virtuous city to tell a "larger lie" (*meizon hamartêma*) than that of a sailor lying to his captain (*kubernêtês*) about his own or a fellow sailor's state (*praxeôs ekhei*). See also Book 1 of the *Laws* and its statement that the worthy navigator (*khrêstos . . . arkhon . . . ean tên nautikên ekhei epistêmên monon*)—that is, the ruler—must not be subject to the pathos of seasickness (639b). The ruler must be master of himself before he can master others, a familiar topos given additional resonance by Plato's insistent parallels between the individual and the city (see below, on the passage from Book 9 of the *Republic*, and see Michel Foucault, *The History of Sexuality*, trans. Richard Hurley [New York: Pantheon, 1985], 2:81).

For a summary of the use of the *kubernêtês* as an image of a city's ruler, see Fraenkel, *Agamemnon* commentary, 2:109 and n. For the historical background of the image, see Koester in Kromayer-Veith, *Heerwesen . . . der Griechen und Römen* (*Handbuch der Altertumswissenschaft* 4:3.2, 1928), 188, and Foucault, 2:139. Cicero in his *De Finibus* 4.14 argues against Stoicism by claiming that "cum autem assumpta est ratio" to *sensus*, "tanto in dominatu locatur ut omnia illa prima naturae huius tutelae subiciantur. Itaque non discedit ab eorum curatione quibus praeposita vitam omnem debet gubernare:" the verb *gubernare* is the equivalent of *kubernein*.

6. The lie is "larger" because the republic is bigger than its citizens: it is a topos in which the truths of nature can more clearly and authoritatively be read than in the individual *psychê*. In Book 10 of the *Republic* Plato makes explicit his concern with scale or size, drawing a connection between the perspectival distortions of desire and those of tragic poetry. Poetry, as if by magic, makes things appear larger or smaller than they actually are; the deception is discovered when objects are measured by the definitive, mathematical perception of the *logismos* (Rep. 602c–d). For a treatment of the idea of authoritative perception as a question of scale, a consideration that involves Plato's use of the terms *haplôs* and *hêmin*, see Wesley Trimpi, *Muses of One Mind* (Princeton: Princeton University Press, 1983), and Kathy Eden, *Poetic and Legal Fiction in the Aristotelian Tradition* (Princeton: Princeton University Press, 1986). For the connection between the big and the beautiful, and Plato's effort to formulate the latter as an absolute rather than a relative standard in the Hippias Major and the Sophist, see Seth Benardete's introduction to his translation of the *Theaetetus*, the *Sophist*, and the *Statesman* (*The Being of the Beautiful* [Chicago: University of Chicago Press, 1984]), xxvii–xxxv.

7. Stanford notes the echo in his edition.

8. The martial service that Ajax laments is, of course, one of the central formative duties for Athenian civic consciousness and one that Plato wanted to preserve in his republic. For an evocative description of the importance of Athenian military service for Athens's self-image, see Simon Goldhill, *Reading Greek Tragedy* (Cambridge: Cambridge University Press, 1986), 63–64.

9. For Plato's ambivalence toward poetry in the *Republic*, see Paul Vicaire, *Platon: Critique Litteraire* (Paris: Klincksieck, 1960), 48ff.

10. In the following discussion, to make clear the Homeric basis of this issue, I have used the word *thumos* rather than *thumoeides* (see Rep. 440e–441a: Plato uses both terms). On the *thumos* in Plato, see Bruno Snell, *The Discovery of the Mind*, trans. T. G. Rosenmeyer (Cambridge: Harvard University Press, 1953), 1–22, 198–200.

11. However, some of Plato's examples of the way *thumos* do rationalize it by transforming it into a kind of angry bodyguard for the *logismos* (Rep. 586d and ff. is very relevant here). The phrase *exôthen pathos* (Book 2, 381a) is significant: as in the Book 3 passage (mentioned earlier), which rejects grief for dead relatives in the name of autarchy (387d), Plato here sees the affections as foreign invaders to be resisted by an integral, unitary *psychê*. See 390d,439e–440a, and 441b (the examples of Leontius and Odysseus). Interestingly, Aristotle in his *Poetics* parallels or echoes the Leontius example. Aristotle uses Plato's image of looking at corpses as an instance of cheap theatrical spectacle (*opsis*), the level of artistic response that corresponds to Plato's *epithumia*.

12. Interestingly, Aristotle in Rhet. 1359a cites praises of Achilles for the inexpediency of his return to combat. Such neglect of one's own interests *can* be a normative value in Aristotle's *Rhetoric*, though he makes it clear that political speeches must answer to an audience's desire for expediency or results, not any generosity they might have. On Achilles' reputation in literary history, see Derek Hughes, *Dryden's Heroic Plays* (Lincoln: University of Nebraska Press, 1982), 15, and John M. Steadman, "Achilles in Renaissance Tradition," in his *Milton and the Paradoxes of Renais-*

*sance Heroism* (Baton Rouge: Louisiana State University Press, 1987). Adam Parry discusses the inchoate or inexpressible nature of Achilles' desire in "The Language of Achilles," repr. in *The Language and Background of Homer*, ed. G. S. Kirk(Cambridge, Mass.: W. Heffer, 1964), James Redfield, *Nature and Culture in the Iliad* (Chicago: University of Chicago Press,1975), and the article by P. Friedrich and Redfield in *Language* 54 (1978): 263–88, "Speech as a Personality Symbol: The Case of Achilles." Finally, the article by David Claus in *Transactions of the American Philological Association* 105 (1975): 13–28, "*Aidos* and the Language of Achilles," which I discovered after writing this chapter, shares much with my own approach and offers an important refinement of Parry.

13. The full passage runs as follows: "We shall not deem it worthy of Achilles himself, or think him so fond of possessions that he accepts the gifts of Agamemnon, or that he will release the corpse of Hector for ransom, but not otherwise" (390e–391a; trans. Grube, 61).

14. Socrates is himself tainted by the materialistic distortion committed by his interlocutor Glaucon. Glaucon, in Book 2, overlooked the desire for justice in his desire for commodified luxury. Socrates, in his conviction that human desire is always materialistic in this way—that Achilles is like Glaucon—overlooks the more serious threat to the *Republic*'s vision of justice, Achilles' passion for his *philos* Patroklos. Socrates' interrogation of Achilles, and of Homer's heroic poetics in general, must be set in the context of his debate over whether virtue is material or extramaterial in nature. This controversy, which occupies the first three books of the *Republic*, tends in the direction of identifying reason with antimaterialism and passion with the coveting of material goods: an either/or in which *logismos* opposes *epithumia* to leave no room for the *thumos*. There is, of course, considerable tension in the post-Homeric period between individual ambition and what Adkins calls "cooperative virtue," but, despite the increasing stress on cooperation, competitive effort remains prior. As Adkins points out, the competitive excellence that results from an individual's striving to acquire more wealth for his household is still the necessary basis for Greek society. See A. W. H. Adkins, *Moral Values and Political Behavior in Ancient Greece* (New York: Norton, 1972), passim, but especially 29–31; and his *Merit and Responsibility*, 164ff., 283ff. (on Plato). See also Dover, *Greek Popular Morality*, 180ff.

Aristotle's statement, in Book 3 of his *Nicomachean Ethics*, that courage (*andreia*) must be on account of (*dia*) virtue (*arêtê*) and desire (*orexis*) of honor to be noble (1117a, 3.8.3–4), along with his comment that if the appetite(s) for pleasure (*hê tou hêdeos orexis*) are intense they push aside (*ekkrouousin*) the *logismos* (1119b, 3.12), suggests vestiges of the Platonic tripartite soul, despite the usual Aristotelian attempt at a more harmonious relation between desire and reason via the mediating faculty of choice (for which, see Nussbaum, 275, 286, on the treatment of the tripartite soul in *De Anima* 3.9). For another somewhat "Platonic" passage, see EN 1102a–1103b.

15. Posidonius's later Stoicism, which sometimes abandons the unitary integrity of the soul and reverts to the Platonic tripartite model, is described in A. A. Long, "Posidonius on Emotions," in *Problems in Stoicism*, ed. A. A. Long (London: Athlone Press, 1971), 203, 205–6. Braden, 228, comments on the persistence of the unitary model even in later Stoic thought: it is especially visible in Seneca (Braden, 228). For a different Platonic view of intrapsychic conflict, see the *Sophist*, 227ff. For discussions of the unitary and the tripartite models of the soul as opposing formulations, with reference to the *Phaedo* and the *Republic*, see Eric Dodds, "Plato and the Irrational Soul," in *Plato: A Collection of Critical Essays*, vol. 2, ed. Gregory Vlastos (1971; reprint, Notre Dame, Ind.: Notre Dame University Press, 1978), 213 and n. See also G.M.A. Grube, *Plato's Thought* (1935; reprint, Indianapolis: Hackett, 1980),

120–49. Thomas Gould presents readings of Plato's thought as dualistic (that is, as assuming a unitary *psychê* attacked by external pathos) in his "Plato's Hostility to Art," *Arion* 3 (1964): 86. Also instructive is Gould's "Aristotle and the Irrational," *Arion* 2 (1963): 61. In Book 4 Plato describes the affections as internal elements of the *psychê*. For a sharper version of the conflict between reason and passion (here *phronêsis* and *andreia*, "prudence" and "courage"), see Book 12 of the *Laws* (963e). Foucault discusses the difference between the idea of intrapsychic combat and that of psychic integrity conceived in terms of a *sophrosunê/enkrateia* distinction in *The History of Sexuality*, 2:64–65, 67.

16. Does Achilles renounce these questions when he returns to battle? A central argument for Achilles' interest in conventional *timê* is Achilles' speech to Patroclus in Book 16, when he allows Patroclus to go out to battle (16.84–86, 90). Achilles here invokes the heroic code and the materialism it involves. But it is the sympathy for the dying Greek warriors impressed on him by Patroclus, not the prospect of war prizes, that makes him decide to send Patroclus into battle (16.66ff.).

17. Another instance will illustrate how the *Republic* exiles the *thumos*'s difficult questions, producing rational alternatives to the unuseful, unreasonable doubts such emotion causes. In Book 2 of his dialogue, Plato envisions a benign alternative to *thumos* in order to illustrate the kind of useful pathos proper to his ideal republic. He cites the example of the dog, whose feeling toward men is "philosophical" ("*kompson ge phainetai to pathos autou tês phuseôs kai hôs alethôs philosophon*") because it is based on whether it recognizes the men it encounters (*katamathein* or *agnoêsai*)—not on the memory of the good or bad deeds it has experienced at their hands (376a–c). Plato's use of the dog as an example enforces his claim for the larger value of recognition in his system: *anagnôrisis*, recognition, is the acknowledging of truth. Such recognition, Plato implies, if it is based on objective knowledge rather than personal advantage, may offer escape from the cycle of revenge and guilt that characterizes tragedies like the *Oresteia* or epics like the *Iliad*. The Socratic passion for justice, unlike the Achillean kind, is not based on destructive resentment. The dog responds to an impersonal cognitive truth, not to the memory of reward and punishment that distorts men's judgments, making them crave the vengeance that would ruin the possibility of a cohesive, rational society.

18. Jaeger and Havelock have argued that the Homeric poems served as textbooks of a sort for Greek society. See Werner Jaeger, *Paideia*, vol. 1 (1939; reprint, New York: Oxford University Press, 1945), and Eric Havelock, *Preface to Plato* (Cambridge: Harvard University Press, 1963). Jaeger argues that the critique of material wealth as inimical to true virtue stems from the shift from a landed aristocracy to a monetary one—a shift that postdates Homer (203). Plato's antimaterialist attack on Homer is then, in a sense, anachronistic.

19. Martha Nussbaum's essay "Love and the Individual," in her *Love's Knowledge* (Oxford: Oxford University Press, 1990), shows how Diotima turns the fact of loss into a lesson about values.

20. See Hertz, "Wordsworth and the Tears of Adam," 34–35.

21. The Epicurean and Stoic ideas in Virgil's poem set an important context for its use of pathos. For Epicurus (*via* Lucretius) and the *Aeneid* see Gordon Williams, *Technique and Ideas in Virgil's Aeneid* (New Haven: Yale University Press, 1983). Max Pohlenz, *Die Stoa* (1943; reprint, Göttingen: Vandenhoeck und Ruprecht, 1947), 276, claims a Stoic aspect in Book 6, because instead of Epicurean blind fate Virgil here displays the providential future of Roman history. But it is crucial that Aeneas himself does not understand this future; he is not in harmony with the divine will as the Stoic sage is.

22. It is impossible to survey in a footnote the vast number of critical reflections on Virgilian morals, but here is a sample. Don Cameron Allen, *Mysteriously Meant* (Baltimore: Johns Hopkins University Press, 1970), 147 (on Landino), and the introduction by Earl Schreiber and Thomas Maresca to Bernardus Silvestris' *Commentary on the First Six Books of Virgil's Aeneid* (Lincoln: University of Nebraska Press, 1979), xxi, xxxi; Thomas Lodge's "Defense of Poetry" (1579) and William Webbe, "A Discourse of English Poetry" (1586) in *Elizabethan Critical Essays*, ed. J. E. Spingarn(Oxford: Clarendon Press, 1908), 1:65 and 237. See also passages by Harington and Peacham on Virgil's didacticism (in Spingarn, ed., 1:121, and 2:210), as well as Girolamo Fracastoro, *Naugerius*, trans. Ruth Kelso (Urbana: University of Illinois Press, 1924), 73.

The notion of *enargeia,* the notion that the poetic text is a speaking and vividly impressive picture, can be seen in English Renaissance criticism in, for example, Peacham (in Spingarn, ed., 1:122): the poet's "efficacie" is "a power of speech, which representeth a thing after an excellent manner: neither by bare words onely, but by presenting to our minds the lively Ideaes or formes of things so truly, as if we saw them with our eyes." See also William Webbe (Spingarn, ed., 1:299–300). (For the "effective" definition of energeia, see Giovanni Pontano, *De Prudentia* [Venice: Aldus, 1518], 162.) For the ancient context see Longinus, *On the Sublime*, 15.1, 26.2; and D. A. Russell's notes on these passages in his edition of Longinus (Oxford: Clarendon Press, 1964). See also Aristotle's Rhet. 1411b38, Rhet. ad Her. 4.68, Quintilian's Inst. 6.2.29 and Augustine's *De Doctrina* 2.6.4. For enargeia in Sidney and his Renaissance context, see Forrest Robinson, *The Shape of Things* (Cambridge: Harvard University Press, 1972).

An important related concept is that of *ekplêxis* (Poet. 1460b25, 1454a4), which is far less adapted to the clarity necessary for persuasion. See Longinus 13.2 (and Russell's notes on p. 122), Cicero's *de Or.* 2.194 and Plutarch's *De Audiendis Poetis* 25d. The defense of poetic pathos in Sidney might be said to founder on his conflation of *ekplêxis* and enargeia: see the discussion of Sidney later in this chapter. The kind of enargeia approved by Seneca, by contrast, is sharply distinguished from *ekplêxis:* it moves the will without disturbing the passions. See Eden, *Poetic and Legal Fiction*, 108–9.

23. There is a theological issue concerning the division between pathos and moral judgment that parallels the literary-critical one. For the emphasis given the idea of conversion through affect by Bullinger, Rogers, Greenham, and others, see Pettit, *The Heart Prepared.*

24. Pietro Pucci, *The Violence of Pity in Euripides' Medea* (Ithaca: Cornell University Press, 1980), 171. Pucci's analysis is evidently indebted to Nietzsche's opposition between Apollo and Dionysus. Nietzsche's ecstatic communal description of Dionysus in *The Birth of Tragedy* can be seen as a defensive gesture against other moments in his work when Dionysian vulnerability is more genuinely risky in its recognition of the horror of the other's suffering, and the suffering present more generally in history itself. It is this latter version of Dionysus, present in the early "Der griechische Staat," *The Gay Science*, and elsewhere, and not the communal Dionysus of *The Birth of Tragedy*, that I refer to throughout this book. See Henry Staten, *Nietzsche's Voice* (Ithaca: Cornell University Press, 1990)—a persuasive reading, though one might take issue with Staten's Bataillean urge to treat *any* version of ascesis as a dangerously restricted economy.

One of the most compelling aspects of Pucci's discussion is its (mostly implicit) critique of Gerald Else's Aristotelian moralization of tragedy. Else emphasizes Aristotle's idea that the spectator makes a decision to pity the tragic hero on the basis of a knowledge that the hero's suffering is undeserved; however, Pucci makes it clear that such rationalization is secondary and in fact represses a primal spectatorial fear for self and other that has nothing to do with conscious judgments about the hero's guilt or innocence (see Pucci, 170). Pucci's "pity" is closer to *clementia* than *misericordia*. For a brief account of the *clementia/misericordia* distinction in Stoicism see Thomas G. Rosenmeyer, *Senecan Drama and Stoic Cosmology* (Berkeley: University of California Press, 1990), 24.

25. Pucci himself does not use Lacanian terms in his discussion; however, I believe that Lacan is a relevant context here.

26. Samuel Weber, *Return to Freud*, trans. Michael Levine (Cambridge: Cambridge University Press, 1991), 103. In addition to Weber and Lacan's own writings, I have relied for this summary on Ellie Ragland-Sullivan, *Jacques Lacan and the Philosophy of Psychoanalysis* (Urbana: University of Illinois Press, 1986), and Joseph H. Smith, *Arguing with Lacan* (New Haven: Yale University Press, 1991).

27. The requirement begins in antiquity: Trimpi notes in *Muses of One Mind,* 58, that Aristotle closes the gap between "ethical significance and formal structure" noticed by Plato. (See also 63, 71, 164, 234.) Although my discussion has been substantially influenced by Trimpi's brilliantly useful division of literature into cognitive, judicative, and formal aspects, I am inclined to see less harmony among the aspects than he does. For a similar division into outward (or rhetorical) and the inward (or formal) aspects, see James Coulter's study of Neoplatonist allegory, *The Literary Microcosm* (Leiden: E. J. Brill, 1976). For a different view of poetic didacticism in the Renaissance, see Robert L. Montgomery, *The Reader's Eye* (Berkeley: University of California Press, 1979). See Torquato Tasso, *Discourses on the Heroic Poem*, trans. Mariella Cavalchini and Irene Samuel (Oxford: Clarendon Press, 1973), Book 1, 10–12, for the exalting of virtuous poetry like that of Virgil over Homeric epic and Greek tragedy (which aim only to delight, Tasso claims). For the emphasis in Renaissance literary criticism on reading the epic hero in moral terms, see Bernard Weinberg, *A History of Literary Criticism in the Italian Renaissance*, 2 vols. (Chicago: University of Chicago Press, 1961), 1:389 (on Robortelli), and Brian Vickers, "Epideictic and Epic in the Renaissance," *New Literary History* 14 (1983): 497–538. (For Castelvetro's idiosyncratic critique of Scaliger's moral emphasis, see Vickers, 524–25.)

28. When Longinus states that he is against the kind of pathos that is manifested in a weak character but approves noble pathos (*to gennaion pathos* [*On the Sublime*, 8.4]), he clearly reveals that he, like Aristotle, wants to ensure the moral value of poetic effects. For the aestheticist or amoral prejudice of the Alexandrian critics, see George A. Kennedy, "Classics and Canons," *South Atlantic Quarterly* 89:1 (Winter 1990): 218–25 and Rudolf Pfeiffer, *History of Classical Scholarship*, vol. 1 (Oxford: Clarendon Press, 1968). For an aestheticizing view of Longinus, see Paul Fry, *The Reach of Criticism* (New Haven: Yale University Press, 1980).

29. The Renaissance was persistent in its efforts to moralize tragic catharsis from sthe time of Hermannus Alemannus' translation (Venice, 1481) of Averroes's synopsis of Aristotle's *Poetics*; see Weinberg, 359n. On catharsis in the Renaissance see Weinberg,1:467, 2:658ff. and 506, and Eden, 154–55nn. The introduction of moral use into Aristotelian catharsis is an aspect of the sixteenth-century conflation of Aristotle and Horace discussed by Marvin T. Herrick in *The Fusion of Horatian and Aristotelian Literary Criticism, 1531–1555* (Urbana: University of Illinois Press,1946). Weinberg also discusses this subject (1:398, 416–76). For the difference between the moralizing Renaissance reading of catharsis and modern clinical readings that rely on Aristotle's statements in *Politics* 8.6–7, see Stephen Halliwell, *Aristotle's Poetics* (London: Duckworth, 1986), 97–98 and Herrick, 42–43.

30. Sebastian Regulus, *In primum Aeneidos Virgilii Librum ex Aristotelis de Arte Poetica* (1563), 157–58 (and, for comments on Virgil's moral import, 9–10). Regulus is less allegorical than, but otherwise in line with, the ancient commentaries on this episode (see, for example, the notes to Aen. Book 1 in Virgil, *Opera*, 2 vols. [Venice, 1544; reprint. New York: Garland, 1976]): both Servius and Tiberius Claudius Donatus claim that Aeneas is not frightened of death, but resistant to the undignified or inappropriate kind of death that drowning would represent (since the soul is composed of fire). In all these cases the ostensible concern for decorum veils a moralizing motive on the part of the critic.

Aristotle's original moralism (unlike Regulus') is developed from, instead of forcibly imposed on, a tragedy like Oedipus. Halliwell, 26, 163, 173, 196, and Nussbaum, 382–83, stress the way in which Aristotle's *Poetics* define moral judgment within, not against, the pathos experienced by tragedy's spectator. But emotion is not always linked to judgment in Aristotle: see Poetics 1453b7–10 and Fry, *The Reach of Criticism*, 18ff. Nussbaum, *Fragility*, 373ff., offers a supporting interpretation.

31. Aristotle in EN 1115b states that the courageous man (*ho andreios*) "finds the thought of such an inglorious [*duskherainousin*, ill-mannered, loathsome] death"—from shipwreck—"revolting ... circumstances which bring out courage are those in which a man can show his prowess or where he can die a noble [*kalon*] death, neither of which is true of death by drowning or illness" (Aristotle, *Nicomachean Ethics*, trans. Martin Ostwald [Indianapolis: Hackett, 1962].) Ostwald notes that Aristotle here seems to be arguing with Plato, who writes that courage *is* applicable to such situations (*Laches* 191d-e).

32. The tripartite division of rhetorical functions into *movere, docere*, and *delectare* is derived from Cicero's *Brutus* (49.185). For one interesting statement of the difference between sublime *enargeia* and tragic pathos see Longinus, *On the Sublime*, 8.2–4. Longinus in fact often blends the two categories, defining tragic pathos as sublime.

33. Weinberg, 1:122, provides illustration. The notion of decorum is largely derived from Horace, though it is applied to Aristotle's *Poetics*. See Weinberg, 1:365, on Giorgio Valla's translation of the Poetics' *di' eikotôn* (1455a18: "plausibly") as "per decorum." Some idea of the large impact of Scaliger's *Poetices* is given by Herrick, 46, and Neil Rudenstine, "Scaliger and Sidney," in Alpers, ed., *Elizabethan Poetry*, 224–26.

34. Julius Caesar Scaliger, *Poetices* (Lyons, 1561), 3.2: 83.

35. Scaliger, 3.20: 106.

36. The epic informs us about (to choose a few of the chapter headings from Book 3) *Aetas, Oeconomia, Officia*, and *Gens*. For the connection between decorum and pathos, see Horace, *Ars Poetica*, 100ff. (Horace also stresses the social use of poetry at 391ff.; see Lodge in Spingarn, 1:74, and Philip Sidney, *The Apology for Poetry* [Oxford: Clarendon Press, 1907], 3.) Another example is Aristotle, Rhet. 1413. For the treatment of pathos and ethos as the purely technical, amoral terms of a contrast between Thucydides and Lysias, see Dionysius of Halicarnassus's treatise on Demosthenes, reprinted in D. A. Russell and M. Winterbottom, eds., *Ancient Literary Criticism* (Oxford: Clarendon Press, 1972), 307. See Seneca, Ep. 6.5 and 59.6 for the choice of persuading through pathos or ethos; for the choice as analyzed in Mazzoni and Quintilian (Inst. 11.3.61–63, 170–74), see Baxter Hathaway, *The Age of Criticism* (Ithaca: Cornell University Press, 1962), 264.

For a more harmonious view than Trimpi's (or mine) of the relation between decorum and morality in Renaissance criticism, see Victoria Kahn, *Rhetoric, Prudence and Skepticism in the Renaissance* (Ithaca: Cornell University Press, 1985), 44–45; also Kahn, 189, for a modification.

37. Scaliger, 3.20: 106. Regulus, 15, emphasizes the moralizing opposition of characters in the *Aeneid*: "Mores perspiciuntur in Aenea potissimum, et in his personis quas facit loquentes, quibus vel boni, vel mali ii iudicantur." (For the more general effort of Renaissance criticism to establish poetry as a moral art, see Weinberg, 1:6–26.)

38. A later important example of this disjunction, this time centering on eros rather than violent rage, occurs in chapter 20 of Book 3 (titled "Mores"). Here, Scaliger considers first the good passions of filial/paternal piety and hospitality, then the bad passion of love exemplified in Dido. The poetic *imago* created for the reader by the emotional reunion of Helenus, Aeneas, and Andromache in Buthrotum (Aen. Book 3) can be taken as genuine, writes Scaliger; the *imago* of Dido's disappointed love cannot. But, for the inauthenticity of Dido's passion to be established, Virgil's depiction of her love must be supplemented by a moralizing aside: "Paulo diversior ab hac amicitiae simplicitate Amor ille qui Veneris causa coniungit nos. Cum tamen Amicitiae verae imaginem quampiam repraesentet: hic apponamus praeceptiones"

39. Scaliger, 3.20: 106: "Somewhat different from this forthright friendship [that is, that of Aeneas with Helenus and Andromache] is that love which joins us on account of Venus. Yet it nevertheless represents some sort of image of true friendship: here we must apply precepts." *Paulo* and *quampiam*, "somewhat" and "some sort of," betray Scaliger's worry about the precise difference between Aeneas's pained sympathy for his lost compatriots and the illness of Dido's love.

40. Scaliger, 3.20: 105.

41. Here is Augustine's *Confessions*, 1.13: "Quid enim miserius misero non miserante se ipsum et flente Didonis mortem, quae fiebat amando Aenean, non flente autem mortem suam, quae fiebat non amando te, deus" ("For what could be more miserable than a wretch that pities not himself; one bemoaning Dido's death, caused by loving of Aeneas, and yet not lamenting his own death, caused by not loving of thee, O God." Augustine, *Confessions*, trans. William Watts [1631; reprint, Cambridge: Harvard University Press, 1960]). Eden (135, 173) notes that, in Augustine, emotional pursuit of an *imago* is congruent with ethical imitation, but such imitation may be sinful (as here) instead of good. See De Trin. 11.5.8. For another early and frank acknowledgment of the importance of pathos in Virgil see Macrobius' *Saturnalia* 4.3–4 (Paris: Garnier Frères,1937).

42. See Scaliger, 3. 20: 104: "Affectus sunt qualitates quae proficiscuntur a moribus." At 7.3: 348 he notes, similarly, "Docet affectus poeta per actiones: ut bonos amplectamur atque imitemur ad agendum: malos aspernemur ob abstinendum. Est igitur actio docendi modus: affectus, quem docemur ad agendum. Quare erit actio quasi exemplar, aut instrumentum in fabula: affectus vero finis." (Compare Sidney on the relation between "moving" and "teaching" in his *Apology*, 11ff.) The desire to establish harmony between the reader's moral judgment and his emotional reactions stems partly from the ancient analogy between the use of emotion in oratory and poetry: see Aristotle's Rhet. 1419b–1420a and his Poetics 1456a; see also Cicero's *Brutus* 185–86 and Quintilian, Inst. 10.1.65–68. (For Quintilian's argument against those who derogate the use of emotion in oratory, see the preface to his Book 5). Scaliger therefore argues against the Stoic view of emotion as an external influence separate from human personality. (For the Stoics, emotion reaches us before the intervention of moral will in the form of *propatheia*, the preliminary shock of affect.) Instead, Scaliger relies on Aristotle's claim in the *Nicomachean Ethics* that emotion is firmly linked to, and even constitutive of, moral disposition. A virtuous *hexis* (moral habit) is bound up with pathos (EN 1105b20,26). Scaliger follows Aristotle's effort to align the various kinds of courageous emotion with degrees of moral approbation (see pp. 106–7 of the

*Poetices*). For a similar approach, see Marco Girolamo Vida's discussion of the Aeneid in *De Arte Poetica* (1517), ed. and trans. Ralph Williams (New York: Columbia University Press, 1976), ll: 482–85.

Nussbaum, *Fragility*, 383–84 and 309, outlines an opposition between Plato's rejection of common or everyday pathos and Aristotle's embracing of it as incipiently reasonable (see, for example, EN 1119a6 –10). But see also Nussbaum, 373ff., for Aristotle's transcendent "Platonizing" strain and his occasional rejection of worldly emotion. Aristotle is sometimes nervous in the presence of passion: he writes, for example, that it is hard to judge the correct degree of pleasure [*hêdonê*] and that it is therefore better to renounce it whenever possible (EN 1109b: "If we send it away, we will make fewer mistakes:" *houtô gar autên apopempomenoi hêtton hamartêsometha*). See also EN 1119 (3.12). Aristotle's personification of pleasure in this passage is Helen; his opinion will be alluded to, and reversed, by Tasso (see later). See also Halliwell, 15n, 16n, 50, and Pontano's *De Prudentia* [Venice, 1518], 174, for a Renaissance definition of the effect of Helen's beauty. For Pontano on the tempering of emotion see *De Prudentia*, 173. See also Scaliger, 3. 1: 83: "Et fit pathos *tou ethous* fundamentum" (pathos makes the basis of ethos). Scaliger uses the examples of Sympathy (*misericondis*) and the suffering of injuries.

43. Scaliger, *Poetices* 3.20: 104.

44. Pallas's welcome of the Trojans (8.122–24) and Aeneas's desire to kill Helen (2.567–88, a famously disputed passage). The former is a lucky example of virtuous emotion: Pallas combines martial courage, hospitality, and respect for the gods (Pallas rushes to prevent his men from breaking off their sacrifice and fleeing from the Trojans). Pallas's brave challenging of the Trojans to declare their intentions, hostile or peaceful, swiftly modulates into a display of *xeinia* (hospitality): he tempers his courage (*audacia*) and checks himself as Turnus does not. Aeneas's desire to kill Helen is less admirable: at this point in the epic he is as *amens* as Dido or Turnus.

45. Scaliger, *Poetices* 3.20: 104.

46. Scaliger, Poetices 3.20: 104 –5. See 106 for Scaliger's approval of Turnus's pious supplication to be returned to his parents for burial (he also mentions, less emphatically, Mezentius's similar request at Aen. 10.904): the "supplex" (12.935–36) Turnus "se prosternit ad Aeneae genua . . . sed negavit se deprecari. Quinetiam non pro se, quippe magnanimus: sed pro patre, ut sit pius."

47. In a nearby passage, a description of the parental anxieties of Aeneas and Amata and the filial ones of Ascanius and Lavinia, Scaliger again cites Lausus's concern for his father Mezentius: "Protexit enim Lausus patrem, quemadmodum et nos nostrum, quanquam alio et fato et facto. Amicitiae igitur ius, aut inter aequales, aut inter inaequales."

48. "Indeed, Lausus defended his father, just as we would ours, even if his deeds and his destiny were different [from his son's—an allusion to Virgil's comment at 7.653–54 that Lausus deserved a better father]. There is, then, a law of friendship, either among those who are similar or those who are dissimilar." Emotion now seems explicitly to vanquish moral judgment: Lausus's concern for his father overrides the father's barbarous character. Scaliger's Aristotelian attempt to state *amicitia* as a kind of moral law is frustrated; he must admit that the significant aspect of such affection is its violation of moral categories. Scaliger here seems forced to recognize the moral ambiguity entailed by Virgilian pathos, because even Mezentius is both object and subject of piety. Conversely, Aeneas's "mad" anger in Books 2 and 12 is quite similar to Dido's or Turnus's, despite the binary morality that separates him from them: but Scaliger will not acknowledge this difficulty.

49. Plato, *Laws* 4.719d, trans. A. E. Taylor, in *The Collected Dialogues of Plato*, eds. E. Hamilton and H. Cairns (Princeton: Princeton University Press, 1961).

50. Tasso, 12.

51. Ibid.

52. Tasso, 78. For the similarity between epic poetry's magnificence and that of nature, see Tasso, 78, 134–36, 173. See also Pontano's *Actius* (in *Opera Omnia* [Florence, 1520], vol. 3), 100, and his *De Prudentia* (at 1:174 of his *Opera*): "Et veloces quidem, et lacertosi, et forma qui praestant, laudantur a natura, deque bonis corporis, ut ab Homero de pertinacitate quidem Achilles, de forma vero Helena." Pontano goes on to draw a distinction between the external qualities he admires in Helen and Achilles and the more internal virtues—between "laus formae" and "laus virtutis" (174).

53. Tasso, 13.

54. Tasso, 12. For Tasso's Italian text I have relied on *Discorsi dell'Arte Poetica e del Poema Eroica* (Bari, 1964, ed. Luigi Poma), the edition used by Cavalchini and Samuel in their translation.

55. Tasso, 11.

56. Tasso, 14. The distinction between pathos and moral point as literary goals is explicitly stated by Tasso, 82. Weinberg, 1:25, discussing Mazzoni, describes the controversy over admitting bad characters as well as good to poetry.

57. Tasso, 46.

58. Tasso, 93.

59. Tasso, 46. Tasso shifts here, as he not uncommonly does, between a relativist argument for approving "wrath and love" as epic subjects ("as Proclus ... says, [the heroes] were especially subject to [these] two feelings" [45; italics added]) and a universally moralizing Christian argument ("if love is ... a highly noble habit of the will, as St. Thomas held, love will be more praiseworthy [than wrath] in heroes.... This kind of love the ancients either did not know or did not wish to describe in their heroes, but ... they should ... have esteemed no other [passion] more appropriate for heroes."

60. Tasso, 46. In the section of the passage I have elided, Tasso champions decorum over morality, writing that "beauty is superior to justice as a theme, according to Proclus himself, a philosopher most highly esteemed among the Platonists. He put goodness or the good in the highest rank, the beautiful in the second, and the just in the third. But this is to be understood only of the principles of things, for in our souls there can be no beauty without justice." Tasso realizes that the Platonist Proclus, like the Platonist in himself, must rebel on some level against the acknowledgment of a disjunction between beauty and virtue: this is why Plato insists that the beauties of immoral poetry are not really beautiful. So Tasso states that the disjunction between beauty and justice "is to be understood only of the principles of things, for in our souls there can be no beauty without justice." But Tasso departs from Platonism when he emphasizes that Proclus has conceded the difference between beauty and justice— and preferred beauty. Tasso began by stating that the love of Helen is beautiful and not just; he now cites the judgments of Proclus and Isocrates to the effect that beauty does not need morality or justice. The continuation of the passage is interesting as well in light of the passage from Aristotle's *Ethics* cited earlier (n. 23), which says the opposite of what Tasso claims it does: "No wonder then if the Trojans, in order to keep her, fought so many years against justice, disregarding the wiser citizens' advice that she be returned to Menelaus, as Aristotle remarks in his *Ethics*—and we should trust him more than any other philosopher."

61. Similarly, Tasso in his Book 3 defends Virgil's Dido episode from the point of view of decorum: "Perhaps he sought occasion to intermix with the severity of other

matters the pleasing converse of love" (59). But in Book 1 Tasso applies a moral criterion to praise Virgil's treatment of love and condemn Ariosto's and Trissino's: "Virgil is decidedly modest [*modestissimo*] about the love-making of Aeneas and Dido" (12).

62. Tasso, 94. For a contrasting celebration of Virgil along with Homer on the basis of their comprehension of epic's aesthetic technicalities, see Tasso, 51–52—and Tasso's Books 4 – 6, nearly passim.

63. Like Scaliger, though, Tasso continues to sustain the idea of decorum even under the pressure of restrictive morality. Violating the prejudices of Christian morals to accommodate decorum, Tasso defends Aeneas' killing of Turnus: "Revenge was then righteous, permissible to the gentle knight (who would not have seemed cruel to the pagans)."

64. Tasso, 98. Such a cultural-relativist avoidance of the universalizing morality of Christianity shifts the territory of Tasso's argument to that of archaic Greek ethics, which here seems at one with Homeric decorum. But a gap once again appears between aesthetic appropriateness and moral discrimination. When Tasso goes on to claim that Aeneas's revenge is more "appropriate" (*convenevole*) than Achilles's, he means that it is more justified, because Aeneas "took the life of a breaker of pledges"—that is, Turnus is more similar to Paris than Hector is. Aeneas's revenge is more appropriate than Achilles' because it is morally correct (Tasso, 98). A major aspect of classical morality, the need to keep oaths faithfully, is here permitted to determine aesthetic decorum: Tasso subordinates decorum to morality. See Samuel's introduction, xxix, on the way "the decorum of appropriateness shades into the decorum of virtuous propriety." Aristotle's Rhet. 1390a gives a relatively amoral definition of decorum in terms of the rhetorical success to be won by conforming to an audience's character. (Tasso states in his Book 1 [23] that the poet shouldn't defend the guilty as the orator does.)

65. Tasso, 87; Tasso here relies on Aristotle's *Poetics* 1454a16ff. The simile may be pointed, because Tasso here criticizes Ariosto's Marfisa (if not his Bradamante).

66. See Tasso, 43.

67. Tasso implies his knowledge of, but fails to acknowledge openly, the way in which Virgil confounds our moral judgment of Turnus. After calling Turnus a breaker of pledges who deserved to be killed by Aeneas (98), Tasso shows him in a noble light by citing his brave speech to Drances in Book 10 and juxtaposing it with unequivocal examples of virtue (100 –1). Tasso's uncertainty about Turnus's moral character is a telling indication of the moral ambiguities that Virgil has written into his narrative. When Tasso and Scaliger, recognizing the danger that sympathy with characters like Dido and Turnus poses to a moral reading, try to escape that sympathy by means of moral judgment, they are trying to evade an ambivalence prominently staged by the poem itself. Virgil, with his genius for dramatic perspectivalism, makes us respond favorably to Dido's passion from one point of view even as he makes us morally censure it from another (see Williams, *Technique and Ideas*, 215–31). The moralizing critic cannot rest in such uncertainty.

Despite his allowance that tragic plays may legitimately be less didactic than epic poems, Tasso's statements on tragedy in the *Discorsi* also sometimes try to integrate morality and affect. Tasso claims that Oedipus's misfortunes arouse more pity than Medea's because he is ethically superior to her. See Tasso, 25. An influential modern version of the integration of morality and poetic affect in the criticism of tragedy is Gerald Else's influential reading of Aristotle, which claims that we pity the tragic hero because we know that he or she is not *miaron* (polluted) on the level of motive— an ethical criterion (Else, *Aristotle's Poetics* [Cambridge: Harvard University Press,1957], 433–39).

For the importance Renaissance criticism placed on integrating *utile* and *dulce*, see Fracastoro, 58 (which defines *admiratio* as a superior category that joins affect and morality) and Pontano's *Actius*. Tasso, 17, discusses the relation between "wonder" (*maraviglia*), "being useful" (*giovare*); he also treats his substitution of "pleasure directed to usefulness" for both *dulce* and *utile* ("il diletto è fine della poesia, è fine ordinato al giovamento") (10). For a discussion of Pontano's notion of *admiratio* and its importance for humanist poetics see Concetta Greenfield, *Humanist and Scholastic Poetics* (London: Associated University Presses, 1981), 280–81. Tasso deals with Pontano and Fracastoro on 173.

68. See Greenfield, 48ff., for the scholastic critique of poetry. Aquinas, though he provided the basis for the scholastic critique by classifying poetry as the lowest of the disciplines of logic, also defended poetic admiratio as a moral instrument. See Aquinas, *Summa Theologica* 1a.2ae.32 and his *Praeclarissima commentaria* (Venice, 1553), 36. Ronald Levao, in *Renaissance Minds and Their Fictions* (Berkeley: University of California Press, 1985), 119ff., discusses the dangerous possibility of the fable becoming divorced from the moral in Sidney and Renaissance criticism in general; he states the danger in epistemological terms, however, whereas my argument is based on the ethical question of persuasion and the role that emotion plays in poetry's persuasive effects.

69. Sidney, 18–19. The word *enargeia* or *energeia* can itself represent the connection between striking clarity and persuasion to moral action that the Renaissance critics desire: in the spelling *energeia* the term can be taken as derived from *ergon*, "deed," and when spelled *enargeia*, from *argês*, "clear" or "bright." The former derivation is clearly implied by the way Aristotle uses the concept of energeia in its original definition (in his *Metaphysics*).

70. Seneca's *Thyestes* casts doubt on its author's idea that the sage can utterly and steadfastly resist the assaults of passion. Here, Seneca depicts the wholesale capitulation of the philosophical attitude, represented by Thyestes, to the rage of Atreus. Mirelle Armisen-Marchetti, *Sapientiae Facies: Étude sur les images de Sénèque* (Paris: Belles Lettres, 1989), 366, is very helpful on this subject.

71. Armisen-Marchetti 50–52, 60. For a similar distinction between passion as *morbus*, or disease of the soul, and *affectus*, see Epistle 85.1. In *De Ira* 2.1, Seneca draws a distinction between the superficial level of ordinary, momentary emotional sensations, which cannot be avoided even by the wise man, and the fierce, passionate affect that develops out of sensation if it is welcomed by the mind.

68. W. B. Stanford, in his edition of the play (London: Macmillan, 1963), emphasizes the increasing signs of *sophrosunê* that Ajax shows (xxxiv–xxxvii): but Ajax's invocation of the Furies at 835ff. creates a contrary impression.

69. For a notable instance of critical nervousness concerning Medea, see Plutarch's *Moralia* 18: Plutarch tries to assert that, in the case of Medea, the spectator will applaud the poet's skill without approving of the action he depicts. But Plutarch, writing after Plato's criticism of poetry's amoral effects, seems quite conscious of the difficulty of making such a separation.

70. Of course, Augustine expresses his later *amor Dei* in the same terms he uses for his earlier earthly loves; however, his movement from secular to divine desire is not motivated by the force of secular desire.

71. On the disjunction between love and honor in medieval romance, see Joan Ferrante in Ferrante, George Economou et al., *In Pursuit of Perfection* (Port Washington, N.Y.: Kennikat Press, 1975), 164–65. Not all Renaissance critics agreed that Spenser's fable won out over his moral. Henry Reynolds, in *Mythomystes* (1633?), writes that "some good judgments have wisht, and perhaps not without cause, that

[Spenser] had . . . bene a little freer of his fiction, and not so closely rivetted to his Morall" (Spingarn, ed., 2:146 –47). But Reynolds's defense of a poetry of delight, in the tradition of Ovid's *Tristia,* 2.353ff., and the Eratosthenes condemned by Strabo (*Geography,* 1.2.3–9; see Russell and Winterbottom, 300 –5), is unusual in the Renaissance. Tasso mentions the Strabo passage (Tasso, *Discourses,* 11).

## Chapter 2. *The Faerie Queene*, Book 1

1. Spenser here responds to the relation between pathos and moral subjectivity in Christian thought, as I shall argue. Augustine, Valla, and other ancestors of the Protestant tradition asserted that the experience of pathos is necessary to the achievement of virtue; Book 2's treatment of Guyon's emotions, and his attempt to resist them, will confront this idea with the opposing mode of Christian-Stoicism, which Guyon endorses. See Charles Trinkaus, *In Our Image and Likeness* (Chicago: University of Chicago Press, 1970), 1:160 –80., and Augustine, *City of God* Book 14. Also helpful is Nancy Struever, *The Language of History in the Renaissance* (Princeton: Princeton University Press, 1970), 58–59. This Renaissance tradition of moralizing through pathos culminates in the "affective" or "dramatic" mode of English puritan writers; see John R. Knott, *The Sword of the Spirit* (Chicago: University of Chicago Press, 1980), 71–72, and Strier, *Love Known,* 174 –217. In Book 2, pathos often blurs the hero's perception of a moral point, and this emotional ambiguity itself becomes a lesson about the shakiness of a human nature like Guyon's, and ours.

2. For a discussion of the three books added in 1596, see "From Milton to Spenser," Chapter 5. MacCaffrey, 81ff., and Paul Alpers, *The Poetry of the Faerie Queene* (Princeton: Princeton University Press, 1967), 343, note that Spenser frequently writes his poem "over the head" of his protagonists. See also Nohrnberg, 148, and Berger, who calls attention to the difference between "what [Red Crosse] sees and what interpretation elicits" ("Spenser's *Faerie Queene,*" 31). I would dispute MacCaffrey's argument for what she sees as Guyon's virtually complete inability to respond to the poem's ethical and allegorical examples; see Chapter 3.

3. The romance genre cannot simply be identified with a choice of plot over character. There is a double possibility within romance in regard to these two base terms. Some readers, like Jameson, view romance as the rule of plot and place over character; others, like Vinaver and Hanning, have pointed out that twelfth-century romance, by placing the hero on his own in a fictive world in which authoritative direction is either relatively invisible or doubtful, opens the possibility of character psychology as divinely directed allegories (for example, medieval morality plays) do not. See Eugene Vinaver, *The Rise of Romance* (New York: Oxford University Press, 1971) and Robert Hanning, *The Individual in Twelfth Century Romance* (New Haven: Yale University Press, 1977).

4. Nohrnberg, 261.

5. Thomas Greene's statement about the submission of Ariostan characters like Ruggiero to the *Orlando Furioso*'s narrative is equally applicable to Spenser's Book 1: "Chance is the mainspring of the plot, controlled by Ariosto's [here Spenser's] mind but almost never by the individual character" (Greene, *The Descent from Heaven* [New Haven: Yale University Press, 1963], 141).

6. Parker, 65.

7. Nohrnberg, 263. In a similar vein, Harry Berger writes, "We may in general wonder why, when Redcross has conquered a dragon-lady named Error, he spends nine

cantos falling into deeper error? If he overcomes Error, why should he succumb to Hypocrisy? If he abandons Una, why should he then conquer Faithlessness? If he conquers Faithlessness, why should he succumb to Falsehood?" ("Spenser's *Faerie Queene*, Book I," *Southern Review* [Adelaide] 2 [1966]: 26–27). Like Nohrnberg, Berger wants to psychologize Red Crosse in order to overcome these problems, arguing that he is a fuller character than, for example, Guyon (21) and that he recognizes his own redemption at the end of Book 1 (48). See Nohrnberg, 124: "The ostensible success of the knight's opening campaign yields to the perception that there are kinds of error that can only be destroyed through hindsight, and from within." It is doubtful, I think, that Red Crosse himself ever achieves this perception. For another psychologizing of Red Crosse see Kenneth Gross, *Spenserian Poetics* (Ithaca: Cornell University Press, 1985), 118, and 57–58. Gross concludes that Red Crosse "becomes by the end of Book I a more complex personification as well as a 'better person,' and ... learn[s] after his early defeat of a monster labeled 'Errour' that the forces of error tend to exceed any limiting names that culture or poetry might find to contain them." It is very debatable, I will argue, that Red Crosse learns any such lesson.

8. Norman Maclean, ed., *Selected Poetry of Edmund Spenser* (1968; reprint, New York: Norton, 1982), 97n.

9. I have been influenced here by Berger's important essay, "'Kidnapped Romance': Discourse in the *Faerie Queene*," in *Unfolded Tales: Essays on Renaissance Romance*, eds. George M. Logan and Gordon Teskey (Ithaca: Cornell University Press, 1989).

10. See Charles Taylor, *Sources of the Self* (Cambridge: Harvard University Press, 1989), 115–42.

11. See Peter Brown, *The Body and Society* (New York: Columbia University Press, 1988), 387–427. As Brown points out, the radical examination of the self's inner desires as a test of religious faith is a central aspect of Judaic tradition, but because such attention to pathos is more often associated in the Reformation with Augustine and Paul than with the Old Testament prophets, I refer to it in this book as "Pauline-Augustinian" or "Augustinian."

12. The classical Stoic aims to adapt himself to the cosmic order, but Christian Stoicism stands between this aspiration and the Augustinian focus on character. Like Augustine, the Christian Stoic often asserts that virtue must stem from an intimate attention to and wish to transform a particular self and its desires; however, at moments of crisis he often returns, as do Guyon and the Palmer in Spenser's Book 2, to classical Stoicism's reliance on a categorical vision of order that transcends the first-person responses of particular individuals. As Gerhard Oestreich notes, the influential Neostoic Justus Lipsius departs from ancient Stoicism by stressing man's free will (Oestreich, *Neostoicism and the Early Modern State* [Cambridge: Cambridge University Press, 1982], 29). Lipsius thus opens up the gap between individual and cosmos that ancient Stoicism means to heal with its insistence on providence.

13. For the hackneyed, comic book quality of the St. George legend—criticized, like St. Christopher's story, as an obvious phony—see William Nelson, *The Poetry of Spenser* (New York: Columbia University Press, 1963), 150–51; for George's official role in the Order of the Garter and Accession Day tilts, see Frances Yates, *Astraea* (London: Routledge and Kegan Paul, 1975) and "Elizabethan Chivalry: the Romance of the Accession Day Tilt," 22, in *Journal of the Warburg and Courtauld Institutes*, 1957: 4–25. Jeffrey Knapp gives good reasons for assuming a mirroring between Red Crosse and Error in "Error as a Means of Empire in the *Faerie Queene* 1," *ELH* 54, no.4 (1987): 801–34. David Lee Miller follows A. C. Hamilton in suggesting that Charissa, the "correct" version of charity who appears in the House of Holiness, is

the symbolic mother of Red Crosse (Miller, *The Poem's Two Bodies* [Princeton: Princeton University Press, 1986], 248–49). In this case, I would add, Error is Red Crosse's original "mother," the starting point and pattern of his adventures.

14. Red Crosse sees, or thinks he sees, Error "plaine" because of "the glooming light, much a shade" (1.1.14) cast by his armor. The symbolic darkness of this gleam is a paradox that Red Crosse programmatically ignores.

15. See Knapp, "Error as a Means of Empire."

16. In contrast to the case of Red Crosse and Error, Guyon's meeting with Mammon illustrates the inability of allegory's sights to define Guyon's character.

17. Error also subverts allegorical authority by demonstrating for us its slippery, dramatically shifting nature: she plays on and contorts whatever stabilizing effect allegory might have.

18. In Mammon's Cave, in exact contrast, Mammon fails because he tempts Guyon with the outward rather than the inward. Guyon resists the possession and knowing perception of external objects, but is sensitive to internal desires, as the Bower demonstrates.

19. For the acceptance of a mixing of tragic and comic in Medieval texts (*ludicra seriis miscere*), see E. R. Curtius, *European Literature and the Latin Middle Ages*, trans. Willard Trask (1948; reprint [German], Princeton: Princeton University Press, 1973), 429ff. J. V. Cunningham, in *Woe or Wonder* (Denver: University of Colorado Press, 1951), 49–51, 55, points out proclaimed sharp distinctions between comedy and tragedy in *Mucedorus* and *Henry VIII*, along with the paradox of "tragical mirth" as described in *A Midsummer Night's Dream*. The comic elements in the *Faerie Queene* have been amply documented by William Nelson in "Spenser *ludens*," in *A Theatre for Spenserians*, ed. Judith Kennedy and James Reither (Toronto: University of Toronto Press, 1973), 83–100.

20. Weinberg, 2: 995. In a less overtly moralizing vein, Thomas Browne writes of Athenaeus that "being miscellaneous in many things, he is to be received with suspition; for such as amass all relations, must erre in some" (cited in Rosalie Colie, *The Resources of Kind* [Berkeley: University of California Press, 1973], 87). Interestingly in this context, Weinberg concludes that the Renaissance defense of Guarini's use of mixed genres culminates in a position that deemphasizes the moral aspect of poetry in favor of the aesthetic: 2:1104–5.

21. Ascoli, *Ariosto's Bitter Harmony* (Princeton: Princeton University Press, 1987), 121–224.

22. See Frye's *Anatomy of Criticism* (Princeton: Princeton University Press, 1957) and *The Secular Scripture* (Cambridge: Harvard University Press, 1976); Lewalski, *Paradise Lost and the Rhetoric of Literary Forms* (Princeton: Princeton University Press, 1985); Bakhtin, *The Dialogic Imagination* (Austin: University of Texas Press, 1981).

23. English romance of the Middle Ages, in distinction to its French sources, tends to eliminate introspection and psychological nuance in favor of a pragmatic emphasis on earthly action (see Sandra N. Ihle, *Malory's Grail Quest* [Madison: University of Wisconsin Press, 1983], 52–53.); in the case of Malory's imitation of the thirteenth-century *Queste del Saint Graal*, much of the French poem's allegorical commentary is omitted as well. The medieval tendency toward abbreviation and laconic, repetitive action is present as well in the English versions of many popular Renaissance romances.

24. See Susan Crane's chapter on pious romance in her *Insular Romance* (Berkeley: University of California Press, 1986).

25. *The Boke of Duke Huon of Burdeux*, trans. John Bourchier, Lord Berners; ed. S.L. Lee (London: Early English Text Society, 1887), 375.

26. Spenser conspicuously alludes to *Huon*: see *Faerie Queene* 2.1.6 for one of his references to it.

27. Vinaver and Hanning and Nohrnberg all see romance as a form that prizes subjectivity rather than providential plot. As Nohrnberg points out, implicit in the romance form is a celebration of the individual psyche's freedom. This liberty is visible in the romance hero's lack of direction by any controlling narrative authority, in contrast to the quintessentially directed hero of epic. See Vinaver, *The Rise of Romance*; Hanning, *The Individual in Twelfth-Century Romance*; Nohrnberg, 5–22.

28. See Parker, *Inescapable Romance* and, for a historicizing interpretation, David Quint, "The Boat of Romance and the Renaissance Epic," in *Romance*, eds. Kevin and Marina Brownlee (Hanover, N.H.: Dartmouth University Press, 1985).

29. One Renaissance commentator, Archbishop Laud's protege Peter Heylyn, reports that Guy of Warwick is rumored to be George's son. Peter Heylyn, *The History of that Most Famous Saynt and Souldier of Christ Jesus St. George of Cappadocia, Asserted from the Fictions of the Middle Ages of the Church and Opposition of the Present* (London, 1631), 139; see also 27, where George is compared with Sir Bevis. Spenser proudly associates St. George with romance, in contrast to Heylyn, who wants to minimize George's affinities with romance tradition. Heylyn wants to assert the reality of St. George, who had been declared a mere fable since the fifth century. To do so he must divorce the legend from its romance features. George did not actually kill any dragon, writes Heylyn; the representations of him doing so are merely allegorical, intended to express George's symbolic victory in standing up for God against Rome. Heylyn, 46–47. The same air of fictionality is attached to St. Christopher very early in the Christian era; see William Camden, *Remaines Concerning Britaine* (1636), 65 and Heylyn, 45. George had been condemned as a fiction by the Nicean council of 492, and more recently by Calvin in his *Institutes* (Heylyn, 43).

30. See *The Hystory of the Two Valyaunte Brethren Valentyne and Orson* (1565?), Chs. 62–63; Samuel Rowland, *The Famous History of Guy Earl of Warwick* (1679), Canto 7, and the similar version in Humphrey Crouch, *The Heroic History of Guy Earl of Warwick* (1671), A 4(v); *Huon of Burdeux*, 379–82.

31. Barclay explicitly sets up this distinction between the militant and the passive kinds of Christian example, reporting first George's pledge "From hens forwarde / I purpose for to fyght / Agayne fals Idollys of Fendes infernal / In chrystys quarrel," and then driving home the vast difference between this heroism of suffering and George's earlier heroics: "Nowe is this knight/ryght bolde and valyant / Bounde without favour / in utter shame / and payne / Thoughe he oftyne / in batayle triumphant / Had won great laude." Alexander Barclay, *Life of St. George* (1515), ed. William Nelson (1955; reprint, Oxford: Early English Text Society, 1960), 74–75. See also John Lydgate, "The Legend of St. George" in Lydgate, *Minor Works*, 1:145ff.; Caxton's version of the George legend from his *Golden Legend* is included as an appendix to Nelson's edition. There are traces of a St. George play from 1456; for the popularity of drama based on this and other romance themes in the Renaissance, see F. P. Wilson, *The English Drama 1485–1585*, ed. G. K. Hunter (Oxford: Clarendon Press, 1969), 7, 120–21.

32. Rowland, N2 (r); Crouch, C 3 (v); *Valentyne and Orson*, Ch. 63ff.; Chrestien de Troyes, *Perceval*, trans. Ruth H. Cline (Athens: University of Georgia Press, 1983), 170–76; and Sir Thomas Malory, *Le Morte d'Arthur*, Book 17, chap. 23.

33. In this respect, Ruggiero's conversion in Canto 41 seems a mere interlude, the hermit who baptizes him an incidental figure rather than the voice of another, higher realm of existence, the role traditionally played by the moralizing anchorites of medieval romance. Instead, the worldly, dynastic destiny of Ruggiero is emphasized;

his conversion is a technicality, allowing him to wed Bradamante and generate the line that will culminate in the house of d'Este, which is itself subject to historical vicissitudes more than divine sanction. See 41.67: "The holy old man spoke to Ruggiero about many an Azzo, Alberto and Obice and their fine posterity up to . . . Ercole and Alfonso, Hippolytus and Isabel." *Orlando Furioso*, trans. Guido Waldman (London: Oxford, 1974). For an analysis of the ways in which Ariosto subverts his celebration of the d'Este, see Ascoli, 380–89.

34. See 1.4.36 for a Latinate pun along these lines: "laesie" (*laesus*).

35. Red Crosse's involvement with Arthurian legend, frequently attacked in the Elizabethan age as both outworn and immoral, is a bad sign (if a delightful one). See the passages from Nashe, Ascham and others assembled in Nelson, "Spenser *ludens*," 84.

36. The turn from light comedy to potential tragedy that we see when we enter the foreboding and eerie wood of Errour is the inverse of another moment a few cantos later, when the author himself strays from a fitting mood to a trifling one. Spenser turns the tragic pathos of Una's distress into an Ariostan ornamental delight:

> The pitteous maiden carefull comfortlesse,
>   Does throw out thrilling shriekes, and shrieking cryes,
> The last vaine helpe of womens great distresse,
>   And with loud plaints importuneth the skyes,
>   That molten starres do drop like weeping eyes;
> And *Phoebus* flying so most shamefull sight,
>   His blushing face in foggy cloud implyes,
>   And hides for shame. What wit of mortall wight
> Can now devise to quit a thrall from such a plight?
>         (*FQ* 1.6.6)

In this passage, which describes Una's vulnerability before Sans-loy, who is trying to rape her, the poet's use of hyperbole serves the purpose of trivializing. Spenser begins by delicately mocking Una's plaints as "thrilling shrieks, and shrieking cryes"—an overly finicky distinction, given the situation—and thus reducing to mere comedy "the last vaine helpe of womens great distress" (a longwinded pomposity of a moralism, here spoken with an ironic smile). He concludes with the coy, overactive personifications of sun, stars, and sky. (In an opposite mood is the image of the stars' witness in 3.11.45, where the description of Cupid's numberless warlike "spoiles" is edged with chill melancholy: "More eath to number, with how many eyes / High heauen beholds sad louers nightly theeveryes.") The authorial self-address of the stanza's last two lines—in effect, "what plot twist should I come up with next?"—completes the deliciously comic frisson. We are left with the impression of a slightly bored author searching, like Archimago, for some casual, malevolent amusement.

37. The double meanings of "sad" (serious or contemplative as well as unhappy) and "silly" (innocent as well as foolish) are important here: the ambiguities of both words are heavily exploited by Spenser.

38. See Knapp, "Error as a Means of Empire."

39. In Canto 2 Red Crosse errs by taking Duessa's tragic tale as a flirtatious occasion: her invented "woes and sorrowes" lead Red Crosse to "feign seemely merth" (1.2.26–27). Red Crosse flirts in similar fashion with Britomart in Book 3. Duessa presents a grotesque exaggeration of Red Crosse's courtly humor. In the House of Pride, Duessa makes her interest in trifling delight obvious when she, who has recently been mourning Sans-ioy's brother Sans-foy, addresses Sans-joy with jolly excitement as "cause of my new joy" (1.4.45). When she adds, "I learne that little sweet / Oft tempred is . . . with muchell smart"—that is, her grief for Sans-foy

(1.4.46)—the niceness of the term "tempred" gives away Duessa's basic callousness by showing her readiness to mix her emotions. Duessa's too-rapid shift in tone from grief to happy exclamation demonstrates her manipulative confusing of distinct kinds of pathos. The rather jaunty opening of combative festivities in the House of Pride indicates a similarly improper mixing of emotional tones. The contest of Red Crosse and Sans-ioy is accompanied by "Minstrales" who "maken melody, / To drive away the dull melancholy" (1.5.3; see also 1.5.17). The suggestion of "great ruth" (1.5.9) in the spectators' reactions to the battle is largely vitiated by the poet's presentation of the encounter as spectacular entertainment. Archimago himself delights in cruelty; he "much rejoyce[s]" that the "bloudy fray" occurs between Sans-loy and Satyrane (1.6.48, 43) and presumably enjoys as well causing "stony horrour" in Una with his false report of Red Crosse's death (1.6.37).

40. The most immediate of epic precedents is Tasso's wood in GL, 13.5–15.

41. In contrast to Red Crosse's misrecognitions, Canto 3 of the poem treats us to an emphatic version of a correct, moralized pathos in the form of Spenser's pity for the abandoned Una who "euermore does steepe / Her tender brest in bitter tears all night" (1.3.15). "When such I see," announces the poet, "all for pittie I could die" (1.3.1). But Una's univocity, and our univocal response to her as readers, is an exception in Spenser (it is significant that Una is absent for most of Book 1).

For the most part in Book 1 we see example after example of skewed emotion, cases that induce an uneasiness in the reader very unlike the straightforward sympathy for Una. The evil Corceca's "dread" is "needlesse" (even when faced with a very violent lion!) because it is based on the elevating of a trifle (the telling of the rosary) into a matter of high emotion (1.3.13–14). With Duessa's crocodile tears in the House of Pride (1.5.18), or Lucifera's praise of Red Crosse's victory over Sans-ioy as "gay chevalree" (1.5.16) when it is actually grievous sin, a misstating of the genre of emotion is a sure sign of distorted morals.

42. Red Crosse's externalizing is subject to critique. In the House of Pride (Canto 4) Spenser criticizes from a didactic point of view Red Crosse's projection of his own sins onto another, the innocent Una. The canto opens with the stern warning: "Young knight, what ever that dost armes professe, / And through long labours huntest after fame, / Beware of fraud, beware of ficklenesse, / In choice, and change of thy deare loved Dame, / Least thou of her beleeve too lightly blame" (1.4.1). Until the final line of the passage I have quoted the meaning of "choice, and change of" is unclear—is "of" subjective or objective, does it refer to Red Crosse's "change" of Una for Duessa or to the "change" that he assumes in Una herself? In narrative context, of course, and given the final line quoted, the genitive must be subjective, charging Red Crosse's own fickleness, but the fleeting ambiguity reminds us that Red Crosse has projected onto Una the exact failing present in himself, "fickleness," or tendency to "change," to err.

43. On allegory and reification, see Stephen Barney, *Allegories of History, Allegories of Love* (New Haven: Yale University Press, 1977), 37.

44. Harry Berger, "The Prospect of Imagination: Spenser and the Limits of Poetry," *SEL* 1, no.1 (1961): 93–120, describes Spenser's imaging evil as restless "nonbeing." Lucifera's pageant, for Berger, is a "turning, or withdrawal . . . from a true to a false image of actuality," a representation of the danger of becoming a slave to transitory things that Paul warns against in Gal. 4:3–9.

45. For the concept of the "big Other," see Lacan, *The Seminar of Jacques Lacan*, Book 2, trans. Sylvana Tomaselli, ed. J.-A. Miller, (1978; reprint [French], New York: Norton, 1988), 241–47. In the House of Pride, the lure of allegorical fixity is, once again, linked to a deceptive mixing of moods. Red Crosse begins by resisting the "joy-

## Notes 219

aunce vaine" of Lucifera's pageant (1.4.37) on the basis of its tone, not its theological meaning—he sees himself as a "warlike swaine" who doesn't belong in this play—but he quickly succumbs to Lucifera's martial pomp. Red Crosse cannot perceive the paradoxical contamination of giddy entertainment and warlike seriousness that proves the essential triviality, and serious danger, of Lucifera's House.

46. See Stanley Fish, *Surprised by Sin* (Berkeley: University of Caliornia Press, 1966), 317 (and elsewhere): Milton's reader "come[s] to regard the time-space mould of experience as an unfortunate consequence of our finitude and mortality, a refraction of reality rather than reality itself."

47. Fish, 20-21.

48. See Pettit, 9-10: "The earliest Puritans were determined to show that grace came not from God as a removed creator but through a personal experience of the direct operation of the spirit"—that is, the sinner's emotions. For examples, see Luther, "Commentary on Galatians," in *Martin Luther: Selections from his Writings*, ed. John Dillenberger (Garden City, N.Y.: Doubeday, 1961), 109-10; also William A. Clebsch, "The Elizabethans on Luther," in *Interpreters of Luther*, ed. Jaroslav Pelikan (Philadelphia: Fortress Press, 1968), 113, and Clebsch's *England's Earliest Protestants* (New Haven: Yale University Press, 1964), 146, on the influence of this commentary in the English Reformation; and see John Bunyan, *Grace Abounding*, ed. Roger Sharrock (Oxford: Clarendon Press, 1962), 40-41, for an important citation of the Luther commentary. For Luther's influence on Tyndale and others, see also J. E. McGoldrick, *Luther's English Connection* (Milwaukee: Northwestern Publishing House, 1979).

For a parallel to Luther's attack on Stoic virtue in this commentary, see John Foxe's taunting of the self-proclaimed righteous in his *Of Free Justification by Christ* (1583; reprint, London, 1694), 100: "No perturbation of affections throws you down from your state of constancy? No concupiscence of the eyes defiles the purity of your mind?" Finally, see Augustine, *On Christian Doctrine*, trans. D.W. Robertson, Jr. (Indianapolis: Bobbs-Merrill, 1958), 39 (a passage influential on the Reformation examples I have mentioned).

49. For the dichotomy between external and efficient grace, see Norman Pettit, *The Heart Prepared* (New Haven: Yale University Press, 1966), 40-85; see also Augustine, "On Grace and Free Will," in *Writings of St. Paul*, ed. Wayne Meeks,(New York: Norton, 1972), 229-30, and the passages cited there (Phil. 2:13, 1:6).

The role of preachers such as Bullinger, Greenham 5, and Rogers in stressing external grace and preparedness will be relevant to my analysis of Book 2; more in line with Book 1 is the more strictly Calvinist emphasis on the efficient grace of a removed God. For the application of these terms to Lutheran theology, see the important study by James S. Preus, *From Shadow to Promise* (Cambridge: Harvard University Press, 1969). According to Preus, the early "Medieval" Luther insists on a tropological reading of Scripture 5, which emphasizes God's action in conforming man to the image of Christ rather than man's moral effort in the direction of God. During his Psalms course, however, Luther moves from *intellectus* to *affectus* as a mode of interpretation, from Christ as a distant, unattainable model of faith to "the 'faithful synagogue' and the expectant, petitioning Israelite, the *purus homo* who is altogether like other men, who 'faints' and 'hopes exceedingly against hope'" (248, 226ff.).

50. Damrosch, *God's Plot*, 149, 145.

51. Ibid., 66.

52. Ibid., 39.

53. It is true that Fish emphasizes the way the reader is shaken up during this didactic process of reading; however, the goal of the process provides a security in

which the reader is able (for example) to reject the "dangerous" connotations of Milton's Eden. Other readers have suggested that such connotations, though liable to "fallen" interpretation, are nevertheless integral to Milton's vision of a divine union of flesh and spirit. See William Kerrigan and Gordon Braden, "Milton's Coy Eve," *ELH* 53 (1986): 27–52, and Kerrigan, *The Sacred Complex* (Cambridge: Harvard University Press, 1983), 98–99.

54. See Augustine, *Confessions* 10 para. 49; Perkins, *Two Treatises*, 2d ed. (London, 1597), 39.

55. See Parker, 58, for a definition of Christian romance.

56. An important source is the rebuke of Job's counsellor Eliphaz in Job 22:5: "Is not thy wickedness great? And thine iniquities infinite?" On the "day of wrath," see Romans 2: 3–5. The answer to Despair comes not only in Paul but in Psalm 130: "If thou, O Lord, straitly markest iniquities, O Lord, who shal stand? . . . [But] with the Lord is mercie, and with him is great redemption" (Geneva Bible).

57. See the similar effect at Amavia's mention of her husband Mordant's death brings on her own in 2.1. As I will note in the next chapter, Spenser uses such parallels between the two episodes to bring out significant differences.

58. Red Crosse's fainting will find its parallel not only in Mordant's surrender to sensuality but in Guyon's swoon after his encounter with Mammon—though Guyon, unlike Red Crosse, will be able to marshal the necessary arguments against his tempter.

59. John Bunyan, *Pilgrim's Progress*, ed. Roger Sharrock (Harmondsworth: Penguin, 1965), 92. Christian's later encounters with the giant named Despair (148ff., 338ff.) are easier and less indicative of the nature of Puritan temptation. See the discussion of Damrosch below, 81–82. I am of course not claiming Spenser's influence on Bunyan, given the conventional nature of the scene, despite the many similarities between them. For an argument against a Spenserian influence on Bunyan, see Harold Golder, "Bunyan and Spenser," *PMLA* 45 (1930): 216–37.

60. Compare Samson in *Samson Agonistes*, 1169–73: "All these indignities . . . / . . . these evils I deserve and more, / Acknowledge them from God inflcited on me / Justly, yet despair not of his final pardon / Whose ear is ever open; and his eye / Gracious to re-admit the suppliant."

61. Foxe, 404, remarks, "Who knows not that, in us, and our Works, there is nothing whereof we ought not to be greatly afraid? . . . We cannot be so perfectly rid of this fear, which is placed in our Nature, but that it will sometimes return and cause trouble to the most eminent saints." See also Luther, "Preface to Romans," in Dillenberger, ed., 29 and 149–50; Calvin, *Institutes*, 3.14 (786), 820, 778, and Melancthon, *Loci Communes* (Philadelphia: Westminster Press, 1969), 80–83, 105; William Perkins, *Two Treatises,* 2d ed.(London, 1597), 39; Augustine, *Confessions* 10.49, trans. R.S. Pine-Coffin (Harmondsworth: Penguin, 1961), 248. Richard Baxter in *The Saints Everlasting Rest* (repr. London, 1803), 80, writes, "God shall cast a man into languishing sickness, and inflict wounds on his heart, and stir up against him his own conscience." Erik H. Erikson, *Young Man Luther* (1958; reprint, New York: Norton, 1962), 155–58, and Haller, *The Rise of Puritanism* provide historical context. Haller (141) writes that "puritan sermons before the revolution were chiefly concerned with charting in infinite detail and tireless reiteration the course of the godly soul out of hardness and indifference to the consciousness of its lost condition, and so out of despair and repentance to faith in God."

A related issue is that of the wound that defines humanity. Foxe, in *Of Free Justification . . .* , 63–64, names this wound as both original sin and the imputed righteousness that heals it through an equally unimaginable pain, Christ's excruciating death: "For as the wound is infinite that is inflicted on our nature, so it is just, that a remedy of the like nature should be applied." See also 73–74, on Christ as the brazen serpent whose sting is medicinal. For the tradition of the Christian *vulnus* (concupiscence), see John Freccero's summary in *Dante: The Poetics of Conversion,* 50–51; Freccero cites Pseudo-Alexander of Hales, *Summa Theologiae* 4, tract 3, q. 3, 1, 510 (Quaracchi, 1928), 746. For the common Christian critique of Stoicism, see Trinkaus, 47–49 (on Petrarch), 107ff., 121 (on Valla), 317–18 (on Brandolini); Struever, 58–59; and Gordon Braden, *Renaissance Tragedy and the Senecan Tradition* (New Haven: Yale University Press, 1986), 92ff.

62. This point is emphasized in Paul Ricoeur, *The Symbolism of Evil* (Boston: Beacon Press, 1967), 147–48, and Freccero, 68–69.

63. For an apt critique of Una's advice, which resurrects Red Crosse against Despair by spurring him on to the glorious knightly deeds that despair has just undermined, see Foxe, 18. Foxe complains that his polemical opponent Osorius treats faith as if "it self profited nothing for the obtaining of Life upon any other account, but that it may procure Grace, which may stir us up to the praise-worthy performances of works."

64. Red Crosse was reported dead in 1.6.38, and Una is his Mary Magdalene (whom, ironically, he has falsely accused of illicit sexuality); he also "dies" at the hands of Orgoglio. For more of the resurrection motif in Book 1, see 1.7.15, 24 and 48–50 (as well as, of course, Sans-ioy's death snd resurrection in canto 5).

65. St. George, revealed to Red Crosse by Contemplation in stanza. 61, is traditionally associated with the earth: William Camden notes that George signifies "Husbandman, the same as *Agricola*" (Camden, *Remaines,* 71—cf. Greek *geôrgia,* the tilling of the earth). See also the life of St. George in Caxton's *Golden Legend* (reprinted in Nelson's edition of Barclay, 112).

66. In a more chivalric vein, Red Crosse asks Contemplation a few stanzas later "how shall I quight / The many favours" done for him by the hermit (1.10.67).

67. Knapp, 822.

68. One might also compare Spenser's suspiciously similar coupling in the Bower episode of "sweet *Parnasse,* the haunt of Muses faire" and "*Eden* selfe, if ought with *Eden* mote compaire," both as analogies to the Bower (2.12.52).

69. See the entry "Mt. of Olives" in *International Standard Bible Encyclopedia,* ed. Geoffrey Bromiley et al. (Grand Rapids, Mich.: Wm. B. Eerdmans, 1979– ).

70. The assimilation of the Mount of Olives to Parnassus conveys a confusion of the poetic power of place associated with romance narrative and the aura of divinity attached to holy places. A similar confusion occurs in canto 11, Red Crosse's battle with the dragon, in which the well and tree of life become magical, quasi-pagan places. There is an interesting analogy in Richard Johnson's *Most Famous History of the Seaven Champions of Christendome* (1596), in which St. George, wounded and fainting, has "yet . . . that good memorie remayning that he tumbled under the branches of the Orange tree; in which place the Dragon could proffer him no further violence." Quoted in Helen C. White, *Tudor Books of Saints and Martyrs* (Madison: University of Wisconsin Press, 1963), 287. During the battle we see a recurrence of the same passivity that afflicted Red Crosse with Despair: "Faint, wearie, sore . . . / Death better were, death did he oft desire" (1.11.28). Red Crosse is saved from death by the intervention of the well of life (st. 29) and later the tree of life (st. 46). Both the well and the tree are the product of a plot of which Red Crosse himself has no consciousness, a plot which creates a mysterious air of suspense by finessing the distinction between God and "fortune" (st. 29): "It chaunst (eternall God that chaunce did guide)" that Red Crosse slips in the mire, allowing the tree to appear (1.11.46).

71. Amid overtones of Odysseus in Phaiakia and Aeneas in Carthage, Una's parents in Canto 12 "blame the too importune fate," which has "tossed" Red Crosse "in fortunes cruell freakes" (1.12.16). The implication of passivity, of narrative machinery obliterating subjective action, continues with Red Crosse's statement that he is "bounden" to return to Gloriana (1.12.18) and, finally, in his overtly passive response to Duessa's accusation. One might also cite, as evidence of the power of narrative over character in this scene, the king's strangely impersonal and juridical offer of Una to Red Crosse, which reads almost as if the plot itself were doing the offering: "In sort as through the world I did proclame, / That who so kild that monster most deforme, / . . . Should haue mine onely daughter to his Dame, / . . . Therefore since now to thee perteines the same, / By dew desert of noble cheualree, / Both daughter and eke kingdome, lo I yield to thee" (1.12.20).

72. Similarly, when Caelia welcomes Red Crosse to the House of Holiness the scene remains focused on his and Una's passivity. Caelia asks Una whether "grace hath thee now hither brought this way? / Or doen thy feeble feet vnweeting hither stray?" (1.10.9). If Una can be led astray, a victim of deceiving fate and Archimago, this is much more true of Red Crosse, whom Caelia explicitly criticizes in the next stanza as a misguided "errant knight" (1.10.10). Significantly, the option of a consciously willed path is not offered to Red Crosse (or Una) by Caelia any more than it was offered by Despair. Either grace or deception, Caelia or Archimago, may guide Red Crosse, but the drama of these two forces' conflict is not based in Red Crosse's own desires.

73. Interestingly in this connection Keith Thomas writes that in Reformation England "many of the old holy wells . . . retained their semi-magical associations, even though Protestants preferred to regard them as medicinal springs working by natural means" (Thomas, *Religion and the Decline of Magic*, 70). Because Spenser, in Book 1, construes grace as an addition to the law rather than an answer to it, the drama of the conflict between the law and grace that is central to one aspect of Protestant thought is absent in Book 1. For the continuing relevance of the law and of works as a moral category in English Protestantism, see Clebsch, *England's Earliest Protestants*, 158–59, 168, 314. English Protestantism did not demand the rejection of works, merely an attention to their moral, internally motivated nature. (See Calvin, *Institutes*, 3.14 [770], and Melancthon, *Loci Communes*, 107–8, for the importance of the intention behind works.) For a contrasting point of view on this episode, see Robin Headlam Wells, *Spenser's Faerie Queene and the Cult of Elizabeth* (London: Croom Helm, 1983), 36ff. Like Ernst Cassirer in *The Platonic Renaissance in England* (Austin: University of Texas Press, 1953), 112–13, Wells overestimates Red Crosse's character. According to Wells, the Despair episode proves "the individual's ability to control his spiritual destiny through self-knowledge and self-discipline," harmonizing the demands of faith and works in the manner of a moderate puritan like Baro (44ff.). I would argue that Red Crosse possesses very little such self-knowledge; the real effort at conscious control comes in Book 2.

# Chapter 3. *The Faerie Queene*, Book 2

1. Interestingly, at the end of the Despair episode Red Crosse is unable to choose how or whether to kill himself (1.9.50–51).

2. William Bouwsma, in *A Usable Past* (Berkeley: University of California Press, 1990), 19–73, sees Stoicism and Augustinianism as the two poles of Renaissance thought.

3. For a cogent argument for Spenser as a Protestant poet, see Anthea Hume, *Edmund Spenser, Protestant Poet* (Cambridge: Cambridge University Press, 1984); also Norbrook.

4. For a convincing recent argument against the identification of Spenser with puritanism see John N. King, *Spenser's Poetry and the Reformation Tradition* (Princeton: Princeton University Press, 1990).

5. See, for example, Cicero, *Tusculan Disputations*, 4.9.

6. See Charles Schmitt, Quentin Skinner and Eckhard Kessler, eds., *The Cambridge History of Renaissance Philosophy* (Cambridge: Cambridge University Press, 1988), 360ff.

7. The Stoic position that we are (potentially) in control of our impulses, though not of our bodies, does not help to resolve the question of the persistence of desire, since our impulses are deeply implicated in the mortal weakness of our bodies. See Jason Saunders, *Justus Lipsius* (New York: Liberal Arts Press, 1955), 102 and 71n (with its reference to a key text, Augustine's *City of God* 9.4). For the theme of allegorical immobility, see my discussion of the Seven Deadly Sins in the previous chapter, on Book 1.

8. To use the Aristotelian terms that Spenser foregrounds: in Book 2 Guyon is an *enkratês* or temperate type in opposition to Acrasia, a well-mixed man. As such, he can be tempted by her intoxicating potions. Guyon wants, at times, to be a *sôphrôn*, a sage who, as Aristotle describes him, is untemptable, in contrast to the *enkratês* (EN 1146a). Mammon, like Stoicism itself, holds out the bait of the *sôphrôn*'s impervious, unbeatable character.

9. Such pathos of vulnerability plays a central role in Reformation thought. The Reformation displays a painful perception of the integral, difficult bond between the self and its desires. Augustine, who was in this respect a vastly important influence on Protestantism, recognizes the problem of eros as a permanent one, an indication of our essential human imperfection. Though Protestantism is in many ways influenced by the championing of Stoic discipline in Christianity that begins with Origen, Protestants often choose Augustine's emphasis on sinful weakness over Origen's belief in self-improvement. For example, the Reformation generally sees baptism not as Origen did, as a ritual of askesis that promises a way of directing oneself into a God-given freedom, as Origen did, but as an Augustinian reminder that the attainment of purity through such moral self-regulation is finally impossible, however desirable it may be. This is not to deny, of course, that there are significant Stoic strain in Augustine. On baptism, see Jean Daniélou, *From Shadows to Reality* (London: Burns and Oates, 1960), J. N. D. Kelly, *Jerome* (London: Burns and Oates, 1975), 181–86, 314–15, and Perkins, *Two Treatises*, 180, 132. For Protestants, the sprinkling of water in baptism commemorates the shedding of Christ's blood and is thus a reminder of moral imperatives, not a ritual of "works" that can automatically remove guilt (see Calvin, *Institutes*, 773, 802, 1305, and the Geneva Bible gloss on Acts 19:4). "Paule would not so greatly bewaile his originall sinne, if after Baptisme it ceased any more to bee sinne," Perkins writes (180). See also Pettit, 74–75, and John Jewel, in *Works* (Cambridge: Cambridge University Press, 1845–50), 751. The purpose of baptism is not to remove sin, but to cause reflection on sin's motives; for the application to Guyon see Carol V. Kaske, "The Bacchus Who Wouldn't Wash: Faerie Queene II.i–ii," *Renaissance Quarterly* 29 (1976): 195–209, and Alastair Fowler, "The Image of Mortality." The general background is Augustine's reading of Romans 7 to enforce a pessimism about the possibility of temperate sexuality: see Pagels, *Adam, Eve and the Serpent*, 143–44, and Brown, *Augustine of Hippo*, 390.

For a critique of opus operatum, see Erasmus's commentary on Romans 8:9 in *Collected Works of Erasmus*, vol. 42, ed. Robert D. Sider (Toronto: University of

Toronto Press, 1984), 46, and his *Enchiridion*, 110ff., 116ff. For the Protestant critique of opus operatum, see also Keith Thomas, *Religion and the Decline of Magic* (New York: Scribner's, 1971), 51ff. Much earlier background is outlined by W. H. C. Frend, *The Donatist Church* (Oxford: Clarendon Press,1971), 137–39, 167–68.

10. See Ricoeur, *The Symbolism of Evil*, 15–17. On 47–150 Ricoeur considers the movement from Old Testament legalism to an internalized, Pauline view of sin as a shift from allegory to symbol.

11. Fish describes an analogous contrast between external and internal in his analysis of Formalist's and Hyprocrisy's challenge to Christian in *Pilgrim's Progress*: "[Formalist and Hypocrisy] say to Christian, [we are] in the same place as you; are we not therefore in the same way? Christian answers by internalizing the metaphor within which they are confined; for him, the 'way' refers to an inner commitment of the spirit." Stanley Fish, *Self-Consuming Artifacts* (Berkeley: University of California Press, 1972), 223.

12. See, for example, Thomas Goodwin's *Patience and Its Perfect Work* (1666?), with its posing of Christian patience against "the violence of the affections" (in his *Works* [Edinburgh: James Nichol, 1861], 2:446–47). Goodwin approves a more rational kind of religious emotion: "reason yourselves into joy" (436–37).

13. See Perkins, 180.

14. For the issue of bodily control, see Nohrnberg, 191ff., Erikson, *Young Man Luther*, 192–93, and (for a brilliant parallel) Bunyan, *Grace Abounding*, 90ff. (A major subtext is Romans 7:15–25.)

15. Guyon's naming of the babe distances him from the coolly allegorical reading of Ruddymane's significance that the Palmer offers in the previous canto. The Palmer, while suggesting an analogy between Amavia and the chaste purity of Diana's nymph, paradoxically insists on Ruddymane's bloody hands as the impure "Symbole" of this chastity. The Palmer says that the babe's hands should remain bloody so that Amavia's "innocence" "may dwell / In her sonnes flesh, to minde reuengement, / And be for all chaste Dames an endlesse moniment" (2.2.10). The "reuengement" that the Palmer refers to here is, I suggest, the revenge of the flesh symbolized by the tale of Mordant, a revenge for which the babe's bloody hands are now a "sacred Symbole." The Palmer gives an Augustinian reading: even innocence is tainted by the blood guilt of original sin. But the Palmer's words, the "reason" to which Guyon "heark[ens]" in 2.2.11, are dramatized and distorted by Guyon in the following canto when he imagines a literal revenge on "them, that had ... wrought" his parents' death. Spenser here may be punning on the Palmer's "sacred Symbole" in its Greek meaning of *sumbolê*, the token of a contractual agreement. Guyon enacts a compact with the babe.

16. On the general issue of Guyon's psychic vulnerability, see Harry Berger, Jr., *The Allegorical Temper* (1957; reprint, Hamden, Conn.: Archon, 1967), 229ff. Contrast 2.12.26, when the Palmer makes the monsters outside the Bower vanish, and 2.12.85–86, when he turns Acrasia's beasts back into still troublesome men.

17. The difference between the two books can also be seen in the ways in which Red Crosse and Guyon approach their respective "doubles." Red Crosse is unaware of the similarities between himself, Sans-ioy and the dragon, but Guyon seems eager to differentiate himself from characters like Pyrochles. Pyrochles mimics Guyon when he cites his obligation to the distressed maiden Occasion as his reason for combat (2.5.17). But Guyon's advice in the preceding stanzas downplays chivalric obligation and the wrath it enjoins in favor of a self-mastery that ostensibly, at least, divides him from Pyrochles.

18. The posture of the "stedfast" Speranza in the House of Holiness is also indicative as an analogy to Red Crosse and a contrast to Guyon: "euer vp to heauen, as she did pray, / Her stedfast eyes were bent, ne swarued other way" (1.10.14).

19. It is Una, not Red Crosse himself, who releases him by reinterpreting his errors: 1.12.33–35.

20. It is significant that one of Red Crosse's rare attempts to undo one of his actions, and thus rewrite his career, takes a clumsy and frantically ineffective form: after "thrust[ing]" the "bleeding bough" of Fradubio "into the ground," Red Crosse "with fresh clay did close the wooden wound" (1.2.44).

21. Mikkel Borch-Jacobsen, *The Freudian Subject* (Stanford, Calif.: Stanford University Press, 1991), 178. Borch-Jacobsen's version of identification is distinct from Lacan's (despite his protestations to the contrary, it is much indebted to Girard). Lacan sees the frustration in the encounter with the other not as a desire for the proper, but as an epistemological issue stemming from the sense that the other reflects one's own lack of knowledge or mastery.

22. As Michel Foucault remarks, this Stoic paradigm sees in a virtuous self, calmly distant from pathos, the basis for a calmly virtuous attitude toward others, and conversely, "The risk of dominating others and exercising over them a tyrannical power only comes from the fact that one did not care for one's self and that one has become a slave to his desires." Michel Foucault, Interview (January 20, 1984), in James Bernauer and David Rasmussen, eds., *The Final Foucault* (Cambridge: MIT Press, 1988), 8.

Guyon reaches the moral power that temperance implies only gradually and temporarily. He begins Book 2 with a capitulation to instinctive passion much like Red Crosse's in Book 1: Guyon is "inflam'd with wrathfulness" against Red Crosse as a result of Una's and Archimago's accusations (2.1.25). Guyon tempers his anger against Red Crosse, but the same anger recurs in Canto 4, when Guyon is "enfierced" by Furor's wrath (2.4.8).

23. See Justus Lipsius's *De Constantia* (1584), trans. Sir John Stradling as *Two Books of Constancie* (1594), ed. and intro. Rudolf Kirk (New Brunswick, N.J.: Rutgers University Press, 1939). Lipsius, glancing at Horace's "Coelum non animum mutant qui trans mare currunt," writes in a characteristic passage, "As they that be holden with a fever, doe tosse and turn themselves unquietlie, and often change their beds through a vain hope of remedie: In like case we wee, who being sicke in our mindes doe without any fruite, wander from one countrey to another. This is indeede to bewray our griefe, but not to allay it. To discouer this inward flame, but not to quench it" (*De Constantia*, 73 [Chapter 2]).

24. See Berger, *The Allegorical Temper*, 230ff. This threat is symbolized by the image of pure (*akratês*, unmixed) passion. Since this image persuades because of the potent Aristotelian idea of our nature as a mixture, a better name for Acrasia might be Kakrasia, bad mixing, just as Malecasta is bad chastity. Aristotle's description of *acrasia* implies a perverse or unbalanced version of virtue, rather than an absence of it.

25. See Tuve, *Allegorical Imagery* (Princeton: Princeton University Press, 1966), 283, 248n. See also Thomas P. Roche, Jr., *The Kindly Flame* (Princeton: Princeton University Press, 1964), 12. For the important debate over whether Guyon in Mammon's Cave is an allegorical or a psychological character, see Tuve, 348n., Berger, *The Allegorical Temper*, 3–38, and Alpers, *Poetry of the Faerie Queene*, 235–75. My own view follows Alpers but adds that the Mammon episode is an uncharacteristic one for Guyon exactly because it shows him as an allegorical figure.

26. Imminent disaster is avoided only by Mammon's own clumsy shift to the offer of Philotime, who, in contrast to Disdaine, does not look at all tempting to Guyon. Philotime appeals to a more grasping and theoretical type of ambition than Guyon's (the exact relation between covetous ambition and theorizing, between Tantalus and Socrates, is one of the mysteries of the Mammon episode). We might try to explain his

unsusceptibility to her, like his lack of interest in Mammon's final test, the silver seat, by his failure to want to brood Mammon-like over the fact of his desire. Guyon is not tempted to inquire, as Mammon inquires all too incessantly, into the meaning of his attractions.

27. The role of experience is greater in Book 2 than in Book 1, and internal emotion comprises an important part in it. At 2.12.68, when Guyon's "courage cold" is excited by the Bower's bathing maidens, Spenser may be hinting in his oxymoronic phrase at the frigid death to which desire's ("courage['s]") heat led Mordant. See the discussion of 2.1.42 below and 1.7.6 in the previous chapter. See also Arthur's reaction to Praysdesire in 2.9.39: "Now seeming flaming whot, now stony cold." In the same scene, Guyon meets his ruling spirit, Shamefastnesse, and her reaction ("bashfull bloud her snowy cheekes did dye" [2.9.41]) mirrors his own. Contrast Fidelia's constant mood (1.10.13). Red Crosse's feverishly chill response to the well in 1.7.6, like his initial lustful pity for Duessa, is less reflective, more of a reflex than Guyon's sympathy: it suggests a reductive reading of emotional compulsion as mere physiology in a way that Guyon's desire does not.

28. The "piteous spectacle" (1.9.37), for which Red Crosse was prepared by Trevisan's account of Despair (1.9.25–32), is similar in its effect to Fradubio's scene: it sparks not pity but vengeful rage in the knight. Red Crosse, instead of considering the possible exemplary relevance of Terwin's case to his own—thinking about how, and why, this could happen to him, too—immediately threatens Despair in a manner as vociferous as it is foolhardy. Red Crosse, we are reminded, approaches dangers as strictly external obstacles, never as questions about the self. Red Crosse's proud courage, here as elsewhere, finds its basis in an unthinking composure. Red Crosse's lack of consciousness means that he fails to provoke the reader's tragic sympathy. For Renaissance theory's discussion of tragic sympathy see Weinberg, 2:648, 652–53; also Weinberg's discussions of Robortello, Cinthio and Guarini. All three critics link catharsis and Christian education through the spectator's identification with the tragic hero. As spectators, Guarini writes, we feel "buona compasione" (good pity) "quando noi ci attristiamo di chi s'affligge nell'animo, perche troppo si sia compiaciuto nel corpo" (when we are saddened for someone who is harmed in his soul because he is too given to pleasure in the body).

The use of exemplary characters in Puritanism, and the difference between exemplary and allegorical modes, is discussed by U. Milo Kaufmann, *The Pilgrim's Progress and Traditions in Puritan Meditation* (New Haven: Yale University Press, 1966), 89–105 (especially 90–94); on other senses of the example, see Seneca's Epistle 6.5, Claude Bremond and Jacques Le Goff, *L'Exemplum* (Biepols Turnhout-Belgium, 1982), 45, 114–16, Joseph Albert Mosher, *The Exemplum in the Early Religious and Didactic Literature of England* (New York: A.M.S. Press, 1966), 108–9, 122–25, 139, and G. W. Owst, *Literature and Pulpit in Medieval England* (Cambridge: Cambridge University Press, 1933), 155ff., 168, 188. The historical exemplum is described in Puttenham, 3.19 (252–53), who suggests the *de casibus* mode of *The Mirror for Magistrates* and Spenser's own 2.10 and 3.9. See also Owst, 160–61. I am attempting to pinpoint, in contrast to these proverbial and historical uses of the example, a poetic sense of it that incorporates the passionate energy that, for example, Sidney evokes in his *Apology*. Richard Helgerson hints at the potential for strife between the proverbial and the dramatic senses of the example when he identifies the struggle between didactic precept and experience as a major theme of Renaissance stories of "self-fashioning" (*The Elizabethan Prodigals* [Berkeley: University of California Press, 1976], 1–5.).

29. See Tuve, 108: "There is no repetition in Book 1 except as men eternally repeat the first sin, never recognizing it again when they see it—surely one of

Spenser's points."Arthur says to Una after his rescue of Red Crosse from Orgoglio's dungeon that "The only good, that grows of passed feare, / Is to be wise, and ware of like agein" (1.8.44). But the content of Arthur's lesson, the usual "That blisse may not abide in state of mortall men" (1.8.44), seems oddly to undermine his claim. How can the unpredictability of misfortune teach one how to act? The realization of mutability, and the fact of original sin that it implies, occurs on a much deeper level in Book 2, and does not there allow a pragmatic response like Arthur's. That is, Guyon cannot hope to avoid "feare" as Red Crosse does. (Red Crosse even wants to manipulate the "time and suffised fates" that Fradubio pronounces inexplicable and inflexible in 1.2.43.)

30. Fradubio describes his fall as a predetermined lot or chance: "It was my lot," Fradubio says, "To loue this gentle lady," he says, when "we chancéd of a knight encountred be." Duessa, who chances to accompany the knight, proceeds to use her "hellish science" on an unsuspecting Fradubio (1.2.35, 38). See Nohrnberg, 287–88, and A. C. Hamilton, *The Structure of Allegory in The Faerie Queene* (Oxford: Clarendon Press, 1961), 94–95.

31. Compare Red Crosse's instinctive, raging reaction to Terwin, Despair's victim in Book 1. Despair has turned Terwin into "a drearie corse, whose life away did pas, / All wallowd in his owne yet luke-warme blood" (1.9.36)—a description that parallels the one of Mordant.

32. In connection with imagery of heat and cold, Fowler, "Image of Mortality," 141–42, notes Bersuire's allegory of the cool water of the stream Diana (Scripture) that tempers the heat of concupiscence. The prototypical moments for this kind of weak reaction in an epic hero are *Odyssey* 5.406–7 and *Aeneid* 1.92–94 (and other places in the two poems).

33. The image of the mourning lion that Spenser applies to Guyon here echoes Red Crosse's agonizing penance in the House of Holinesse, "In which his torment often was so great, / That like a Lyon he would cry and rore, / And rend his flesh, and his owne synewes eat" (1.10.28). The Achillean image of the lion, applied to Red Crosse in the first martial encounter of the poem, his battle with Error ("he lept / As Lion fierce vpon the flying pray" [1.1.17]), is turned against Red Crosse's own "flesh" in the House of Holinesse. The lion only becomes an emblem of inwardness, however, in Guyon's scene. In the House of Holinesse Red Crosse, though he suffers from "inward corruption," is tormented by an outward, physical discipline of the the body (1.10.25–27). Guyon, by contrast, is subject to "ruth and fraile affection," not Red Crosse's monastic mortification of the flesh.

34. See Berger, *The Allegorical Temper*, 198–99; see also 14–15, 216–17.

35. See Kenneth Burke, "On Catharsis, or Resolution," *Kenyon Review* 21 (1959): 346–47.

36. When Red Crosse forces his counterpart Sans-ioy to stoop before him, his emotional reaction, though apparently similar to Guyon's, partakes of a shame that is competitive rather than empathic as in 2.1. Red Crosse's pride keeps him unaware of the similarity between him and his enemy that Spenser, writing behind his hero's back, obviously suggests. Red Crosse, unlike Guyon with Pyrochles and Mordant, is ignorant of the secret bond that ties him to his fellow knight, the weakness that their desire for glory entails, when he

> ... with so'exceeding furie at him [i.e., Sans-ioy] strake,
> That forced him to stoupe vpon his knee;
> Had he not stouped so, he should have clouen bee.
> (*FQ* 1.5.12)

The difference between Red Crosse's errors and Guyon's has a lot to do with the fact that Acrasia, unlike Archimago and Duessa in Book 1, is not a stand-in for the poet in his engineering of the narrative. Acrasia is so immediately *there* that she does not need to pursue her targets or actively change the course of events. Rather than casting narrative snares, she preys on the intimate fact of character, the palpable sensitivity that elicits desire without her needing to make an effort. Archimago's and Duessa's plotting, by contrast, works because they energetically exploit deceptive appearances. Book 1, again, is centered on plot; Book 2, on character.

37. "Pleasure in the conscious exercise of virtue," writes Richard Strier, "is a deeply Aristotelian conception and, of course, a deeply self-satisfied state of mind." As such, it must conflict with the Christian awareness of original sin. Strier, *Love Known*, 20 (on Herbert's "Unkindnesse").

38. See the exchange between Arthur and Una in 1.7.41: "No faith so fast (quoth she) but flesh does paire. / Flesh may empaire (quoth he) but reason can repaire." Arthur wins his argument with Una; Guyon loses his with Amavia. (But Arthur is not immune to passionate vulnerability—see 1.9.12–16, his memory of Gloriana.)

39. There are several other moments in Book 2 that would support such an implication. In 2.12.27–28, the Palmer restrains Guyon from sympathizing with "a seemely Maiden" they see as they approach the Bower. Guyon wants to "know, and ease her sorrow sad," just as he wanted to console Duessa in 2.1. In 2.5.24, similarly, the Palmer prevents Guyon from "succour[ing]" Pyrochles ("Ne let thy stout hart melt in pitty vayne"). Such pity is affective evidence of Guyon's complicity in the fates of these characters: their faults are also his. In Alma's house, Guyon's chivalric offer to aid Shamefastnesse (2.9.42) betrays, in its awkwardness, his own involvement in her "trouble:" "If it be I [who is responsible], of pardon I you pray." For the major problem of pity as a potential obstacle to justice in Book 5, see 5.5.13 and Nohrnberg, 358. In Book 6 pity seems to become safer; it is usually seen as a persuasive device, directed toward other characters, that does not implicate the hero as it does in Book 2 (6.2.41, 6.4.3)

40. Fowler, "Image of Mortality," 147, cites 1 Cor. 5:4 and Romans 8:23, noting Guyon's "burden" in 2.2.11–12 and the fact that his "response to the image of mortality is, like Paul's, a groan."

41. On the persistence of original sin, see, for example, Article 9 of the 39 Articles: "This infection of nature doth remain, yea in them that are regenerated . . ." An important subtext tending in the contrary direction (noted by Fowler, "Image of Mortality") is Isa. 1:15–18: "Though your sins were as crimson, they shall be made white as snow." The striking similarity between Archimago's description of the wounded Duessa in 2.1.11, with its image of her "snowy brest" and her foe's "bloudie word," and Amavia's appearance in 1.1.39 must be noted here. *Pace* Isaiah, the blood persists. (See also Amoret in 3.12.20.)

42. Interestingly, Nohrnberg's comment on this passage, citing Northrop Frye, conjectures that Diana is to be identified with the Old Law (Nohrnberg, 288–89).

43. See Hans-Robert Jauss, *Aesthetic Experience and Literary Hermeneutics* (Minneapolis: University of Minnesota Press, 1982), 92, 106–9, 156–59, 178–79.

44. Elizabeth Freund, *The Return of the Reader: Reader-Response Criticism* (New York: Methuen, 1987), 99–103. Freund proposes a deconstructive alternative to reader-response in which the text becomes the site of "a patient dialogue or interrogation" (154). It does not detract from the acuteness of Freund's critique of Fish to note that she does not raise the question of interpretive didacticism, of theory's role as therapy, in relation to her own deconstructive program. As didacticism, de Manian decon-

struction, with its transformation of nearly every text into a proof of inexorable law, falls victim to the same overestimation of readerly mastery, combined with a bad-faith attribution of this mastery to the text itself, that Freud attacks in Fish. For a compelling consideration of the didactic aspect of deconstruction see Stanley Cavell, "The Politics of Interpretation (Politics as Opposed to What?)," in his *Themes out of School* (Chicago: University of Chicago Press, 1984).

45. Fish, "Withholding the Missing Portion," in *Doing What Comes Naturally* (Durham: Duke University Press, 1989), 552.

46. Here I disagree with the assessments of both Nohrnberg and Greenblatt, who see an enraged, not a cold or steadfast, Guyon "pitiless[ly]" destroying the Bower. See Nohrnberg, 498, and Stephen Greenblatt's chapter on Spenser in *Renaissance Self-Fashioning*, 157–92. Freccero, 47, discusses the related issue of *ira* and *concupiscentia* and their Thomistic separation.

47. See Woodhouse, "Nature and Grace," 366, and A. C. Hamilton in his edition of *The Faerie Queene* (167). Hamilton writes on 2.11.40: "These riddles, which defeat 'reasons reach,' suggest that Maleger is the old Adam in us, against whom Paul laments: 'O wretched man that I am, who shal deliver me from the bodie of this death?' (Rom. 7:24). Woodhouse (366) claims that, because only "the exercise of grace" can destroy Maleger, the latter's death by water "is intended to suggest baptismal regeneration"; see Hamilton, ed., 167.

48. The 1596 version will substitute "this lifeless shadow" for "his lifeless shadow," slightly obscuring the original sense that Arthur is fighting his own death.

49. Woodhouse, 378, writes that Spenser "makes it clear that the Squire's arrival is the effect of Providence, which can on occasion use the weak to save the strong."

50. Arthur is clearly the stand-in for Guyon, who like him wears "bright armour" (st. 3). Guyon, unlike Arthur, is accompanied by the Palmer "in habit sad" (st. 3); as usual in the poem, Arthur represents a brand of action so effective that it does not need to be accompanied by contemplation, though Canto 11 will question his effectiveness.

51. By contrast, Sans-ioy in his battle with the Red Crosse of Book 1 is simply a reflection of Red Crosse's joyous pride (or, rather, Red Crosse reflects Sans-ioy). "Sans-ioy" might be translated as false (or superficial) joy.

52. But Arthur's reaction is unintentionally paradoxical: in his reaction to Maleger, Arthur shows both furious disbelief and susceptibility. As Spenser ambiguously puts it, he is "halfe in rage to be deluded" (st. 38), both raging with the consciousness that he's been deluded and raging with the desire for delusion, for the illusion of superiority that such combat necessarily requires.

53. The punning reference to Arthur's "mortall speare," Mordure (2.11.25), as well as his fury and fear during the contest with Maleger (2.11.33,39), reinforce the impression of his vulnerability.

54. When Spenser depicts Maleger in the final moments of this battle picking up and casting a boundary-stone against Arthur, he conjures up a particular epic context, Turnus' similar action in *Aeneid* 12.896–98. Significantly, in Book 12 of the *Aeneid* Aeneas is closest in the entire poem to merging his emotions, and thus his identity, with the fury of his enemy Turnus. Virgil's two antagonists, like Arthur and Maleger at the end of Canto 11, are frequently difficult to tell apart during their final battle.

55. Ricoeur's notion of the symbolic is remarkably similar to Lewalski's definition of Protestant meditation in *Protestant Poetics*. Lewalski writes that, unlike Catholic meditation, which subjects the believer to a sacred theme, Protestant meditation submits the theme to the spiritual state of the believer (Lewalski, 13–28).

## Chapter 4. *The Faerie Queene*, Book 3

1. See J. G. Turner, *One Flesh* (Oxford: Clarendon Press, 1988).
2. Turner, 194.
3. For the difference between Spenser's Book 3 and Petrarchan poetics in terms of depiction of the feminine, see Berger, *Revisionary Play*, 114–15, and Lauren Silberman, "Unsung Heroines," in *Rewriting the Renaissance*, eds. Margaret W. Ferguson, Maureen Quilligan, and Nancy Vickers (Chicago: University of Chicago Press, 1986). Spenser also reverses the gendered pattern of quest romance, in which female figures like Perceval's sister may aid and abet the quest, but do not lead it (female knights are, of course, represented in Virgil, Ariosto and Tasso). The torture of Amoret seems to be a version of a common enough scene in the quest romances: the bleeding of a maiden to cure a lady Traditionally, a male knight arrives to protest the treatment and rescue the maiden. In Spenser, Britomart takes on the role of the male knight.
4. Mary Nyquist, "The Genesis of Gendered Subjectivity in the Divorce Tracts and *Paradise Lost*," in *Re-membering Milton*, eds. Nyquist and Margaret W. Ferguson (New York: Methuen, 1987), 121.
5. The female children studied in Freud's "'A Child Is Being Beaten,'" through the fantasy of observing a beating which "takes the place of a sexual act" "escape from the demand[s] of the erotic side of [their] li[ves] altogether." Sigmund Freud, "'A Child Is Being Beaten,'" in *Collected Papers*, 2:196. As Freud also notes, however, this phase of the fantasy is erotically gratifying (despite or because of the fact that it represents a release from the trial of occupying a sexual role?).
6. See Miller's psychoanalytic reading of Marlowe's *Hero and Leander*, "The Death of the Modern," *South Atlantic Quarterly* 88, no. 4 (Fall 1989): 779.
7. Scudamour lies passively on the ground outside Busirane's house, helpless in his love. His failed desire has become anger turned against himself: "With huge impatience he inly swelt . . . / And wilfully him throwing on the gras, / Did beat and bounse his head and brest full sore" (3.11.27)—compare Apollo's "rending his golden heare" over the loss of Coronis and Hyacinth, as depicted in the House of Busirane (3.11.37).
8. Britomart's pity when she is "emmoved" by the sight of the Squire of Dames chased by Ollyphant (3.11.4) is of an essentially different sort, a forecast of the public or courteous pathos more characteristic of Book 6. See later, chap. 5.
9. We see the same dangerous mirroring in Britomart's relation to both Malecasta and Amoret. Malecasta's "misconstruing" in lines 8–9 is the mirror image of Britomart's own in the preceding stanza. Like 3.12.37 with its blurring of the distinction between Amoret and Britomart, this stanza confuses Britomart and Malecasta by adroitly shifting the referent of its "she." The continuation of Britomart's journey depends on her refusal to recognize the significance of such mutuality—just as Guyon can only survive the end of Book 2 because he refuses to recognize Acrasia's relevance for him.
10. Jacques Lacan, "Aggressivity in Psychoanalysis," in *Écrits*, 19. Lacan's formulation relates to the beginning stages of the growth of the self. He postulates a connection between narcissism and anger that depends on a mirroring of the other in a self that is not yet inducted into the Symbolic world of social competition among distinct selves (the kind of world that Spenser presents in Book 4).
11. There is a specific parallel between the two episodes: Britomart's phallic upraised sword, which she brandishes in both episodes, defends against her own receptiveness to Busirane and Malecasta. The sword holds off her shocked susceptibility, her realization, as the Enchanter gives her his full attention, that she in her essential personality shares something with Amoret. Britomart's "horror" suggests her unconscious knowledge that she has an Amoret-like aspect which she must heroically resist.

12. Citing Chaucer, Britomart comments on the dueling knights outside Malecasta's castle "Ne may love be compeld by maisterie" (3.1.25). But Britomart does not know that mastery can appear as sensitive, affectionate communion rather than the overt power of chivalric combat.

13. Nohrnberg (445) notes the assumed masculine identity of the attacker here. The episode has its source in Fiordispina's attraction to the disguised Bradamante in canto 25 of the *Orlando Furioso*.

14. Nohrnberg connects these two lines (447).

15. See Burke, "On Catharsis, or Resolution." It is possible, I believe, to see this movement from precathartic to cathartic as a transition from Lacan's Imaginary to his Symbolic stage. In a discussion related to Lacan's theory of the mirror stage, Jean Laplanche suggests that in the autoerotic phase of infantile development sexuality is born—that is, the desiring self comes into being—through its attraction to an internalized image. This image, the first object of desire, is a fantasy reflected within the subject. Britomart's selfhood coincides with her sexual desire. See Laplanche, *Life and Death in Psychoanalysis*, 88. The nonappearance of King Ryence—whose prohibited space Britomart invades, but without ever encountering or being punished by him—and his replacement by the elusive quasi-paternal figure of Merlin, who encourages Britomart's desire, is more evidence for the pre-Oedipal nature of Britomart's education (that is, Spenser's avoidance of the father's presence).

16. For Britomart's "Amoret aspect," see Alpers, 393, 403: "Britomart assumes the integrity of the experience not by exercising her magical prowess but by being assimilated to Amoret's suffering."

17. Nohrnberg, 477, applies the briar-rose image to Malecasta and to Britomart (in a different passage); he adds, "Briar-rose is vulnerable to herself; the same thing is true of Amoret," and links this fairy-tale topos to that of Cupid's self-inflicted wound (3.11.45).

18. In this speech, Britomart also rebels against the common romance mode in which the self is constructed or influenced by place (in Spenser, this happens with the Bower, the Garden of Adonis, the Temple of Venus and the House of Pride).

19. For Lacan's definition of the Symbolic (not to be confused with Ricoeur's use of the term in *The Symbolism of Evil*), see the "Discours du Rome," "The Function and Field of Speech and Language in Psychoanalysis," in *Écrits*.

20. See Baldassare Castiglione, *The Book of the Courtier* (New York: Doubleday, 1967), trans. Thomas Hoby, 61, on the advantages of feigned modesty, which sets up a discord of words and actions: "This in like maner is verified in musicke: where it is a verye greate vice to make two perfecte cordes, the one after the other, so that the verye sense of our hearing abhorreth it, and often times deliteth in a seconde or in a seven, which in it selfe is an unpleasaunt discord and not tollerable."

21. See the first sonnet of Sidney's *Astrophel and Stella* for a similarly intended pun on "fain."

22. See Alpers, p. 395, on the connection between desire and morality: "When we come to the pain and terror that Amoret undergoes in the name of fidelity, we can see what Florimell contributes to Book 3. Spenser makes us aware that fidelity must be the product of erotic desire: precisely because it has its source in problematic human impulses, it has dignity as a moral virtue." I would argue that this comment applies to Britomart as well as Florimell, and that it suggests the central importance in this book of the emotional vulnerability Britomart shows.

23. As Joan Ferrante points out, love in medieval literature can be both the legitimation of the pursuit of honor and an obstacle to honor. See Ferrante, in Ferrante and George Economou eds., *In Pursuit of Perfection* (Port Washington, N.Y.: Kennikat

Press, 1975), 164–65. Britomart's disdain for the fabliau plot occupied by Paridell and Hellenore is also a rejection of courtly love, because this plot here takes the form of a rival, scurrilous literary genre's reduction of such courtly amours to self-parody. For the typical fabliau triangle of foolish husband, sensual wife and clever interloper see Charles Muscatine, *Chaucer and the French Tradition* (Berkeley: University of California Press, 1957), 59, 61; also Per Nykrog, *Les Fabliaux* (1957; reprints, Geneva, 1973), 72–91, for the fabliau as aristocratic self-satire.

24. Tobin Siebers, in *The Mirror of Medusa* (Berkeley: University of California Press, 1983), 13–16, notes some of the parallels between Medusa and Athena/Minerva in classical tradition; he argues for an analogy between the two figures.

25. Interestingly, Medusa stands for a look that is deadly because it cannot be returned; the same kind of power through lack of reciprocity characterizes the gentler Minerva, like Diana a chastely self-sufficient figure. In 3.9, Britomart's reproving eye does not depend on anyone else's gaze; thus she can allow all to wonder at her, to be "smitten" by her appearance, as she could not in Castle Joyeous, when Gardante wounded her. But, as will become apparent in Busirane's House, Britomart has not transcended her earlier, unprotected self: Busirane's House, like the Actaeon-Diana myth of the Mutabilitie Cantos, clearly implies the vulnerability to the other's gaze that is hidden behind such chaste autonomy.

26. Spenser is careful to distinguish between Britomart's doubt and actual dissimulation. Britomart's "secret dout," her practice of "mask[ing]" her mind "so doutful to be wayd," is the elusiveness and confusion that makes for her appeal—a dissimulation distinct from the malicious contrariness of Ate, whose heart "doubly stil [is] guided" as she stirs up trouble (4.1.27; see also 4.1.3, 7–17).

27. The lines are followed by an apology for the use of Hellenore as an example of womankind, and a caution against seeing her as typical of all women (a similar caution was stated in the case of Malecasta, 3.1.49).

28. The blending of identities during Britomart's combat with Paridell might be glossed with a reference to Frank Whigham, *Ambition and Privilege: The Social Tropes of Elizabethan Courtesy Theory* (Berkeley: University of California Press, 1984), who describes courtly competition as a "struggle [that brings] resemblance rather than distinction," in which "moral dignity recedes before martial resemblance" (78–79; here Whigham cites *FQ* 6.1.36–37).

29. Britomart's fury at the beginning of canto 9—she "wex exceeding wroth," we are told, on being denied access to the sty (3.9.13)—contrasts sharply with her steely composure during the rest of the episode.

30. Another variation on this image of unveiling is the vision of Arthegall Britomart sees in her father's looking-glass:

> Eftsoones there was presented to her eye
> A comely knight, all arm'd in complete wize,
> Through whose bright ventayle lifted vp on hye
> His manly face, that did his foes agrize,
> And friends to termes of gentle truce entize,
> Lookt forth, as Phoebus face out of the east,
> Betwixt two shadie mountaines doth arize....
> (3.2.24)

31. The nymph Cymoent, advised by Proteus that her son Marinell would be destroyed by a woman, warned him to fear feminine love ("a lesson too too hard for liuing clay," Spenser wryly laments [3.4.26]), but neglected to consider the danger of feminine wrath. Of course, because Britomart's anger is motivated, in this scene and others, by her love, it is in effect a woman's love that fells Marinell.

32. See Ovid, *Amores* 1.4.29ff., in which the lover offers his girlfriend advice on how to seduce him in her husband's presence, and *Heroides* Books 16 and 17. In the latter account, Paris traces the word "amo" in the spilled wine (Book 17, 87ff.); Helen's watchword to him is "dissimulare potes / lude, sed occulte!" (Book 17, 152–53). Ovid, *Heroides and Amores,* trans. Grant Showerman, 2nd ed. rev. G.P. Goold (1914; reprint, Cambridge: Harvard University Press, 1977).

33. See Mihoko Suzuki, *Metamorphoses of Helen* (Ithaca: Cornell University Press, 1989), 164n; Suzuki cites Castiglione, 277, and, for the Harington passage, *Elizabethan Critical Essays,* ed. G. Gregory Smith (1904; reprints, London: Oxford University Press, 1971), 2:215.

34. For more on Spenser and history in this episode, see Lawrence Manley, "Spenser and the City: The Minor Poems," *MLQ* 43 (1982): 215ff. For the depiction of history in Book 4, see David Quint, *Origin and Originality in Renaissance Literature* (Princeton: Princeton University Press, 1983), 149ff. The very different view of history given in Book 5 is discussed in Angus Fletcher, *The Prophetic Moment* (Chicago: University of Chicago Press, 1971).

Venus's role in sponsoring the concord of Book 4 is a contrasting solution to the problem of eros; see Harry Berger, Jr., "The Spenserean Dynamics," *SEL* 8 (1968): 1–18.

35. See Nohrnberg, 573–74, and MacCaffrey, 353. MacCaffrey defines Paridell's lust in terms of the "meaningless linear[ity]" of his existence (310 –11). His brand of desire might be compared with Argante's; it is symbolized by the hyena that chases Florimell, who is replaced by a series of interchangeable subsitutes—the fantasy-objects that, taken together, comprise the False Florimell. The place of self-directed modelling in the Proem to Book 3 is also notable: Elizabeth, Spenser claims, contains her own praises, inexpressible by him. There is, of course, a continuity between Florimell and False Florimell, and between Florimell and Britomart (see later, chapter 5), that threatens such distinctions in the name of the poem's massively orchestrated rambling, or error (see Parker, passim).

36. See Nohrnberg, Fletcher, p. 99, and Berger, "The Discarding of Malbecco," *Studies in Philology* 66 (1969): 135–54. Berger's persuasive analysis has influenced my own: I add only that he fails to explain why Spenser's emphasis on repetition or "archaism" is necessary, and why it is invoked at this point in Britomart's story. (For a fuller account of archaism elsewhere in Spenser, see Berger's essay on the Mutabilitie Cantos, reprinted in *Revisionary Play*.) I suggest that Spenser presents the crude, archaic character Paridell as a contrast to the psychological finesse of Britomart in order to produce the didactic image of Britomart as an exemplary historical character that the poet has promised from the beginning of Book 3.

37. See Berger, "Discarding of Malbecco," 137–38. Suzuki, 167, suggests a pun on Helen-*or*: the Helen of today.

38. Contrast the prognostication of Guyon's quest that the Palmer gives Red Crosse in 2.1.32: "But wretched we, where ye haue left your marke, / Must now anew begin, like race to runne"—a revisionary reel-to-reel far more sophisticated than Paridell's one-dimensional, black-and-white reproduction.

39. See Hallett Smith, *Elizabethan Poetry* (Cambridge: Harvard University Press, 1952), 4 –10, and Humphrey Tonkin, *Spenser's Courteous Pastoral* (Oxford: Clarendon Press, 1972), 274 –75, 299. Tonkin claims that Spenser, in Book 6, turns Calidore from a morally dubious Paris into a virtuous Hercules figure with his victory over the brigands. But the routing of the brigands is a traditional feature of the Paris legend; see Apollodorus, *The Library* 3.12.5, trans. Sir J. G. Frazer (London: Heinemann, 1921). Moreover, Tonkin's reading implies a questionable narrative teleology: Does Calidore really change for the better in the course of Book 6? If he does, can the change

be described as a conversion of pleasure into virtue rather than a momentary or disjunctive abandoning of the one in favor of the other?

For surveys of the tradition of the shepherd Paris that is referred to here, see Nohrnberg, 721–23, and the introductions to *Excidium Troiae*, eds. E. Bagby Atwood and Virgil K. Whitaker (Cambridge: Harvard University Press, 1944) and *The Seege of Troye*, ed., C. H. A. Wager (New York, 1899). For Medieval material, see C. David Benson, *The History of Troy in Middle English Literature* (Woodbridge, Suffolk, England: D. S. Brewer, 1980); and Robert Mannyng, *The Story of England* (1338), ed. F. J. Furnivall (London, 1887), 459–503. In the Renaissance, the innocence of the shepherd Paris is sometimes contrasted to what Comes calls the "concupiscence charnelle" that arrives with his Judgment; see Natalis Comes, *Mythologie*, trans. Jean Baudouin (1627; reprint [Paris], New York: Garland Press, 1976), 1.6.24 (651–53.), and Charles Stephanus (Charles Estienne), *Dictionarium* (Paris, 1596), entry "Paris." Paris's shepherd life is mentioned but not glorified in Thomas Cooper's *Thesaurus* (London, 1565), entry "Paris." For a negative treatment of Paris the shepherd, see Thomas Heywood's Ovidian *Oenone and Paris* (1594); Peele's *The Arraignment of Paris* (1584) is more complex and ambivalent on the subject. For two contrasting views of Paris's Judgment in Spenser, see in *The Shepheardes Calender* Julye (145–48) and August (138).

40. In Book 4, Spenser wonders whether Paridell is on a par with Duessa (4.1.32: "whether were more false, full hard it is to tell"). Puns on "paragon," "conquests part" (st. 33) and "Paramour" (st. 36) follow. The contest for False Florimell is a par-agon, a competition among unimpressive equals.

41. See Manley, "Spenser and the City," 216.

42. On the Brute connection, see Geoffrey of Monmouth, *Geoffrey's Histories of the Kings of Britain* (London, n.d.), Chapter 1. Geoffrey recounts Brute's accidental slaying of his father, Sylvius, which is mentioned by Paridell in st. 48. Merritt Y. Hughes, in *Virgil and Spenser* (Port Washington, N.Y.: Kennikat Press, 1969), 338, remarks that "the abrupt transition from the legend of Aeneas to that of Brutus in Spenser's stanzas is analogous to Geoffrey's hasty dispatch of Aeneas's story."

43. The definition is given in both Thomas Cooper's *Thesaurus* (1565) and Calepine's *Dictionarium* (1542); Spenser certainly used the former and probably the latter. See DeWitt T. Starnes and E. W. Talbert, *Classical Myth and Legend in Renaissance Dictionaries* (Chapel Hill: University of North Carolina Press, 1955), 88, 81, 47–48.

It is unlikely, but Spenser may even have remembered that, in Calepine's *Dictionarium* (Venice, 1542), RR iii [r], the exemplary definition given for *Parius lapis* is a passage from the first book of the Aeneid in which Aeneas represents both the white marble and the gold that a contemporary touchstone might test. Aeneas, with a completeness unattainable for Spenser's Britomart, needs no opposing vice to carry his historical destiny. (The citation given for "Parius lapis . . . quo aurum probatur" is "Verg. I. Aeneid. Parius ve lapis circundatur auro." The entire passage, Aeneid 1.589–93, runs as follows: "Namque ipsa decoram/caesariem nato genetrix lumenque iuventae/purpureum et laetos oculis adflarat honores: / quale manus addunt ebori decus, aut ubi flavo/argentum Pariusve lapis circundatur auro."

44. The issue is how (as Isabel MacCaffrey puts it) the shadow Arthegall becomes reality—how "the impulse to seal off the psyche in a self-created world of love" gets transmuted into "the impulse to serve a wonder-working natural providence" (MacCaffrey, 312, 299–303).

45. Compare Ariosto's *Orlando Furioso* 34.14, in which the king of Lydia's daughter groups Aeneas with Jason, Theseus and Amnon as a betrayer of women.

46. See, in particular, Frances Yates, *Astraea* (London: Croom Helm, 1975), 29–120.

47. See Fichter, passim.

48. See also Wells, passim. Quint suggests that, in Book 4's river marriage as in 3.9, national history replaces the Church history of Book 1 as a more contingent, truer to experience, and therefore more authentic version of the sacramental (159, 164). As Quint states, 3.9 grounds providential narrative in history as Book 1 does not.

49. Although Glauce's proposal following Merlin's prophecy that the two women join Uther in the British cause stirs "great desire / Of warlike armes" and "generous stout courage" in Britomart (3.3.57), the latter almost immediately reverts to a "pensiue" interior monologue—her "amorous discourse" about Arthegall: "With such self-pleasing thoughts her wound she fed" (3.4.6). Fantasizing Arthegall's gentle nature, Britomart is still a courteous dreamer like Malecasta.

50. Daniel Javitch, *Poetry and Courtliness in Renaissance England* (Princeton: Princeton University Press, 1978), 150. Javitch, 40–41, 49, describes an English courtly rhetoric increasingly governed by *delectare* (pleasing), rather than persuasion, in an era when opportunities for its political use were diminishing; he goes to suggest the congeniality of such purely aesthetic courtliness to Spenser's poetry.

51. Clare Regan Kinney, *Strategies of Poetic Narrative: Chaucer, Spenser, Milton, Eliot* (Cambridge: Cambridge University Press, 1992), 111.

52. Javitch, 151. Thus Tonkin, as noted above, claims that Calidore moves from pleasure (Paris) to virtue (Hercules); however, it is doubtful that pleasure can be made to imply virtue. Active virtue in Book 6, because it implies a confrontation with the Blatant Beast, does not defend poetry, but rather makes the threat to the poem's interest in aesthetic pleasure more prominent. See Tonkin, 315–18, for an optimistic reading in which the aesthetic becomes didactic myth. Norbrook, 147 writes (also, in my opinion, overestimating Spenser's ability to harmonize his political and didactic goals) that "Colin Clout's vision of the Graces is in part a vision of the beautiful poetry which will help to persuade all inhabitants of Ireland that their best interests are served by British rule."

# Chapter 5. From Spenser to Milton

1. There are still gestures toward the earlier internal definition of passion in Books 4 to 6, but on deeper consideration they usually turn out to be public in import. Amoret's sympathy for Aemylia is an exceptional moment (4.7.10, 19).

2. Arthegall's anger does occasionally appear dangerous is the first half of Book 5: Guyon "pacif[ies]" Arthegall's "choler" to wholesome effect at 5.3.36. But this moment is also an exception.

3. Spenser here goes counter to the usual Renaissance judgment that, while mercy is acceptable in the context of justice, pity is not. See Nohrnberg, 382–83, which cites Lipsius, Elyot, and Hooker—also Cicero, *Tusculan Disputations*, 3.3. Despite her name, Spenser ascribes pity rather than mercy to Mercilla.

4. This prospect of a dissolution of the self is also conveyed by a different form of pathos: anger. That there is a dangerous potential for self-frustration, even self-dissolution, in anger is indicated by Arthur's encounter with the angry Souldan, who is "all with furie fraught" (5.8.28). The Souldan's uncontrolled rage leads to his defeat at the hands of the coolly decisive Arthur. The similarly hotheaded Gerioneo unsuccessfully attempts to use his "enraging heat" (5.11.12) as his chief weapon against

Arthur, who again calmly "watch[es] advauntage, how to worke his care" (5.11.13). The uncontrolled rage of the Souldan and Gerioneo in Book 5, a passion that seems to dissolve the consistency of self into an ambient and diffuse energy, appears as well in the excessive violence of Book 6's Calidore-Crudor fight, with both warriors "inflam'd with furious despight" (6.1.36).

5. Here Calidore resembles the Aeneas who shows mercy to Lausus—rather than the Aeneas who angrily kills of Turnus.

6. I should note, however, that the adjective "greedy" is often in *The Faerie Queene* (as elsewhere in Renaissance use) ethically neutral or even positive.

7. Calidore also blatantly misses the point of Melibee's statement that it is the mind, not the power of (in this case, pastoral) place, that determines virtue (a Horatian topos: *Caelum non mentem mutant qui trans mare currunt* [Epistle 1.11, 27]). Calidore answers this philosophy by saying that he has decided to "fashion [his] owne lyfes estate" by choosing "in this shore / To rest [his] barcke:" the place will have a transforming effect on him. Calidore interprets "estate" in external, topographical terms rather than the internal, ethical terms intended by Melibee (6.9.29–31). Here as at Acidale, the lure of the place coincides with the attractions of a beautiful woman.

8. For more on the figure of Paris in relation to Calidore, see Donald Cheney, *Spenser's Image of Nature* (New Haven: Yale University Press, 1966), 219–20.

9. Pastorella is introduced to us, and Calidore, sitting luminously atop a hillock and serenaded by shepherds in 6.9.9, in a clear forecast of Acidale.

10. See Berger's essays on the "paradise principle" in the *Shepheardes Calender* (collected in his *Revisionary Play* [Berkeley: University of California Press, 1988], 325–452).

11. "Hewing off [the beast's] head," Calidore "it presented / Before the feete of the faire Pastorell" (6.10.36): the final line seems to be spoken by Calidore himself with coolly cynical mastery. Much worse is Calidore's manipulation of the disgraced Coridon, who ran from the tiger. Pastorella dislikes Coridon because of a kind of inherent or automatic decorum in which the noble and virtuous are repelled by the "base": "the gentle heart scornes base disparagement" (6.10.37). "Yet," the poet goes on, Calidore's strategic egoism lets him make use of Coridon to impress Pastorella: "Calidore did not despise him quight, / But vsde him friendly for further intent."

12. Berger, in *Revisionary Play* (107), discusses this point.

13. See Goldberg, 86–95.

14. See Goldberg, *Endlesse Worke*, and Frank Whigham, *Ambition and Privilege* (Berkeley: University of California Press, 1984).

15. Jameson, *The Political Unconscious*, 118. On this issue see also Whigham, *Ambition and Privilege*.

16. Radigund also gives evidence of the basic or authorized nature of femininity (*radus*, "root" and *gunê*, "woman"). William Camden, in his *Remaines Concerning Britaine* (London, 1636), offers an interestingly inappropriate etymology, from the Saxon *Gund* (favor), "Favourable counsell."

17. I have noted the lack of coherence between the intriguing or enticing character of the Bower, Malecasta's and Busirane's Houses, and the moral point Spenser draws from such scenes. When critics like C. S. Lewis try to solve Spenser's problem for him by asserting that this incoherence is precisely the moral point, they seriously underestimate the degree to which the poet's investment in poetic affect is equal to, and even precedes, the moralizing of such affect. A similar strategy with Milton is Fish's claim that the poet presents Satan as an attractive figure in order then to deflate him. For a view of heroic poetry and Christian morality as equal alternatives in Milton, see G. K. Hunter, *Paradise Lost* (London: George Allen and Unwin, 1980), 12. See

also the first chapter of Anne Ferry, *Milton's Narrative Voice* (Cambridge: Harvard University Press, 1963).

18. A. Bartlett Giamatti, *The Earthly Paradise and the Renaissance Epic* (Princeton: Princeton University Press, 1966), 289. For the traditional sources of the Garden's celebration of sexuality see Lewis, *Allegory*, 154, and Giamatti, 285n. (on the sixteenth-century notion of a connection between "Adonis" and "Eden"). See Giamatti, 83–86, on the "true" earthly paradises of Dante, Spenser and Milton and how they depart from the false, delusive earthly paradise of tradition.

19. In general, though, the Garden achieves its morality of pleasure by attenuating its erotic force. Spenser, in comparison to Milton, sharply pulls his punches by de-eroticizing the Garden, which, as Greenblatt notes, is much less sensual than the Bower. See *Renaissance Self-Fashioning*, 171.

20. See Nohrnberg, 446–47. The tale of Myrrha appears in Book 10 of Ovid's *Metamorphoses*. Like Chrysogonee, Myrrha prays to Lucina, but, in contrast to her (and like Spenser's Amavia), she gives birth in great pain.

21. Venus similarly exposes her foster-child Amoret, who is "brought forth into the worldes vew" (st. 52).

22. Lewis's analysis is in his *Allegory of Love* (1936; reprint, London: Oxford University Press, 1938), 327–29, 331–33.

23. For the debate over unfallen sexuality in Milton and its debt to Augustine's *City of God*, chap. 14, see C. S. Lewis, *A Preface to Paradise Lost* (London: Oxford University Press, 1942), 118; Edward LeComte, *Milton and Sex* (London: Macmillan, 1978), 93–94; Wolfgang Rudat, "Milton, Freud, St. Augustine: Paradise Lost and the History of Human Sexuality," *Mosaic* 2 (1982): 109–22; Kerrigan, *The Sacred Complex*, 228–29, 309n; and Denis Saurat, *Milton: Man and Thinker* (London: Dent, 1925), 105, 155–59, 275–79. Sources of Eden closer to Spenser, including Carew's "A Rapture," are treated in Kerrigan and Braden, "Milton's Coy Eve."

24. See Kerrigan and Braden, "Milton's Coy Eve," for an account of the way in which Milton revises the Cavaliers' language of amorous flirtation into an innocent, rather than a fallen and lustful, practice.

25. John Milton, *The Reason of Church Government*, in *Complete Prose Works*, ed. Douglas Bush et al. (New Haven: Yale University Press, 1953), 1:817–18. Subsequent quotations of Milton's prose will be from the Yale edition; for the poems, I have relied on John Milton, *Complete Poems and Major Prose*, ed. Merritt Y. Hughes (Indianapolis: Bobbs-Merrill, 1957), 670. I will be citing Hughes's text of Milton's poems throughout this chapter. For a strikingly similar passage that exploits both the image of poetry as clothing for a female allegorical figure and that of the smoothness added by poetry to a moral journey or "way," see Sidney, 23, 25: "For indeed poetry ever setteth Virtue out in her best colors, making Fortune her well-waiting handmaid, that one must needs be enamored of her.... [The poet] doth not only show the way, but giveth so sweet a prospect into the way, as will entice any man to enter into it."

26. See Spenser, Letter to Ralegh, in Hamilton, ed., *The Faerie Queene*, 737, with its reference to "the vse of these dayes seeing all things accounted by their showes, and nothing esteemed of, that is not delightfull and pleasing to commune sense."

27. Milton's use of the term "delight" in this passage suggests a shallowness of emotional response on the reader's part that is untrue to the passionate strength of Milton's poetic effects, the "grave" or even "holy" "passion and admiration" that he invokes in this same discussion. Plato's characterization of Achilles as subject to trivial *epithumia* rather than a *thumos* whose social value would be more equivocal is a comparable critical maneuver (see chapter 1). In both the Plato and the Milton passages, an affect is made more superficial so that it may be more easily defined, and

controlled, by a poetics that stresses didactic intent. This kind of reduction is an attempt to avoid confronting the pathos that characterizes most epic and tragic poetry, whose powerful effect on the reader cannot be reconciled with a straightforward moral message.

For this common version of the *dulce et utile* formula in Renaissance literary criticism, in which the "sweetness" is seen as a way of attracting the reader to a poet's morally useful message, see, Spingarn's selections of Webbe and Harington for example, contrast Milton's formula, also a commonplace, in his Preface to *Samson Agonistes*: "To purge the mind of passions . . . with a kind of delight, stirr'd up by reading or seeing those passions well imitated" (Hughes, ed., 549). For two contrasting interpretations of the "medicinal" image in Milton's *Samson* Preface, see Radzinowicz, *Toward Samson Agonistes*, 358ff., which responds to William Kerrigan, *The Prophetic Milton* (Charlottesville: University Press of Virginia, 1974), 201ff. Eric Rothstein, in his *Restoration Tragedy* (Madison: University of Wisconsin Press, 1967), remarks on Milton's desire to join poetic emotion and morality, in contrast to the Restoration critics' desire to separate them (9, 13). In Rothstein's scheme, the Restoration critics are "fabulists" who separate *dulce* and *utile*, in contrast to "affective" writers like Sidney and Milton, who try to conflate these two effects of poetry, or at least establish a motivated relation between them.

28. See Hughes, ed., 826. For a brilliantly persuasive commentary on this passage in the context of Milton's career, see Kerrigan, *The Sacred Complex*, 257–60. The Second Defense, it should be noted, resists the full acknowledgment of its protagonist's weakness as the major poems do not—probably because its protagonist is Milton himself.

29. *Complete Prose Works*, 1:820.

30. In *Complete Prose Works*, 1:890. For hints as to the autobiographical context of this issue, see *Doctrine and Discipline of Divorce* in *Complete Prose Works*, 2:246 (Book 1, chapter 2). The divorce tracts, despite their ambition for embodied or "carnal knowledge," a spiritual union of flesh, often suffer from a disjoining or paradoxical combination of head and body as severe as the monstrous union of the female head Custom with the male body Error (*Doctrine and Discipline of Divorce*, in *Complete Prose Works*, 2:223–24—an interesting revision of Spenser). The same tract offers an oxymoronic passage in which Time is both the midwife of Truth, who must be purified of the pains of childbirth—an image that, like the maieutic Socrates' recourse to Diotima in the *Symposium*, accents the role of the feminine body in the delivery of truth—and a Zeus from whose head she springs Minerva-like, without the intervention of a woman's body (225). The result is a confusion as painful as the "dizzy megrim[s]" of the libertines whom Milton castigates (226). (On the issue of body and mind in the divorce tracts, see Turner, *One Flesh*.)

31. Hughes, ed., 742–43.

32. *Doctrine and Discipline of Divorce* (Preface), in *Complete Prose Works*, 2:241.

33. As I have noted, Spenser in his Book 6 exploits an "outward" use of pathos in, for example, Calidore's conversion of Crudor and Briana. Spenser does worry about the possible superficiality of this kind of emotional didacticism, but he worries less than Milton does and in a more secular context: that of courtesy and its need to dissemble.

34. See Christopher Hill, *The Experience of Defeat* (Harmondsworth: Penguin, 1984), 318–19, and William Lamont, *Godly Rule* (London: Macmillan, 1969), 123–31. The more radical nonconformists saw the battle of Burford or the coming of the Protectorate as the defeat of Godly rule: Lamont convincingly argues that Cromwell's toleration had no pretensions to being the holy government that was envisioned in the early 1640s by Milton and others.

Notes    239

35. A valuable examination of Milton's attitude toward pathos seen in a patristic context, including the argument over the Son's supposed apathy in *Paradise Regained*, is contained in Arnold Stein, *Heroic Knowledge* (Minneapolis: University of Minnesota Press, 1957), 22–23. For other treatments of Milton's work as an exploration of pathos, see Georgia Christopher, "The Verbal Gate to Paradise," in *PMLA* 90 (1975), especially 73 and 75, and Sherman Hawkins, "Samson's Catharsis," in *Milton Studies* 2 (1970): 211–30. Both Christopher and Hawkins assert a strong connection between the "exemplary" status of Milton's heroes and their ability to elicit a pathetic response from both themselves and the reader. My discussion inquires into the nature of Milton's desire for such connections between hero and reader.

## Chapter 6. *Paradise Lost*

1. My discussion of continuity and discontinuity in Milton has been influenced by Stuart Ende's treatment of the companion poems and *Comus* in *Keats and the Sublime* (New Haven: Yale University Press, 1976), and Regina Schwartz, *Remembering and Repeating* (Cambridge: Cambridge University Press, 1989). Schwartz depicts the force that both interrupts and antithetically generates God's authority in *Paradise Lost* as an evil, primordial chaos; whereas I focus, instead, on the presence of a historical event, the tragedy of Satan's fall.

2. For a richly suggestive discussion of the "enfolded sublime" in Spenser, Milton, and Renaissance science that comes to somewhat different conclusions from my own, see Kerrigan, *The Sacred Complex*, 231ff.

3. See Schwartz, 5ff.

4. For a discussion of the tradition that God creates the world in order to repopulate the universe after the angels' fall, see C. A. Patrides, *Milton and the Christian Tradition* (Oxford: Oxford University Press, 1966), 37ff.—in particular the references to Augustine's *City of God* 22.1 and Spenser's Hymn of Heavenly Love (101ff.) Patrides notes that, while the angels' fall is the accepted occasion for the creation of earth and humanity, it is not the primary motive for this creation; instead, God's creativity stems from an infinite and as it were motiveless goodness.

5. Milton, *Complete Prose Works*, 2:273.

6. Geoffrey Hartman, *Criticism in the Wilderness* (New Haven: Yale University Press, 1979), 146.

7. For the traditional idea of a *creatio continua* or continuing creation, with God's governance of the universe through its history equated to his persistent creation of it, see Patrides, 52–53.

8. In a crucial passage of Book 3, Milton suggests, only to withdraw, a possible parallel between Satan and Jacob. In the Hebrew Bible, Jacob's ladder is an easily legible sign of God's favor that transforms vision into reality: "Dreaming" the ladder "by night under the open Sky," Jacob then "wak[es]" and "cr[ies]," "*This is the Gate of Heavn*" (3.514 –15). The image becomes embodied as Jacob wakes and finds it truth. For Satan, attempting here to play the role of the clever, successful Jacob but really more like the thwarted Esau, the image of the ladder proves delusive: "The Stairs were then let down, whether to dare / The Fiend by easy ascent, or aggravate / His sad exclusion from the doors of Bliss" (3.524 –26). Milton here associates Satan's imprisonment in mere fantasies of power with the poet/artist's inadequacy before a heavenly vision of the kind that God shows Jacob: heaven's gate shines "thick with sparkling orient Gems / . . . inimitable on Earth/By Model, or by shading Pencil drawn"

(3.507–09). Imagining that Satan is like Jacob, we, along with the poet, fall short. Despite Moloch's words at 2.81 ("th'ascent is easy then"), Satan can only go down, whereas the Messiah actually ascends and descends the ladder of creation (see 10.209–24).

9. Christopher Kendrick, "Milton and Sexuality: A Symptomatic Reading of *Comus*," in *Re-membering Milton*, 44, 62.

10. Cavell, *The Claim of Reason*, 356–57.

11. Ibid., 382.

12. See Joseph Loewenstein, *Responsive Readings* (New Haven: Yale University Press, 1984).

13. Milton, *Complete Prose Works*, 2:254–55.

14. Plato, *Phaedrus* 255b-d, trans. C.J. Rowe (Warminster, England: Aris and Phillips, 1986).

15. See also Adam at 10.953: "Death is to me as life."

16. Fallen desire becomes a parody of itself, as we see in Adam and Eve's lustful dalliance at the end of Book 9, and even more in Book 10's apotheosis of Sin and Death. Sin provides a parody of the ascent to Godhead that Eve and Adam had hoped for ("divinity within them breeding wings" [9.1010]) when she feels "wings growing, and Dominion giv'n" (*PL* 10.244). (In their incestuous closeness, Satan, Sin and Death mock not only the Trinity, but also the generation of Eve out of Adam.)

17. On the estranging effect of being called, see Slavoj Zizek, *The Sublime Object of Ideology* (London: Routledge and Kegan Paul, 1989), 115ff.

18. I am indebted to a paper by Neal Dolan (Yale University, 1986) for the comparison with Stevens.

19. Friedrich Nietzsche, *Beyond Good and Evil*, trans. R. J. Hollingdale (Harmondsworth: Penguin, 1990), 55.

20. To cite only a few among many notable recent discussions of the final books: Fish, *Surprised by Sin*, 272–331; Lewalski, "Structure and the Symbolism of Vision in Michael's Prophecy," *Philological Quarterly* 42 (1963): 25–35; Radzinowicz, *Toward Samson Agonistes*, 284–312; George Williamson, "The Education of Adam" and Lawrence Sasek, "The Drama of Paradise Lost, Books 11 and 12" (both in Arthur Barker, ed., *Milton: Modern Essays in Criticism* [New York: Oxford University Press, 1963]).

21. See Fish, *Surprised by Sin*, 272–331.

22. See Fish, *Surprised by Sin*, 317; for the opposition between the false visibility of experience and invisible truth, see Fish, 249, 252, 264, 290, and 294, with its citation of 1 John 2:16 ("For all that is in the world, the lust of the flesh and the lust of the eyes, and the pride of life is not of the Father"). But see Fish, 335, for an interestingly contravening statement: Adam is correct in thinking what he sees of the world is good, because the world's divine source is good. For Christian tradition on the value of invisible religion over visible honors and pleasures see, for example, Erasmus's *Enchiridion* (Bloomington: Indiana University Press, 1962), 105; and see John Phillips, *The Reformation of Images* (Berkeley: University of California Press, 1973), 39. Some of Fish's central insights, it should be noted, are anticipated in Christopher Ricks's great *Milton's Grand Style* (Oxford: Oxford University Press, 1963).

23. Of course, iconolatry also draws a connection between the image and pathos in its assertion that images are powefully persuasive vehicles of Christian truth. See Pope Gregory's letter to the iconoclastic Bishop Serenus of Marseilles (sixth century), and a passage by St. Bonaventure, both cited in William Jones, "Art and Christian Piety," in *The Image and the Word*, ed. Joseph Gutmann (Missoula: University of Montana Press, 1977), 78–79, 84. Also Daniélou, *Origen*, 188; Thomas Harding's *Answer*,

cited in John Jewel, 2:661; and the passages from Harding in Horton Davies, *Worship and Theology in England* (Princeton: Princeton University Press, 1970), 1:352–53. The late fifteenth-century moral dialogue Dives and Pauper defends religious images, because "ofte a manne is more stered by syght then by herynge or redynge." *Dives and Pauper* (London, 1534 [repr.]), chapter 1, "The First Commandment," 12.

24. Beard's was one of the more popular books in seventeenth-century England; Oliver Cromwell was fond of it. See Maurice Ashley, *The Greatness of Oliver Cromwell* (London: Hodder, 1958), 43, cited in Lamont, *Godly Rule*, 123. For the popularity of Beard's *Theatre*, see Lamont, 122. The last books, as their use of theatrical tableaux suggests, have their origin in drama: for the mime that Milton planned as the original form of this section of the poem (in the Trinity Manuscript, final draft) see John Demaray, *Milton's Theatrical Epic* (Cambridge: Harvard University Press, 1980), 46–47 and ff.

25. In his Preface, Beard defines providence as a visible reality: "When the wicked ... doe receive the wages and reward of their iniquities. In this ... shineth out the wonderfull and incomprehensible wisedome of God ..." (*The Theatre of God's Judgements* [London, 1648], A 1 [v]). Five drunken men who "prophaned the name of God," Beard reports, were found the next day "quashed to pieces, as though a whiele had gone over them, bloud running out of theire mouths, nostrils, and eares, to the great astonishment of the beholders" (417).

26. Beard, *Theatre*, 28–29, 35.

27. See *A Second and Third Blast of Retrait from Plaies and Theaters* [1580], in *The English Drama and Stage*, ed. W. C. Hazlitt (London, 1869), 144–45, and George Ridpath, *The Stage Condemn'd* (1698; reprint, New York: Garland, 1972), 5, 11. See also William Prynne, *Histrio-Mastix* (London, 1633), 935. Michael O'Connell, "Iconoclasm and the Elizabethan Theatre," *ELH* 52 (1985): 285, writes that Philip Stubbs and Anthony Munday objected to religious theatre on account of its elaboration of scripture, its humanizing of scriptural characters, and its use of comedy and pathos to establish a connection with the audience. Compare Stephen Gosson's complaint in *Playes Confuted in Fiue Actions* (1582), that both the delight of stage comedy and the pathos of tragedy stir up and corrupt the affections (Gosson, in *Merchants of Bawdrie*, ed. Arthur F. Kinney [Salzburg: Salzburg Studies in English Literature, 1974], 181, 185, 188). See also the chapters on puritanism in Jonas Barish, *The Anti-Theatrical Prejudice* (Berkeley: University of California Press, 1981).

28. Milton, *Complete Prose Works*, 7:461.

29. On this subject see, for example, Michael McKeon, *Politics and Poetry in Restoration England* (Cambridge: Harvard University Press, 1979).

30. Milton, *Complete Prose Works*, 8:439. With high irony Milton here cites idolatry as the punishment appropriate to an age in which God no longer dispenses visible signs.

31. Milton, *Complete Prose Works*, 8:439. Baxter, in *The Life of Faith* (London, 1660), C 2 (v)(p. 16), rebukes those doubters who want to see "a sight of Heaven or Hell" before they will believe. Thomas Goodwin, in *An Unregenerate Man's Guiltiness Before God*, Book 13 (in Goodwin's *Works* [Edinburgh: James Nichol, 1865], 10:490–91), agrees that the Bible's descriptions of heaven and hell are "mere shadows and similitudes," not meant to be taken literally (compare Calvin's Institutes 3.25.10). But in Baxter's *The Saints Everlasting Rest* (London, 1803 [rep.]), he offers us a lush picture of the regained paradise. (For commentary, see Gilman, 151, and William Lamont, *Richard Baxter and the Millenium* [London: Croom Helm, 1979], 288, 297, 318.)

32. See Phillips, 84, on the Edwardian humanists: "Images were rejected not

because they were idols, but because they appealed to a 'grosser' side of man." *The Treatise against Image Worship*, ascribed to Nicholas Ridley, emphasizes that idolatry is mainly a danger for the uneducated (see *Works of Nicholas Ridley*, ed. Henry Christmas [Cambridge: Parker Society, 1843], 86). Compare in Jewel, 1:12 (a sermon of 1560): "he that goeth to the mass, and worshippeth the sacrament, unless he be learned and take good heed, may soon commit idolatry." See also 10–11 and 2:664. For the official Henrician defense of images coupled with a warning against their abuse, see the statement by Bishops Cranmer, Gardiner, Heath and Thirlby known as *The King's Book* [1543] (London: Society for Promoting Christian Knowledge, 1932), 87–89.

33. See *Of Reformation* in Milton, *Complete Prose Works*, 1:590, 592.

34. Martin Luther, "The Pagan Servitude of the Church," in Dillenberger, ed., 300. Calvin's similar interpretation of the rainbow that symbolizes the Covenant as a sacrament that must be mentally comprehended, not merely visually apprehended is relevant to Adam's reaction to the Flood and its aftermath later in the poem (see John Calvin's commentary on *Genesis* [1578], trans. John King [Edinburgh: Banner of Truth, 1979], 1:298, on Gen. 9:12: "If the sacrament be wrested from the word it ceases to be what it is called.... And not only is that administration of sacraments in which the word of God is silent, vain and ludicrous; but it draws with it pure satanic delusions."

Aquinas in *Summa Theologica* 3.60.5 notes that the seven sacraments of the Christian Church, as opposed to the Old Testament sacraments, are all in the form of the spoken word.

35. Calvin, *Genesis* commentary, 197. See also the judgment on the killing of Abel in William du Bartas's *Divine Weekes* [1608], trans. Joshua Sylvester (Waukesha, Wisc.: H. M. Youmans, 1908), 244: "Rein-searching God, thought-sounding Judge, that tries / The will and heart more than the work and guise." Augustine's *City of God* 15.1 identifies Cain with the external or earthly city, Abel with the internal, divine one.

36. Interestingly, the same phrase, "sweet recess," is used by Satan in his praise of Athenian letters in Book 4 of *Paradise Regained* (242).

37. See Radzinowicz, 284–312, on the ethical emphasis of Books 11 and 12: Milton often rejects the typological readings of these scenes that were available to him in favor of more general or universal ethical readings. Thus the killing of Abel is pointedly not construed, as it usually was, as a harbinger of the crucifixion. Unlike Radzinowicz, I would incline to read this particular avoidance of typology on Milton's part as his repression of the true significance of Christ's passion—the visible pathos attached to what seems a permanently irreparable injustice.

## Chapter 7. *Paradise Regained* and *Samson Agonistes*

1. Here, oddly, Milton follows the lead of Satan's "solicitous and blank" address to his audience in Book 1 (1.118–19), his calm reinforced by the obvious irrelevance of Belial's appeal to sensuality: Book 2 begins by emptying out pathos and shifting to preparatory abstraction. Mary's speech begins by adducing the phrase "conceiv'd of God" (67) in a literal, palpably emotional sense—with concrete realism, she speaks of the bleak hardships of her labor and the flight into Egypt—but shifts to an abstract sense of mental conception: "what he meant I mus'd, / Since understand" (99–100). Her rhetorical mode becomes disputatious: "Afflicted I may be, it seems, and blest; / I will not argue that, nor will repine" (93–94). The strong similarity of the disciples' sudden fall "from what high hope" to Satan's description of his loss of heaven at the beginning of *Paradise Lost* might suggest to Milton's reader that such

emotion is here to be rejected, that the disciples' "perplexity and new amaze" (2.38) is not an appropriate response to the Son's disciplined trials. But to reject in this way an emotional response to *Paradise Regained* is to underestimate the necessity of the Son's audience, including the readers of the poem itself—an audience which dwells in emotional reaction.

2. See Kerrigan on need in *Paradise Regained* in *The Sacred Complex*, 109–11.

3. See Lewalski, "Time and History."

4. Satan invokes visible evidence in his speech to his legions (1.79–80: "I saw / the Prophet do him reverence"), as does the Father at 1.130 ("Gabriel this day by proof thou shalt behold"). At the beginning of Book 2 the Messiah who had been "pointed at and shown" (51) is withdrawn from sight. See the important discussion in Kermode, *The Genesis of Secrecy*. Some other versions of Christ's temptation, like John Bale's *The Temptation of Our Lord* (1538), allow Christ a prolix didacticism (see Christ's final speech against Satan in Bale's play: *The Dramatic Writings of John Bale,* ed., John S. Farmer [London, 1907], 166–67).

5. To argue that the Son is now finally able, at the poem's end, to display his power as he has not before because he has succeeded to a new divine role—Stein's interpretation in *Heroic Knowledge*—is to beg the main question of Milton's conclusion, its genuine obscurity. Is the Son obedient and steadfast at the close of *Paradise Regained*, or does he finally give in to Satan's temptation to be vengeful?

6. A *locus classicus* for the image of future salvation as exodus is Jeremiah 31:31–33: but Jeremiah emphasizes, as does Paul, the "inward" nature of salvation, insisting that it will not be a literal exodus. One would expect the Son's treatment of the exodus as a symbol to be more Pauline, in keeping with his insistence on inner discipline over the external facts of history. Paul's revisionary stress on the "inward" nature of the messianic antitype is significant throughout his writings; see, for example, 1 Cor. 3:3. (For the early Pauline Christians' literal apocalypticism, though, see Meeks, *The First Urban Christians*, 182.) Herbert Marks explores the revisionary nature of Paul's view of typology in "Pauline Typology and Revisionary Criticism," reprinted in *The Bible: Modern Critical Views,* ed. Harold Bloom (New York: Chelsea House, 1987). Interesting in relation to this issue is the idea of Christ's *exitus* from life on the cross as the fulfillment of the Old Testament exodus (see Donne, *Death's Duel*, 35, 37–42).

7. The Son conspicuously mentions Job's patience (1.426); as Lewalski has demonstrated, Job is an important model for the Son (Lewalski, *Milton's Brief Epic*). For discussions of the Son's patience in its opposition to Satan's hurried desire, see Brisman, *Milton's Poetry of Choice*, 190–91, and Stein, *Heroic Knowledge*, 85–86. For discussion of the Son's reticent interpretation of apocalypse in the historical context of millenarian zeal for a prophetic outcome to history and the Puritan debate over the conversion of the Jews, see Michael Fixler, *Milton and the Kingdoms of God* (Evanston, Ill.: Northwestern University Press, 1964), especially 234ff.

8. A notable parallel is *Paradise Lost* 12.310, with its reference to "Joshua whom the Gentiles Jesus call" in the context of Old Testament miracles performed by two types of Christ: Mose's Exodus and Joshua's stopping of the sun.

9. The Son's own argument, ostensibly along the same lines, in *Paradise Regained* Book 2, is in fact significantly different: he denounces Satan's interpretation of "Empire" as overly literal. The Stoic sage's true empire is not necessarily political, the Son points out, but rather an idea of personal "government" that succeeds in the world by refraining from the effort to overpower the world in such a crude, forceful way. The Son aspires to the status, not of military commander, but of religious "guide" who will rule mankind by teaching them to rule themselves as he does:

> Yet he who reigns within himself, and rules
> Passions, Desires, and Fears, is more a King;
> Which every wise and virtuous man attains:
> And who attains not, ill aspires to rule
> Cities of men, or headstrong Multitudes,
> Subject himself to Anarchy within,
> Or lawless passions in him, which he serves.
> But to guide Nations in the way of truth
> By saving Doctrine, and from error lead
> To know, and knowing worship God aright,
> Is yet more Kingly; this attracts the Soul,
> Governs the inner man, the nobler part. . . .
> (*PR* 2.466–77)

10. Satan's reference to the Son as a potential "king" draws on the analogy between wise man and monarch present in the Stoic tradition. For the Son's relation to Stoicism, see Lewalski, 229ff.; see also Stein, *Heroic Knowledge* 17–35, and my discussion of Stoicism in relation to Samson, chapters 8 and 9. Boethius in his *Consolation of Philosophy* 4.Pr.7 offers a classic statement of Christian Stoic ambition as he compares the sage and the warrior. Boethius implies that the contemplative, just as much as the active type, is strongly attracted to the goal of worldly success, even though success is redefined by Stoic contemplation as a purely internal phenomenon. See Braden, *Renaissance Tragedy*, 70–71.

11. The final angelic chorus drives home this point by sandwiching the final temptation on the pinnacle between Satan's fall, when the savior "down from heaven cast [Satan] / With all his army," and the equally militant Gadarene swine episode (4.600–30).

12. Milton cannot afford to let the Lady display the "flame of sacred vehemence" with which she threatens Comus (795): it would too much resemble Comus's own Orphic skill. The Lady is left to her irritated, closely reasoned praises of virtue, and the summoning of Sabrina's chaste magic saves her from the dangers of wielding a sensual, seductive power. A. S. P. Woodhouse, "Theme and Structure in *Paradise Regained*" (*University of Toronto Quarterly* 25 [1955–56]: 181, writes that, at the end of Book 4, "For the first and only time, [the Son] complies with Satan's suggestion; however, it is not in surrender to Satan: it is in obedience to God—like Samson's going to the festival of Dagon." Frye ("Typology of Paradise Regained," 319) writes that this moment is like both Samson's refusal and his acceptance of the Philistine games; the kairos is merely more extenuated for Samson than for the Son.

13. Stein, *Heroic Knowledge*, 128–30.

14. Stein, 130.

15. For the theatrical metaphor in *Paradise Regained*, see Satan's instructions to his colleagues at 2.237–40, when he chooses "spirits likest to himself in guile / If cause were to unfold some active scene / Of various persons each to know his part." Satan's temptations are, in fact, a series of increasingly spectacular scenes (see John Carey's commentary in Milton, *Complete Shorter Poems* [London: Longman's, 1971], 237, 240), but they culminate in the Son's stealing the stage.

16. See Fish, *Surprised by Sin*, 268. As usual, Kerrigan's reading of *Paradise Regained* in *The Sacred Complex* does remarkable justice to the complexities of the text, including the ambiguity I have discussed.

17. At times, the similarity between Satan and the Son is rhetorical as well. Satan's final temptation of the Son suggests that he is mimicking the savior's own ver-

bal elusiveness, and thus enforcing the impression of a potential similarity between the two characters that is suggested by the shifting "him" in the angelic rescue. Satan's challenge on the pinnacle is not simply "cast thyself down," as it is often summarized, but "There stand, if thou wilt stand . . . if not to stand, / Cast thy self down." Satan's words are reminiscent of the Son's own earlier answers in the way they deliver their ambiguity over to the addressee in order to make him responsible for his mistakes (compare the Son's "Think not but that I know these things; or think / I know them not" [4.286 – 87]). Satan imitates the Son's elusive speech in order to persuade him, in turn, to imitate Satanic action—falling.

18. Augustine, *City of God,* trans. Marcus Dods (New York: Modern Library, 1950), 16.37.

19. See Kerrigan's remarks on this ambiguity (*The Sacred Complex*, 90).

20. Notable here is Satan's attempt to deceive the Son by casting him as an accommodating, merciful New Testament God who will offer the "shading cool" of pastoral refuge. Satan's appeal to the Son's mercy seems to stand as a warning to readers looking for a gentle messiah—a caution reinforced by the intransigent personality and icy sarcasm of the Son throughout this poem. See the Son's words at 4.147–53., with their evocation of the ruthless, warlike prophecy of Daniel 2:35: "and the stone that smote the image [of the four kingdoms preceding Christ] became a great mountain, and filled the whole earth." Here Milton refuses the Gospels' image of the kingdom as a sheltering tree in favor of a fiercer Old Testament vision. Lewalski, *Milton's Brief Epic* 279, mentions the Christian revision of the Daniel 2 passage.

21. Another place will, of course, be the ending of Book 4.

22. See *Paradise Lost* 4.114 –21 (discussed in the conclusion).

23. The importance of occasion in the biblical narrative has been emphasized by Hermann Gunkel in respect to the award of the blessing to Jacob: "Esau kommt, sobald Jaqob gegangen ist . . . wäre er einen Augenblick eher erschienen, so wäre alles anders gekommen" (*Genesis, übersetzt und erklärt von Hermann Gunkel* [Göttingen, 1964], 313). Here, of course, the favorable occasion is the work of chance; Jacob is not the master of this moment. See *Rabbi Samuel Ben Meir's Commentary on Genesis*, trans. Martin Lockshin (Lampeter, Wales: Edwin Mellen Press, 1989), 157.

24. The question of the truth of images is important in the angelic rescue scene. The luxurious rest that surrounds and embowers the Son (4.585ff.) seems suspiciously similar to Satan's depictions of Greek and Asian comforts. It also includes a banquet somewhat like the one offered by Satan in Book 2 (338ff.). But we are reminded just after the picture of the embowered Son that, though the future saviour may condescend to linger in such seemingly pagan locales, he is not *of* them. Instead, he is the "true Image" (4.596) of his father alone. Milton thus tries to rescue the *locus amoenus* of Christian rest, along with the Son himself, from the potentially corrupting association with paganism. Is this "a fairer Paradise" (4.613)? For Christ as the true image of his father, see Hebrews 1:3.

See the Son's comparison of Greek and Hebrew literature at 4.334 –49.: the Hebrews' "terms" are even more (or more subtly) "artful" than the Greeks'. Carey, *Complete Shorter Poems*, 430, notes the way in which the desert gradually blooms in the course of the poem, until it too is a locus amoenus: see 4.433–41. (after Satan's storm).

25. For the Gospel subtext, see Mark 5 and Matt. 8: "And all the devils besought him, saying, Send us into the swine" (Mark 5:12; cf. Matthew 8:31). Milton's insistence that it is the true Son who conquers the false is evident in this passage's emphatic "hee[s]" and "thee[s]"—the opposite of the earlier pronominal confusion when the

Son is rescued by angels at line 583. See Christopher Ricks on the significance of Milton's emphatic "hee," "mee" and others in the prefatory note to his edition of *Paradise Lost* and *Paradise Regained* (New York: New American Library, 1969), xxxiii.

26. See Weber, *Return to Freud*, 133.

27. Paul Ricoeur, *Essays on Biblical Interpretation*, ed. and trans. Lewis S. Mudge (Philadelphia: Fortress Press, 1980), 81.

28. David Damrosch, *The Narrative Covenant* (San Francisco: Harper and Row, 1987), 48–49. My discussion of *Samson* has been influenced throughout by Mieke Bal's account of the biblical story in *Lethal Love* (Bloomington: Indiana University Press, 1987), 37–67.

29. Near the beginning of the play, Samson says at the Chorus's approach, "I hear the sound of words" (176): the hero's blindness allows him to discern the blurriness or uncertainty of words as sensory phenomena, before they are resolved or reduced into definite significance. The mystery of physical shape and sound seems both antithetical to idolatry (because it sees images in their unclarity, not the authority they derive from fixed meaning) and somehow idolatrous (because it emphasizes the level of sensual appearance). This sheer perceptual impact is present most of all in Samson's pulling down the Temple of Dagon.

30. Samson speaks out what should stay concealed and unrevealable (*muein*, to keep one's eyes and mouth shut, is the source of the Greek mysteries; the *fanum* [temple] in *profanus* is evidently related to *fari*, to speak).

31. Interestingly, the aged Manoa enters during this discussion of the stain with locks "white as down" (327).

32. Jean-Luc Nancy, *The Inoperative Community* (Minneapolis: University of Minnesota Press, 1991), 32–33.

33. See William Kerrigan, "The Irrational Coherence of *Samson Agonistes*," in *Milton Studies* 22 (1986): 217–32.

34. It is interesting in this respect that, meditating on an appropriate punishment for himself, Samson considers the "outward pains" of "Gentile" legend—the punishments of Hades (501)—and not the ethical sentences of Hebrew law.

35. The Chorus implies still another comparison between Samson and Dalila in stating that Dalila promises a change (753)—at the end it is Samson who will, of course, produce the spectacular visual change that Dalila foreshadows here.

36. Samson resists this parallelism in his debate with Dalila by suggesting an asymmetry: a wife leaves her home to cleave to her husband. But Samson left his home also, alienating his parents, by marrying Philistine women; and he, like Dalila, did this for a national purpose.

37. See Bal, 41ff.

38. See J. A. Wittreich, *Interpreting Samson Agonistes* (Princeton: Princeton University Press, 1986), particularly 187–88 and 210, and Wittreich's *Visionary Poetics*, 198.

39. Bal (37–38) discusses this question.

40. For Manoa's deficiencies as a reader of Samson's triumph, see Radzinowicz, 107: "From the correct lesson in the noble death, Manoa proceeds to a less correct" when he describes the future celebrations to occur at Samson's tomb. I would go further than Radzinowicz and argue that the extravagance of Manoa's ceremonial planning casts doubt on the correctness of the lesson he infers from his son's "noble death." See also Wittreich, *Interpreting Samson Agonistes*, 221–22. Perhaps the most notable example of interpretive difficulty in *Samson* is the continuing controversy over the character of Dalila. Is Dalila really a malicious "serpent," as Samson charges, or is she sincerely concerned for Samson's well-being—her concern taking a second place

only to her national responsibility to the Philistines? Given the striking similarities between her subordination of her marriage to her political loyalty and Samson's own decision to marry Dalila for political reasons (to "seek an occasion against" the Philistines, as he puts it), Samson's excoriation of his wife looks less persuasive than has traditionally been supposed. Dalila voices the idea of fame as necessarily "double-mouthed" (971), dependent on the position of the interpreter—man or woman, Hebrew or Philistine. See, for two contrasting readings of Dalila, John C. Ulreich, "The Tragedy of Dalila." and Jackie DiSalvo, "Intestine Thorn," both in Julia Walker, ed., *Milton and the Idea of Woman* (Carbondale: Southern Illinois University Press, 1988).The seminal attempt to rehabilitate Dalila's reputation is William Empson's chapter on *Samson* in *Milton's God*.

41. Samson's isolation from his audience at the play's end is like an echo of the distance from Dalila that Samson wills throughout most of the play. But this final isolation is the site of pathos, not an escape from it.

42. *Doctrine and Discipline of Divorce*, in Milton, *Complete Prose Works*, 2:669.

43. On the latter aspect of the divorce tracts, I have been influenced by James G. Turner's unsurpassed treatment (in *One Flesh*, 188–229).

44. See, in particular, chapters 2 to 4 of *Doctrine and Discipline of Divorce* (1643).

45. Lewalski, introduction to Milton, *Treatise*, in *Selected Prose*, ed. Max Patrick, 446.

46. Milton, *Treatise*, in *Complete Prose Works*, 7:249.

47. *First Defense* in *Complete Prose Works,* 4:402. John Donne, in *Death's Duel* (27) writes that God "received *Sampson*, who went out of this world in such a manner as was subject to interpretation hard enough. Yet the holy Ghost hath moued S. Paul to celebrate Sampson in his great Catalogue, and so doth all the Church." By contrast, Donne in *Biathanatos* 3.5.4 criticizes Samson as a suicide (cited in Hughes, ed., 591). See also J. A. Wittreich, *Visionary Poetics* (San Marino, Calif.: Huntington Library, 1979), 196. For an illuminating discussion of the *Samson* passage cited here see John Guillory, *Poetic Authority*, 172–73.

48. This is especially true of Dalila's repeated attempts to discover Samson's secret: see Judges 16:4ff. The false etymology of Samson, "in the same place twice" (well-known in the Renaissance) is relevant here (see Radzinowicz, 99).

49. Yet the Messenger's position, "aloof obscurely st[anding]" amid the Philistine crowd (1611), makes him a near mirror of the self-isolating, internalized Samson, just as the disciples echo the Son's emotions in Book 2 of *Paradise Regained*.

50. The conclusion of the Samson story is negatively associated with the dangers of tragic pathos, and the Philistine rites compared to a tragic theatre, even before Milton: see John Rainoldes, *Th'Overthrow of Stage Playes* (1599; reprint, New York: Garland, 1974), 23.

51. Samson's efforts during most of the play to make inward decision control outward events have something in common with the Stoic's strategy. Stoicism asserts the link between the disciplining of pathos and the command over a predictable narrative that I have been discussing. The Stoic acts out an anxiety over the way that worldly consequences escape the self's intentions: virtue is only really virtue, Stoicism implies, if its rewards can be ensured in advance. For the Stoic, internal morality is prior to and therefore a way of commanding one's external circumstances, if only by reducing one's hold on the world to the small area an individual can plausibly control: the mind's decisions. The stringent mastery of mind over passion that Stoicism demands is repaid by the mastery over events that it promises. In narrowing his perspective to a personal regime of virtue that (he hopes) will shield him against the world's ambient risks, the Stoic sage tries to order events that are, for the rest of us,

irrational and uncontrollable. The Stoic can thus act within an orderly universe. See C. John Herington, "Senecan Tragedy," *Arion* 5 (1966): 460. In a similar vein, A. W. H. Adkins writes that Stoicism is a philosophy for kings as Epicureanism is a philosophy for slaves, noting the parallel between Stoic philosopher and king. A. W. H. Adkins, *From the Many to the One* (Ithaca: Cornell University Press, 1970), 264. Eliot remarks contrarily in his famous essay on Seneca that Stoicism is appropriate for a society of slaves (see his introduction to *Seneca His Tenne Tragedies translated into English*, ed. Thomas Newton [1581; reprint, New York, 1927], vol. 1). (Milton's desire to secure his own career by preventing unforeseen disaster can be detected in *Lycidas*, along with other works.) In Book 4 of *Paradise Regained*, the Son condemns Satan's suggestion that he seize the Roman empire and redeem it, "A victor people free[ing] from servile yoke" (4.102), by claiming that the soul of the empire, not merely its visible body, is corrupt. Rome can only be saved if such corruption is realized and remedied internally by each Roman subject, not by the messiah's external subjugation of the empire. "What wise and valiant man would seek to free / These thus degenerate, by themselves enslav'd, / Or could of inward slaves make outward free?" the Son asks (4.142–45). Virtue's seat is within the mind; "outward" liberation must stem from moral reflection rather than the reverse. The Son makes "outward" bondage morally explicable by construing it as the result of an "inward," ethical state. In *Paradise Lost* 12.90–93, Michael similarly justifies God's allowing of historical evil by remarking that, "Since [man] permits / Within himself unworthy Powers to reign / Over free Reason, God in Judgment just / Subjects him from without to violent Lords."

52. See Judges 14:4: "But [Samson's] father and his mother knew not that [Samson's first marriage] was of the Lord, that he sought an occasion against the Philistines."

53. Stoic virtue, which prides itself on its self-sufficient inwardness, yet remains dependent on its reactions to the external world—as is evident in Samson's revulsion at the grotesqueness of Philistine idolatry. Samson's disgust with Philistia is not unlike Harapha's opinion that Samson must be unworthy of God's grace because he is bound and filthy. When he initially refuses to take part in the Philistine rites, Samson repeats his identification of his strength with his hair, calling it a gift not to be "abused" (1355–56). Like Manoa's locating of Samson's strength in his lost eyesight, Samson's resistance to the abuse of his body here reduces spiritual power to external fact: the presence of his hair. The same kind of literalism makes Samson sees contact with Philistine deities as fatally contaminating, unlike the "honest and lawful" labor he now performs for them (12365–66).

54. See Georges Bataille, "The Notion of Expenditure," in *Visions of Excess*, ed. Allan Stoekl (Minneapolis: University of Minnesota Press, 1985).

55. I owe this point to a lecture given by Leslie Brisman (Yale University, 1986).

56. Slavoj Žižek, *Looking Awry* (Cambridge: Harvard University Press, 1991), 159 (alluding to, among other texts, Freud's *The Ego and the Id*).

57. On discontinuous history and *Samson*, see Northrop Frye, "Agon and Logos," in *The Prison and the Pinnacle*, 150–51.

# Conclusion

1. One influential critique of this assumption is Lionel Trilling's "The Meaning of a Literary Idea," in *The Liberal Imagination* (New York: Doubleday, 1950).

2. For example, Dryden submits secular and sacred to the same poetic standard when he compares Virgil's description of the Trojans' drunken sleep in Book 2 of the

*Aeneid* ("Invadunt urbem, somno vinoque sepultam") with Cowley's picture of angels "dissolv'd in Hallelujahs:" "A Cities being buried [sepultam]," writes Dryden, "is just as proper an occasion, as an Angel's being dissolv'd in Ease, and Songs of Triumph." Watson, ed., 1:205. In the Preface to his theatrical version of *Paradise Lost, The State of Innocence* (1677), Dryden writes, "If Poetry be imitation, that part of it must needs be best, which describes most lively our Actions and Passions; our Virtues and Vices." The passage is from John Dryden, *Of Dramatic Poesy and Other Essays*,ed. George Watson (1962; reprint, London: Dent, 1968), 1:203. As his Preface continues, Dryden makes it clear that he judges poetic "Virtue" and "Vice," both pagan and sacred, by the same purely aesthetic criteria. "How are Poetical Fictions, how are Hippocentaures and Chymaeras, or how are Angels and immaterial Substances, to be Imaged?" Dryden asks (Watson, ed., 1:204). Dryden here sees the problem of imaging angels as one of poetic technique, not moral belief; he equates Christian poetry's angels with the classical writers' depictions of "Hippocentaures and Chimaeras."

In a similar vein, Dryden in his Preface to *The Conquest of Granada* (1672) applauds Spenser's use of supernatural creatures in *The Faerie Queene*, stating that "the whole doctrine of separated beings, whether those spirits are incorporeal substances . . . or that they are a thinner and more aerial sort of bodies (as some of the Fathers have conjectured) may better be explained by poets than by philosophers or divines. For their speculations on this subject are wholly poetic: they have only their fancy for their guide" ("Of Heroic Plays" [the Preface to *The Conquest of Granada*], in Watson, ed., 2:161). In Dryden's criticism the secularizing of inspiration has occurred: poetic imagination or "fancy" decisively overtakes religion. For Dryden in the *State of Innocence* preface the biblical notion of accommodation is comparable with Homer's. "For Incorporeal Substances we are authoriz'd by Scripture in their description: and herein the Text accommodates it self to vulgar apprehension, in giving angels the likeness of beautiful young men. Thus, after the Pagan divinity, has Homer drawn his Gods with humane Faces" (Watson, ed., 1:204). Dryden here stands in strong opposition to Milton's desire, in *Paradise Lost*, to condemn pagan imagination as the false antagonist of Christian inspiration's truth. For Dryden, all of poetry, including Christian epic, is imagination. Comparably, Addison writes that "As Homer has introduced into his Battle of the Gods everything that is great and terrible in Nature, Milton has fill'd his Fight of good and bad Angels with all the like Circumstances of Horror" (cited in John Dennis, *Critical Works*, ed. E. N. Hooker [Baltimore: Johns Hopkins University Press, 1943], 2:224). Dennis writes of Milton's war in heaven that he "do[es] not believe one Syllable" of it—"I would sooner believe the greatest Absurdities of the Alcoran"—and goes on to praise its sublimity (224).

3. Dryden in Watson, ed., 2:274. The *Conquest of Granada* preface at 2:164-65 offers Dryden's similar championing of Tasso's Achillean Rinaldo over his more moralized hero Goffredo.

4. Dryden, "Discourse," in Watson, ed., 2:84.

5. "Discourse," 86. See Dennis, 228-29: Christian machines are more "wonderful" and "terrible," but less "delightful," than pagan ones.

6. Dryden, in Watson, ed., 2:233. At 228 Dryden introduces a moralizing discrimination between Achilles' cruelty and his courage; yet this moral emphasis to me to be far less important in his criticism, especially by the time of the Preface to *Fables*, than in that of Scaliger, Tasso and Sidney.

7. See Thomas M. Greene, *The Descent from Heaven* (New Haven: Yale University Press, 1963), 411-18, for some remarks on the decline in epic after Milton with reference to the growing gap between poetic imagination and ideas of the divine.

8. On modernism's aestheticizing tendency and its negative effect on the critical

reputations of Spenser and Milton, see John Hollander, "A Poetry of Restitution," *Yale Review* 70 (1981): 161.

9. William Hazlitt, from *Lectures on the English Poets* (1818), in Alpers, ed., *Edmund Spenser*, 133, 138.

10. Hazlitt in Alpers, ed., *Edmund Spenser*, 138. Compare the passage from Thomas Warton's *Observations* in Alpers, ed., 102. (On the aestheticized Spenser and Hazlitt's place in this critical tradition, see Alpers's introduction, 69.) In contrast to his criticism of Spenser, Hazlitt was careful to assert the moral character of Milton's poetry. See his *Lectures on the English Poets* (1818), in his *Complete Works*, P. P. Howe, ed. (1930; reprint, New York: AMS Press, 1967), 5:46, 56 – 65 and ff.; also 4: 110 ("On the Character of Milton's Eve").

11. Alpers, ed., 131.

12. See Ende, *Keats and the Sublime*, 88–96, Geoffrey Hartman, "Milton's Counterplot," in *Beyond Formalism* (New Haven: Yale University Press, 1970), and Brisman, *Milton's Poetry of Choice*.

13. Radzinowicz, *Toward Samson Agonistes*, 4.

14. See John Guillory, "The Father's House: *Samson Agonistes* in its Historical Moment," in *Re-Membering Milton*, 148, 168, 171–72.

15. Kerrigan's remarks on Books 11 and 12 of *Paradise Lost* at the end of *The Sacred Complex*, 274 –75, acknowledge this tension. See also Saurat, *Milton: Man and Thinker*, 199–200.

16. Kerrigan is more equivocal on Milton's transformation of personal pathos to faith in God: in *The Sacred Complex* (241) he notes, for example, that the traces of Milton's Oedipus complex remain even after he formulates his "sacred complex." Fish's reading separates Milton's drama from his moral message instead of harmonizing them as these critics do, but like them Fish often wants to assert that there is little or no ambivalence in Milton's poetic religion. For Fish's Milton, the abstract message is unequivocally superior to the experiential drama. Fish discusses the puritan subordination of aesthetics to doctrine in *Self-Consuming Artifacts*, 224 –25.

17. Kerrigan, *The Sacred Complex*, 273, evokes the virtuous obstinacy of the "one just man," who "seems locked into conflict with external evil." Kerrigan writes that "the opposed forces begin to look alike: Satan himself is unshaken, unterrified, relentless and obstinate in the service of evil." An important comment on the division I have been discussing is provided by Kerrigan's discussion of the final books of *Paradise Lost* in *The Sacred Complex*, 274 –75, in which he brilliantly illuminates Milton's contrary investments in mundane experience and apocalyptic doctrine.

18. David Quint, *Origin and Originality in Renaissance Literature* (Princeton: Princeton University Press, 1983), 216.

# Works Cited

Adelman, Janet. *The Common Liar*. New Haven: Yale University Press, 1973.
Adkins, A. W. H. *From the Many to the One*. Ithaca: Cornell University Press, 1970.
———. *Merit and Responsibility*. Oxford: Clarendon Press, 1960.
———. *Moral Values and Political Behavior in Ancient Greece*. New York: Norton, 1972.
Aeschylus. *Agamemnon*. Edited by J. D. Denniston and Denys Page. 1957. Reprint. Oxford: Clarendon Press, 1979 (1st ed. 1957).
Allen, Don Cameron. *Mysteriously Meant*. Baltimore: Johns Hopkins University Press, 1970.
Alpers, Paul J., ed. *Edmund Spenser: A Critical Anthology*. Harmondsworth: Penguin, 1969.
———, ed. *Elizabethan Poetry*. New York: Oxford University Press, 1967.
———. *The Poetry of The Faerie Queene*. Princeton: Princeton University Press, 1967.
Apollodorus. *The Library*. Translated by Sir J. G. Frazer. London: William Heinemann, 1921.
Aquinas, St. Thomas. *Summa Theologica*. Edited by Thomas Gilby. Garden City, N.Y.: Image Books, 1969.
———. *Praeclarissima Commentaria in Libri Aristotelis Peri Hermeneis et Posteriorum Analyticorum*. Venice, 1553.
Arendt, Hannah. *Willing*. Vol. 2 of *The Life of the Mind*. New York: Harcourt Brace, 1978.
Ariosto, Ludovico. *Orlando Furioso*. Translated by Sir John Herington (1591). Ed. R. McNulty. Oxford: Clarendon Press, 1972.
———. *Orlando Furioso*. Translated by Guido Waldman. London: Oxford University Press, 1974.
Aristotle. *De Anima*. Edited by R. D. Hicks. Amsterdam: Adolf M. Hakkert, 1965.
———. *Nicomachean Ethics*. With a translation by H. Rackham. 1926. Reprint. 1934. Rev. ed. Cambridge: Harvard University Press, 1982.
———. *Poetics (Aristotle's Theory of Poetry and Fine Art)*. Edited and translated by S. H. Butcher. 4th ed. New York: Dover, 1951.
———. *Politics*. With a translation by H. Rackham. London: William Heinemann, 1932.
———. *Rhetoric*. Edited and translated by J. H. Freese. 1926. Reprint. Cambridge: Harvard University Press, 1944.
Armisen-Marchetti, Mirelle. *Sapientiae Facies: Étude sur les images de Sénèque*. Paris: Belles Lettres, 1989.

Ascoli, Albert. *Ariosto's Bitter Harmony*. Princeton: Princeton University Press, 1987.
Ashley, Maurice. *The Greatness of Oliver Cromwell*. London: Hodder, 1958.
Athanasius. *The Life of Antony and the Letter to Marcellinus*. Translated and with an introduction by Robert C. Gregg, New York: Paulist Press, 1980.
Atwood, E. Bagby, and Virgil K. Whitaker, eds. *Excidium Troiae*. Cambridge, Mass.: Medieval Academy of America, 1944.
Auerbach, Erich. *Literary Language and Its Public in Late Latin Antiquity and in the Middle Ages*. New York: Random House, 1965.
———. *Scenes from the Drama of European Literature*. Gloucester, Mass.: Peter Smith, 1973.
Augustine. *The City of God*. Translated by H. Bettenson. Harmondsworth: Penguin, 1972.
———. *The City of God*. Translated by Marcus Dods. New York: Modern Library, 1950.
———. *Confessions*. Translated by R. S. Pine-Coffin. Harmondsworth: Penguin, 1961.
———. *Confessions*. Translated by William Watts. 1631. Reprint. Cambridge: Harvard University Press, 1960.
———. *De Vera Religione*. In *Corpus Christianorum: Series Latina*, vol. 32. Turnhold, 1962.
———. *On Christian Doctrine*. Translated by D. W. Robertson, Jr. Indianapolis: Bobbs-Merrill, 1958.
———. *On the Trinity*. Translated by Stephen McKenna. Washington: Catholic University of America Press, 1963.
Averroes. *Poetics* (synopsis of Aristotle). Translated by Jacob Mantino. Reprint Jahrbucher für Classische Philologie, Supplementband 17, 367 (Leipzig, 1890).
Baker, Herschel. *The Race of Time*. Toronto: University of Toronto Press, 1967.
Bakhtin, M. M. *The Dialogic Imagination*. Translated by Michael Holquist and Caryl Emerson. Austin: University of Texas Press, 1981.
Bal, Mieke. *Lethal Love*. Bloomington: Indiana University Press, 1987.
Bale, John. *A Brefe Chronycle Concerning the Examination and Death of John Oldecastle the Lord Cobham*. London, ca. 1548.
———. *Dramatic Writings*. Edited by John S. Farmer. London: Early English Drama Society, 1907.
Barclay, Alexander. *The Life of St. George* (1515). Edited by William Nelson. Oxford: Early English Text Society, 1960.
Barnes, Robert,William Tyndale, and John Frith. *The Whole Workes of William Tyndale, John Frith, and Doctor Barnes*. London, 1573.
Barney, Stephen. *Allegories of History, Allegories of Love*. New Haven: Yale University Press, 1977.
Bataille, Georges. *Visions of Excess*. Edited by Allan Stoekl. Minneapolis: University of Minnesota Press, 1985.
Baxter, Richard. *The Life of Faith*. London, 1660.
———. *The Saints Everlasting Rest*. Reprint. London, 1803.
Beard, Thomas. *The Theatre of God's Judgements* (1598). Reprint. London, 1648.
Bennett, J. A. W. *Poetry of the Passion*. Oxford: Clarendon Press, 1982.
Bennett, Josephine Waters. *The Evolution of the Faerie Queene*. Chicago: University of Chicago Press, 1942.
Benson, C. David. *The History of Troy in Middle English Literature*. Woodbridge, Suffolk, England: D. S. Brewer, 1980.
Berger, Harry, Jr. *The Allegorical Temper*. 1957. Reprint. Hamden, Conn.: Archon, 1967.

―――. "The Discarding of Malbecco." *Studies in Philology* 66 (1969): 135–54.
―――. "'Kidnapped Romance': Discourse in the Faerie Queene." In *Unfolded Tales: Essays on Renaissance Romance,* edited by George M. Logan and Gordon Teskey. Ithaca: Cornell University Press, 1989.
―――. "The Spenserean Dynamics." SEL 8 (1968): 1–18.
―――. "Spenser's Faerie Queene, Book I." *Southern Review* (Adelaide) 2 (1966): 18–48.
―――. *Revisionary Play: Studies in the Spenserian Dynamics.* Berkeley: University of California Press, 1988.
Besserman, Lawrence L. *The Legend of Job in the Middle Ages.* Cambridge: Harvard University Press, 1979.
Bèze, Theodor (Theodore Beza). *Job Expounded.* Cambridge, Mass.: John Leggatt, [1593?].
Bloom, Harold, ed. *Marlowe.* New York: Chelsea House, 1986.
Boethius. *Consolation of Philosophy.* Translated by S. J. Tester. London: Macmillan, 1973.
*The Boke of Duke Huon of Burdeux.* Translated by Sir John Bouchier, Lord Berners. Edited by S. L. Lee. London: Early English Text Society, 1887.
Borch-Jacobsen, Mikkel. *The Freudian Subject.* Stanford, Calif.: Stanford University Press, 1991.
Boulger, James D. *The Calvinist Temper in English Poetry.* The Hague: Mouton, 1980.
Bouwsma, William. *A Usable Past.* Berkeley: University of California Press, 1990.
―――. *John Calvin.* New York: Oxford University Press, 1988.
Braden, Gordon. *Renaissance Tragedy and the Senecan Tradition.* New Haven: Yale University Press, 1986.
Brandon, S. G. F. *The Judgment of the Dead.* London: Weidenfeld and Nicolson, 1967.
Bremond, Claude, and Jacques Le Goff. *L'Exemplum.* Biepols Turnhout-Belgium, 1982.
Brisman, Leslie. *Milton's Poetry of Choice and Its Romantic Heirs.* Ithaca: Cornell University Press, 1973.
Brown, Peter. *Augustine of Hippo.* 1967. Reprint. Berkeley: University of California Press, 1975.
―――. *The Body and Society.* New York: Columbia University Press, 1988.
―――. *The Making of Late Antiquity.* Cambridge: Harvard University Press, 1978.
Bunyan, John. *Grace Abounding.* Edited by Roger Sharrock. Oxford: Clarendon Press, 1962.
―――. *Pilgrim's Progress.* Edited by Roger Sharrock. Harmondsworth: Penguin, 1965.
Burke, Edmund. *Enquiry Into the Sublime and the Beautiful.* Edited by J. T. Boulton. London: Routledge and Kegan Paul, 1967.
Burke, Kenneth. "On Catharsis, or Resolution." *Kenyon Review* 21 (1959): 346–47.
Calepine. *Dictionarium.* Venice: Aldus, 1542.
Calvin, Jean. *Commentaries.* Edited by Joseph Haroutunian and Louise P. Smith. Philadelphia: Westminster Press, 1958.
―――. *Genesis* (commentary). Translated by John King. 1578. Reprint. Edinburgh: Banner of Truth, 1979.
―――. *Institutes.* Edited by J. T. McNeill. Translated by Ford Lewis Buttles. Philadelphia: Westminster Press, 1960.
―――. *Opera.* Edited by G. Baum, E. Cunitz, and E. Reiss. Berlin, 1863–1900.
Camden, William. *Remaines Concerning Britaine.* London, 1636.
Cantor, Norman. *Medieval History.* 1963. Reprint. New York: Macmillan, 1967.

Cassirer, Ernst. *The Platonic Renaissance in England*. Austin: University of Texas Press, 1953.
Castiglione, Baldassare. *The Book of the Courtier*. Translated by Thomas Hoby. New York: A. M. S. Press, 1967.
Cavell, Stanley. *The Claim of Reason*. New York: Oxford University Press, 1979.
———. *Themes Out of School*. Chicago: University of Chicago Press, 1984.
Caxton, William. *The Golden Legend*. Translated by of Jacobus de Voragine, *Legenda Aurea*. London: J. M. Dent, 1900.
Cheney, Donald. "Spenser's Hermaphrodite and the 1590 Faerie Queene." *PMLA* 87 (1972): 192–200.
Chrestien de Troyes. *Perceval*. Translated by Ruth H. Cline. Athens: University of Georgia Press, 1983.
Christopher, Georgia. "The Verbal Gate to Paradise." *PMLA* 90 (1975): 69–77.
Cicero. *De Finibus Bonorum et Malorum*. With a translation by H. Rackham. 1914. Reprint. London: William Heinemann, 1931.
———. *De Oratore*. 2 vol. With a translation by E. W. Sulton and H. Rackham. 1942. Reprint. Cambridge: Harvard University Press, 1979.
Claus, David. "Aidôs and the Language of Achilles." *Transactions of the American Philological Association* 105 (1975): 13–28.
Clebsch, William. "The Elizabethans on Luther." In *Interpreters of Luther*, edited by Jaroslav Pelikan. Philadelphia: Fortress Press, 1968.
———. *England's Earliest Protestants*. New Haven: Yale University Press, 1964.
Collinson, Patrick. *The Religion of Protestants*. Oxford: Clarendon Press, 1982.
Comes, Natalis. *Mythologie*. Translated by Jean Baudouin. Paris, 1627. Reprint. New York: Garland Publishing, 1976.
Coolidge, John S. *The Pauline Renaissance in England*. Oxford: Clarendon Press, 1970.
Cooper, Thomas. *Thesaurus*. London, 1565.
Coulter, James. *The Literary Microcosm*. Leiden: E. J. Brill, 1976.
Cowley, Abraham. *Poems*. Edited by A. R. Waller. Cambridge, 1905.
Crane, Susan. *Insular Romance*. Berkeley: University of California Press, 1986.
Cranmer, Thomas, et al. *The King's Book* (1543). Introduction by T. A. Lacey. London: Society for Promoting Christian Knowledge, 1932.
Cranz, Edward. "The Development of Augustine's Ideas on Society before the Donatist Controversy." *Harvard Theological Review* 47 (1954): 254–316.
Crouch, Humphrey. *The Heroic History of Guy Earl of Warwick*. London, 1671.
Cunningham, J. V. *Woe or Wonder*. Denver: University of Colorado, 1951.
Damrosch, David. *The Narrative Covenant*. San Francisco: Harper and Row, 1987.
Damrosch, Leopold. *God's Plot and Man's Stories*. Chicago: University of Chicago Press, ca. 1986.
Daniélou, Jean. *From Shadows to Reality*. Translated by Wulston Hubbard. London: Burns and Oates, 1960.
———. *Origen*. Translated by Walter Mitchell. New York: Sheed and Ward, 1955.
Davies, Horton. *Worship and Theology in England*. Princeton: Princeton University Press, 1970.
Demaray, John. *Milton's Theatrical Epic*. Cambridge: Harvard University Press, 1980.
Dennis, John. *Critical Works*. 2 vols. Edited by Edward Niles Hooker. Baltimore: Johns Hopkins University Press, 1943.
*Dives and Pauper*. Reprint. London, 1534.
Dodds, Eric. "Plato and the Irrational Soul." In *Plato: A Collection of Critical Essays*, edited by Gregory Vlastos. 2 vols. 1971. Reprint. Notre Dame, 1978.
Dollimore, Jonathan. *Radical Tragedy*. Brighton: Harvester Press, 1984.

Donne, John. *Death's Duel* (1632). Menston, England: Scolar Press, 1969.
Dover, Kenneth. *Greek Popular Morality*. Oxford: Basil Blackwell, 1974.
Drayton, Michael. *Noah's Flood*. In Michael Drayton, *Poems*, edited by Alexander Chalmers. 1810. Reprint. New York: Greenwood Press, 1969.
Dryden, John. *Dramatic Works*. Edited by Montague Summers. London: Nonesuch, 1932–33.
———. *An Essay of Dramatic Poesy and Other Works*. 2 vols. Edited by George Watson. 1962. Reprint. London: Dent, 1968.
du Bartas, William de Saluste. *Divine Weekes*. Translated by Joshuah Sylvester. Edited by T. W. Haight. 1608. Reprint. Waukesha, Wisc.: H. M. Youmans, 1908.
Earl, James W. "Identification and Catharsis." In *Pragmatism's Freud*, edited by Joseph H. Smith and William Kerrigan. Baltimore: Johns Hopkins University Press, 1986.
Eden, Kathy. *Poetic and Legal Fiction in the Aristotelian Tradition*. Princeton: Princeton University Press, 1986.
Else, Gerald. *Aristotle's Poetics*. Cambridge: Harvard University Press, 1957.
Elyot, Thomas. *The Boke Named the Governor*. 2 vols. Edited by H. H. S. Croft. New York: Brent Franklin, 1967.
Ende, Stuart. *Keats and the Sublime*. New Haven: Yale University Press, 1976.
Erasmus, Desiderius. *Collected Works*. Edited by Robert D. Sider. Toronto: University of Toronto Press, 1984.
———. *Enchiridion*. Edited by Raymond Himelick. Bloomington: Indiana University Press, 1963.
Erikson, Erik H. *Young Man Luther*. 1958. Reprint. New York: Norton, 1962.
Ferguson, Margaret W., Maureen Quilligan, and Nancy Vickers, eds. *Rewriting the Renaissance*. Chicago: University of Chicago Press, 1986.
Ferrante, Joan, George Economou, et al. *In Pursuit of Perfection*. Port Washington, N.Y.: Kennikat Press, 1975.
Ferrari, Giovanni. *Listening to the Cicadas*. Cambridge: Cambridge University Press, 1987.
Ferry, Anne. *Milton's Narrative Voice*. Cambridge: Harvard University Press, 1963.
Fichter, Andrew. *Poets Historicall*. New Haven: Yale University Press, 1982.
Fiore, Peter A. *Milton and Augustine*. University Park: Pennsylvania State University Press, 1981.
Fish, Stanley. *Doing What Comes Naturally*. Durham, N.C.: Duke University Press, 1989.
———. "Question and Answer in Samson Agonistes." In *Comus and Samson Agonistes*, edited by Julian Lovelock. London: Macmillan, 1975.
———. "Reasons that Imply Themselves: Imagery, Argument and the Reader in Milton's Reason of Church Government." In *Seventeenth-Century Imagery*, edited by Earl Miner. Berkeley: University of California Press, 1971.
———. *Self-Consuming Artifacts*. Berkeley: University of California Press, 1972.
———. *Surprised by Sin*. Berkeley: University of California Press, 1966.
Fixler, Michael. *Milton and the Kingdoms of God*. Evanston, Ill.: Northwestern University Press, 1964.
Fletcher, Angus. *Allegory*. Ithaca: Cornell University Press, 1964.
Fletcher, Angus. *The Prophetic Moment*. Chicago: University of Chicago Press, 1971.
Foucault, Michel. *The History of Sexuality*. Vol. 2. Translated by Richard Hurley. New York: Pantheon, 1985.
Foucault, Michel. *Power/Knowledge*. Translated and edited by Colin Gordon. New York: Pantheon, 1980.

Foucault, Michel. *Technologies of the Self: A Seminar with Michel Foucault*. Edited by Luther Martin, Huck Gutman, and Patrick Hutton. Amherst: University of Massachusetts Press, 1988.
Fowler, Alistair. "The Image of Mortality: The Faerie Queene 2.1–2." In *Essential Articles for the Study of Edmund Spenser*. Hamden, Conn.: Shoe String Press, 1972.
———. *Spenser and the Numbers of Time*. New York: Barnes and Noble, 1964.
Foxe, John. *Of Free Justification by Christ*. 1583. Reprint (Latin). London, 1694.
Fracastoro, Girolamo. *Naugerius*. Translated by Ruth Kelso. Urbana: University of Illinois Press, 1924.
Fraenkel, Eduard. *Aeschylus's Agamemnon* (commentary). 2 vols. 1950. Reprint. Oxford: Clarendon Press, 1974.
Freccero, John. *Dante: The Poetics of Conversion*. Cambridge: Harvard University Press, 1986.
Frend, W. H. C. *The Donatist Church*. Oxford: Clarendon Press, 1971.
Freud, Anna. *The Ego and the Mechanisms of Defense*. London: Hogarth Press, 1968.
Freud, Sigmund. *Collected Papers*. 5 vols. Edited by Joan Rivière. New York: International Psycho-analytical Press, 1924–50.
Freund, Elizabeth. *The Return of the Reader: Reader-Response Criticism*. New York: Methuen, 1987.
Fry, Paul H. *The Reach of Criticism*. New Haven: Yale University Press, 1980.
Frye, Northrop. "Agon and Logos." In *The Prison and the Pinnacle*, edited by Balachandra Rajan. Toronto: University of Toronto Press, 1973.
———. *Anatomy of Criticism*. Princeton: Princeton University Press, 1987.
———. *The Great Code*. New York: Harcourt Brace Jovanovich, 1982.
———. *The Secular Scripture*. Cambridge: Harvard University Press, 1976.
———. "The Typology of Paradise Regained." In *Milton's Epic Poetry*, edited by C. A. Patrides. Warmondsworth: Penguin, 1967.
Geoffrey of Monmouth. *Geoffrey's Histories of the Kings of Britain*. London: J. M. Dent, n.d.
Giamatti, A. Bartlett. *The Earthly Paradise and the Renaissance Epic*. Princeton: Princeton University Press, 1966.
Gilman, Ernest B. *Iconoclasm and Poetry in the English Reformation*. Chicago: University of Chicago Press, 1986.
Goldberg, Jonathan. "The Voicing of Power." In *Shakespeare and the Question of Theory*, edited by Patricia Parker and Geoffrey Hartman. New York: Methuen, 1985.
Goldhill, Simon. *Reading Greek Tragedy*. Cambridge: Cambridge University Press, 1986.
Goodwin, Thomas. *Works*. Edinburgh: James Nichol, 1865.
Gorday, Peter. *Principles of Patristic Exegesis*. New York: Edwin Mellen, 1983.
Gosson, Stephen. *Playes Confuted in Fiue Actions* (1582). In *Markets of Bawdrie: The Dramatic Criticism of Stephen Gosson*, edited by Arthur F. Kinney. Salzburg: Salzburg Studies in English Literature, 1974.
Gould, Thomas. *The Ancient Quarrel Between Poetry and Philosophy*. Princeton: Princeton University Press, 1991.
Gould, Thomas. "Aristotle and the Irrational." *Arion* 2 (Summer 1963): 55–74.
———. "Plato's Hostility to Art." *Arion* 3 (Spring 1964): 70–91.
Grant, Patrick. *Images and Ideas in Literature of the English Renaissance*. Amherst: University of Massachusetts Press, 1979.
Greenblatt, Stephen. "Psychoanalysis and Renaissance Culture." In *Literary Theory/Renaissance Texts*, edited by Patricia Parker and David Quint. Baltimore: Johns Hopkins University Press, 1986.

———. *Renaissance Self-Fashioning.* Chicago: University of Chicago Press, 1980.
Greene, Thomas M. *The Descent from Heaven.* New Haven: Yale University Press, 1963.
Greenfield, Concetta. *Humanist and Scholastic Poetics.* London: Associated University Presses, 1981.
Gross, Kenneth. *Spenserian Poetics.* Ithaca: Cornell University Press, 1985.
Grube, G. M. A. *Plato's Thought.* 1935. Reprint. Indianapolis: Hackett, 1980.
Guillory, John. *Poetic Authority.* New York: Columbia University Press, 1983.
Gunkel, Hermann. *Genesis, übersetzt and erklärt von Hermann Gunkel.* Göttingen, 1964.
Gutmann, Joseph, ed. *The Image and the Word.* Missoula: University of Montana Press, 1977.
Haller, William. *The Rise of Puritanism.* New York: Columbia University Press, 1938.
Halliwell, Stephen. *Aristotle's Poetics.* London: Duckworth, 1986.
Hamilton, A. C., ed. *Essential Articles for the Study of Edmund Spenser.* Hamden, Conn.: Shoe String Press, 1972.
———. *The Structure of Allegory in The Faerie Queene.* Oxford: Clarendon Press, 1961.
Hankins, John E. *Source and Meaning in Spenser's Allegory.* Oxford: Clarendon Press, 1971.
Hanning, Robert. *The Individual in Twelfth-Century Romance.* New Haven: Yale University Press, 1977.
Hartman, Geoffrey. *Beyond Formalism.* New Haven: Yale University Press, 1976.
Hathaway, Baxter. *The Age of Criticism.* Ithaca: Cornell University Press, 1962.
Hawkins, Sherman. "Samson's Catharsis." *Milton Studies* 2 (1970): 211–30.
Hazlitt, William. *Complete Works.* Edited by P. P. Howe after the edition of A. R. Waller and Arnold Glover. 1930. Reprint. New York: AMS Press, 1967.
Heidegger, Martin. *Nietzsche.* 2 vols. Translated by D. F. Krell. San Francisco: Harper and Row, 1979.
Helgerson, Richard. *The Elizabethan Prodigals.* Berkeley: University of California Press, 1976.
Heller, Thomas, et al, ed. *Reconstructing Individualism.* Stanford, Calif.: Stanford University Press, 1986.
Herington, C. John. "Senecan Tragedy." *Arion* 5 (Winter 1966): 422–71.
Herrick, Marvin. *The Fusion of Horatian and Aristotelian Literary Criticism, 1531–1555.* Illinois Studies in Language and Literature 32:1. Urbana: University of Illinois, 1946.
Heylyn, Peter. *The History of that Most Famous Saynt and Souldier of Christ Jesus St. George of Cappadocia, Asserted from the Fictions of the Middle Ages of the Church and Opposition of the Present.* London, 1631.
Heywood, Thomas. *Oenone and Paris.* London, 1594.
Hill, Christopher. *The Experience of Defeat: Milton and Some Contemporaries.* Harmondsworth: Penguin, 1984.
Hollander, John. "A Poetry of Restitution." *Yale Review* 70 (1981): 161–86.
Hollander, Robert. *Allegory in Dante's Commedia.* Princeton: Princeton University Press, 1969.
Homer. *Iliad.* London: William Heinemann, 1924.
———. *Odyssey.* Edited by W. B. Stanford. 2 vols. 1948. Reprint. New York: St. Martin's, 1978.
Horace. *Odes*, Book 1. Edited by R. G. M. Nisbet and Margaret Hubbard. 1970. Reprint. Oxford: Clarendon Press, 1975.

Hughes, Derek. *Dryden's Heroic Plays*. Lincoln: University of Nebraska Press, 1982.
Hughes, Merritt Y. *Virgil and Spenser*. Port Washington, N.Y.: Kennikat Press, 1969.
Hume, Anthea. *Edmund Spenser, Protestant Poet*. Cambridge: Cambridge University Press, 1984.
Hunter, G. K. *Paradise Lost*. London: George Allen and Unwin, 1980.
*The Hystory of the Two Valyaunte Brethren Valentyne and Orson*. London, 1565.
Ihle, Sandra N. *Malory's Grail Quest*. Madison: University of Wisconsin Press, 1983.
Jauss, Hans-Robert. *Aesthetic Experience and Literary Hermeneutics*. Minneapolis: University of Minnesota Press, 1982.
Javitch, Daniel. *Poetry and Courtliness in Renaissance England*. Princeton: Princeton University Press, 1978.
Jewel, John. *Works*. Edited by John Ayer. Cambridge: Parker Society, 1845-50.
Johnson, W. R. *Darkness Visible*. Berkeley: University of California Press, 1976.
Jones, John. *On Aristotle and Greek Tragedy*. London: Chatto and Windus, 1967.
Jones, William. "Art and Christian Piety." In *The Image and the Word*, edited by Missoula, Joseph Gutmann. Montana: Scholars Press, 1977.
Kahn, Victoria. *Rhetoric, Prudence and Skepticism in the Renaissance*. Ithaca: Cornell University Press, 1985.
Kaske, Carol V. "The Bacchus Who Wouldn't Wash: Faerie Queene 2. 1-2." *Renaissance Quarterly* 29 (1976): 195-209.
Kennedy, George A. "Classics and Canons." *South Atlantic Quarterly* 89, no. 1 (Winter 1990): 218-25.
Kermode, Frank. *The Genesis of Secrecy*. Cambridge: Harvard University Press, 1979.
Kerrigan, William. "The Irrational Coherence of Samson Agonistes." *Milton Studies* 22 (1986): 217-32.
———, and Gordon Braden. "Milton's Coy Eve." *ELH* 53 (1986): 27-52.
———. *The Prophetic Milton*. Charlottesville: University of Virginia Press, 1974.
———. "The Riddle of Paradise Regained." In *Poetic Prophecy in Western Literature*, edited by Jan Wojcik and Raymond-Jean Frontain. Cranbury, N.J.: Associated University Presses, 1984.
———. *The Sacred Complex: On the Psychogenesis of Paradise Lost*. Cambridge: Harvard University Press, 1983.
King, John N. *Spenser's Poetry and the Reformation Tradition*. Princeton: Princeton University Press, 1990.
Kinney, Clare Regan. *Strategies of Poetic Narrative: Chaucer, Spenser, Milton, Eliot*. Cambridge: Cambridge University Press, 1992.
Kirk, Geoffrey S. *The Language and Background of Homer*. Cambridge: W. Heffer, 1964.
Knapp, Jeffrey. "Error as a Means of Empire in the *Faerie Queene* 1." *ELH* 54, no.4 (1987): 801-34.
Knott, John R. *The Sword of the Spirit*. Chicago: University of Chicago Press, 1980.
Koester, August. In , *Heerwesen und Kriegführung der Griechen und Römer: Handbüch der Geisteswissenschaft*, edited by Johannes Kromayer and Georg Veith. Vol.3, part 2. Munich: Beck, 1928.
Korshin, Paul A. "Queuing and Waiting: The Apocalypse in England, 1660-1750." In *The Apocalypse in English Renaissance Thought and Literature*, edited by J. A. Wittreich and C. A. Patrides. Ithaca: Cornell University Press, 1984.
Kugel, James, and Rowan Greer. *Early Biblical Interpretation*. Philadelphia: Westminster Press, 1986.
Lacan, Jacques. *Écrits: A Selection*. Translated by Alan Sheridan. New York: Norton, 1977.

---. *The Seminar of Jacques Lacan*. Translated by Jacques-Alain Miller, Sylvana Tomaselli, and John Forrester. New York: Norton, 1988– .
Lake, Peter. *Moderate Puritans and the Elizabethan Church*. Cambridge: Cambridge University Press, 1982.
Lamont, William. *Godly Rule*. London: Macmillan, 1969.
---. *Richard Baxter and the Millenium*. London: Croom Helm, 1979.
Landes, Paula Fredriksen, trans. *Augustine on Romans*. Chico, Calif.: Scholars Press, 1982.
Langland, William. *Piers Plowman*. Edited by Walter Skeat. Oxford, 1886.
Laplanche, Jean. *Life and Death in Psychoanalysis*. Translated by Jeffrey Mehlman. Baltimore: Johns Hopkins University Press, 1976.
Latimer, Hugh. *Sermons and Remains*. Edited by G. E. Corrie. Cambridge: Parker Society, 1845.
LeComte, Edward. *Milton and Sex*. London: Macmillan, 1978.
Levao, Ronald. *Renaissance Minds and Their Fictions*. Berkeley: University of California Press, 1985.
Lewalski, Barbara. *Milton's Brief Epic*. Providence, R.I.: Brown University Press, 1966.
---. *Paradise Lost and the Rhetoric of Literary Forms*. Princeton: Princeton University Press, 1985.
---. *Protestant Poetics and the Seventeenth Century Religious Lyric*. Princeton: Princeton University Press, 1979.
---. "Structure and the Symbolism of Vision in Michael's Prophecy." *Philological Quarterly* 42 (1963): 25–35.
---. "Time and History in Paradise Regained." In *The Prison and the Pinnacle*, edited by Balachandra Rajan. Toronto: University of Toronto Press, 1973.
Lewis, C. S. *The Allegory of Love*. 1936. Reprint. London: Oxford University Press, 1967.
---. *A Preface to Paradise Lost*. London: Oxford University Press, 1942.
Lipsius, Justus. *Two Books of Constancie*. Translated by Sir John Stradling of *De Constantia*. Edited with an introduction by Rudolf Kirk. 1594. Reprint. New Brunswick, N.J.: Rutgers University Press, 1939.
Lloyd, A. C. "Emotion and Decision in Stoic Philosophy." In *The Stoics*, edited by J. M. Rist. Berkeley: University of California Press, 1978.
Loewenstein, Joseph. *Responsive Readings*. New Haven: Yale University Press, 1984.
Long, A. A., ed. *Problems in Stoicism*. London: Athlone Press, 1971.
Longinus. *On the Sublime*. Edited by D. A. Russell. Oxford: Clarendon Press, 1964.
Luther, Martin. *Martin Luther: Selections from his Writings*. Edited by John Dillenberger. Garden City, N.Y.: Doubleday, 1961.
Lydgate, John. "The Legend of St. George." In *Minor Poems*. London: Early English Text Society, 1900.
MacCaffrey, Isabel G. *Spenser's Allegory*. Princeton: Princeton University Press, 1976.
MacCallum, H. R. "Milton and Sacred History." In *Essays in English Literature Presented to A. S. P. Woodhouse*, edited by M. Maclure and F. W. Watt. Toronto: University of Toronto Press, 1964.
McClure, George. "The Art of Mourning." *Renaissance Quarterly* 39 (1986): 440–75.
McGoldrick, J. E. *Luther's English Connection*. Milwaukee, Wisc.: Northwestern Publishing House, 1979.
McKeon, Michael. *Politics and Poetry in Restoration England*. Cambridge: Harvard University Press, 1979.

Macrobius. *Saturnalia*. Paris: Garnier Frères, 1937.
Malory, Sir. Thomas. *Le Morte d'Arthur*. London: Dent, 1906.
Manley, Lawrence. "Spenser and the City: the Minor Poems." *Modern Language Quarterly* 43 (1982): 203–27.
Mannyng, Robert. *The Story of England* (1338). Edited by F. J. Furnivall. London, 1887.
Marcus Aurelius Antoninus. *Meditations*. Edited by A. S. L. Farquharson. 2 vols. Oxford: Clarendon Press, 1944.
Marks, Herbert. "Pauline Typology and Revisionary Criticism." Reprint. in *The Bible: Modern Critical Views,* edited by Harold Bloom. New York: Chelsea House, 1987.
Marshall, William H. "Calvin, Spenser, and the Major Sacraments." *MLN* 74 (1959): 97–101.
Meeks, Wayne. *The First Urban Christians*. New Haven: Yale University Press, 1983.
Melancthon, Philip. *Loci Communes*. In *Melancthon and Bucer*, edited by Wilhelm Pauck. Philadelphia: Westminster Press, 1969.
Miller, David Lee. "The Death of the Modern." *South Atlantic Quarterly* 88, no. 4 (Fall 1989): 757–88.
Miller, David Lee. *The Poem's Two Bodies*. Princeton: Princeton University Press, 1986.
Milton, John. *Complete Poems and Major Prose*. Edited by Merritt Y. Hughes. Indianapolis: Bobbs-Merrill, 1957.
———. *Complete Prose Works*. Edited by Douglas Bush et al. New Haven: Yale University Press, 1953–.
———. *Complete Shorter Poems*. Edited by John Carey. 1968. Reprint. London: Longman's, 1971.
———. *Paradise Lost*. Edited by Alistair Fowler. 1968. Reprint. London: Longman's, 1971.
———. *Paradise Lost and Paradise Regained*. Edited by Christopher Ricks. New York: New American Library, 1969.
———. *Selected Prose*. Edited by Max Patrick. Garden City, N.Y.: Doubleday, 1967.
Montgomery, Robert L. *The Reader's Eye*. Berkeley: University of California Press, ca. 1979.
More, St. Thomas. *Complete Works*. Vol. 13. Edited by Garry E. Haupt. New Haven: Yale University Press, 1976.
Mosher, Joseph Albert. *The Exemplum in the Early Religious and Didactic Literature of England*. New York: AMS Press, 1966.
Mueller, Martin. "Pathos and Katharsis in Samson Agonistes." In *Critical Essays on Milton from ELH*. Baltimore: Johns Hopkins University Press, 1969.
Muscatine, Charles. *Chaucer and the French Tradition*. Berkeley: University of California Press, 1957.
Nancy, Jean-Luc. *The Inoperative Community*. Minneapolis: University of Minnesota Press, 1991.
Nelson, William. *The Poetry of Spenser*. New York: Columbia University Press, 1963.
———. "Spenser *ludens*." In *A Theatre for Spenserians*, edited by Judith Kennedy and James Reither. Toronto: University of Toronto Press, 1973.
Nohrnberg, James. *The Analogy of The Faerie Queene*. Princeton: Princeton University Press, 1976.
Norbrook, David. *Poetry and Politics in the English Renaissance*. London: Routledge and Kegan Paul, 1984.
Nussbaum, Martha. *The Fragility of Goodness*. Cambridge: Cambridge University Press, 1986.

Nussbaum, Martha. *Love's Knowledge*. Oxford: Oxford University Press, 1990.
Nussbaum, Martha. "The Stoics on the Extirpation of the Passions." *Apeiron* 20 (1987): 128–77.
Nykrog, Per. *Les Fabliaux*. 1957. Reprint. Geneva, 1973.
O'Connell, Michael. "Iconoclasm and the Elizabethan Theatre." *ELH* 52 (1985): 279–310.
Oestreich, Gerhard. *Neostoicism and the Early Modern State*. Cambridge: Cambridge University Press, 1982.
Ong, Walter. *The Presence of the Word*. New Haven: Yale University Press, 1967.
Oulton, J. E. L., and Henry Chadwick, eds. *Alexandrian Christianity*. Philadelphia: Westminster Press, 1954.
Ovid. *Heroides and Amores*. Translated by Grant Showerman. 2d. ed., rev. by G. P. Goold. 1914. Reprint. Cambridge: Harvard University Press, 1977.
Owst, G. W. *Literature and Pulpit in Medieval England*. Cambridge: Cambridge University Press, 1933.
Padelford, F. M. "Spenser and the Puritan Propaganda." *MP* 11 (1913–14): 85–106.
———. "Spenser and the Spirit of Puritanism." *MP* 14 (1916–17): 31–44.
———. "Spenser and the Theology of Calvin." *MP* 12 (1914–15): 1–18.
———. "The Spiritual Allegory of The Faerie Queene, Book One." *JEGP* 22 (1923): 1–17.
Pagels, Elaine. *Adam, Eve and the Serpent*. New York: Random House, 1988.
Parry, Adam. "The Language of Achilles." Reprint in *The Language and Background of Homer*, edited by G. S. Kirk. New York: Barnes and Noble, 1964.
Patrides, C. A. *Milton and the Christian Tradition*. Oxford: Clarendon Press, 1966.
Patterson, Annabel. "Couples, Canons and the Uncouth: Spenser- and-Milton in Educational Theory." *Critical Inquiry* 16, no. 4 (Summer 1990): 773–93.
Patterson, Lee W. "'Rapt with Pleasaunce': Vision and Narration in the Epic." *ELH* 48 (1981): 455–75.
Paul of Tarsus, Saint. *The Writings of Saint Paul*. Edited by Wayne Meeks. New York: Norton, 1972.
Peele, George. *The Araygnment of Paris* (1584). In *The Dramatic Works of George Peele*. Vol. 3. Edited by R. Mark Benbow. New Haven: Yale University Press, 1970.
Perkins, William. *Two Treatises*. 2d ed. London, 1597.
Pettit, Norman. *The Heart Prepared*. New Haven: Yale University Press, 1966.
Phillips, John. *The Reformation of Images*. Berkeley: University of California Press, 1973.
Philo of Judaeus. *The Essential Philo*. Edited by Nahum N. Glatzer. New York: Schocken, 1971.
Pigman, George W. III. *Grief and English Renaissance Elegy*. New York: Cambridge University Press, 1985.
Plato. *The Being of the Beautiful (Theaetetus, Sophist, and Statesman)*. Translated by Seth Benardete. Chicago: University of Chicago Press, 1984.
———. *Laws*. Translated by Thomas L. Pangle. New York: Basic, 1980.
———. *Opera*. Edited by John Burnet. 5 vols. 1907. Reprint. Oxford: Clarendon Press, 1976.
———. *Republic*. Edited by James Adam. 1902. Reprint. London: Cambridge University Press, 1965.
———. *Republic*. Translated by G. M. A. Grube. Indianapolis: Hackett, 1974.
Plutarch. *Moralia*. 14 vols. Cambridge: Harvard University Press (Loeb Classical Library), 1936.
Pohlenz, Max. *Die Stoa*. Göttingen: Vandenhoeck and Ruprecht, 1948.

Pontano, Giovanni. *De Prudentia*. Venice: Aldus, 1518.

———. *Opera Omnia*. Florence, 1520.

Pope, Marvin H., ed. and intro. *Job*. 1965. Reprint. Garden City, N.Y.: Doubleday, 1973.

Preus, James. *From Shadow to Promise*. Cambridge: Harvard University Press, 1969.

Prynne, William. *Histrio-Mastix*. London, 1633.

Puttenham, George. *The Arte of English Poesy*. Edited by Baxter Hathaway. 1589. Reprint. Kent, Ohio: Kent State University Press, 1970.

Quint, David. "The Boat of Romance and the Renaissance Epic." In *Romance*, edited by Kevin and Marina Brownlee. Hanover, N.H.: Dartmouth University Press, 1985.

Quint, David. *Origin and Originality in Renaissance Literature*. Princeton: Princeton University Press, 1983.

Quintilian. *Institutio Oratoria*. With a translation by H. E. Butler. 1922. Reprint. London: William Heinemann, 1936.

*Rabbi Samuel Ben Meir's Commentary on Genesis*. Translated by Martin Lockshin. Lampeter, Wales: Edwin Mellen Press, 1989.

Radzinowicz, Mary Anne. *Toward Samson Agonistes*. Princeton: Princeton University Press, 1978.

Rainoldes, John. *Th'Overthrow of Stage Playes* (1599). New York: Garland, 1974.

Redfield, James. *Nature and Culture in the Iliad*. Chicago: University of Chicago Press, 1975.

——— and P. Friedrich. "Speech as a Personality Symbol: The Case of Achilles." *Language* 54 (1978): 263–88.

Regulus, Sebastian. *In primum Aeneidos Virgilii Librum ex Aristotelis de Arte Poetica*. 1563.

*Rhetorica ad Herennium*. With a translation by Harry Caplan. 1954. Reprint. Cambridge: Harvard University Press, 1968.

Ricoeur, Paul. *Essays on Biblical Hermeneutics*. Edited by Lewis Mudge. Philadelphia: Fortress Press, 1980.

Ricoeur, Paul. *The Symbolism of Evil*. Translated by Emerson Buchanan. Boston: Beacon Press, 1967.

Ridley, Nicholas. *Works*. Edited by Henry Christmas. Cambridge: Parker Society, 1843.

Ridpath, George. *The Stage Condemn'd* (1698). New York: Garland, 1972.

Riggs, William. *The Christian Poet in Paradise Lost*. Berkeley: University of California Press, 1973.

Rist, J. M. *Stoic Philosophy*. New York: Cambridge University Press, 1969.

Robinson, Forrest. *The Shape of Things*. Cambridge: Harvard University Press, 1972.

Roche, Thomas P., Jr. *The Kindly Flame*. Princeton: Princeton University Press, 1964.

Rose, Mark. *Heroic Love*. 1968. Reprint. Cambridge: Harvard University Press, 1970.

Rothstein, Eric. *Restoration Tragedy*. Madison: University of Wisconsin Press, 1967.

Rowland, Samuel. *The Famous History of Guy Earl of Warwick*. London, 1679.

Rudat, Wolfgang. "Milton, Freud, St. Augustine: Paradise Lost and the History of Human Sexuality." *Mosaic* 2 (1982): 109–22.

Rudenstine, Neil. "Sidney and Energeia." In *Elizabethan Poetry*, edited by Paul J. Alpers. New York: Oxford University Press, 1967.

Russell, D. A., and Martin Winterbottom, eds. *Ancient Literary Criticism*. Oxford: Clarendon Press, 1972.

Sackville, Thomas, Earl of Dorset. *The Complaint of Henry, Duke of Buckingham*. (From *The Mirror for Magistrates*.) Edited by Marguerite Hearsey. New Haven: Yale University Press, 1936.

Sahas, Daniel J., trans. *Icon and Image.* Toronto: University of Toronto Press, 1986.
Sanders, Wilbur. *John Donne's Poetry.* Cambridge: Cambridge University Press, 1971.
Sasek, Lawrence. "The Drama of Education of Adam." In *Milton: Modern Essays in Criticism,* edited by Arthur Barker. New York: Oxford University Press, 1963.
Saurat, Denis. *Milton: Man and Thinker.* London: J. M. Dent, 1925.
Scaliger, Julius Caesar. *Poetices.* Lyons, 1561.
Schmitt, Charles, Quentin Skinner and Eckhard Kessler, eds. *The Cambridge History of Renaissance Philosophy.* Cambridge: Cambridge University Press, 1988.
Screech, M. A. *Ecstasy and the Praise of Folly.* London: Duckworth, 1980.
*A Second and Third Blast of Retrait from Plaies and Theaters.* In *The English Drama and Stage,* edited by W. C. Hazlitt. London, 1869.
*The Seege of Troye.* Edited by C. H. Wager. New York, 1899.
Senault, J. F. *The Use of Passions.* Translated by Henry, Earl of Monmouth. London, 1649.
Seneca. *Agamemnon.* Edited by R. J. Tarrant. London: Cambridge University Press, 1976.
———. *De Ira.* In *Moral Essays.* 3 vols. 1925. Reprint. Cambridge: Harvard University Press, 1970.
———. *Epistolae Morales.* 3 vols. 1917. Reprint. Cambridge: Harvard University Press, 1979.
———. *Medea.* Edited by C. D. N. Costa. Oxford: Clarendon Press, 1973.
———. *Seneca His Tenne Tragedies Translated into English.* Edited by Thomas Newton. 1581. Reprint. New York: Knopf, 1927.
Sibbes, Richard. *The Bruised Reede.* London, 1632.
Sidney, Philip. *The Apology for Poetry.* Oxford: Clarendon Press, 1907.
———. *Poems.* Edited by William A. Ringler, Jr. Oxford: Clarendon Press, 1962.
Siebers, Tobin. *The Mirror of Medusa.* Berkeley: University of California Press, 1983.
Siegel, Paul N. "Spenser and the Calvinist View of Life." *Studies in Philology* 41 (1944): 201–22.
Silvestris, Bernardus. *Commentary on the First Six Books of Virgil's Aeneid.* Edited and translated by Earl Schreiber and Thomas Maresca. Lincoln: University of Nebraska Press, 1979.
Sinfield, Alan. *Literature in Protestant England.* London: Croom Helm, 1983.
Smith, G. Gregory, ed. *Elizabethan Critical Essays.* 2 vols. 1904. Reprint. London: Oxford University Press, 1971.
Smith, Hallett. *Elizabethan Poetry.* Cambridge: Harvard University Press, 1952.
Smith, Paul. *Discerning the Subject.* Minneapolis: University of Minnesota Press, 1988.
Snell, Bruno. *The Discovery of the Mind.* Translated by T. G. Rosenmeyer. Cambridge: Harvard University Press, 1953.
Sophocles. *Ajax.* Edited by W. B. Stanford. London: Macmillan, 1963.
Spenser, Edmund. *The Faerie Queene.* Edited by A. C. Hamilton. New York: Longman's, 1977.
———. *The Faerie Queene.* Edited by Thomas P. Roche, Jr. 1978. Reprint. New Haven: Yale University Press, 1981.
———. *The Shepheardes Calender.* 1579. Reprint. New York: Burt Franklin, 1967.
Spingarn, J. E., ed. *Elizabethan Critical Essays.* 2 vols. Oxford: Clarendon Press, 1908.
Starnes, DeWitt T,. and E. W. Talbert. *Classical Myth and Legend in Renaissance Dictionaries.* Chapel Hill: University of North Carolina Press, 1955.
Steadman, John. *Epic and Tragic Structure in Paradise Lost.* Chicago: University of Chicago Press, 1976.

———. *Milton and the Paradoxes of Renaissance Heroism.* Baton Rouge: Louisiana State University Press, 1987.
Stein, Arnold. *Answerable Style.* 1953. Reprint. Seattle: University of Washington Press, 1967.
———. *Heroic Knowledge.* Minneapolis: University of Minnesota Press, 1957.
Stephanus, Charles (Charles Estienne). *Dictionarium.* Paris, 1596.
Strauss, Leo. *The City and Man.* 1964. Reprint. Chicago: University of Chicago Press, 1977.
Strier, Richard. *Love Known.* Chicago: Chicago University Press, 1983.
Strong, Roy. *The Cult of Elizabeth.* London: Thames and Hudson, 1977.
Struever, Nancy. *The Language of History in the Renaissance.* Princeton: Princeton University Press, 1970.
Summers, Joseph. *The Muse's Method.* London: Chatto and Windus, 1962.
Suzuki, Mihoko. *Metamorphoses of Helen.* Ithaca: Cornell University Press, 1989.
Tasso, Torquato. *Discorsi dell'Arte Poetica e del Poema Eroica.* Bari, 1964.
———. *Discourses on the Heroic Poem.* Translated by Mariella Cavalchini and Irene Samuel. Oxford: Clarendon Press, 1973.
Tayler, Edward. *Milton's Poetry.* Pittsburgh: Duquesne University Press, 1979.
Taylor, Charles. *Sources of the Self.* Cambridge: Harvard University Press, 1989.
Thomas, Keith. *Religion and the Decline of Magic.* New York: Scribner's, 1971.
Tillyard, E. M. W. *The Elizabethan World Picture.* New York: Random House, n.d.
Tonkin, Humphrey. *Spenser's Courteous Pastoral.* Oxford: Clarendon Press, 1972.
Trimpi, Wesley. *Muses of One Mind.* Princeton: Princeton University Press, 1983.
Trinkaus, Charles. *In Our Image and Likeness.* 2 vols. Chicago: University of Chicago Press, 1970.
Trinterud, Leonard J. *Elizabethan Puritanism.* New York: Oxford University Press, 1971.
Turner, James Grantham. *One Flesh: Paradisal Marriage and Sexual Relations in the Age of Milton.* Oxford: Clarendon Press, 1988.
Tuve, Rosemond. *Allegorical Imagery.* Princeton: Princeton University Press, 1966.
Veeser, H. Aram, ed. *The New Historicism.* New York: Routledge, 1988.
Vicaire, Paul. *Platon: Critique Litteraire.* Paris: Klincksieck, 1960.
Vickers, Brian. "Epideictic and Epic in the Renaissance." *NLH* 14 (1983): 497–538.
Vida, Marco Girolamo. *De Arte Poetica* (1517). Edited and translated by Ralph Williams. New York: Columbia University Press, 1976.
Virgil. *Opera.* 2 vols. Venice, 1544. Reprint. New York: Garland Publishing, 1976.
———. *Aeneid.* 2 vols. Edited by R. D. Williams. 1973. Reprint. New York: St. Martin's, 1985.
Von Arnim, Hans Friedrich August. *Stoicorum Veterum Fragmenta.* Stuttgart: Teubner, 1903–24.
Weinberg, Bernard. *A History of Literary Criticism in the Italian Renaissance.* 2 vols. Chicago: University of Chicago Press, 1961.
Weiner, Andrew. *Sir Philip Sidney and the Poetics of Protestantism.* Minneapolis: University of Minnesota Press, 1978.
Wells, Robin Headlam. *Spenser's Faerie Queene and the Cult of Elizabeth.* London: Croom Helm, 1983.
Whigham, Frank. *Ambition and Privilege: The Social Tropes of Elizabethan Courtesy.* Berkeley: University of California Press, 1984.
Whitaker, Virgil K. *The Religious Basis of Spenser's Thought.* Stanford, Calif.: Stanford University Press, 1950.

Widmer, Kingsley. "The Iconography of Renunciation." In *Milton's Epic Poetry*, edited by C. A. Patrides. Harmondsworth: Penguin, 1967.
Williams, Gordon. *Technique and Ideas in the Aeneid*. New Haven: Yale University Press, 1983.
Wilson, F. P. *The English Drama 1485–1585*. Edited by G. K. Hunter. Oxford: Clarendon Press, 1969.
Wittreich, Joseph Anthony. *Interpreting Samson Agonistes*. Princeton: Princeton University Press, 1986.
———. *Visionary Poetics*. San Marino, Calif.: Huntington Library, 1979.
Wolfson, Harry. 2 vols.1947. Reprint. Cambridge: Harvard University Press, 1982.
Woodhouse, A. S. P. "Nature and Grace in the Faerie Queene. In *Elizabethan Poetry*, edited by Paul J. Alpers. New York: Oxford University Press, 1967.
———. "Theme and Structure in *Paradise Regained*." University of Toronto Quarterly 25 (1955–56): 167–82.
Yates, Frances. *Astraea*. London: Routledge and Kegan Paul, 1975.
Yates, Frances. "Elizabethan Chivalry: the Romance of the Accession Day Tilt." *Journal of the Warburg and Courtauld Institutes* (1957): 4–25.
Žižek, Slavoj. *Looking Awry*. Cambridge: MIT Press, 1991.
———. *The Sublime Object of Ideology*. London: Routledge and Kegan Paul, 1989.

# Author and Subject Index

Adkins, A. W. H., 19
Aeschylus, 24
Allegory, 40, 42, 52–53, 70–72
Althusser, Louis, 12
Apuleius, 97
Ariosto, Ludovico, 35, 40, 46, 48–50
Aristotle, 16, 26, 33, 64, 109–10
Ascesis, 67, 161
Ascoli, Albert, 46
Ashbery, John, ix
Augustine, Saint, 3, 29–30, 42, 55, 58, 64–65, 81, 166

Badger, Anne, ix
Bakhtin, Mikhail, 46
Bal, Mieke, 179
Baptism, 65–67
Barclay, Alexander, 48
Bataille, Georges, 192
Baxter, Richard, 153
Beard, Thomas, 152
Berger, Harry, 71, 74, 107
Bernard, John, ix
Bers, Victor, ix
Bloom, Harold, ix
Borch-Jacobsen, Mikkel, 69
Brisman, Leslie, ix
Bunyan, John, 57–58
Burckhardt, Jacob, 11–13
Burke, Kenneth, 96, 109

Calvin, Jean, 155
Catharsis (pity and fear), 24–25, 78, 96–97, 109–10, 114–16
Cavell, Stanley, 140–41

Caxton, William, 48
Chastity, 77, 97, 102–3, 140, 143
Chaucer, Geoffrey, 36
Cheney, Donald, ix
Chrétien de Troyes, 40, 48
Collinson, Patrick, 5
Courtesy, 100–102, 116–19
Creation, 131, 134–36, 138

Damrosch, David, 175
Damrosch, Leopold, 3–4, 14, 54
Dante, 16, 29
Decorum, 44–46, 49, 68–69, 190
Dillon, Steven, ix
Discontinuity, 5–6, 8, 131, 134–36, 163, 192
Dollimore, Jonathan, 7, 13
Dryden, John, 189–90
Duncan, Ian, ix

Empson, William, 6, 167, 191–92

Fichter, Andrew, 112
Fish, Stanley, 6–7, 26, 53–55, 78–80, 150–51, 155, 167, 189
Foucault, Michel, 7–8, 12
Freud, Sigmund, 6–7, 16, 23–26, 79, 92, 173
Freund, Elizabeth, 78
Frye, Northrop, 5, 46, 166–67

Galileo, 134
Gender, 86–96, 137, 146, 177–78, 181–82
Genre, 41, 46

Giamatti, A. Bartlett, 124
Gilman, Ernest, ix
Goldberg, Jonathan, 13
Goodwin, Thomas, 153
Greenblatt, Stephen, 8–13
Greene, Thomas M., ix
Gregory, Elizabeth, ix
Guillory, John, ix, 192

Hamilton, A. C., 81
Harington, Sir John, 50–51
Hartman, Geoffrey, 136–37, 191
Hazlitt, William, 190–91
Heidegger, Martin, 7
Hirst, Derek, 5
History, 102, 109–12, 129–30, 160–61, 174, 188, 189
Hollander, John, ix
Homer, 6, 15–16, 18–21, 23, 34, 36, 50–51, 190
Houlihan, James, ix

Imaginary and Symbolic (Lacan), 5, 24–25, 39, 69, 75, 85, 87, 89, 92, 95, 97, 103, 122, 133, 138–39, 146, 161–62, 166, 173–74, 176–77, 193, 195

Jameson, Fredric, 7–10, 77–78
Jauss, Hans-Robert, 78
Javitch, Daniel, ix, 112–13
Joyce, James, 145

Kaplan, Lindsay, ix
Kaufmann, David, ix
Keats, John, 6, 191
Kendrick, Christopher, 139–40
Kerrigan, William, 6, 167, 177
Kierkegaard, Søren, 176
Kinney, Clare, 113
Knapp, Jeffrey, 60–61

Lacan, Jacques, 5, 9, 24–26, 39, 55, 92, 97, 133
Lake, Peter, 5
Law, 7, 58–59, 156–57, 163, 176, 185–86, 192
Lear, Jonathan, 16
Lewalski, Barbara Kiefer, 46, 150–51, 182
Lewis, C. S., 125

Lupton, Julia, ix
Luther, Martin, 155
Lydgate, John, 48

Maclean, Norman, 41
Malory, Sir Thomas, 40, 48
Manley, Lawrence, ix
Marriage, 87–88, 129, 143–45
Martin, Mary Pat, ix
Marx, Karl, 7, 9, 192
Meisel, Perry, ix
Mikics, Lewis J., ix
Miller, David Lee, 89–90
Milton, John, 3–8, 15–16, 21–22, 79, 88–8, 125–95

Nancy, Jean-Luc, 176–77
Narcissism, 147
Narcissus, 142
Nietzsche, Friedrich, 7, 4, 97, 150
Nohrnberg, James, 39–40, 107
Norbrook, David, 4
Nyquist, Mary, 89

Original sin, 67, 81

Parker, Patricia, 40
Pastoral, 61
Paul, Saint, 3, 5, 55, 64–65, 81
Pellegrino, Cesare, 46
Perkins, William, 55
Petrarch, 88
Plato, 6, 15–21, 32, 36–37, 41–42, 122, 143–45
Price, Martin, ix
Protestantism, 4–5, 54–55, 65–66, 129–30, 153–55, 180, 190
Providence, 41–42, 47–48, 58, 129, 156–58, 164, 170, 174–75, 180, 183
Pucci, Pietro, 24, 96

Quinlan, Alexis, ix
Quint, David, 112, 194

Rabelais, François, 46
Radzinowicz, Mary Ann, 150, 189, 191–93
Regulus, Sebastian, 27
Reiss, Tom, ix
Ricoeur, Paul, 174

# Index

Romance, 47, 50, 60, 63, 73, 77
Romanticism, 6, 191

Scaliger, Julius Caesar, 15, 23, 27–33, 37, 189
Schiffer, Edward, ix
Scodel, Joshua, ix
Seneca, 36–37
Shakespeare, William, 13
Sidney, Sir Philip, 15, 23, 113, 189
Skelton, John, 54
Sophocles, 18, 36–37
Spenser, Edmund, 3–6, 10, 24, 27, 37–127, 131–34, 175, 191, 195
Spivak, Gayatri Chakravorty, 7
Stein, Arnold, 166–67
Stevens, Wallace, 149–50
Stoicism, 16, 65–66, 77, 80, 165
Sublime, 132–34
Superego, 6, 177, 188

Tasso, Torquato, 15, 23, 33–35, 37, 120–21, 189
Tayler, Edward, 167

Taylor, Charles, 41, 158
Temperance, 65–66, 75–76, 82–83, 90
Tennyson, Alfred, Lord, 16
Thernstrom, Melanie, ix
*Thumos* (Plato), 17–19, 37
Turner, James G., 87–88
Tuve, Rosemond, 71
Tyndale, William, 12–13
Typology, 164

Virgil, 6, 15, 22–35, 166, 190
Voyeurism, 125–26

Weber, Samuel, 24–26
Williamson, George, 150
Wittgenstein, Ludwig, 7
Wittreich, Joseph A., 180
Woodhouse, A. S. P., 81, 166–67
Wordsworth, William, 136–37
Wright, Nancy, ix
Wyatt, Sir Thomas, 12–13
Yates, Frances, 112

Žižek, Slavoj, 187

# Index to Works by Spenser and Milton

## By Edmund Spenser

*Faerie Queene, The*
   Letter to Ralegh, 45, 127
   Book 1:
      Canto 1: 43–45, 49–50, 63, 95, 108
      Canto 2: 45, 50–51
      Canto 4: 52
      Canto 5: 52
      Canto 6: 123
      Canto 9: 52–53, 55–60, 64
      Canto 10: 59–62
      Canto 11: 63, 66
      Canto 12: 57, 62
   Book 2:
      Canto 1: 66, 68–69, 73–76, 90, 95
      Canto 2: 66, 72–73, 76–77
      Canto 3: 67
      Canto 4: 69, 71
      Canto 5: 69–71
      Canto 6: 69, 71
      Canto 7: 65, 72, 79
      Canto 8: 80
      Canto 9: 74
      Canto 11: 81–85
      Canto 12: 71, 76, 80, 85, 90, 93, 123
   Book 3:
      Canto 1: 87, 91, 94–98, 104, 106
      Canto 2: 95–96, 98–101, 103
      Canto 3: 87
      Canto 4: 98, 101, 105, 119
      Canto 5: 87, 119
      Canto 6: 119, 124–25
      Canto 7: 119
      Canto 8: 107–8, 119, 123
      Canto 9: 90, 102–11, 118–19, 122
      Canto 10: 107–8
      Canto 11: 91–92
      Canto 12: 91, 97
   Book 4:
      Canto 6: 102, 121–22
      Canto 8: 115
      Canto 9: 114
   Book 5:
      Canto 2: 115
      Canto 5: 122
      Canto 6: 115
      Canto 7: 123
      Canto 8: 115, 123
      Canto 9: 115–16
      Canto 10: 115
   Book 6:
      Canto 1: 116
      Canto 3: 116
      Canto 4: 116
      Canto 6: 115
      Canto 7: 116
      Canto 8: 116
      Canto 9: 117–18
      Canto 10: 113, 118–19, 134
   Mutabilitie Cantos, 131
*Shephardes Calender, The*, 118

## By John Milton

*Areopagitica*, 65, 128
*Doctrine and Discipline of Divorce, The*, 129, 143–45, 148, 181–82

# Index

*Hymn on the Morning of Christ's Nativity* (Nativity Ode), 139–40
*Maske Presented at Ludlow Castle, A* (Comus), 140–42, 155
*Of Reformation touching Christ–Discipline*, 153–54
*Of True Religion,* 153
*Paradise Lost*
   Book 1: 132, 134
   Book 2: 135, 151
   Book 3: 134, 148, 151, 195
   Book 4: 89, 126, 135–37, 146–47, 194–95
   Book 5: 132, 134–35, 146
   Book 7: 135
   Book 8: 136, 138, 149, 195
   Book 9: 148–49
   Book 10: 15–16, 21, 147–48
   Book 11: 22, 148, 150–59
   Book 12: 150–59, 183
*Paradise Regained*
   Book 1: 160–65
   Book 2: 160, 163, 166–67, 169, 172
   Book 3: 163–64, 168–70
   Book 4: 164–65, 167–68, 170–74
*Pro populo anglicano defensio* (First Defense of the English People), 183
*Readie and Easie Way to Establish a Free Commonwealth, The,* 153
*Reason of Church Government urg'd against Prelaty, The,* 122–28
*Samson Agonistes,* 175–88, 192–93
*Treatise of Civil Power, A,* 182–83